EXAM CRAM

D0726481

MCSE™ SQL Server™ 2000 Database Design

Richard Alan McMahon, Sr.
Sean Chase

MCSE™ SQL Server™ 2000 Database Design Exam Cram

The Coriolis Group, LLC
14455 N. Hayden Road
Suite 220
Scottsdale, Arizona 85260

(480)483-0192
FAX (480)483-0193
www.coriolis.com

Library of Congress Cataloging-in-Publication Data
McMahon, Richard.
    MCSE SQL Server 2000 database design / Richard McMahon and Sean Chase.
        p. cm. -- (Exam cram)
        Includes index.
        ISBN 1-58880-034-2
    1.   Electronic data processing personnel--Certification. 2. Microsoft Software--Examinations--Study guides. 3. SQL (Computer program language) 4. Database management--Examinations--Study guides. I. Title. II. Series

QA76.3 .G553 2001
005.75'65--dc21

                                                2001028387
                                                CIP

Printed in the United States of America
10 9 8 7 6 5 4 3 2 1

President and CEO
Roland Elgey

Publisher
Steve Sayre

Associate Publisher
Katherine Hartlove

Acquisitions Editor
Hilary Long

Product Marketing Manager
Jeff Johnson

Project Editor
Sybil Ihrig,
Helios Productions

Technical Reviewer
John S. Green

Production Coordinator
Sybil Ihrig,
Helios Productions

Cover Designer
Jesse Dunn

Layout Designer
April Nielsen

The Coriolis Group, LLC • 14455 North Hayden Road, Suite 220 • Scottsdale, Arizona 85260

A Note from Coriolis

Our goal has always been to provide you with the best study tools on the planet to help you achieve your certification in record time. Time is so valuable these days that none of us can afford to waste a second of it, especially when it comes to exam preparation.

Over the past few years, we've created an extensive line of *Exam Cram* and *Exam Prep* study guides, practice exams, and interactive training. To help you study even better, we have now created an e-learning and certification destination called **ExamCram.com**. (You can access the site at **www.examcram.com**.) Now, with every study product you purchase from us, you'll be connected to a large community of people like yourself who are actively studying for their certifications, developing their careers, seeking advice, and sharing their insights and stories.

We believe that the future is all about collaborative learning. Our **ExamCram.com** destination is our approach to creating a highly interactive, easily accessible collaborative environment, where you can take practice exams and discuss your experiences with others, sign up for features like "Questions of the Day," plan your certifications using our interactive planners, create your own personal study pages, and keep up with all of the latest study tips and techniques.

We hope that whatever study products you purchase from us—*Exam Cram* or *Exam Prep* study guides, *Personal Trainers*, *Personal Test Centers*, or one of our interactive Web courses—will make your studying fun and productive. Our commitment is to build the kind of learning tools that will allow you to study the way you want to, whenever you want to.

Visit ExamCram.com now to enhance your study program.

Help us continue to provide the very best certification study materials possible. Write us or email us at **learn@examcram.com** and let us know how our study products have helped you study. Tell us about new features that you'd like us to add. Send us a story about how we've helped you. We're listening!

Good luck with your certification exam and your career. Thank you for allowing us to help you achieve your goals.

ExamCram.com Connects You to the Ultimate Study Center!

Look for these related products from The Coriolis Group:

MCSE SQL 2000 Administration Exam Cram
By Kalani Kirk Hausman

SQL Server 2000 Black Book
By Patrick Dalton and Paul Whitehead

SQL Server 2000 On Site
By Anthony Sequeira

Oracle8i DBA: SQL and PL/SQL Exam Cram
By Michael Ault

MCSE Administering SQL Server 7 Exam Prep
By Brian Talbert

MCSE Database Design on SQL Server 7 Exam Cram
By Jeffrey R. Garbus and David Pascuzzi

Also recently published by Coriolis Certification Insider Press:

Oracle 8i DBA: Architecture and Administration Exam Cram
By Peter Sharman

MCSE Supporting and Maintaining NT Server 4 Exam Cram
By J. Peter Bruzzese and Christian Wolf

MCSE Exchange 2000 Design Exam Prep
By Michael Shannon and Dennis Suhanovs

About the Authors

. . . .

Richard Alan McMahon, Sr. (MCSE, MCT, MCP, MCP+I, CTT, CNE, CNI, CNA) was introduced to computing in the early 1970s during the enlisted portion of his military career, as he worked on his college degree on the way to becoming a commissioned officer in the United States Air Force. Rich graduated from the University of Arizona with bachelor's degrees in both Operations Management (OM) and Management Information Systems (MIS). He earned his first master's degree in Operations Management at the University of Arkansas and, later, his dual-emphasis MBA (through Hardin-Simmons University) in Systems Analysis and Marketing. When, as a Major, he retired from the Air Force, Rich's interests in computing and teaching about computers intensified. He became a business teacher in the Texas secondary school system with an emphasis in computer education. After advancing to district-level IT positions in various school districts, his involvement in networking began with the local school district in Conroe, Texas. At about the same time, he started the certification path and wrote a NetWare 5 text for SouthWestern Educational Publishing. Later he started his MCSE training, became involved in Microsoft's worldwide pilot "Train-The-Trainer" program, and became a national spokesperson as one of the first nine AATP mentors while teaching both high school and college networking courses. Rich was invited to participate in Microsoft's Windows 2000 beta testing program and, as an OEM provider, has played an active part in the rollout of each new Microsoft product. Currently a full-time CIS faculty member at the University of Houston, Rich is responsible for teaching advanced courses in telecommunications and networking, systems analysis, MIS, and database design, and introductory courses in computer-based systems. He recently co-authored Coriolis' *Windows 2000 Security Design Exam Prep* and will be using that book as the primary text in a graduate-level networking security design course.

Sean Chase (MCP) has been working as a software engineer specializing in Microsoft development tools since 1995. He has a bachelor's degree in Computer Information Systems and has been a Microsoft Certified Professional (MCP) since 1997. Sean currently works as an IT consultant for Analysts International in Phoenix, Arizona. As a former Microsoft Certified Trainer (MCT) and Microsoft Certified Solution Developer (MCSD), Sean developed Microsoft Official Curriculum (MOC) courses and has authored self-paced training kits for Microsoft Press on such topics as Windows architecture for developers, Windows 2000, Visual Basic, and Visual InterDev.

Acknowledgments

First and foremost, I would like to express sincerest thanks to my loving family. Without the undying support from Sheronna, Lauren, and Ricky, this book could never have been completed. Once again, they endured long, painstaking stretches of writing project proposals, negotiating contracts, outlining, drafting, editing, researching, and compiling the never-ending sources of information that go into an Exam Cram. My family put up with long evenings and the project's tendency to sap all semblance of potential relaxation or quiet time from our existence.

Nearly every day, I thank the insights of the people who were instrumental in helping me choose studies in the newly forming computer field. Special thanks go to Drs. Chase and Aquilano, my University of Arizona advisors, who had the foresight to suggest that I become an MIS student in that school's then-newest degree plan. Their insistence that my studies include heavy emphasis on data structures and manipulation planted the seed for significant career development opportunities.

Finally, I would like to thank my mom, dad, and sister (and her family) for their continued support. Their critiques of these works are more important than any critical technical review.
—*Rich McMahon*

I would like to thank Lee Anderson, Scott Tetmyer, Steve Chase, Eric Griesser, Glee Spurlock, Dave Schatzel, Nader Kutub, and the great people at The Coriolis Group for all of their help and support.
—*Sean Chase*

Without any one of these individuals (especially in our families), neither our careers nor this book would have happened. It is, therefore, in sincere and grateful appreciation that both authors offer their resounding thanks.

And finally, we would like to thank Coriolis's staff. Without Shari Hehr, this project never would have surfaced. Without Lee Anderson, it never would have reached contract stage. Without Catherine Oliver as the copyeditor, it would not be grammatically correct. Without John S. Green as the technical reviewer, it would not mean what we expected. And, without Sybil Ihrig as the project manager, much less would have gotten accomplished. Thank you all!
—*Both of us*

Contents at a Glance

Table of Contents

. . . .

Introduction

Welcome to *MCSE SQL Server 2000 Database Design Exam Cram*! Whether this is your first or your fifteenth *Exam Cram* book, you'll find information here and in Chapter 1 that will help ensure your success as you pursue knowledge, experience, and certification. This book aims to help you get ready to take—and pass—the Microsoft certification Exam 70-229, titled "Designing and Implementing Databases with Microsoft SQL Server 2000 Enterprise Edition." This Introduction explains Microsoft's certification programs in general and talks about how the *Exam Cram* series can help you prepare for Microsoft's Windows 2000 certification exams.

Exam Cram books help you understand and appreciate the subjects and materials you need to pass Microsoft certification exams. *Exam Cram* books are aimed strictly at test preparation and review. They do not teach you everything you need to know about a topic. Instead, we (the authors) present and dissect the questions and problems we've found that you're likely to encounter on a test. We've worked to bring together as much information as possible about Microsoft certification exams.

Nevertheless, to completely prepare yourself for any Microsoft test, we recommend that you begin by taking the Self-Assessment included in this book, immediately following this Introduction. This tool will help you evaluate your knowledge against the requirements for an MCSE under both ideal and real circumstances.

Based on what you learn from that exercise, you might decide to begin your studies with some classroom training or some background reading. On the other hand, you might decide to pick up and read one of the many study guides available from Microsoft or third-party vendors on certain topics, including The Coriolis Group's *Exam Prep* series. We also recommend that you supplement your study program with visits to **ExamCram.com** to receive additional practice questions, get advice, and track the Windows 2000 MCSE program.

We also strongly recommend that you install, configure, and fool around with the software that you'll be tested on, because nothing beats hands-on experience and familiarity when it comes to understanding the questions you're likely to encounter on a certification test. Book learning is essential, but hands-on experience is the best teacher of all!

The Microsoft Certified Professional (MCP) Program

The MCP Program currently includes the following separate tracks, each of which boasts its own special acronym (as a certification candidate, you need to have a high tolerance for alphabet soup of all kinds):

➤ *MCP (Microsoft Certified Professional)*—This is the least prestigious of all the certification tracks from Microsoft. Passing one of the major Microsoft exams qualifies an individual for the MCP credential. Individuals can demonstrate proficiency with additional Microsoft products by passing additional certification exams.

➤ *MCP+SB (Microsoft Certified Professional + Site Building)*—This certification program is designed for individuals who are planning, building, managing, and maintaining Web sites. Individuals with the MCP+SB credential will have demonstrated the ability to develop Web sites that include multimedia and searchable content and Web sites that connect to and communicate with a back-end database. This certification requires one MCP exam, plus two of these three exams: Exam 70-055, "Designing and Implementing Web Sites with Microsoft FrontPage 98;" Exam 70-057, "Designing and Implementing Commerce Solutions with Microsoft Site Server 3.0, Commerce Edition;" and Exam 70-152, "Designing and Implementing Web Solutions with Microsoft Visual InterDev 6.0."

➤ *MCSE (Microsoft Certified Systems Engineer)*—Anyone who has a current MCSE is warranted to possess a high level of networking expertise with Microsoft operating systems and products. This credential is designed to prepare individuals to plan, implement, maintain, and support information systems, networks, and internetworks built around Microsoft Windows 2000 and its BackOffice Server 2000 family of products.

To obtain an MCSE, an individual must pass four core operating system exams, one optional core exam, and two elective exams. The operating system exams require individuals to prove their competence with desktop and server operating systems and networking/internetworking components.

For Windows NT 4 MCSEs, the Accelerated Exam 70-240, "Microsoft Windows 2000 Accelerated Exam for MCPs Certified on Microsoft Windows NT 4.0," is an option. This free exam covers all of the material tested in the Core Four exams. The hitch in this plan is that you can take the test only once. If you fail, you must take all four core exams to recertify. The Core Four exams are: Exam 70-210, "Installing, Configuring, and Administering

Microsoft Windows 2000 Professional;" Exam 70-215, "Installing, Configuring, and Administering Microsoft Windows 2000 Server;" Exam 70-216, "Implementing and Administering a Microsoft Windows 2000 Network Infrastructure;" and Exam 70-217, "Implementing and Administering a Microsoft Windows 2000 Directory Services Infrastructure."

To fulfill the fifth core exam requirement, you can choose from three design exams: Exam 70-219, "Designing a Microsoft Windows 2000 Directory Services Infrastructure;" Exam 70-220, "Designing Security for a Microsoft Windows 2000 Network;" or Exam 70-221, "Designing a Microsoft Windows 2000 Network Infrastructure." You are also required to take two elective exams. An elective exam can fall in any number of subject or product areas, primarily BackOffice Server 2000 components. The two design exams that you don't select as your fifth core exam also qualify as electives. If you are on your way to becoming an MCSE and have already taken some exams, visit **www.microsoft.com/trainingandservices/** for information about how to complete your MCSE certification.

Individuals who wish to remain certified MCSEs after 12/31/2001 must "upgrade" their certifications on or before 12/31/2001. For more detailed information than is included here, visit **www.microsoft.com/trainingandservices/**.

New MCSE candidates must pass seven tests to meet the MCSE requirements. It's not uncommon for the entire process to take a year or so, and many individuals find that they must take a test more than once to pass. The primary goal of the *Exam Prep* and *Exam Cram* test preparation books is to make it possible, given proper study and preparation, to pass all Microsoft certification tests on the first try. Table 1 shows the required and elective exams for the Windows 2000 MCSE certification.

➤ *MCSD (Microsoft Certified Solution Developer)*—The MCSD credential reflects the skills required to create multitier, distributed, and COM-based solutions, in addition to desktop and Internet applications, using new technologies. To obtain an MCSD, an individual must demonstrate the ability to analyze and interpret user requirements; select and integrate products, platforms, tools, and technologies; design and implement code, and customize applications; and perform necessary software tests and quality assurance operations.

To become an MCSD, you must pass a total of four exams: three core exams and one elective exam. Each candidate must choose one of these three desktop application exams—Exam 70-016, "Designing and Implementing Desktop Applications with Microsoft Visual C++ 6.0;" Exam 70-156, "Designing and Implementing Desktop Applications with Microsoft Visual FoxPro 6.0;" or Exam 70-176, "Designing and Implementing Desktop Applications with

Table 1 MCSE Windows 2000 Requirements

Core

If you have not passed these 3 Windows NT 4 exams	
Exam 70-067	Implementing and Supporting Microsoft Windows NT Server 4.0
Exam 70-068	Implementing and Supporting Microsoft Windows NT Server 4.0 in the Enterprise
Exam 70-073	Microsoft Windows NT Workstation 4.0
then you must take these 4 exams	
Exam 70-210	Installing, Configuring, and Administering Microsoft Windows 2000 Professional
Exam 70-215	Installing, Configuring, and Administering Microsoft Windows 2000 Server
Exam 70-216	Implementing and Administering a Microsoft Windows 2000 Network Infrastructure
Exam 70-217	Implementing and Administering a Microsoft Windows 2000 Directory Services Infrastructure
If you have already passed exams 70-067, 70-068, and 70-073, you may take this exam	
Exam 70-240	Microsoft Windows 2000 Accelerated Exam for MCPs Certified on Microsoft Windows NT 4.0

5th Core Option

Choose 1 from this group	
Exam 70-219	Designing a Microsoft Windows 2000 Directory Services Infrastructure
Exam 70-220	Designing Security for a Microsoft Windows 2000 Network
Exam 70-221	Designing a Microsoft Windows 2000 Network Infrastructure
Exam 70-226	Designing Highly Available Web Solutions with Microsoft Windows 2000 Server Technologies

Elective*

Choose 2 from this group	
Exam 70-019	Designing and Implementing Data Warehouse with Microsoft SQL Server 7.0
Exam 70-056	Implementing and Supporting Web Sites Using Microsoft Site Server 3.0
Exam 70-080	Implementing and Supporting Microsoft Internet Explorer 5.0 by Using the Internet Explorer Administration Kit
Exam 70-085	Implementing and Supporting Microsoft SNA Server 4.0
Exam 70-086	Implementing and Supporting Microsoft Systems Management Server 2.0
Exam 70-222	Migrating from Microsoft Windows NT 4.0 to Microsoft Windows 2000
Exam 70-223	Installing, Configuring, and Administering Microsoft Clustering Services by Using Microsoft Windows 2000 Advanced Server
Exam 70-224	Installing, Configuring, and Administering Microsoft Exchange 2000 Server
Exam 70-225	Designing and Deploying a Messaging Infrastructure with Microsoft Exchange 2000 Server
Exam 70-227	Installing, Configuring, and Administering Microsoft Internet Security and Acceleration (ISA) Server 2000 Enterprise Edition
Exam 70-228	Installing, Configuring, and Administering Microsoft SQL Server 2000 Enterprise Edition
► **Exam 70-229**	Designing and Implementing Databases with Microsoft SQL Server 2000 Enterprise Edition
Exam 70-244	Supporting and Maintaining a Microsoft Windows NT Server 4.0 Network

This is not a complete listing—you can still be tested on some earlier versions of these products. However, we have included mainly the most recent versions so that you may test on these versions and thus be certified longer. We have not included any tests that are scheduled to be retired.

* 5th Core Option exams may also be used as electives, but can only be counted once toward a certification. You cannot receive credit for an exam as both a core and an elective in the same track.

Microsoft Visual Basic 6.0"—*plus* one of these three distributed application exams—Exam 70-015, "Designing and Implementing Distributed Applications with Microsoft Visual C++ 6.0;" Exam 70-155, "Designing and Implementing Distributed Applications with Microsoft Visual FoxPro 6.0;" or Exam 70-175, "Designing and Implementing Distributed Applications with Microsoft Visual Basic 6.0." The third core exam is Exam 70-100, "Analyzing Requirements and Defining Solution Architectures." Elective exams cover specific Microsoft applications and languages, including Visual Basic, C++, the Microsoft Foundation Classes, Access, SQL Server, Excel, and more.

➤ *MCDBA (Microsoft Certified Database Administrator)*—The MCDBA credential reflects the skills required to implement and administer Microsoft SQL Server databases. To obtain an MCDBA, an individual must demonstrate the ability to derive physical database designs, develop logical data models, create physical databases, create data services by using Transact-SQL, manage and maintain databases, configure and manage security, monitor and optimize databases, and install and configure Microsoft SQL Server.

To become an MCDBA, you must pass a total of three core exams and one elective exam. The required core exams are: Exam 70-028, "Administering Microsoft SQL Server 7.0" or 70-228, "Installing, Configuring, and Administering Microsoft SQL Server 2000 Enterprise Edition;" Exam 70-029, "Designing and Implementing Databases with Microsoft SQL Server 7.0" or 70-229: "Designing and Implementing Databases with Microsoft SQL Server 2000 Enterprise Edition;" and Exam 70-215, "Installing, Configuring, and Administering Microsoft Windows 2000 Server."

The elective exams that you can choose from cover specific uses of SQL Server and include: Exam70-015, "Designing and Implementing Distributed Applications with Microsoft Visual C++ 6.0;" Exam 70-019, "Designing and Implementing Data Warehouses with Microsoft SQL Server 7.0;" Exam 70-155, "Designing and Implementing Distributed Applications with Microsoft Visual FoxPro 6.0;" Exam 70-175, "Designing and Implementing Distributed Applications with Microsoft Visual Basic 6.0;" and Exam 70-216, "Implementing and Administering a Microsoft Windows 2000 Network Infrastructure."

If you have taken the three core Windows NT 4 exams on your path to becoming an MCSE, you qualify for the Accelerated exam (it replaces the Network Infrastructure exam requirement). The Accelerated exam (Exam 70-240) covers the objectives of all four of the Windows 2000 core exams. In addition to taking the Accelerated exam, you must take only the two SQL exams—Administering (70-228) and Database Design (70-229).

Note that the exam covered by this book is a core requirement for the MCDBA certification. Table 2 shows the requirements for the MCDBA certification.

Table 2 MCDBA Requirements
Core

If you have not passed these 3 Windows NT 4 exams	
Exam 70-067	Implementing and Supporting Microsoft Windows NT Server 4.0
Exam 70-068	Implementing and Supporting Microsoft Windows NT Server 4.0 in the Enterprise
Exam 70-073	Microsoft Windows NT Workstation 4.0
you must take this exam	
Exam 70-215	Installing, Configuring and Administering Microsoft Windows 2000 Server
plus these 2 exams	
Exam 70-228	Installing, Configuring, and Administering Microsoft SQL Server 2000 Enterprise Edition
➤ **Exam 70-229**	Designing and Implementing Databases with Microsoft SQL Server 2000 Enterprise Edition

Elective

Choose 1 of the following exams	
Exam 70-015	Designing and Implementing Distributed Applications with Microsoft Visual C++ 6.0
Exam 70-019	Designing and Implementing Data Warehouses with Microsoft SQL Server 7.0
Exam 70-155	Designing and Implementing Distributed Applications with Microsoft Visual FoxPro 6.0
Exam 70-175	Designing and Implementing Distributed Applications with Microsoft Visual Basic 6.0
Exam 70-216	Implementing and Administering a Microsoft Windows 2000 Network Infrastructure

OR

If you have already passed exams 70-067, 70-068, and 70-073, you may take this exam	
Exam 70-240	Microsoft Windows 2000 Accelerated Exam for MCPs Certified on Microsoft Windows NT 4.0
plus these 2 exams	
Exam 70-228	Installing, Configuring, and Administering Microsoft SQL Server 2000 Enterprise Edition
➤ **Exam 70-229**	Designing and Implementing Databases with Microsoft SQL Server 2000 Enterprise Edition

This is not a complete listing—you can still be tested on some earlier versions of these products. However, we have tried to include the most recent versions so that you may test on these versions and thus be certified longer.

> ➤ *MCT (Microsoft Certified Trainer)*—Microsoft Certified Trainers are deemed able to deliver elements of the official Microsoft curriculum, based on technical knowledge and instructional ability. Thus, it is necessary for an individual seeking MCT credentials (which are granted on a course-by-course basis) to pass the related certification exam for a course, complete the official Microsoft training in the subject area, and demonstrate an ability to teach.

This teaching-skill criterion may be satisfied by proving that one has already attained training certification from Novell, Banyan, Lotus, the Santa Cruz Operation, or Cisco, or by taking a Microsoft-sanctioned workshop on instruction. Microsoft makes it clear that MCTs are important cogs in the wheels of the Microsoft training channels. Instructors must be MCTs before Microsoft will allow them to teach in any of its official training channels, including Microsoft's affiliated Certified Technical Education Centers (CTECs) and its online training partner network. As of January 1, 2001, MCT candidates must possess a current MCSE, but the requirement for them to pass applicable tests for each course taught has been lifted (although it is still recommended by Microsoft).

Microsoft has announced that the MCP+I and MCSE+I credentials will not be continued when the MCSE exams for Windows 2000 are in full swing because the skill set for the Internet portion of the program has been included in the new MCSE program. Therefore, details on these tracks are not provided here; go to **www.microsoft.com/trainingandservices/** if you need more information.

When a Microsoft product becomes obsolete, MCPs typically have to get recertified on current versions. (If individuals do not get recertified, their certifications become invalid.) Because technology keeps changing and new products continually supplant old ones, this should come as no surprise. This explains why Microsoft has announced that MCSEs have 12 months past the scheduled retirement date for the Windows NT 4 exams to get recertified on Windows 2000 topics. (Note that this means taking at least two exams, if not more.)

The best place to keep tabs on the MCP program and its related certifications is on the Web. The URL for the MCP program is **www.microsoft.com/ trainingandservices/**. But Microsoft's Web site changes often, so if this URL doesn't work, try using the Search tool on Microsoft's site with either "MCP" or the quoted phrase "Microsoft Certified Professional" as a search string. This will help you find the latest and most accurate information about Microsoft's certification programs.

Taking a Certification Exam

Once you've prepared for your exam, you need to register with a testing center. Each computer-based MCP exam costs $100, and if you don't pass, you may retest for an additional $100 for each additional try. In the United States and Canada, tests are administered by Prometric and by Virtual University Enterprises (VUE). Here's how you can contact them:

➤ *Prometric*—You can sign up for a test through the company's Web site at **www.prometric.com**. Within the United States and Canada, you can register by phone at 800-755-3926. If you live outside this region, check the company's Web site for the appropriate phone number.

➤ *Virtual University Enterprises*—You can sign up for a test or get the phone numbers for local testing centers through the Web page at **www.vue.com/ms/**.

To sign up for a test, you must possess a valid credit card, or contact either company for mailing instructions to send them a check (in the U.S.). Only when payment is verified, or a check has cleared, can you actually register for a test.

To schedule an exam, call the number or visit either of the Web pages at least one day in advance. To cancel or reschedule an exam, you must call before 7 P.M. Pacific standard time the day before the scheduled test time (or you may be charged, even if you don't take the test). When you want to schedule a test, have the following information ready:

➤ Your name, organization, and mailing address.

➤ Your Microsoft Test ID. (Inside the United States, this means your Social Security number; citizens of other nations should call ahead to find out what type of identification number is required to register for a test.)

➤ The name and number of the exam you wish to take.

➤ A method of payment. (As we've already mentioned, a credit card is the most convenient method, but alternate means can be arranged in advance, if necessary.)

Once you sign up for a test, you'll be informed as to when and where the test is scheduled. Try to arrive at least 15 minutes early. You must supply two forms of identification—one of which must be a photo ID—to be admitted into the testing room.

All exams are completely closed-book. In fact, you will not be permitted to take anything with you into the testing area, but you will be furnished with a blank sheet of paper and a pen or, in some cases, an erasable plastic sheet and an erasable pen. We suggest that you immediately write down on that sheet of paper all the information you've memorized for the test. In *Exam Cram* books, this information appears on a tear-out sheet inside the front cover of each book. You will have some time to compose yourself, record this information, and take a sample orientation exam before you begin the real thing. We suggest you take the orientation test before taking your first exam, but because they're all more or less identical in layout, behavior, and controls, you probably won't need to do this more than once.

When you complete a Microsoft certification exam, the software will tell you whether you've passed or failed. If you need to retake an exam, you'll have to schedule a new test with Prometric or VUE and pay another $100.

 The first time you fail a test, you can retake the test the next day. However, if you fail a second time, you must wait 14 days before retaking that test. The 14-day waiting period remains in effect for all retakes after the second failure.

Tracking MCP Status

As soon as you pass any Microsoft Certification track exam (except Networking Essentials), you'll attain Microsoft Certified Professional (MCP) status. Microsoft also generates transcripts that indicate which exams you have passed. You can view a copy of your transcript at any time by going to the MCP secured site and selecting Transcript Tool. This tool will allow you to print a copy of your current transcript and confirm your certification status.

Once you pass the necessary set of exams, you'll be certified. Official certification normally takes anywhere from six to eight weeks, so don't expect to get your credentials overnight. When the package for a qualified certification arrives, it includes a Welcome Kit that contains a number of elements (see Microsoft's Web site for other benefits of specific certifications):

➤ A certificate suitable for framing, along with a wallet card and lapel pin.

➤ A license to use the MCP logo, thereby allowing you to use the logo in advertisements, promotions, and documents, and on letterhead, business cards, and so on. Along with the license comes an MCP logo sheet, which includes camera-ready artwork. (Note: Before using any of the artwork, individuals must sign and return a licensing agreement that indicates they'll abide by its terms and conditions.)

➤ A subscription to *Microsoft Certified Professional Magazine*, which provides ongoing data about testing and certification activities, requirements, and changes to the program.

Many people believe that the benefits of MCP certification go well beyond the perks that Microsoft provides to newly anointed members of this elite group. We're starting to see more job listings that request or require applicants to have an MCP, MCSE, and so on, and many individuals who complete the program can qualify for increases in pay and/or responsibility. As an official recognition of hard work and broad knowledge, one of the MCP credentials is a badge of honor in many IT organizations.

How to Prepare for an Exam

Preparing for any Windows 2000 or SQL Server 2000-related test (including Exam 70-229, "Designing and Implementing Databases with Microsoft SQL Server 2000 Enterprise Edition") requires that you obtain and study materials designed to provide comprehensive information about the product and its capabilities; such information will appear on the specific exam for which you are preparing. The following list of materials will help you study and prepare:

➤ The Windows 2000 or SQL Server 2000 product CD includes comprehensive online documentation and related materials; it should be a primary resource when you are preparing for the test.

➤ The exam preparation materials, practice tests, and self-assessment exams on the Microsoft Training & Services page at **www.microsoft.com/trainingandservices/ default.asp?PageID=mcp**. The Testing Innovations link offers samples of the new question types found on the Windows 2000 MCSE exams. Find the materials, download them, and use them!

➤ The exam preparation advice, practice tests, questions of the day, and discussion groups on the **ExamCram.com** e-learning and certification destination Web site (**www.examcram.com**).

In addition, you'll probably find any or all of the following materials useful in your quest for Exam 70-229, "Designing and Implementing Databases with Microsoft SQL Server 2000 Enterprise Edition" expertise:

➤ *Microsoft training kits*—Microsoft Press offers a training kit that specifically targets Exam 70-229. For more information, visit: **http://mspress.microsoft.com/ findabook /list/series_ak.htm**. This training kit contains information that you will find useful in preparing for the test.

➤ *Microsoft TechNet CD*—This monthly CD-based publication delivers numerous electronic titles that include coverage of Exam 70-229, "Designing and Implementing Databases with Microsoft SQL Server 2000 Enterprise Edition" and related topics. This CD's offerings include product facts, technical notes, tools and utilities, and information on how to access the Seminars Online training materials for Exam 70-229, "Designing and Implementing Databases with Microsoft SQL Server 2000 Enterprise Edition." A subscription to TechNet costs $299 per year, but it is well worth the price. Visit **www.microsoft.com/technet/** and check out the information under the "TechNet Subscription" menu entry for more details.

➤ *Study guides*—Several publishers—including The Coriolis Group—offer Windows 2000 or SQL Server 2000 titles. The Coriolis Group series includes the following:

➤ *The Exam Cram series*—These books give you information about the material you need to know to pass the tests.

➤ *The Exam Prep series*—These books provide a greater level of detail than the *Exam Cram* books and are designed to teach you everything you need to know from an exam perspective. Each book comes with a CD that contains interactive practice exams in a variety of testing formats.

Together, the two series make a perfect pair.

➤ *Multimedia*—These Coriolis Group materials are designed to support learners of all types—whether you learn best by reading or by doing:

➤ *The Exam Cram Personal Trainer*—Offers a unique, personalized self-paced training course based on the exam.

➤ *The Exam Cram Personal Test Center*—Features multiple test options that simulate the actual exam, including Fixed-Length, Random, Review, and Test All. Explanations of correct and incorrect answers reinforce concepts learned.

➤ *Classroom training*—CTECs, online partners, and third-party training companies (like Wave Technologies, Learning Tree, Data-Tech, and others) all offer classroom training on Windows 2000 or SQL Server 2000. These companies aim to help you prepare to pass Exam 70-229. Although such training runs upwards of $350 per day in class, most of the individuals lucky enough to partake find it to be quite worthwhile.

➤ *Other publications*—There's no shortage of materials available about SQL Server 2000 design. The resource sections at the end of each chapter should give you an idea of where we think you should look for further discussion.

By far, this set of required and recommended materials represents a nonpareil collection of sources and resources for SQL Server 2000 design and related topics. We anticipate that you'll find that this book belongs in this company

About this Book

Each topical *Exam Cram* chapter follows a regular structure, along with graphical cues about important or useful information. Here's the structure of a typical chapter:

➤ *Opening hotlists*—Each chapter begins with a list of the terms, tools, and techniques that you must learn and understand before you can be fully conversant with that chapter's subject matter. We follow the hotlists with one or two introductory paragraphs to set the stage for the rest of the chapter.

➤ *Topical coverage*—After the opening hotlists, each chapter covers a series of topics related to the chapter's subject title. Throughout this section, to highlight topics or concepts likely to appear on a test, we use a special Exam Alert layout, like this:

This is what an Exam Alert looks like. Normally, an Exam Alert stresses concepts, terms, software, or activities that are likely to relate to one or more certification test questions. For that reason, we think any information found offset in Exam Alert format is worthy of unusual attentiveness on your part. Indeed, most of the information that appears on The Cram Sheet appears as Exam Alerts within the text.

Pay close attention to material flagged as an Exam Alert; although all the information in this book pertains to what you need to know to pass the exam, we flag certain items that are really important. You'll find what appears in the meat of each chapter to be worth knowing, too, when preparing for the test. Because this book's material is very condensed, we recommend that you use this book along with other resources to achieve the maximum benefit.

Now that you know what an Exam Alert looks like, here is one of which you should be *very* aware:

You should be comfortable working with long, complex T-SQL queries: **SELECT**, **UNIONS**, **JOINS**, grouping, aggregate functions, and so on. Microsoft expects you to have knowledge in this area, and several questions on exam 70-229 test your background in T-SQL.

In addition to the Exam Alerts, we have provided tips that will help you build a better foundation for SQL Server 2000 design knowledge. Although the information may not be on the exam, it is certainly related and will help you become a better test-taker.

This is how tips are formatted. Keep your eyes open for these, and you'll become a SQL Server design guru in no time!

➤ *Practice questions*—Although we talk about test questions and topics throughout the book, a section at the end of each chapter presents a series of mock test questions and explanations of both correct and incorrect answers.

➤ *Details and resources*—Every chapter ends with a section titled "Need to Know More?". This section provides direct pointers to Microsoft and third-party resources offering more details on the chapter's subject. In addition, this section tries to rank or at least rate the quality and thoroughness of the topic's coverage by each resource. If you find a resource you like in this collection, use it, but don't feel compelled to use all the resources. On the other hand, we recommend only resources we use on a regular basis, so none of our recommendations will be a waste of your time or money. (Purchasing them all at once, however, probably represents an expense that many network administrators and would-be MCPs and MCSEs might find hard to justify.)

The bulk of the book follows this chapter structure slavishly, but there are a few other elements that we'd like to point out. Chapter 15 includes a sample test that provides a good review of the material presented throughout the book to ensure that you're ready for the exam. Chapter 16 is an answer key to the sample test that appears in Chapter 15. In addition, you'll find a handy glossary and an index.

Finally, the tear-out Cram Sheet attached next to the inside front cover of this *Exam Cram* book represents a condensed and compiled collection of facts and tips that we think you should memorize before taking the test. Because you can dump this information out of your head onto a piece of paper before taking the exam, you can master this information by brute force—you need to remember it only long enough to write it down when you walk into the test room. You might even want to look at it in the car or in the lobby of the testing center just before you walk in to take the test.

How to Use this Book

We've structured the topics in this book to build on one another. Therefore, some topics in later chapters make more sense after you've read earlier chapters. That's why we suggest you read this book from front to back for your initial test preparation. If you need to brush up on a topic or you have to bone up for a second try, use the index or table of contents to go straight to the topics and questions that you need to study. Beyond helping you prepare for the test, we think you'll find this book useful as a tightly focused reference to some of the most important aspects of Exam 70-229, "Designing and Implementing Databases with Microsoft SQL Server Enterprise Edition 2000."

Given all the book's elements and its specialized focus, we've tried to create a tool that will help you prepare for—and pass—Microsoft Exam 70-219. Please share your feedback on the book with us, especially if you have ideas about how we can improve it for future test-takers. We'll consider everything you say carefully, and we'll respond to all suggestions.

Send your questions or comments to us at **learn@examcram.com**. Please remember to include the title of the book in your message; otherwise, we'll be forced to guess which book you're writing about. And we don't like to guess—we want to *know*! Also, be sure to check out the Web pages at **www.examcram.com**, where you'll find information updates, commentary, and certification information.

Thanks, and enjoy the book!

Self-Assessment

The purpose of this Self-Assessment is to help you evaluate your readiness to tackle Microsoft Certified Systems Engineer (MCSE) certification. It should also help you understand what you need to know to master the topic of this book—namely, Exam 70-229, "Designing and Implementing Databases with Microsoft SQL Server 2000 Enterprise Edition." Before you take this Self-Assessment, you should think about the concerns you have about pursuing an MCSE for Windows 2000 and what an "ideal" MCSE candidate is.

MCSEs in the Real World

The next section describes the "ideal" MCSE candidate, although very few real candidates meet all of the requirements. In fact, some of those requirements may seem impossible to fulfill, especially with the ongoing changes made to the program to support Windows 2000. Although the requirements for obtaining an MCSE may seem formidable, they are by no means unattainable. However, it does take time, involves some expense, and requires real effort to get through the process.

Increasing numbers of people are attaining Microsoft certifications, and you can also reach that goal. If you're willing to tackle the process seriously and work toward obtaining the necessary experience and knowledge, you can take—and pass—all of the certification tests involved in obtaining an MCSE. In fact, Coriolis has designed *Exam Preps*, the companion *Exam Crams*, *Exam Cram Personal Trainers*, and *Exam Cram Personal Test Centers* to assist you in studying for these exams. Coriolis has also greatly expanded its Web site, **www.examcram.com**, to provide a host of resources to help you prepare for the complexities of Windows 2000.

In addition to MCSE, other Microsoft certifications include the following:

➤ Microsoft Certified Solution Developer (MCSD), which is aimed at software developers and requires one specific exam, two more exams on client and distributed topics, plus a fourth elective exam drawn from a different, but limited, pool of options.

➤ Microsoft certifications that require one test, such as Microsoft Certified Professional (MCP), or several tests, such as Microsoft Certified Professional + Site Building (MCP+SB) and Microsoft Certified Database Administrator (MCDBA).

Who Is an Ideal Windows 2000 MCSE Candidate?

Just to give you some idea of the qualifications an ideal MCSE candidate should have, here are some relevant statistics about background and experience. Don't worry if you don't meet these qualifications, or don't come that close—this is a far from ideal world, and if you fall short, it just means that you simply have more work to do in those areas.

➤ Academic or professional training in network theory, concepts, and operations. This includes everything from networking media and transmission techniques through network operating systems, services, and applications.

➤ Three-plus years of professional networking experience, including experience with Ethernet, token ring, modems, and other networking media. This must include installation, configuration, upgrade, and troubleshooting experience.

Note: The Windows 2000 MCSE program is much more rigorous than the previous NT MCSE program; therefore, you'll really need some hands-on experience. Some of the exams require you to solve real-world case studies and network design issues, so the more hands-on experience you have, the better.

➤ Two-plus years in a networked environment that includes hands-on experience with Windows 2000 Server, Windows 2000 Professional, Windows NT Server, Windows NT Workstation, and Windows 95 or Windows 98. A solid understanding of each system's architecture, installation, configuration, maintenance, and troubleshooting is also essential.

➤ Knowledge of the various methods for installing Windows 2000, including manual and unattended installations.

➤ A thorough understanding of key networking protocols, addressing, and name resolution, including TCP/IP, IPX/SPX, and NetBEUI.

➤ A thorough understanding of NetBIOS naming, browsing, and file and print services.

➤ Familiarity with key Windows 2000 TCP/IP-based services, including hypertext transfer protocol (HTTP), dynamic host configuration protocol (DHCP), windows internet naming server (WINS), domain name service (DNS), plus familiarity with one or more of the following: Internet Information Server (IIS), Index Server, and Proxy Server.

➤ An understanding of how to implement security for key network data in a Windows 2000 environment.

➤ Working knowledge of NetWare 3.x and 4.x, including IPX/SPX frame formats; NetWare file, print, and directory services; and both Novell and Microsoft client software. Working knowledge of Microsoft's Client Service for NetWare (CSNW), Gateway Service for NetWare (GSNW), NetWare Migration Tool (NWCONV), and NetWare Client For Windows (NT, 95, and 98) is essential.

➤ A good working understanding of Active Directory. The more you work with Windows 2000, the more you'll realize that this new operating system is quite different from Windows NT. New technologies such as Active Directory have really changed the way that Windows is configured and used. I recommend that you find out as much as you can about Active Directory and acquire as much experience using this technology as possible. The time you take learning about Active Directory will be time very well spent!

Fundamentally, this boils down to a bachelor's degree in computer science, plus three years' experience working in a position involving network design, installation, configuration, and maintenance. The Coriolis Group believes that well under half of all certification candidates meet these requirements, and that most meet less than half of these requirements—at least, when they begin the certification process. However, many candidates have survived this ordeal and become certified. You can also survive it—especially if you heed what our Self-Assessment can tell you about what you already know and what you need to learn.

Put Yourself to the Test

The following series of questions and observations is designed to help you determine what you must do to pursue Microsoft certification and what kinds of resources you may consult on your quest. Be absolutely honest in your answers, or you'll end up wasting money on exams that you're not yet ready to take. There are no right or wrong answers—only steps along the path to certification. Only you can decide where you really belong in the broad spectrum of aspiring candidates.

At the very minimum, you should have the following:

➤ Some background in computer science, even a limited one

➤ Hands-on experience with Microsoft products and technologies

Educational Background

Following are some questions to help you determine if you need further education and training before attempting to take an exam:

1. Have you ever taken any computer-related classes? [Yes or No]

   ➤ If Yes, proceed to Question 2; if No, proceed to Question 4.

2. Have you taken any classes on computer operating systems? [Yes or No]

➤ If Yes, you will probably be able to handle Microsoft's architecture and system component discussions. If you're rusty, brush up on basic operating system concepts, especially virtual memory, multitasking regimes, user mode versus kernel mode operation, and general computer security topics.

➤ If No, consider some basic reading in this area. We strongly recommend a good general operating systems book, such as *Operating System Concepts, 5th Edition*, by Abraham Silberschatz and Peter Baer Galvin (John Wiley & Sons, 1998, ISBN 0-471-36414-2). If this title doesn't appeal to you, check out reviews for other, similar titles at your favorite online bookstore.

3. Have you taken any networking concepts or technologies classes? [Yes or No]

➤ If Yes, you will probably be able to handle Microsoft's networking terminology, concepts, and technologies (brace yourself for frequent departures from normal usage). If you're rusty, brush up on basic networking concepts and terminology, especially networking media, transmission types, the OSI Reference Model, and networking technologies such as Ethernet, Token Ring, FDDI, and WAN links.

➤ If No, you may want to read one or two books in this topic area. The two best books that we know of are *Computer Networks, 3rd Edition*, by Andrew S. Tanenbaum (Prentice Hall, 1996, ISBN 0-13-083617-6) and *Computer Networks and Internets, 2nd Edition*, by Douglas E. Comer and Ralph E. Droms (Prentice Hall, 1998, ISBN 0-130-83617-6).

➤ Skip to the next section, "Hands-on Experience."

4. Have you done any reading on operating systems or networks? [Yes or No]

➤ If Yes, review the requirements stated in the first paragraphs after Questions 2 and 3. If you meet those requirements, move on to the next section. If No, consult the recommended reading for both topics. A strong background will help you prepare for the Microsoft exams better than anything else.

Hands-On Experience

The most important key to success on all of the Microsoft tests is hands-on experience, especially with Windows 2000 Server and Professional, plus the many add-on services and BackOffice components around which so many of the Microsoft certification exams revolve. After taking this Self-Assessment, you should learn at least this—there's no substitute for time spent installing, configuring, and using the various Microsoft products on which you'll be tested repeatedly and in depth.

5. Have you installed, configured, and worked with the following:

➤ Windows 2000 Server? [Yes or No]

If Yes, make sure that you understand the basic concepts as covered in Exam 70-215. You should also study the TCP/IP interfaces, utilities, and services for Exam 70-216, plus implementing security features for Exam 70-220.

You can download objectives, practice exams, and other data about Microsoft exams from the Training and Certification page at **www.microsoft.com/trainingandservices/default.asp?PageID=mcp**. Use the "Exams" link to obtain specific exam information.

If you haven't worked with Windows 2000 Server, you must obtain one or two machines and a copy of Windows 2000 Server. Then, learn the operating system and whatever other software components on which you'll also be tested.

In fact, we recommend that you obtain two computers—each with a network interface—and set up a two-node network on which to practice. With decent Windows 2000-capable computers selling for about $500 to $600 apiece these days, this shouldn't be too much of a financial hardship. You may have to scrounge to come up with the necessary software, but if you scour the Microsoft Web site you can usually find low-cost options to obtain evaluation copies of most of the software that you'll need.

➤ Windows 2000 Professional? [Yes or No]

If Yes, make sure you understand the concepts covered in Exam 70-210.

If No, you should obtain a copy of Windows 2000 Professional and learn how to install, configure, and maintain it. You can use *MCSE Windows 2000 Professional Exam Cram* to guide your activities and studies or work straight from Microsoft's test objectives if you prefer.

For any and all of these Microsoft exams, the Resource Kits for the topics involved are a good study resource. You can purchase softcover Resource Kits from Microsoft Press (search for them at **http://mspress.microsoft.com**), but they also appear on the TechNet CDs (**www.microsoft.com/technet/**). Along with *Exam Crams* and *Exam Preps*, we believe that Resource Kits are among the best tools you can use to prepare for Microsoft exams.

6. For any specific Microsoft product that is not itself an operating system (for example, SQL Server), have you installed, configured, used, and upgraded this software? [Yes or No]

➤ If Yes, skip to the next section. If No, you must get some experience. Read on for suggestions on how to do this.

Experience is a must with any Microsoft product exam, be it something as simple as FrontPage 2000 or as challenging as SQL Server 2000. For trial copies of other software, search Microsoft's Web site using the name of the product as your search term. Also, search for bundles like "BackOffice" or "Small Business Server."

 If you have the funds, or your employer will pay your way, consider taking a class at a Certified Training and Education Center (CTEC) or at an Authorized Academic Training Partner (AATP). In addition to classroom exposure to the topic of your choice, you get a copy of the software that is the focus of your course, along with a trial version of whatever operating system it needs and the training materials for that class.

Before you even think about taking any Microsoft exam, make sure that you've spent enough time with the related software to understand how it may be installed and configured, how to maintain such an installation, and how to troubleshoot that software when things go wrong. This will help you in the exam, and in real life!

Testing Your Exam-Readiness

Whether you attend a formal class on a specific topic to get ready for an exam or use written materials to study on your own, some preparation for the Microsoft certification exams is essential. At $100 a try, pass or fail, you want to do everything you can to pass on your first try. That's where studying comes in.

We have included a practice exam in this book, so if you don't score that well on the test, you can study more and then take the test again. The Coriolis Group also has exams that you can take online through the **ExamCram.com** Web site at **www.examcram.com**. If you still don't hit a score of at least 70 percent after these tests, you'll want to investigate the other practice test resources mentioned in this section.

For any given subject, consider taking a class if you've tackled self-study materials, taken the test, and failed. The opportunity to interact with an instructor and fellow students can make all the difference in the world, if you can afford that privilege. For information about Microsoft classes, visit the Training and

Certification page at **www.microsoft.com/education/partners/ctec.asp** for Microsoft Certified Education Centers or **www.microsoft.com/aatp/default.htm** for Microsoft Authorized Training Providers.

If you can't afford to take a class, visit the Training and Certification page anyway, because it also includes pointers to free practice exams and to Microsoft Certified Professional Approved Study Guides and other self-study tools. If you can't afford to spend much at all, you should still invest in some low-cost practice exams from commercial vendors.

7. Have you taken a practice exam on your chosen test subject? [Yes or No]

> ➤ If Yes, and you scored 70 percent or better, you're probably ready to tackle the real thing. If your score isn't above that threshold, keep at it until you break that barrier.

> ➤ If No, obtain all of the free and low-budget practice tests you can find and start working. Keep at it until you can break the passing threshold comfortably.

When it comes to assessing your test readiness, there is no better way than to take a good-quality practice exam and pass with a score of 70 percent or better. When we prepare ourselves, we shoot for 80-plus percent, just to leave room for the "weirdness factor" that sometimes shows up on Microsoft exams.

Assessing Readiness for Exam 70-229

In addition to the general exam-readiness information in the previous section, there are several things you can do to prepare for the "Designing and Implementing Databases with Microsoft SQL Server 2000 Enterprise Edition" exam. As you're getting ready for Exam 70-229, visit the Exam Cram Resource Center at **www.examcram.com/studyresource/**. Another valuable resource is the Exam Cram Insider newsletter. Sign up at **www.examcram.com** or send a blank email message to **subscribe-ec@mars.coriolis.com**. We also suggest that you join an active MCSE or MCDBA mailing list. One of the better ones is managed by Sunbelt Software. Sign up at **www.sunbelt-software.com** (look for the Subscribe button).

You can also cruise the Web looking for "braindumps" (recollections of test topics and experiences recorded by others) to help you anticipate topics that you're likely to encounter on the test. The MCSE mailing list is a good place to ask where the useful braindumps are.

You can't be sure that a braindump's author can provide correct answers. Thus, use the questions to guide your studies, but don't rely on the answers in a braindump to lead you to the truth. Double-check everything you find in any braindump.

Microsoft also recommends checking the Microsoft Knowledge Base (available on its own CD-ROM as part of the TechNet collection or on the Microsoft Web site at **http://support.microsoft.com/support/**) for "meaningful technical support issues" that relate to your exam's topics. Although we're not sure exactly what the quoted phrase means, we have also noticed some overlap between technical support questions on particular products and troubleshooting questions on the exams for those products.

Onward, through the Fog!

Once you've assessed your readiness, undertaken the right background studies, obtained the hands-on experience that will help you understand the products and technologies at work, and reviewed the many sources of information to help you prepare for a test, you'll be ready to take a round of practice tests. When your scores come back positive enough to get you through the exam, you're ready to go after the real thing. If you follow this assessment regime, you'll know what you need to study and when you're ready to make a test date at Prometric or VUE. Good luck!

Microsoft
Certification Exams

. . . .

Terms you'll need to understand:

✓ Case study

✓ Multiple-choice question formats

✓ Build-list-and-reorder question format

✓ Create-a-tree question format

✓ Drag-and-connect question format

✓ Select-and-place question format

✓ Fixed-length tests

✓ Simulations

✓ Adaptive tests

✓ Short-form tests

Techniques you'll need to master:

✓ Assessing your exam readiness

✓ Answering Microsoft's questions of varying types

✓ Altering your test strategy depending on the exam format

✓ Practicing (to make perfect)

✓ Making the best use of the testing software

✓ Budgeting your time

✓ Guessing (as a last resort)

Exam taking is not something that most people anticipate eagerly, no matter how well prepared they may be. In most cases, familiarity helps offset test anxiety. In plain English, this means you probably won't be as nervous when you take your fourth or fifth Microsoft certification exam as you'll be when you take your first one.

Whether it's your first exam or your tenth, understanding the details of taking the new exams (how much time to spend on questions, the environment you'll be in, and so on) and of using the new exam software will help you concentrate on the material rather than on the setting. Likewise, mastering a few basic exam-taking skills should help you recognize—and perhaps even outfox—some of the tricks and snares you're bound to find in some exam questions.

This chapter, besides explaining the exam environment and software, describes some proven exam-taking strategies that you should be able to use to your advantage.

Assessing Exam-Readiness

We strongly recommend that you read through and take the Self-Assessment included with this book (it appears just before this chapter, in fact). This will help you compare your knowledge base to the requirements for obtaining an MCSE; this assessment will also help you identify parts of your background or experience that may need improvement, enhancement, or further learning. If you get the right set of basics under your belt, obtaining Microsoft certification will be that much easier.

Once you've gone through the Self-Assessment, you can remedy those topical areas where your background or experience may not measure up to an ideal certification candidate. But you can also tackle subject matter for individual tests at the same time, so you can continue making progress while you're catching up in some areas.

Once you've worked through an *Exam Cram*, have read the supplementary materials, and have taken the practice test, you'll have a pretty clear idea of when you should be ready to take the real exam. Although we strongly recommend that you keep practicing until your scores top the 80 percent mark, 85 percent would be a good goal to give yourself some margin for error in a real exam situation (where stress will play more of a role than when you practice). Once you hit that point, you should be ready to go. But if you get through the practice exam in this book without attaining that score, you should keep taking practice tests and studying the materials until you get there. You'll find more pointers on how to study and prepare in the Self-Assessment. But now, on to the exam itself!

The Exam Situation

When you arrive at the testing center where you scheduled your exam, you'll need to sign in with an exam coordinator. He or she will ask you to show two forms of identification, one of which must be a photo ID. After you've signed in and your time slot arrives, you'll be asked to deposit any books, bags, or other items you brought with you. Then, you'll be escorted into a closed room.

All exams are completely closed book. In fact, you will not be permitted to take anything with you into the testing area, but you will be furnished with a blank sheet of paper and a pen or, in some cases, an erasable plastic sheet and an erasable pen. Before the exam, you should memorize as much of the important material as you can, so you can write that information on the blank sheet as soon as you are seated in front of the computer. You can refer to this piece of paper anytime you like during the test, but you'll have to surrender the sheet when you leave the room.

You will have some time to compose yourself, to record this information, and to take a sample orientation exam before you begin the real thing. We suggest you take the orientation test before taking your first exam, but because they're all more or less identical in layout, behavior, and controls, you probably won't need to do this more than once.

Typically, the room will be furnished with anywhere from one to half a dozen computers, and each workstation will be separated from the others by dividers designed to keep you from seeing what's happening on someone else's computer. Most test rooms feature a wall with a large picture window. This permits the exam coordinator to monitor the room, to prevent exam-takers from talking to one another, and to observe anything out of the ordinary that might go on. The exam coordinator will have loaded the appropriate Microsoft certification exam— for this book, that's Exam 70-229—and you'll be permitted to start as soon as you're seated in front of the computer.

All Microsoft certification exams allow a certain maximum amount of time in which to complete your work (this time is indicated on the exam by an on-screen counter/clock, so you can check the time remaining whenever you like). All Microsoft certification exams are computer generated. Questions take a variety of formats. In addition to multiple choice, you'll encounter select and place (drag and drop), create a tree (categorization and prioritization), drag and connect, and build list and reorder (list prioritization) on most exams. Although these constructions may sound quite simple, the questions not only check your mastery of basic facts and figures about Designing and Implementing Databases with Microsoft SQL Server 2000 Enterprise Edition but also require you to evaluate one or more sets of circumstances or requirements. Often, you'll be asked to give more than one answer to a question. Likewise, you might be asked to select the best or most effective solution to a problem from a range of choices, all of which technically are correct. Taking the exam is quite an adventure, and it involves real thinking. This book shows you what to expect and how to deal with the potential problems, puzzles, and predicaments.

In the next section, you'll learn more about how Microsoft test questions look and how they must be answered.

Exam Layout and Design: New Case Study Format

The format of Microsoft's Windows 2000 exams is different from that of its previous exams. For the design exams (70-219, 70-220, 70-221, 70-229), each exam consists entirely of a series of case studies, and the questions can be of six types. For the Core Four exams (70-210, 70-215, 70-216, 70-217), the same six types of questions can appear, but you are not likely to encounter complex multiquestion case studies.

For design exams, each case study or "testlet" presents a detailed problem that you must read and analyze. Figure 1.1 shows an example of what a case study looks like. You must select the different tabs in the case study to view the entire case.

Following each case study is a set of questions related to the case study; these questions can be one of six types (which are discussed next). Careful attention to details provided in the case study is the key to success. Be prepared to toggle frequently between the case study and the questions as you work. Some of the

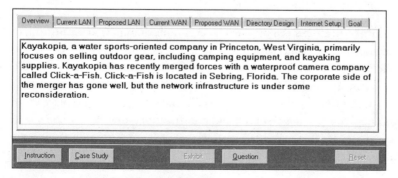

Figure 1.1 This is how case studies appear.

case studies also include diagrams, which are called *exhibits*, that you'll need to examine closely to understand how to answer the questions.

After you complete a case study, you can review all the questions and your answers. However, once you move on to the next case study, you may not be able to return to the previous case study and make any changes.

The six types of question formats are:

➤ Multiple choice, single answer

➤ Multiple choice, multiple answers

➤ Build list and reorder (list prioritization)

➤ Create a tree

➤ Drag and connect

➤ Select and place (drag and drop)

Note: Exam formats may vary by test center location. Although most design exams consist entirely of a series of case studies or testlets, a test-taker may occasionally encounter a strictly multiple-choice test. You may want to call the test center or visit ExamCram.com to see if you can find out which type of test you'll encounter.

Multiple-Choice Question Format

Some exam questions require you to select a single answer, whereas others ask you to select multiple correct answers. The following multiple-choice question requires you to select a single correct answer. Following the question is a brief summary of each potential answer and why it is either right or wrong.

Question 1

You have three domains connected to an empty root domain under one contiguous domain name: **tutu.com**. This organization is formed into a forest arrangement with a secondary domain called **frog.com**. How many Schema Masters exist for this arrangement?

❍ a. 1

❍ b. 2

❍ c. 3

❍ d. 4

The correct answer is a. Only one Schema Master is necessary for a forest arrangement. The other answers (b, c, and d) are misleading because they try to make you believe that Schema Masters might be in each domain or perhaps that you should have one for each contiguous namespaced domain.

This sample question format corresponds closely to the Microsoft certification exam format—the only difference on the exam is that questions are not followed by answer keys. To select an answer, you position the cursor over the radio button next to the answer. Then, click the mouse button to select the answer.

Let's examine a question for which one or more answers are possible. This type of question provides checkboxes rather than radio buttons for marking all appropriate selections.

Question 2

How can you seize FSMO roles? [Check all correct answers]

❑ a. The ntdsutil.exe utility

❑ b. The Replication Monitor

❑ c. The secedit.exe utility

❑ d. Active Directory Domains and FSMOs

Answers a and b are correct. You can seize roles from a server that is still running through the Replication Monitor, or, in the case of a server failure, you can seize roles with the ntdsutil.exe utility. The secedit utility is used to force group policies into play; therefore, answer c is incorrect. Active Directory Domains and FSMOs is a combination of truth and fiction (the correct name of this MMC snap-in is Active Directory Domains and Trusts); therefore, answer d is incorrect.

For this particular question, two answers are required. Microsoft sometimes gives partial credit for partially correct answers. For Question 2, you have to check the boxes next to items a and b to obtain credit for a correct answer. Notice that picking the right answers also means knowing why the other answers are wrong!

Build-List-and-Reorder Question Format

Questions in the build-list-and-reorder format present two lists of items—one on the left and one on the right. To answer the question, you must move items from the list on the right to the list on the left. The final list must then be reordered into a specific order.

These questions can best be characterized as "From the following list of choices, pick the choices that answer the question. Arrange the list in a certain order." To give you practice with this type of question, this study guide includes some questions of this type. Here's an example of how they appear in this book; for a sample of how they appear on the test, see Figure 1.2.

Question 3

From the following list of famous people, pick those who have been elected President of the United States. Arrange the list in the order that they served.

Thomas Jefferson

Ben Franklin

Abe Lincoln

George Washington

Andrew Jackson

Paul Revere

The correct answer is:

George Washington

Thomas Jefferson

Andrew Jackson

Abe Lincoln

On an actual exam, the entire list of famous people would initially appear in the list on the right. You would move the four correct answers to the list on the left, and then reorder the list on the left. Notice that the answer to the question did not include all items from the initial list. However, this may not always be the case.

To move an item from the right list to the left list, first select the item by clicking on it, and then click on the Add button (left arrow). Once you move an item from one list to the other, you can move the item back by first selecting the item and then clicking on the appropriate button (either the Add button or the Remove button). After you have moved items to the left list, you can reorder an item by selecting the item and clicking on the up or down button.

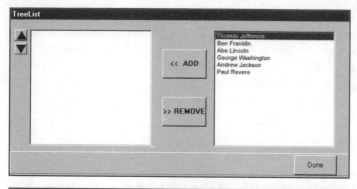

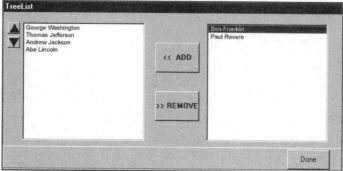

Figure 1.2 This is how build-list-and-reorder questions appear.

Create-a-Tree Question Format

Questions in the create-a-tree format also present two lists—one on the left side of the screen and one on the right side of the screen. The list on the right consists of individual items, and the list on the left consists of nodes in a tree. To answer the question, you must move items from the list on the right to the appropriate node in the tree.

These questions can best be characterized as simply a matching exercise. Items from the list on the right are placed under the appropriate category in the list on the left. Here's an example of how they appear in this book; for a sample of how they appear on the test, see Figure 1.3.

Question 4

The calendar year is divided into four seasons:

Winter

Spring

Summer

Fall

Identify the season when each of the following holidays occurs:

Christmas

Fourth of July

Labor Day

Flag Day

Memorial Day

Washington's Birthday

Thanksgiving

Easter

The correct answer is:

Winter

Christmas

Washington's Birthday

Spring

Flag Day

Memorial Day

Easter

Summer

Fourth of July

Labor Day

Fall

Thanksgiving

In this case, all the items in the list were used. However, this may not always be the case.

To move an item from the right list to its appropriate location in the tree, you must first select the appropriate tree node by clicking on it. Then, you select the item to be moved and click on the Add button. If one or more items have been added to a tree node, the node will be displayed with a "+" icon to the left of the node name. You can click on this icon to expand the node and view the items that have been added. If any item has been added to the wrong tree node, you can remove the item by selecting it and clicking on the Remove button.

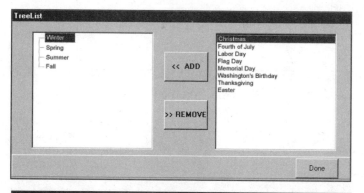

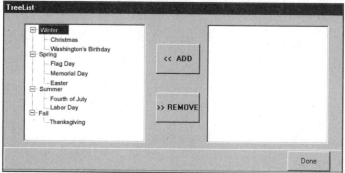

Figure 1.3   This is how create-a-tree questions appear.

Drag-and-Connect Question Format

Questions in the drag-and-connect format present a group of objects and a list of "connections." To answer the question, you must move the appropriate connections between the objects.

This type of question is best described using graphics. Here's an example.

Question 5

The following objects represent the different states of water:

| Ice | Water Vapor | Water | Steam |

Use items from the following list to connect the objects so that they are scientifically correct.

Sublimates to form

Freezes to form

Evaporates to form

Boils to form

Condenses to form

Melts to form

The correct answer is:

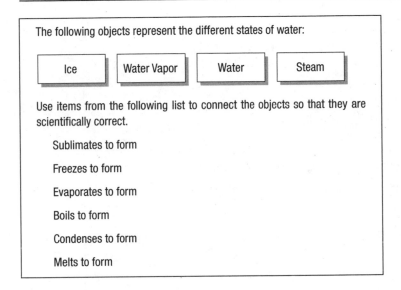

For this type of question, it's not necessary to use every object, and each connection can be used multiple times.

Select-and-Place Question Format

Questions in the select-and-place (drag-and-drop) format present a diagram with blank boxes, and a list of labels that need to be dragged to correctly fill in the blank boxes. To answer the question, you must move the labels to their appropriate positions on the diagram.

This type of question is best described using graphics. Here's an example.

Question 6

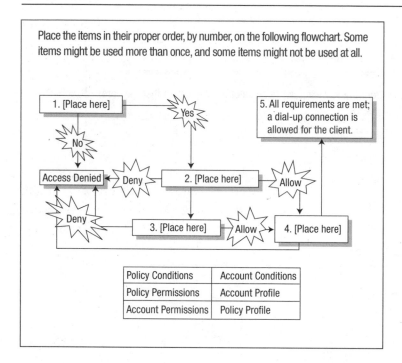

The correct answer is:

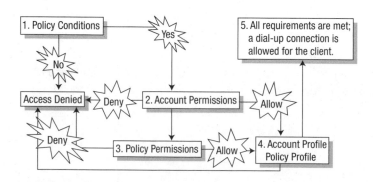

Microsoft's Testing Formats

Currently, Microsoft uses four testing formats:

➤ Case study

➤ Fixed length

➤ Adaptive

➤ Short form

As we mentioned earlier, the case study approach is used with Microsoft's design exams, such as the one covered by this book (Exam 70-229). These exams consist of a set of case studies that you must analyze so you can answer questions related to the case studies. Such exams include one or more case studies (tabbed topic areas), each of which is followed by 4 to 10 questions. The question types for design exams and for Core Four Windows 2000 exams are multiple choice, build list and reorder, create a tree, drag and connect, and select and place. Depending on the test topic, some exams are totally case-based, whereas others are not.

Other Microsoft exams employ advanced testing capabilities that might not be immediately apparent. Although the questions that appear are primarily multiple choice, the logic that drives them is more complex than that used in older Microsoft tests, which use a fixed sequence of questions called a *fixed-length test*. Some questions employ a sophisticated user interface, which Microsoft calls a *simulation*, to test your knowledge of the software and systems under consideration in a more or less "live" environment that behaves just like the original. The Testing Innovations link at **www.microsoft.com/trainingandservices/default.asp?PageID=mcp/** includes a downloadable practice simulation.

For some exams, Microsoft has turned to a well-known technique, called *adaptive testing*, to establish a test-taker's level of knowledge and product competence. Adaptive exams look the same as fixed-length exams, but adaptive exams discover the level of difficulty at which an individual test-taker can correctly answer questions. Test-takers with differing levels of knowledge or ability therefore see different sets of questions; individuals with high levels of knowledge or ability are presented with a smaller set of more difficult questions, whereas individuals with lower levels of knowledge are presented with a larger set of easier questions. Two individuals may answer the same percentage of questions correctly, but the test-taker with a higher knowledge or ability level will score higher because his or her questions are worth more.

Also, the lower-level test-taker will probably answer more questions than will his or her more-knowledgeable colleague. This explains why adaptive tests use ranges of values to define the number of questions and the amount of time it takes to complete the test.

Adaptive tests work by evaluating the test-taker's most recent answer. A correct answer leads to a more difficult question (and the test software's estimate of the test-taker's knowledge and ability level is raised). An incorrect answer leads to a less difficult question (and the test software's estimate of the test-taker's knowledge and ability level is lowered). This process continues until the test targets the test-taker's true ability level. The exam ends when the test-taker's level of accuracy meets a statistically acceptable value (in other words, when his or her performance demonstrates an acceptable level of knowledge and ability), or when the maximum number of items has been presented (in which case, the test-taker is almost certain to fail).

Microsoft also introduced a short-form test for its most popular tests. This test delivers 25 to 30 questions to its takers, giving them exactly 60 minutes to complete the exam. This type of exam is similar to a fixed-length test in that it allows readers to jump ahead or return to earlier questions and to cycle through the questions until the test is done. Microsoft does not use adaptive logic in this test, but claims that statistical analysis of the question pool is such that the 25 to 30 questions delivered during a short-form exam conclusively measure a test-taker's knowledge of the subject matter in much the same way as an adaptive test. You can think of the short-form test as a kind of "greatest hits exam" (that is, the most important questions are covered) version of an adaptive exam on the same topic.

Note: Some of the Microsoft exams can contain a combination of adaptive and fixed-length questions.

Microsoft tests can come in any one of these forms. Whatever you encounter, you must take the test in whichever form it appears; you can't choose one form over another. If anything, it pays more to prepare thoroughly for an adaptive exam than for a fixed-length or a short-form exam: The penalties for answering incorrectly are built into the test itself on an adaptive exam, whereas the layout remains the same for a fixed-length or short-form test, no matter how many questions you answer incorrectly.

The biggest difference between an adaptive test and a fixed-length or short-form test is that on a fixed-length or short-form test, you can revisit questions after you've read them over one or more times. On an adaptive test, you must answer the question when it's presented; you will have no opportunities to revisit that question thereafter.

Strategies for Different Testing Formats

Before you choose a test-taking strategy, you must know if your test is case study based, fixed length, short form, or adaptive. When you begin your exam, you'll know right away if the test is based on case studies. The interface will consist of a tabbed window that allows you to navigate easily through the sections of the case.

If you are taking a test that is not based on case studies, the software will tell you that the test is adaptive, if in fact the version you're taking is an adaptive test. If your introductory materials fail to mention this, you're probably taking a fixed-length test (50 to 70 questions). If the total number of questions involved is 25 to 30, you're taking a short-form test. Some tests announce themselves by indicating that they will start with a set of adaptive questions, followed by fixed-length questions.

You'll be able to tell for sure if you are taking an adaptive, fixed-length, or short-form test by the first question. If it includes a checkbox that lets you mark the question for later review, you're taking a fixed-length or short-form test. If the total number of questions is 25 to 30, it's a short-form test; if more than 30, it's a fixed-length test. Adaptive test questions can be visited (and answered) only once, and they include no such checkbox.

The Case-Study Exam Strategy

Most test-takers find that the case study type of test used for the design exams (70-219, 70-220, 70-221, and 70-229) is the most difficult to master. When it comes to studying for a case study test, your best bet is to approach each case study as a standalone test. The biggest challenge you'll encounter is that you'll feel that you won't have enough time to get through all of the cases that are presented.

Each case provides a lot of material that you'll need to read and study before you can effectively answer the questions that follow. The trick to taking a case study exam is to first scan the case study to get the highlights. Make sure you read the overview section of the case so that you understand the context of the problem at hand. Then, quickly move on and scan the questions.

As you are scanning the questions, make mental notes to yourself so that you'll remember which sections of the case study you should focus on. Some case studies may provide a fair amount of extra information that you don't really need to answer the questions. The goal with this scanning approach is to avoid having to study and analyze material that is not completely relevant.

When studying a case, carefully read the tabbed information. It is important to answer each and every question. You will be able to toggle back and forth from case to questions and from question to question within a case testlet. However, once you leave the case and move on, you might not be able to return to it. You may want to take notes while reading useful information so you can refer to them when you tackle the test questions. It is hard to go wrong with this strategy when taking any kind of Microsoft certification test.

The Fixed-Length and Short-Form Exam Strategy

A well-known principle when taking fixed-length or short-form exams is to first read over the entire exam from start to finish while answering only those questions you feel absolutely sure of. On subsequent passes, you can dive into more complex questions more deeply, knowing how many such questions you have left.

Fortunately, the Microsoft exam software for fixed-length and short-form tests makes the multiple-visit approach easy to implement. At the top-left corner of each question is a checkbox that permits you to mark that question for a later visit.

Note: Marking questions makes review easier, but you can return to any question by clicking the Forward or Back button repeatedly.

As you read each question, if you answer only those you're sure of and mark for review those that you're not sure of, you can keep working through a decreasing list of questions as you answer the trickier ones in order.

There's at least one potential benefit to reading the exam completely before answering the trickier questions: Sometimes, information supplied in later questions sheds more light on earlier questions. At other times, information you read in later questions might jog your memory about Designing and Implementing Databases with Microsoft SQL Server 2000 facts, figures, or behavior that helps you answer earlier questions. Either way, you'll come out ahead if you defer those questions about which you're not absolutely sure.

Here are some question-handling strategies that apply to fixed-length and short-form tests. Use these strategies if you have the chance:

➤ When returning to a question after your initial read-through, read every word again—otherwise, your mind can fall quickly into a rut. Sometimes, revisiting a question after turning your attention elsewhere lets you see something you missed, but the strong tendency is to see what you've seen before. Try to avoid that tendency at all costs.

➤ If you return to a question more than twice, try to articulate to yourself what you don't understand about the question, why answers don't appear to make sense, or what appears to be missing. If you chew on the subject awhile, your subconscious might provide the details you lack, or you might notice a "trick" that points to the right answer.

As you work your way through the exam, another counter that Microsoft provides will come in handy—the number of questions completed and questions outstanding. For fixed-length and short-form tests, it's wise to budget your time by making sure that you've completed one-quarter of the questions by one-quarter of the way through the exam period, and three-quarters of the questions by three-quarters of the way through.

If you're not finished when only five minutes remain, use that time to guess your way through any remaining questions. Remember, guessing is potentially more valuable than not answering, because blank answers are always wrong, but a guess may turn out to be right. If you don't have a clue about any of the remaining questions, pick answers at random, or choose all a's, b's, and so on. The important thing is to submit an exam for scoring that has an answer for every question.

 At the very end of your exam period, you're better off guessing than leaving questions unanswered.

The Adaptive Exam Strategy

If there's one principle that applies to taking an adaptive test, it can be summed up as "Get it right the first time." You cannot elect to skip a question and move on to the next one when taking an adaptive test, because the testing software uses your answer to the current question to select whatever question it plans to present next. Nor can you return to a question once you've moved on, because the software gives you only one chance to answer the question. You can, however, take notes, because sometimes information supplied in earlier questions will shed more light on later questions.

Also, when you answer a question correctly, you are presented with a more difficult question next to help the software gauge your level of skill and ability. When you answer a question incorrectly, you are presented with a less difficult question, and the software lowers its current estimate of your skill and ability. Continuing until the program settles into a reasonably accurate estimate of what you know and can do, this process takes you on average through somewhere between 15 and 30 questions as you complete the test.

The good news is that if you know your stuff, you'll probably finish most adaptive tests in 30 minutes or so. The bad news is that you must really, really know your stuff to do your best on an adaptive test. That's because some questions are so convoluted, complex, or hard to follow that you're bound to miss one or two, at a minimum, even if you do know your stuff. So the more you know, the better you'll do on an adaptive test, even accounting for the occasionally weird or unfathomable questions that appear on these exams.

Because you can't always tell in advance if a test is fixed length, short form, or adaptive, you will be best served by preparing for the exam as if it were adaptive. That way, you should be prepared to pass no matter what kind of test you take. But if you do take a fixed-length or short-form test, remember the tips from the preceding section. They should help you improve on what you could do on an adaptive test.

If you encounter a question on an adaptive test that you can't answer, you must guess an answer immediately. Because of how the software works, you may suffer for your guess on the next question if you guess right, because you'll get a more difficult question next!

Question-Handling Strategies

For those questions that take only a single answer, usually two or three of the answers will be obviously incorrect, and two of the answers will be plausible—of course, only one can be correct. Unless the answer leaps out at you (if it does, reread the question to look for a trick; sometimes those are the ones you're most likely to get wrong), begin the process of answering by eliminating those answers that are most obviously wrong.

Almost always, at least one answer out of the possible choices for a question can be eliminated immediately because it matches one of these conditions:

➤ The answer does not apply to the situation.

➤ The answer describes a nonexistent issue, an invalid option, or an imaginary state.

After you eliminate all answers that are obviously wrong, you can apply your retained knowledge to eliminate further answers. Look for items that sound correct but refer to actions, commands, or features that are not present or not available in the situation that the question describes.

If you're still faced with a blind guess among two or more potentially correct answers, reread the question. Try to picture how each of the possible remaining answers would alter the situation. Be especially sensitive to terminology; sometimes the choice of words ("remove" instead of "disable") can make the difference between a right answer and a wrong one.

Only when you've exhausted your ability to eliminate answers, but you remain unclear about which of the remaining possibilities is correct, should you guess at an answer. An unanswered question offers you no points, but guessing gives you at least some chance of getting a question right; just don't be too hasty when making a blind guess.

Note: If you're taking a fixed-length or a short-form test, you can wait until the last round of reviewing marked questions (just as you're about to run out of time or out of unanswered questions) before you start making guesses. You will have the same option within each case study testlet (but once you leave a testlet, you might not be allowed to return to it). If you're taking an adaptive test, you'll have to guess to move on to the next question if you can't figure out an answer some other way. Either way, guessing should be your technique of last resort!

Numerous questions assume that the default behavior of a particular utility is in effect. If you know the defaults and understand what they mean, this knowledge will help you cut through many Gordian knots.

Mastering the Inner Game

In the final analysis, knowledge breeds confidence, and confidence breeds success. If you study the materials in this book carefully and review all the practice questions at the end of each chapter, you should become aware of those areas where additional learning and study are required.

After you've worked your way through the book, take the practice exam in the back of the book. Taking this test will provide a reality check and help you identify areas to study further. Make sure you follow up and review materials related to the questions you miss on the practice exam before scheduling a real exam. Only when you've covered that ground and feel comfortable with the whole scope of the practice exam should you set an exam appointment. Only if you score 80 percent or better should you proceed to the real thing (otherwise, obtain some additional practice tests so you can keep trying until you hit this magic number).

 If you take a practice exam and don't score at least 80 to 85 percent correct, you'll want to practice further. Microsoft provides links to practice exam providers and also offers self-assessment exams at **www.microsoft.com/trainingandservices/**. You should also check out **ExamCram.com** for downloadable practice questions.

Armed with the information in this book and with the determination to augment your knowledge, you should be able to pass the certification exam. However, you need to work at it, or you'll spend the exam fee more than once before you finally pass. If you prepare seriously, you should do well. We are confident that you can do it!

The next section covers other sources you can use to prepare for the Microsoft certification exams.

Additional Resources

A good source of information about Microsoft certification exams comes from Microsoft itself. Because its products and technologies—and the exams that go with them—change frequently, the best place to go for exam-related information is online.

If you haven't already visited the Microsoft Certified Professional site, do so right now. The MCP home page resides at **www.microsoft.com/trainingandservices/** (see Figure 1.4).

Note: This page might not be there by the time you read this, or might be replaced by something new and different, because things change regularly on the Microsoft site. Should this happen, please read the sidebar titled "Coping with Change on the Web."

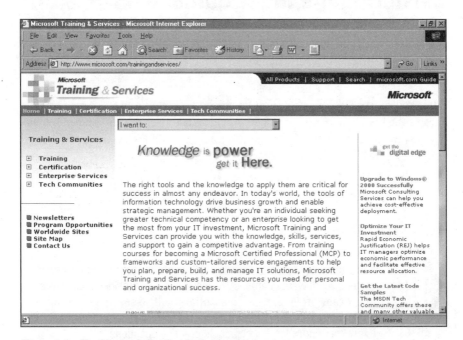

Figure 1.4 The Microsoft Certified Professional home page.

Coping with Change on the Web

Sooner or later, all the information we've shared with you about the Microsoft Certified Professional pages and the other Web-based resources mentioned throughout this book will go stale or be replaced by newer information. In some cases, the URLs you find here might lead you to their replacements; in other cases, the URLs will go nowhere, leaving you with the dreaded "404 File not found" error message. When that happens, don't give up.

There's always a way to find what you want on the Web if you're willing to invest some time and energy. Most large or complex Web sites—and Microsoft's qualifies on both counts—offer a search engine. On all of Microsoft's Web pages, a Search button appears along the top edge of the page. As long as you can get to Microsoft's site (it should stay at **www.microsoft.com** for a long time), use this tool to help you find what you need.

The more focused you can make a search request, the more likely it is that the results will include information you can use. For example, you can search for the string

```
"training and certification"
```

to produce a lot of data about the subject in general, but if you're looking for the preparation guide for Exam 70-229, "Designing and Implementing Databases with Microsoft SQL Server 2000," you'll be more likely to get there quickly if you use a search string similar to the following:

```
"Exam 70-229" AND "preparation guide"
```

Likewise, if you want to find the Training and Certification downloads, try a search string such as this:

```
"training and certification" AND "download page"
```

Finally, feel free to use general search tools—such as **www.search.com**, **www.altavista.com**, and **www.excite.com**—to look for related information. Although Microsoft offers great information about its certification exams online, there are plenty of third-party sources of information and assistance that need not follow Microsoft's party line. Therefore, if you can't find something where the book says it lives, intensify your search.

Data Modeling

Terms you'll need to understand:

- ✓ Data modeling
- ✓ Relational database management system (RDBMS)
- ✓ Online transaction processing (OLTP) and online analytical processing (OLAP)
- ✓ Entity relationship diagrams (ERD)
- ✓ Entities
- ✓ Attributes
- ✓ Primary keys
- ✓ Foreign keys
- ✓ Referential integrity
- ✓ Relationships
- ✓ Normalization
- ✓ Denormalization
- ✓ Data integrity
- ✓ Constraints

Techniques you'll need to master:

- ✓ Understanding database design
- ✓ Gathering the database requirements
- ✓ Defining the modeling elements
- ✓ Building a logical data model
- ✓ Understanding normalization and denormalization
- ✓ Deriving a physical data model from a logical model
- ✓ Designing for performance
- ✓ Designing for availability and maintainability
- ✓ Understanding the role of security

Models are supposed to represent reality. Because this book deals with an enterprise's data, the emphasis here will be on different methods for representing that data so as to simulate what really occurs.

In this book, the database will be the desired model, which depicts how company information is organized. It's important to note, however, that the methods discussed in this book reflect Microsoft's constricted view of model development concerning databases design. Rather than considering all of what is commonly referred to as the *system development life cycle (SDLC)*, in which systems are planned, analyzed, designed, implemented, and then operated and maintained, Microsoft simply focuses on the actual design portion (phase 3) of that cycle. Microsoft then breaks the system's development (or the company database, in this case) apart and forms two distinct modeling views—the logical and the physical models.

As a result, when we're discussing the logical model, it already includes all actions of a conceptual nature (i.e., planning and analysis) leading up to a system's ultimate creation—at least from Microsoft's perspective, that is. Similarly, when we're developing the physical model, all concrete activities such as implementation, operation, and maintenance are considered to be included there as well. Microsoft's viewpoint, therefore, is a simplistic form of the SDLC.

Now let's look at data modeling with an emphasis on the relational database system, Microsoft's basis for SQL Server 2000. Use of relational database systems such as SQL Server 2000 has become standard practice for enterprise data processing.

Using Data Models (Data Modeling)

Data modeling is the process of identifying, documenting, and implementing the data requirements for your application. It is an iterative process, repeatedly involving refinement of the following tasks:

➤ Identifying each piece of data required to perform the business operations for your application. Some examples include **Customer Name, ZIP Code**, and **Employee ID**.

➤ Defining the type, size, and other traits for each piece of data. An example would be that the **Customer Name** field can contain 20 alphanumeric characters and must not be null (or empty).

➤ Defining how one data item relates to another. For example, **Customers** buy **Products**.

➤ Defining all constraints required by each piece of data. For example, the **ZIP Code** can be required to contain exactly five numeric characters, or each **Employee ID** can be required to contain a unique numeric identifier.

➤ Defining the operational processes required to effectively maintain the data. Examples include activities such as security audits and scheduled backups.

➤ Choosing a data storage technology for implementing the model. Examples include relational, hierarchical, or indexed sequential access method (ISAM) databases.

➤ Organizing the data to avoid redundancy and inconsistency while maintaining optimal overall performance—a process referred to as *normalization*.

Whether you are creating a database to store all the information for a company's continued operation or you are simply developing a new application to use that data, your actions should follow a basic systems-design plan. This plan involves developing the logical and physical design models. The logical design phase includes gathering the requirements for the database you're going to develop. The logical model also defines entities as well as their attributes and their interrelationships.

During the logical model's development, the data requirements themselves are determined, and no concern is given to how data will be stored or what vendor's product will be used. With the completion of the logical model's development (which can actually be thought of as the beginning of the physical model's design), the process of finding a particular vendor's product should be started. That product should be the one found to optimally support the system's logical design.

During the physical phase, you map the logical design's elements into the database. Where the logical design decided "what" had to occur, the physical design specifies "how" it occurs. This is also when the database's supportive objects are actually developed. At this point, it becomes clear whether the selection process for choosing the best database product actually occurred or whether the constraints placed upon the design (cost, speed, ease of transition, and so on) had the process settling for less than the best.

Review of Database Types

Before we proceed, it might help to clarify some important terminology. It's important to understand the following database types: *transaction processing*, *decision support*, and *relational*:

➤ *Transaction processing database*—Also known as an *online transaction processing (OLTP)* database, this is the most common type of database and will be the one primarily discussed in this book. This type of database contains the active set of data that a company uses. If the database will have a high access rate, it is normalized for optimal performance during the read and write functions.

➤ *Decision support database*—Also known as an *online analytical processing (OLAP)* database, this is used to help companies analyze all the data they have acquired. This is usually historical data, whose purpose is to help companies predict future business scenarios. This type of database is often used in data warehousing and data mining. The data itself is usually not modified and is typically denormalized to gain optimum read performance.

➤ *Relational database*—Also known as a *relational database management system (RDBMS)*, this is a set of data that is based on relationships. The relationships associate various information items to applicable database components. Thus, relationships are denoted by use of tables whose columns are logically interconnected, or linked.

Logical Design

With that slight review of database types behind us, it should be obvious that any questions about what is to be accomplished should come before you decide how it is undertaken. Determining a system's desired outcomes involves developing that system's logical design. It is during this development that requirements are gathered for the database's components and goals. To determine these requirements, the system users and the management team are interviewed. It is also important, at this point, to review any existing systems and see what data (if any) is already available from that system's use.

When the logical design is being developed, no details should be decided about what database engine (or specific vendor product) will be used. Rather, the process should emphasize gathering the information that is needed to optimally support the application and meet the users' needs. In fact, at this point, databases, tables, constraints, or anything else "database-oriented" should not even be considered. Effort should be concentrated primarily on gathering the requirements for data and determining how all the pieces should ultimately work together.

The process of gathering and defining the data is iterative. You'll need to repeatedly gather such information as:

➤ *Item name*—How does one refer to the item?

➤ *Description*—What is the item?

➤ *Responsible person*—Who is responsible for the item?

➤ *Data traits or characteristics*—What does the item look like?

➤ *Processing and relationships*—How and when is the data concerning the item created, modified, or used? Does one item relate to or depend on another item?

Data (like the people, places, and things it usually describes) comes in many types and forms. Data can have various features (or attributes), such as:

➤ *Conceptual*—Name, serial number, or title

➤ *Physical*—Color, texture, weight, or dimension

➤ *Location*—Address, country, or shelf

➤ *Value*—Currency, quantity, or dates

➤ *Relational*—Orders that are made up of multiple products, customers who order products, or employees who work on projects

After you (and your fellow developers) gather the requirements for the application (or database) being developed, you put the collected data into meaningful, related groups. Again, during this part of the design, no thought should be given to determining specific database structures. Rather, the emphasis should be on putting similar items together, defining associations between those items, and defining any restrictions on them. This particular model's creation includes analyzing the gathered data, separating it into entities and attributes, and defining the relationships between each of these items.

The Database Model

Now that you have gathered the information, you need to present it in a meaningful way so that you and the end users can all agree on the final design. This is usually best accomplished by creating a visual representation of the desired logical design. This visual representation is called the *database model* or an *entity relationship diagram (ERD)*.

To create these database models, you can use pen and paper, a word processing program, a drawing program, or any other method that will depict the logic of your data flow. You can also use one of the many software packages designed specifically for creating database models. Visio, now owned by Microsoft, is an example of such a software package. It offers database-modeling assistance in the form of wizards or templates that essentially provide stencils of typical models to help get the job started.

In addition, the newest edition—Visio 2000 Enterprise version (and only this version)—can generate the scripts necessary to create the physical database as well as reverse-engineer an existing database so you can develop the ERD. Visio "senses" the network and creates graphical depictions and much of the typically needed documentation, such as equipment inventory sheets, router schemes, and subnet populations.

The resultant diagram is a pictorial view of the system's data and its associated relationships. Many of the more widely used modeling tools use their own conventions and symbols for defining the various components in the diagram. One common set of these ERD symbols is shown in Figure 2.1. It doesn't matter, however, what symbols are used as long as they are used consistently and the end users understand what the graphics are trying to portray. Remember, the goal of the model is to help the developers and the end users agree on the design of the database.

Next, let's look at some of the more important items that make up the database's logical model. In the database model discussion to follow, we'll discuss entities, attributes, keys, and entity relationships.

Entities

An *entity* is a unit of data that can be classified or described and that can have a relationship with another entity. An entity usually represents a person (such as an employee), a place (such as an office location), or a thing (such as a product). One occurrence of an entity is called an *instance* or a *tuple*. For example, John Doe is a single instance of the entity **Employees**. Instances, then, become the rows within the tables.

 When entities are being defined, the end users being interviewed might see something as needing to be classified as an entity when it actually should not be one. Remember, it is ultimately the job of the designer to determine what is and what is not an entity.

Attributes

Something's characteristics become the *attributes* of its entity. Attributes are data objects that either identify or describe an entity. An attribute is considered a *key attribute* if it uniquely defines or identifies the entity; an attribute is considered a

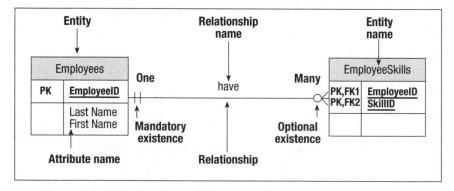

Figure 2.1 ERD notation.

non-key attribute if it simply describes the entity without doing so uniquely. For example, let's say that the **Employees** entity has the attributes of **ID Number, First Name, Last Name, Birth Date,** and **Email Address.** The **ID Number** and **Email Address** could be key attributes, but the **Birth Date, First Name,** or **Last Name** would likely be non-key attributes. Both key and non-key attributes become the columns of your table.

Attributes should be *atomic*; that is, they should present a single fact about an entity. If you keep this in mind and define attributes accordingly, normalizing your database will be easier. An example of a non-atomic attribute could be **Full Name** (first plus last). In this case, to present the attributes as atomic, it is better to have two attributes: **First Name** and **Last Name.**

 For the exam, you need to know what entities and attributes are and what makes up key attributes and non-key attributes. If no single column in a table identifies each row uniquely, you should create a primary key. That is known as a *primary key constraint* to ensure uniqueness.

Keys

Keys are one or more attributes that further define an entity so that one instance of the entity is distinguishable from any other instance. Keys can be *singular*, involving only one attribute, or *composite*, involving more than one attribute. Keys are essentially classified into three categories: primary keys, candidate (or alternate) keys, and foreign keys.

Here is what you need to know about each of these key types:

➤ *Primary keys*—In a relational database, every entity (table) should have a primary key. A *primary key* is one or more attributes (columns) that uniquely identify an instance of the entity (a row in the table). When multiple attributes are combined to form a primary key, the result is called a *composite attribute.*

Primary keys must adhere to certain rules:

➤ The value must be unique for each instance of the entity.

➤ The value must not be null.

➤ The value cannot change or become null during the life of the instance.

➤ *Candidate keys and alternate keys*—When reviewing an entity and its associated attributes, you might determine that more than one attribute could serve as a primary key. These attributes become your *candidate keys.* From these, you can select one or more to create a primary key. The candidate keys that do *not* become the primary key are called *alternate keys*. All candidate keys adhere to the same rules as primary keys.

An example of an entity with several candidate keys is **Employees**. An **Employees** entity can have **Employee ID, Social Security Number, Full Name** (first name plus last name combination), and **Email Address** fields. Each of these could uniquely identify an instance of the **Employees** entity (i.e., one employee) in small companies. If the organization always assigns unique employee IDs, then the **Employee ID** column would be a good candidate to become the primary key. However, you should note that although a name combination might uniquely identify an employee in a small company, the name would probably not remain unique in a large organization; therefore, this would not always be a good candidate. A better choice may be the **Social Security Number** column.

➤ *Foreign keys*—A *foreign key* is an attribute or composite attribute that completes the relationship between two entities. This key, then, relates one entity to its parent entity. Foreign keys can relate to a primary key or to one of the alternate keys in another entity. If a foreign key points to a primary key, then the foreign key must be non-null. Otherwise, it can be null. Foreign keys are used to maintain data integrity—called *referential integrity*—and will be discussed later in the chapter.

Entity Relationships

The association between two or more entities that is discovered during data gathering becomes the *relationship* in the ERD. If two entities can be joined with a verb, it is usually true that a relationship exists. For example, **Customers** *buy* **Products**, and **Employees** *have* **Skills**.

 The exam will ask you about creating a foreign key constraint using transaction SQL. The following is an example of creating a foreign key constraint on the **Products** table.

```
ALTER TABLE Products
ADD CONSTRAINT FK FOREIGN KEY(CategoryID)
REFERENCES CATEGORIES(CategoryID)
```

A relationship is classified in terms of cardinality. There are four basic types:

➤ *One-to-one*—For each instance in the first entity, there is one and only one instance in the second entity; and for each instance in the second entity, there is one and only one instance in the first entity. This type is rarely used; you would usually combine these entities into one entity. An example would be an

Employees entity and a **Legal Residence** entity. An employee is really supposed to have only a single legal residence. One of the most important things to remember about the one-to-one relationship is that the two entities involved in the relationship share the same primary key attribute.

➤ *Many-to-many*—For each instance in the first entity, there can be one or more instances in the second entity. Moreover, for each instance in the second entity, there can be one or more instances in the first entity. An author can write many books, and books can have multiple authors. Usually, a many-to-many relationship cannot be handled in a relational database, so you will have to create associated relationships. An associated relationship is an intermediate relationship between the two entities. An example would be an **Authors-Titles** entity. The primary keys of both entities (**Authors** and **Titles**) become attributes of this associative entity.

➤ *Zero-to-many*—There may be instances in the second entity that do not have a corresponding instance in the first entity. For example, you might have an **Employees** table and a **Department** table, where a department exists but does not have any employees. You usually do not see this type of relationship in RDBMSs because it violates *referential integrity* (discussed in the next section).

➤ *One-to-many*—This is probably the most common type of relationship. For each instance in the first entity, there can be one or more instances in the second entity. However, for each instance in the second entity, there can be one and only one instance in the first entity. An employee can exist in only one department, but a department can have many employees. In a one-to-many relationship, the primary key of the first entity usually becomes a foreign key attribute on the "many" side, although the foreign key could point to one of the alternate keys on the "one" side.

The components within the database model are important, but they do not explain the entire logical design process. Another important concept regarding that portion of the design is normalization.

Normalization

One of the last tasks of the logical design phase is *normalization*. Normalization is a refinement process that occurs after you have identified all of the data objects. The goal of normalization is to create a set of relational entities or tables that are free of duplicate data and that can be correctly modified in a consistent manner. Although normalization appears to create redundant data as you create the additional entities or tables, its goal is to eliminate unnecessary duplication. The process usually results in the creation of additional entities/tables.

Why should designs be normalized? Normalization makes a database more efficient in several ways. First, it provides more efficient indexes, and this results in improved updates, deletions, and insertions. Next, normalization aids in eliminating redundant data and protecting against missed data. This helps provide referential integrity constraints. Finally, normalization reduces null values, thereby decreasing inconsistencies and making the database more compact.

In normalization theory, there are five *normal forms* or *degrees*, with each level dependent on the previous one. In other words, each subsequent normal form must meet the previous normal form's requirements plus some additional requirements. Most databases are taken out only to third normal form. When you're looking at the different normalization forms, note that the entities/tables are two-dimensional with instances and attributes (rows and columns, respectively).

First Normal Form

An entity is in first normal form (1NF) if there are no repeating attributes or groups of attributes and if the columns present atomic information. Thus, an entity is in 1NF if:

➤ There are no duplicated rows in the table.

➤ Each column is single-valued (i.e., there are no repeating groups).

➤ Entries in an attribute (column, field) are of the same kind.

As we stated earlier, an attribute should present only one fact about an entity (which makes it atomic). If you follow this practice, entities will be in first normal form. An example of first normal form is shown in Figure 2.2. This example contains repeating data—the skills and their descriptions. If a fourth skill were required, two new columns would be needed. The better design would be to add two tables (one that stores the skill definitions and one that tracks the employees with their skills). Then, when an employee acquires a new skill, new columns don't have to be added to the **Employee** table. Rather, only an instance in the **EmployeeSkills** table is needed.

Second Normal Form

A relational table is in second normal form (2NF) if it is in 1NF and every non-key attribute is fully dependent upon the primary key. Second normal form has no redundant data. Remember that a non-key attribute is an attribute that describes, but does not define, the entity. What should become apparent from this rule is that all tables in second normal form require a primary key. An example of second normal form is shown in Figure 2.3. In Figure 2.3, the **Skill Description** (shown in the upper, incorrect section) has nothing to do with the composite primary key of **EmployeeID** and **SkillID**. The **Description** (shown in the lower, correct section), however, actually belongs only in the **Skills** table.

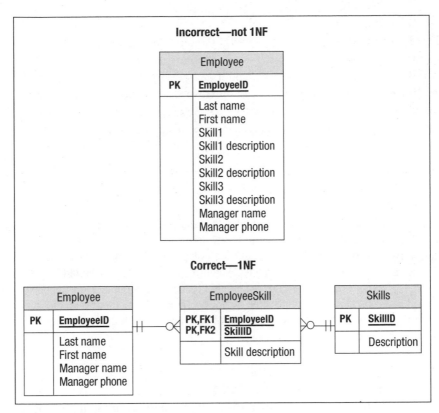

Figure 2.2   First normal form.

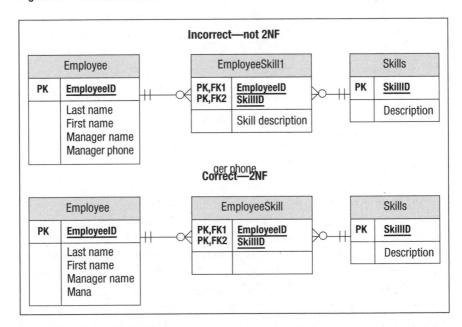

Figure 2.3   Second normal form.

Third Normal Form

Third normal form (3NF) is the most common of the relational tables. Third normal form removes data that is not dependent on the primary key. An entity is in third normal form if it is in 2NF and if no non-key attributes are transitively dependent upon their primary keys. In other words, values of non-key attributes are not dependent on any non-key attributes. An example of third normal form is shown in Figure 2.4. In this example, the manager's name and phone number do not depend on the employee and therefore should not exist in the **Employee** table.

Note: Because managers are also employees, rather than create another table, you could join the Employee table back to itself.

It is important that you understand the definitions of the first three normal forms for the exam. First normal form means that no table contains multivalue columns or multiple columns for the same type of information. 2NF is in effect when you have already converted to 1NF and each column that is not part of a composite primary key depends on the full PK rather than part of it. 3NF is implemented when 2NF has been achieved and columns not covered by the PK do not depend on each other.

Boyce-Codd Normal Form (BCNF)

The Boyce-Codd normal form (BCNF) is a more restrictive 3NF. It's sometimes called the *3 1/2 normal form*. An entity is in BCNF if the entity is in 3NF and if every determinant is a candidate key. In the definitions of second and third normal forms, it is assumed that all attributes not actually part of the candidate keys nonetheless depend on the candidate keys. BCNF goes one step further and states that dependencies within keys must also be dependent on the keys. Most 3NF relationships are also BCNF. Anomalies occur in BCNF when:

➤ The candidate keys are composite keys (that is, they are not single attributes).

➤ There is more than one candidate key in the relation.

➤ The keys are not disjointed (that is, some attributes in the keys are common).

Fourth Normal Form

Fourth normal form (4NF) deals with multivalued normalization. An entity is in 4NF if it is in BCNF and if it has no multivalued dependencies. In other words, an entity is in 4NF if all dependencies are a result of keys. For example, employees can have many skills and take many courses. Fourth normal form would not result in combining the skills and courses into the same table. Rather, 4NF would have two tables created: one for skills and one for courses.

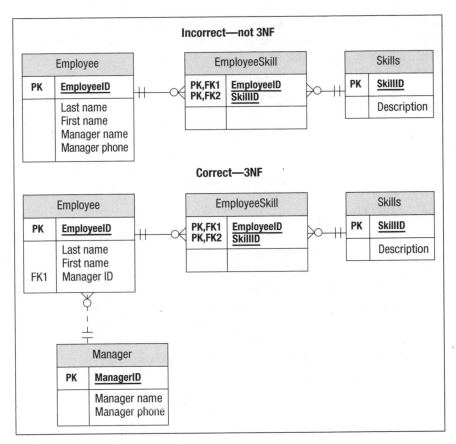

Figure 2.4   Third normal form.

Fifth Normal Form

Fifth normal form (5NF) is also called *projection-join normal form (PJNF)*. An entity is in 5NF if it is in 4NF and if every *join dependency* in the entity is a consequence of the candidate keys of that entity. In other words, the goal is to have relationships that cannot be broken down (decomposed) any further. Although it is usually a goal to keep related attributes together, sometimes it is better to place these attributes in separate tables.

The third aspect of logical design is whether data integrity can be maintained. That is the next section of our discussion.

Data Integrity

The requirements analysis (part of what is commonly referred to as the conceptual phase), included not only discovering which items the system should track but also determining the data's characteristics or traits. When the logical model is designed, these requirements become what are called *data integrity* rules. Data integrity ensures that the data values in the database are correct and consistent. Data integrity can be divided into four rule types: three standard (entity, referential, and domain) and one user-defined.

Entity Integrity

The *entity integrity* rule states that for every instance of an entity, the value of the primary key must exist, must be unique, and cannot be null. Notice that the definition of entity integrity is the same as the definition of the primary key. Remember that an instance of an entity becomes a row in a table.

Referential Integrity

The *referential integrity* rule states that every foreign key value must match a primary key value in an associated table. Referential integrity ensures that the data stays consistent between the two tables after you use an **INSERT, DELETE,** or **UPDATE** command. When you add a foreign key to link two tables, you form a parent-child hierarchy. The foreign key of the child refers to the primary key of the parent. Referential integrity preserves this relationship. Referential integrity ensures that you do not delete from the parent a record that would leave the child an orphan, and that you do not add a child without adding its parent, too.

Note: A foreign key can also refer to one of the candidate keys instead of the primary key.

Domain Integrity

Domain integrity rules ensure that there is a valid set of values for an attribute. You should gather the following types of information for each attribute:

➤ *Data Type*—Basic data types are integer, decimal, character, and date-time. Most databases support variants of these.

➤ *Length/Size*—This is the number of digits or characters, such as 20 characters or 5 digits.

➤ *Date Format*—This is the format for date values, such as dd/mm/yy or yy/mm/dd.

➤ *Range*—The range specifies the lower and upper boundaries of an attribute. For instance, you could specify that a quantity must be greater than 100 and less than 10,000.

➤ *Constraints*—These are special restrictions on allowable values. An example is the typical use of ZIP codes, where they should be all numeric and the value must be unique.

➤ *Null Support*—This indicates whether the attribute can have null values.

➤ *Default Value (if any)*—This is the value used if none is entered. For instance, a quantity attribute might have a default of zero instead of null or blank.

User-Defined Integrity

In addition to the three integrity rules just described, more *user-defined integrity* rules can be placed on the data so that applicable business restrictions are enforced. Such restrictions should be unique to an organization. They enforce rules that would make otherwise valid data invalid for that specific organization. For instance, a company in a particular region might require that its employees live within the region. An integrity rule could be used that verifies this requirement before allowing the data to be entered into the system.

Database Size

After completing the ERD model and determining the data integrity rules for entities and attributes, you need to determine which database product will optimally suit the system's needs. The principal factor in making this selection is the size of the database. Any estimates of the database's size should be based upon the database when it's filled with the data. Estimating the size helps you determine not only which vendor to choose but also which type of hardware will be required. Estimating the size also helps you determine whether the database design needs refining.

Determining the size of a database involves estimating the extent of each entity or table as well as determining the types and number of indexes. To calculate the size of the entity or table, you estimate the length of each row (the sum of the size and type of each attribute), and then estimate how many instances should be expected. Microsoft provides several formulas for estimating size based on its engine, either with or without using a clustered index. These formulas are located in the SQL Server Books Online; see "Creating and Maintaining Databases: Estimating the Size of a Database." Go to the following Web site: **http:// msdn.microsoft.com/library/default.asp?URL=/library/psdk/sql/portal_7ap1.htm**. Then, in the left pane (under SQL Server), select the following series of headings: Creating And Maintaining Databases|Databases|Database Design Considerations|Estimating The Size Of A Database.

Physical Design

Now a logical model exists for your data, but it is not a database yet. The logical model still needs to be converted into a physical model. Many sophisticated database design tools can convert your logical design into the actual physical database. That is, they physically build the tables with the constraints determined when the logical model was developed. If the logical model is well thought out, then building the physical database will be straightforward. Entities become tables, attributes become the columns in the table, and relationships define how all the components interact with each other in the database.

The Microsoft SQL Server Database Designer Tool

Microsoft SQL Server 2000 provides a tool—the Database Designer, located in the Enterprise Manager—that will help you create the physical model. This tool redraws the ERD. Each entity becomes a new table, and its attributes become the columns of that table. The tool also applies the specified constraints and defines the desired relationships. When you save this diagram, SQL builds the physical tables in your database. Before you can use the Database Designer, however, the database must already have been created.

To launch the Database Designer, do the following:

1. Start the Enterprise Manager.

2. Either right-click on the diagrams node (located under the database node) and select New Database Diagram (to create a new database); or double-click on an existing diagram (to modify or review it).

When you're creating tables, remember to follow the normalization rules discussed earlier. If they were used when the logical model was designed, then the system's entities will likely have followed those rules, and your tables will be more efficient. Following are the rules for normalizing tables:

➤ All tables should have a primary key (identifier).

➤ All data within a table should refer to one entity and only one entity.

➤ A table should avoid null-value columns.

➤ A table should not have repeating values or columns.

 Although normalizing tables is effective for queries, to improve inserts, updates, and deletes (online transaction processing) you should, in some cases, denormalize and change fewer indexes on tables.

Constraints

The data integrity rules identified when the logical model was designed become the database's constraints. Table 2.1 summarizes how data integrity rules map to database constraint types. *Constraints* ensure that the data within a database is consistent and accurate.

Table 2.1	Data integrity constraints.
Integrity Type	**Constraint Type**
Entity	**PRIMARY KEY** constraint; **UNIQUE** constraint; index; **IDENTITY** property
Domain	Data types; **CHECK** constraints; rules; **DEFAULT** constraint; **NOT NULL** constraint; **FOREIGN KEY** constraint
Referential	**FOREIGN KEY** constraint; **CHECK** constraint; triggers
User-defined	Any of the constraints listed in this table; triggers; stored procedures

The primary key of an entity becomes the primary key of the table. This rule is enforced by virtue of its being a primary key constraint. Because the alternate keys in the entity could have been the primary key, the data is usually unique. To ensure this uniqueness, you should construct a unique index constraint. If the alternate key is not unique, then you might still need to create an index to aid in retrieving this data.

Usually keys (whether primary or alternate) are prime candidates for being criteria in a query, and they might operate more efficiently if an index of them is created. You can also improve performance by adding columns with pre-aggregated data instead of using aggregate functions in queries.

The relationships defined earlier (in the logical model) will be further supplemented by using foreign key constraints. Foreign key constraints maintain referential integrity. Triggers can also help maintain referential integrity. Indexes for foreign key constraints also need to be created. Each foreign key must be unique if it refers to a primary key. However, if the foreign key refers to an alternate key, then it might not necessarily have to be unique.

Performance

In addition to ensuring that a system's data is accurate and consistent, you should ensure that it can be manipulated efficiently. Quality and speed are foremost. Although performance is monitored for the life of the database, an optimized initial design makes subsequent database performance issues less burdensome to incorporate. Planning for database performance issues early in the design phases saves development time, and this ultimately cuts cost. However, if done properly, this planning also limits user stress, and this also saves money.

There are several areas to consider when you're determining potential database performance issues. Using large-volume tables and complex tables with many constraints affects a database's performance. In tables with large volumes of data, consider splitting the data into multiple tables (with the most-used or most important data in one table and lesser-used or non-essential data in another). Consider also the numbers of users who will be accessing this data. Some designs work well with a few users, but as the number of users increases, many designs can be stressed such that they can no longer support the users efficiently. In some cases, indexes can aid database performance. In other cases, however, they can hinder it. Therefore, their impact must be considered both in the initial database creation and as an ongoing task.

Denormalization

Denormalization is the process of taking data that has previously been split into multiple tables and recombining them back into one table. This reduces the overhead of *table joins* when you're performing queries. Denormalization often occurs in data warehousing to reduce complexity and to increase the speed of querying data. A good rule to follow is that a database should be normalized and then selectively denormalized as necessary.

Sometimes in our zeal to follow the database normalization rules, databases can be over-normalized and end up with numerous small, interrelated tables. When the database processes the data (with actions such as retrieve, update, delete, or modify), a great deal of extra work occurs because the database has to recalculate the data's relationships. Usually, a database in third normal form has been taken far enough and is typically considered to be in the optimally normalized state. If higher normal form rules are applied, then usually the database ends up later needing denormalizing to increase its performance.

Hardware Considerations

Obviously, the larger the database, the greater the need for more capable hardware. However, the size of a database is not the only factor in determining hardware needs. Other factors include the number of users accessing the data, the number of transactions and anticipated response times from users, and the types of operations users will be performing. Depending on these factors, increased memory, additional hard disk space, and/or faster processors may be needed. What's more, RAID technology (now commonly defined as "redundant array of independent disks" or what used to be referred to as "redundant array of inexpensive disks") might result in additional hardware that may increase the system's efficiency. Additionally, proper use of filegroups can help achieve increased performance. (Filegroups are discussed in the next chapter.)

Microsoft SQL Server 2000 provides several tools to help you monitor database performance. Such tools include SQL Server Profiler, Performance Monitor (using

NT Performance Monitor with counters designed for SQL Server), and the Index Tuning Wizard. Although these tools are useful for the ongoing task of database monitoring, they cannot substitute for a good database design.

Maintenance

A properly maintained database is essential to its successful use and application. Maintenance is a critical factor that sometimes is overlooked when a new database is rolled out. For instance, during database design, the design team often overlooks answers to such questions as: How often should data backups be conducted? How much of the data must be backed up? How fast must the database come online after a crash? A regular and well-thought-out backup strategy must be put in place to ensure that the database stays available and contains consistent, accurate data.

Another maintenance task is ensuring proper database performance and avoiding built-in choke points. A plan for monitoring the database's use can help you quickly determine the causes of bottlenecks and rectify them. Microsoft SQL Server 2000 provides several tools for performing and automating these tasks. One such tool that can help you set up a monitoring plan is the Database Maintenance Plan Wizard. Another tool that helps with database performance is the Index Tuning Wizard; use it when you're determining whether you need to add or remove indexes.

Again, to minimize database maintenance and its impacts, the importance of a well-designed plan should be emphasized. A database should be as small and as easily maintainable as possible. This is why normalizing the design helps by eliminating redundant data and reducing the overall database size. Breaking up (partitioning) large tables into smaller tables also helps with decreasing the time required for maintenance and with reducing the requirement for detailed monitoring. Additionally, there may be a way that cyclical data could be organized on a yearly basis (or monthly) to reduce the monitoring task as well as to assist when maintenance is required.

Security

Database designers must not only ensure that the data within the database is accurate and consistent but also devise methods to help protect that data. Security measures—such as specifying (and restricting) who can read or modify the data—are important matters. These questions should be addressed early in the design, through the physical implementation, and all the way through continued maintenance and support. The security system within SQL Server helps control user access to the database and uses permissions to control user actions on the data. A database's design should incorporate the security enhancements available through the SQL Server security system. Then, as the database increases in size and objects are added, these security measures will help maintain a secure environment. In addition to SQL Server providing protection at the server level, it also provides security at the database level. At that level, users, roles, and permissions can be defined. These will be discussed in Chapter 14.

Data Modeling Steps

Effectively modeling data before building a database is extremely helpful in determining all system requirements as well as in reducing potential problems. The process of developing a good model includes these steps:

1. Gather requirements.

2. Identify the data objects, characteristics, and any associations.

3. Create the initial ERD with entities and relationships.

4. Refine the ERD (reviewing it with users and making necessary changes).

5. Define the key attributes (keys).

6. Add non-key attributes (descriptive characteristics).

7. Define hierarchical (parent-child) relationships (foreign key relationships).

8. Validate the model through normalization.

9. Add business and integrity rules.

10. Determine which database engine to use.

11. Translate your model to a physical database.

Practice Questions

Case Study

The Best Jewelry store has been running its business with paper and pencil for decades. Store owners have been able to keep track of their employees, customers, and supplies by using the tried and true staples of business—ledgers and lots of paper. With business falling off and the workload increasing at an alarming rate, Asghar Nazemzadeh (the store manager) recently declared that he would like to get the company computerized. Your task is to interview the various people in an effort to clarify the design process. Remember, it is a small store, and the owners have been reluctant to modernize. Remember, too, that they specialize in the field of fine (expensive) jewelry, whose requirements for meticulous detail and volumes of data lend themselves nicely to database use.

The Owners (Lauren and Ricky McMahon)

If we have to do any kind of updating, we want an inexpensive system that will track everything easily and be affordable to maintain. We do agree that there is a need to get a handle on which types of jewelry sell the most (so we know what we should stock more of) and, conversely, which types don't (so we know which we should stop carrying). We would also like to keep track of additional information about our employees.

Accountant (Jonny Antoline)

I need a system that can track employees and their status. I need a system that tracks inventory: who supplies what; who buys what; what is on hand; and when I should reorder. We have fewer than 10 employees, and we have fewer than 50 categories and suppliers, so we don't need a large system.

Store Manager (Asghar Nazemzadeh)

I want a system that lets me know who my customers are and what they are interested in so I can stock those items. I also want to be able to send out special fliers through the mail and email to let customers know that their favorite product is on sale. I want a system that tells me if I have an item stored in the back.

Question 1

Based on the case study, identify some of the entities. [Check all correct answers]

❑ a. Employees

❑ b. Store Manager

❑ c. Customers

❑ d. Products

❑ e. Suppliers

Answers a, c, d, and e are correct. Entities would include **Employees, Customers, Products,** and **Suppliers**. Answer b is incorrect; Store Manager is a type of employee or an employee's title, but not an entity.

Question 2

Following are some of the entities and attributes for the Best Jewelry store:

Employees	Suppliers	Products
LastName	FirstName	Title
ContactName	BirthDate	Address
ProductName	SupplierName	Discount

Place the attributes under the correct entities. You may use an item more than once or not at all.

The correct answer is:

> **Employees**
>
> > **LastName**
> >
> > **FirstName**
> >
> > **Title**
> >
> > **Address**
> >
> > **BirthDate**

Suppliers

>   SupplierName

>   ContactName

>   Address

Products

>   ProductName

>   SupplierName

For **Employees,** you would want their last name and first name, but for **Suppliers,** you would need only the contact name because you would identify a supplier by its company name and not by the contact. You would not necessarily need the **Title** and most likely would not need the **Birthdate** of the supplier, either. A **Discount** would more likely be applied to an order and not to a supplier or employee.

Question 3

The following are some of the attributes of the **Customers** table:

CustomerNo	**CustomerName**	**Address**
City	**PostalCode**	**Phone**
Fax	**Email**	

Which of the following is the best choice for a combination of primary keys (PK) and alternate keys (AK)?

○ a. PK = **CustomerNo**, AK = **Email, CustomerName**

○ b. PK = **CustomerNo**, AK = **Email**

○ c. PK = **Email**, AK = **CustomerNo, CustomerName**

○ d. PK = **CustomerName**, AK = **CustomerNo, Email**

Answer b is the correct response. The primary key would be the **CustomerNo,** and an alternate key would be **Email.** Answer c is incorrect because even though **Email** is unique, users can change their email addresses, so it would not necessarily be a good primary key. Primary keys should never change. Answers a and d are incorrect because **CustomerName** might not be unique and thus would be neither a good primary key nor a good alternate key.

Question 4

Using the case study, assume that you have identified the following entities and attributes:

Products

   ProductNo

   ProductName

   SupplierName1

   SupplierContact1

   SupplierName2

   SupplierContact2

   Category Name

   Category Description

Suppliers

   SupplierNo

Categories

   CategoryNo

Rearrange these so your design is in 3NF.

The correct answer is:

    Categories

       CategoryNo

       CategoryName

       CategoryDescription

    Products

       ProductNo

       ProductName

       SupplierNo

       CategoryNo

    Suppliers

       SupplierNo

       SupplierName1

SupplierContact1

SupplierName2

SupplierContact2

You would separate the **Suppliers** from the **Products** to reduce repeating groups. **CategoryName** and **CategoryDescription** are non-essential to the product. They should be moved and then referenced using a foreign key. Note that **Suppliers** has a one-to-many relationship to **Products** and that **Categories** has a one-to-many relationship to **Products**.

Question 5

Which of the following types of relationships *cannot* be implemented in a relational database?

○ a. One-to-one

○ b. One-to-many

○ c. Zero-to-many

○ d. Many-to-many

Answer d is correct. Most relational databases cannot handle many-to-many relationships. Instead, create an associated relationship that sits between the two entities. The remaining answers (a, b, and c) are valid relationships.

Question 6

What is denormalization?

○ a. Splitting one entity into multiple entities

○ b. Creating an entity that has two primary keys

○ c. Recombining two previously split entities back into one entity

○ d. Removing repeating groups in an entity

Answer c is correct. Denormalization is the process of recombining entities that were split. Answer a is incorrect because it is the process of normalization. Answer b is incorrect because an entity cannot have two primary keys. Answer d is incorrect because it is the definition of 1NF.

Question 7

Rearrange the following items into entities with their attributes, and identify the primary key (PK) and foreign key (FK). Not all items need to be used.

Orders

OrderDetails

OrderNo

CustomerNo

Date

ProductName

ProductNo

Price

Quantity

The correct answer is:

> Orders
>
> > OrderNo (PK)
> >
> > CustomerNo (FK)
> >
> > Date
>
> OrderDetails
>
> > OrderNo (PK, FK)
> >
> > ProductNo (PK, FK)
> >
> > Price
> >
> > Quantity

The **ProductName** would be included in the **Products** entity (which was not identified in the list). The **Orders** entity would have an order number and a reference to the **Customer** table and the date of the order. The **OrderDetails** entity would have a row for each product purchased in the order. The **OrderNo** combined with the **ProductNo** would make up the primary key, and both of these refer to other tables.

Question 8

The **Products** entity defined for this case study is shown below:

Products

   ProductNo

   ProductName

   Price

   SupplierNo

Apply some or all of the following constraints to the attributes shown in the **Products** entity:

- Primary key constraint
- Foreign key constraint
- Check constraint
- Unique constraint
- **IDENTITY** property

The correct answer is:

   Products

      ProductNo: Primary key constraint, **IDENTITY** property

      ProductName: Unique constraint

      Price: Check constraint

      SupplierNo: Foreign key constraint

The **ProductNo** will become the primary key. To generate numbers, you could use the **IDENTITY** property. The **SupplierNo** would refer to the **Supplier** entity. Although it may have the **IDENTITY** property assigned to it, this would be done under the **Supplier** entity. The **Price**, which should have at least a value of zero, would benefit by a default or check constraint. The **ProductName** would most likely be unique.

Question 9

> What are the characteristics of a primary key constraint? [Check all correct answers]
>
> ❑ a. A primary key constraint must be unique.
>
> ❑ b. A primary key constraint can contain foreign key null values.
>
> ❑ c. A primary key's value does not change.
>
> ❑ d. A primary key constraint must not have null values.

Answers a, c, and d are correct. A primary key must be unique, must never change, and must not have any null values. Because a primary key constraint cannot contain null values, answer b is incorrect.

Question 10

> An entity is in second normal form if which of the following statements are true? [Check all correct answers]
>
> ❑ a. Entries in an attribute (column, field) are of the same kind.
>
> ❑ b. There are no duplicated rows in the entity.
>
> ❑ c. There are no repeating groups in the entity.
>
> ❑ d. Data not dependent on the primary key is removed.
>
> ❑ e. Every non-key attribute is fully dependent upon the primary key.

Answers a, b, c, and e are correct. To be in 2NF, the entity must be in 1NF, which has the characteristics identified by answers a, b, and c. In addition, non-key attributes are fully dependent upon the primary key (answer e). Answer d is incorrect because this would make the entity 3NF.

Need to Know More?

 Iseminger, David. *SQL Server 2000 Reference Library*. Redmond, WA: Microsoft Press, 2000. ISBN 0-7356-1280-3. A selected collection of SQL Server Books Online. There are six volumes focused on key areas.

 Microsoft SQL Server Books Online has a section on database design ("Creating and Maintaining Databases"). This is also available online at the following "Getting Started with SQL Server Books Online" page: **http://msdn.microsoft.com/library/default.asp?ShowPane =false&URL=/library/psdk/sql/getstart_4fht.htm**.

 Search the TechNet CD or its online version through **www.microsoft.com/ technet/**. Good keywords to search on are "database design", "modeling", and "Visio".

 www.microsoft.com/sql/ is a good place to find up-to-date information about SQL Server.

SQL Server 2000 Database Formation

Terms you'll need to understand:

- ✓ System databases
- ✓ The **master** database
- ✓ The **model** database
- ✓ The **tempdb** database
- ✓ The **msdb** database
- ✓ System tables
- ✓ Metadata
- ✓ Pages
- ✓ Extents
- ✓ Primary file
- ✓ Secondary file
- ✓ Transaction log
- ✓ Filegroups
- ✓ Database options
- ✓ Recovery model

Techniques you'll need to master:

- ✓ Understanding system databases
- ✓ Creating databases
- ✓ Modifying databases
- ✓ Creating and altering filegroups
- ✓ Configuring databases
- ✓ Retrieving database information

In the previous chapter, we looked at how the process of data modeling helps you define the data requirements of your system. We saw that you first gather as much information as possible and develop the logical design of the system. From there, that data helps you develop the actual physical requirements. After you come up with the data's logical design, followed by its physical model, SQL Server 2000 gets installed, and you must begin the actual task of forming your database from the materials included with Microsoft's software package.

When you're putting your database together, some of the materials in Microsoft's SQL Server 2000 software are necessary components that form the foundation of your physical database. A good example of these components, which will be discussed in the next section, is the set of system databases that Microsoft includes with the installation files. Microsoft also includes other materials, however, as samples that can be used if you need to see properly formed databases. We will take a look at two of these samples. You will also need many other files as you consider space management and file location. For example, you'll use these files when you change your original database structure or its size. These are some of the topics covered in this chapter.

First, let's look at SQL Server 2000 itself and then discuss some of the databases that support SQL Server and the user-defined databases.

SQL Server 2000 Basics

Of the database types discussed in the previous chapter, SQL Server 2000 is a relational database management system (RDBMS) that primarily uses the Transact-SQL query and programming language. SQL Server 2000 is capable of handling high volumes of online transaction processing (OLTP) and the multitudes of decision-support or data-warehousing tasks required of online analytical processing (OLAP). SQL Server 2000 processes client requests for transaction storage or retrieval and handles client applications' requests for analysis on data stored within the database itself. Such requests can be initiated from within SQL Server 2000 but normally are the result of client-initiated applications that request query results. Typically, this client interaction with SQL Server 2000's capabilities is accomplished over a company's computer-based network.

Although SQL Server 2000 can be installed such that it becomes limited to being an individual's personal database, it is more commonly thought of for its capacity to handle large enterprise-wide data storage and retrieval requirements. Microsoft has included installation provisions for SQL Server 2000's client operation on systems ranging from DOS and Windows 3.1 up through Windows 95, 98, ME, NT 4, and, as you'd expect, the entire Windows 2000 family. However, with Microsoft's decision to keep SQL Server 2000 as an open-architecture system, it is also capable of working well with Internet browsers and with many of the other independent operating systems available, such as Unix. Additionally, SQL Server 2000 can have multiple installations on the same system that can be set up to use either the same or totally separate data and system users.

In general, client installation is considered universally available, but some components of SQL Server 2000 (such as the database engine and its Analysis server) are limited as to which operating system they can be installed on. Neither of these components can, for instance, be installed on Windows 2000 Professional or similar single-individual systems, even though most of these systems can operate the client components—some SQL Server 2000 components require that you be running Windows 2000 Server.

System Databases

The system databases are used to store information about the SQL environment and about all the databases that are controlled by SQL Server. Four system databases are installed automatically when the SQL Server 2000 installation process finishes. They are the **master, model, tempdb,** and **msdb** databases. An additional **distribution** database gets created when SQL Server 2000 replication is initiated.

Note: Please be aware that although SQL is normally considered insensitive to capitalization, the names of these databases are indeed case-sensitive.

The master Database

The **master** database is the key to SQL Server; this database stores all system-level information. This information includes login accounts (who can access SQL Server), server initialization and configuration settings, and a list of all databases (including their physical locations) maintained by this instance of SQL Server. If the **master** database gets corrupted, SQL Server ceases to function.

You can, however, use the Rebuild Master utility to fix a corrupt master database if necessary. To rebuild the **master** database:

1. Shut down SQL Server.

2. Run the Rebuildm.exe file in the Tools\Binn folder.

3. Click Browse when the Rebuild Master dialog appears.

4. Select the Data directory from the SQL Server installation CD; then click OK.

5. Click Settings if you want to modify **master** or other database settings. (This step is not required.)

6. When the Rebuild Master dialog appears, click Rebuild to reinstall the **master** database.

Remember that rebuilding a **master** database causes each object in the database and all the data to be deleted. Before you rebuild the **master** database, be sure to have either a backup of the data and log files, or the scripts for each database object (such as stored procedures and tables) and a backup of the data. Reconstruct the database objects and restore the data by using the **sp_attach_db** stored procedure after you rebuild the **master** database.

The model Database

The **model** database—as its name implies—is a template or prototype for building new user databases. The **model** database contains options, settings, and even objects that are applied to all new databases. After a database is created, the **model** database has no effect on it. The **model** database is required for SQL Server to start up because this database is used to create the **tempdb** database, which is created each time SQL Server is started. The size of the **model** database determines the smallest size that a database can be on a server.

The tempdb Database

The **tempdb** database is a temporary storage area that holds temporary tables, stored procedures, and any other temporary needs of SQL Server, such as working tables. This database is global; every resource that has access to SQL Server has access to the **tempdb** database. When a connection is closed, the data that was stored in the **tempdb** database for that connection is lost. When the server is shut down, nothing is retained; this database is created fresh each time SQL Server starts. Because the **tempdb** database is reconstructed each time SQL Server is restarted, you cannot back it up.

The **tempdb** database automatically grows (*autogrows*) while the server is running; however, when the server is shut down and restarted, the **tempdb** database returns to its initial size (unlike all other databases, which retain their new size). With the increased efficiency of the SQL Server engine starting in version 7, the **tempdb** database no longer resides in RAM.

 If your **tempdb** database has to grow each time the server is restarted, consider increasing the initial size by using the **ALTER DATABASE** statement.

The msdb Database

The **msdb** database works with the SQL Server Agent. The **msdb** database stores information about schedules, jobs, alerts, and the operators responsible for these tasks. If this database is missing or corrupt, the SQL Server Agent will not function, but SQL Server will continue to work.

Sample Databases

In addition to the four system databases, two sample databases are installed automatically when you install SQL Server 2000. These samples can be practiced on or removed at any time and rebuilt whenever desired.

The pubs Database

The **pubs** sample database is modeled after a book publishing company, and it seems to be one of Microsoft's favorites to use in certification training courses. You might become very familiar with this database should you take many classes along the certification track. The mere fact that it is widely distributed and recognized, coupled with the fact that it is relatively small and does not take up much room, makes it a good item to leave installed on your system. This database provides excellent common ground for explaining expansion concepts to potential developers, and it is a constant source for continued training examples.

The Northwind Database

Also fairly small and widely used in Microsoft examples during certification training courses and throughout its documentation materials, the **Northwind** sample database contains the sales data for a fictitious company called Northwind Traders. Because it is a bit more complicated, it is also somewhat larger than the **pubs** database (nearly double its size). However, because of its beginnings as a Microsoft Access database, it is also even more widely known by people in the database certification tracks.

Both the **pubs** and **Northwind** databases contain scripts, located in the \Install directory, that will let you rebuild the databases if they are removed. You can simply execute instpubs.sql or instnwnd.sql to reinitiate the database you want to rebuild. This is a handy feature because you can experiment freely upon either sample database (or both) with the comfortable knowledge that you can simply rebuild them and start again.

System Files and Tables

Starting in SQL Server 7, databases are made of individual operating system files located on the drives managed by SQL Server. The default location of the database and log files is Program Files\Microsoft SQL Server\MSSQL\Data. SQL Server program files are located in MSSQL\Binn. You can change these locations when you install SQL Server.

Every database in SQL Server contains *system tables*, which contain data needed by the SQL Server components. This data is known as *metadata*, or information about the properties of the objects contained in SQL Server. (These objects include databases, tables, columns, users, and so on.) There is server-wide data, which is stored in the **master** database, and there is database-specific data, which is stored in each individual database. System tables are analogous to the data dictionaries used in other RDBMSs.

Microsoft does not support users directly updating the information in the system tables. Instead, Microsoft provides a complete set of administrative tools that allow users to fully administer their system tables and to manage all users and objects in a database. We will be looking at some of these tools throughout the book.

 You will notice that all system tables start with the letters "sys" to indicate that they are system tables. Do not start user tables with these letters, or you won't be able to distinguish them from system tables.

Database Considerations

You know that a database is a collection of tables and all the supporting objects, such as views, indexes, stored procedures, and triggers. Before creating a database, you need to be prepared with some important information, such as what the name of the database will be, who owns the database, what its estimated size is, and what file structure (which files and filegroups) will hold your data.

Some points to consider:

➤ By default, only the **sysadmin** and **dbcreator** roles can create databases. Because the user who creates the database becomes the owner, after creating the database, you'll need to change the database owner.

➤ The maximum number of databases on a given SQL server is 32,767.

➤ Databases are stored in operating system files.

➤ The name of the database must follow the rules for creating identifiers.

➤ The **model** database contains defaults that are applied when you create a database.

➤ Information about each database is stored in the **sysdatabases** table in the **master** database. When you issue the **CREATE DATABASE** statement, you must be connected to the **master** database.

Database Files and Filegroups

Microsoft SQL Server maps a database by using a set of operating system files, which store all the objects that make up a database. A database consists of at least two database files—the primary data file and one transaction log. In addition, a database may have secondary data files. The maximum size for a file is 32TB, so typical databases will not require secondary data files. Each file has two name properties: the logical file name, used in Transact-SQL statements; and the physical file name, used by the operating system. The logical file name must conform to the rules for SQL Server identifiers and must be unique to the database. The physical file name must follow the rules for Microsoft Windows operating systems. The file names are stored both in the **sysaltfiles** table of the **master** database and in the **sysfiles** table located in the primary file of the specific database. The maximum number of files per database is the same as the number of allowable databases on a given SQL server: 32,767.

Although SQL Server allows you to change the file extensions for the physical database files, doing so is not recommended.

Understanding how data is organized is key to setting up your database. The following section discusses this topic with an introduction to pages and extents and looks into the different data files and transaction logs. Then we'll conclude our short discussion about this area by investigating filegroups and some general recommendations on their use.

Pages and Extents

Database files are made up of pages. A *page* is a contiguous block of virtual addresses. A page is 8KB; therefore, there are 128 pages per megabyte. The first 96 bytes of each page are reserved for header information, such as the type of page, the amount of free space on the page, and the object ID of the object owning the page. Log files do not contain pages; they contain virtual log records.

Pages are categorized as follows. To manage file space, SQL Server provides two types of pages: PFS (Page Free Space) and GAM and SGAM (Global Allocation Map and Secondary Global Allocation Map). To track tables and indexes, SQL Server provides four types of pages: IAM (Index Allocation Map), Data, Text/Image, and Index. To track backups, SQL Server provides two types of pages: Bulk Changed Map and the Differential Changed Map.

Rows cannot span pages; therefore, the maximum amount of data—not including **text, ntext,** and **image** data—contained in a single row is 8,060 bytes. This limit is important when you're considering the size of your database.

An *extent* is the amount of space allocated for SQL Server objects such as indexes and tables. Extents are 8 contiguous pages, or 64KB. There are 16 extents per megabyte. There are two types of extents: *mixed extents*, which contain more than one object; and *uniform extents*, which contain a single object.

The first extent of a database is reserved for system information and contains the following:

➤ Page 0, the file header, contains file attributes such as the name and owner of the database.

➤ Page 1, the PFS (Page Free Space) page, contains information about the free space available.

➤ Page 2, the GAM (Global Allocation Map), contains information about allocated extents. This page contains a bit for each extent: A value of 0 indicates that the extent is allocated; a value of 1 indicates that it is available.

➤ Page 3, the SGMA (Secondary Global Allocation Map), contains information about allocated mixed extents. A value of 1 indicates that the extent is a mixed extent with one or more free pages. A value of 0 means that the extent is not mixed or is mixed with no free pages.

The Primary Data File

The *primary data file* contains the startup information for the database (tracking all other database files) and usually contains the actual data that users see. Every database has one and only one primary data file. The default file extension is .mdf.

Secondary Data Files

The *secondary data file* or files are optional. They are used when the primary data file cannot hold all of the data or when you want to put certain objects on separate disk drives. The default file extension is .ndf.

The Transaction Log

The *transaction log* is a serial record that has its own cache, separate from the buffer cache used for data pages. Log files hold all of the information used to recover the database; this information includes the start of each transaction, the changes to the data, and enough information to undo the modifications made during each transaction. Each database must have at least one log file. The recommended size is 25 percent of the database. The default file extension is .ldf.

So that you can recover data, you should always create the log files on separate physical disks from the primary or secondary files. If the log file reaches its maximum size and cannot grow further, then all modifications stop until the transaction log is emptied. You can also use log shipping to back up a transaction log from one database to another to maintain a consistent backup.

Filegroups

Filegroups are named collections of files. Filegroups separate specific objects onto separate physical disks. Each database can have up to 256 filegroups.

Some points to remember are:

➤ A file can be in only one filegroup.

➤ Transaction logs are never part of a filegroup.

➤ There are two types of filegroups: primary and user defined (secondary). The primary filegroup contains the primary file, system tables, and other files not specified in the user-defined filegroups.

➤ Tables and indexes can be specified to reside in any filegroup; if their location is not specified, they will be allocated to the default filegroup.

➤ Initially, the default filegroup is the primary filegroup, but the primary filegroup can be reassigned to another filegroup.

➤ With the exception of the primary filegroup, all other filegroups can be marked read-only. This attribute can be used to separate historical data tables from the active data and to place this data on separate disks.

File and Filegroup Recommendations

Following are some general recommendations for files and filegroups:

➤ The performance of SQL Server is quite efficient; most databases need only a primary data file, a primary filegroup, and the transaction log. In most instances, you can obtain the same performance gain by using RAID (redundant array of independent disks) technology as you can by creating files and filegroups.

➤ If you use multiple files, then create a secondary filegroup for the additional files, and make that filegroup the default filegroup. This way, the primary file will contain only system tables and objects.

➤ To maximize performance, create files or filegroups on as many different local physical disks as possible, and place objects that compete heavily for space in different filegroups.

➤ Place different tables used in the same JOIN queries in different filegroups. This improves performance due to parallel disk I/O searching for joined data.

➤ Place heavily accessed tables and their nonclustered indexes in different filegroups on different physical disks. This improves performance due to parallel I/O.

➤ Do not place the transaction log file or files on the same physical disk with the other files (primary or secondary) and filegroups.

➤ Having separate files and filegroups allows you to back up and restore sections of a database rather than the entire database.

A new feature in SQL Server 2000 is the ability to create databases on raw partitions. *Raw partitions* are disk partitions that have *not* been formatted with a Microsoft Windows NT file system, such as FAT or NTFS. The recommended method is to use FAT or NTFS.

Creating Databases

You create databases by using a Transact-SQL statement or the Enterprise Manager. The examples that follow (in the next section and in Listings 3.1 and 3.2) all use the Transact-SQL syntax. The same result, however, is possible if you use the Enterprise Manager when you create a database. The main difference between the two methods is simplicity. Enterprise Manager is basically just a template that acts like Microsoft's now-familiar "assistant" and walks you through creating a database and setting up all the desired properties; the end result is a complete database.

People with the **sysadmin** and **dbcreator** server roles are, by default, the only people who can issue the **CREATE DATABASE** statement in either form. To maintain control over disk usage, you want to minimize the number of people who can create databases. The **sysadmin** or **securityadmin** roles can grant **CREATE DATABASE** permission to other roles. You can also add other logins to the **dbcreator** role. The **GRANT ALL** statement does not grant **CREATE DATABASE** permission; it must be explicitly given.

When SQL Server creates the new database, it starts by initializing the new database based on the **model** database, applying all the objects defined in **model**. Then, SQL Server fills the rest of the database with empty pages. If you do not specify a size for your database, the size of the **model** database is used.

 The smallest size a database can be is the size of the **model** database.

The basic syntax of the **CREATE DATABASE** Transact-SQL statement is as follows (the highlighted area is a new feature in SQL Server 2000):

```
CREATE DATABASE database_name [ ON
    [ PRIMARY ]
    [ < filespec > [ ,...n ] ]
    [FILEGROUP filegroup_name
        ( <filespec> )
        [,( <filespec> )
        [,...n ]
]
[ LOG ON
[( <filespec>) [,...n ]
]
[ COLLATE collation_name ]

< filespec > ::=
        ( NAME = logical_file_name
        [ , FILENAME = 'os_file_name' ]
        [ , SIZE = size ]
        [ , MAXSIZE = { max_size | UNLIMITED } ]
        [ , FILEGROWTH = growth_increment ] )
```

Rules for Identifiers

When you create identifiers, follow these rules:

➤ The first character must be either of the following:

➤ A letter, either uppercase or lowercase (A–Z or a–z)

➤ One of these: underscore (_), "at" sign (@), or number sign (#). Some of these symbols have special meanings: @ indicates a local variable; # indicates a temporary table or procedure. Additionally, ## indicates a global temporary object and @@ is used by some Transact-SQL functions. These final two symbols should be avoided.

➤ Subsequent characters can be any of the following:

   ➤ A letter, either uppercase or lowercase (A–Z or a–z)

   ➤ Decimal numbers

   ➤ The "at" sign (@), dollar sign ($), number sign (#), or underscore (_)

➤ The identifier must *not* be a Transact-SQL reserved word. SQL Server reserves both the uppercase and lowercase versions of reserved words.

➤ Embedded spaces or special characters are not allowed.

Key Arguments

The **CREATE DATABASE** statement has the following key arguments:

➤ *database_name*—Specifies the name of the database. This must be unique for the SQL Server instance and must conform to rules for creating identifiers. The maximum number of characters is 128, but it's recommended that you limit the identifier to 123 characters to accommodate the system-generated log file convention of *databasename*_**log**.

➤ **PRIMARY**—Names the primary filegroup. If this is not specified, then the first file specification becomes the primary filegroup. It's recommended that you specify the primary filegroup first.

➤ **NAME**—Specifies the logical file name, which is used in Transact-SQL statements. It must adhere to the rules for naming identifiers.

➤ **FILENAME**—Specifies the operating-system file name and path. The path must be on the SQL server. The name must adhere to operating system rules.

➤ **SIZE**—Specifies the size of the file. If it is not specified, the primary file defaults to the size of the **model** database, and all others default to 1MB. You cannot use fractions.

Note: Remember to account for the system tables and indexes.

➤ **MAXSIZE**—Specifies the maximum size to which a file can grow. This size can be specified in any of the byte suffixes (KB, MB, GB, TB). **UNLIMITED** is the default if **MAXSIZE** is not specified. **UNLIMITED** means that the file will grow until it runs out of disk space.

 The default byte suffix for **SIZE** and **MAXSIZE** is MB.

➤ FILEGROWTH—Sets the growth increment for the file. This value cannot be greater than the **MAXSIZE** value. This value can be specified in megabytes (the default), in kilobytes, or as a percentage, indicated by the percent symbol (%). The minimum is 64KB (one extent). If **FILEGROWTH** is not specified, the default is 10 percent. Specify a large value to prevent the file from continually having to grow.

➤ COLLATE *collation_name*—Indicates the collation of the database. If this is not specified, it defaults to the collation of SQL Server. A new feature, this argument replaces the code pages and sort orders used in the previous release of SQL Server.

Let's look at some examples of the **CREATE DATABASE** statement. In Listings 3.1 and 3.2, the **FILENAME** specification would be typed on one line.

Listing 3.1   A basic CREATE DATABASE statement, specifying the database file and transaction log.

```
CREATE DATABASE Test
ON
(NAME = test,
    FILENAME = 'c:\program files\microsoft sql server\
                mssql\data\test.mdf',
    SIZE = 50,
    MAXSIZE = 100,
    FILEGROWTH = 5)
LOG ON
(NAME = 'test_log',
    FILENAME = 'c:\program files\microsoft sql server\
                mssql\data\testlog.ldf',
    SIZE = 10MB,
    MAXSIZE = 25MB,
    FILEGROWTH = 5MB)
```

Listing 3.2   Creating a database with filegroups, multiple files, and multiple transaction logs.

```
CREATE DATABASE Test
ON PRIMARY
-- set the database name,
-- source file, and other properties
(NAME = Test1,
    FILENAME = 'c:\program files\microsoft sql server\
                mssql\data\test1.mdf',
```

```
      SIZE = 50,
      MAXSIZE = 100,
      FILEGROWTH = 15% ),
(NAME = Test2,
      FILENAME = 'c:\program files\microsoft sql server\
                 mssql\data\test2.ndf',
      SIZE = 10,
      MAXSIZE = 50,
      FILEGROWTH = 15% ),
-- use a filegroup to simplify administration
FILEGROUP TestGroup
(NAME = TestGroupFile1,
      FILENAME = 'c:\program files\microsoft sql server\
                 mssql\data\testgroupfile1.ndf',
      SIZE = 10,
      MAXSIZE = 50,
      FILEGROWTH = 5 ),
(NAME = TestGroupFile2,
      FILENAME = 'c:\program files\microsoft sql server\
                 mssql\data\testgroupfile2.ndf',
      SIZE = 10,
      MAXSIZE = 50,
      FILEGROWTH = 5 )
LOG ON
(NAME = Testlog1,
      FILENAME = 'c:\program files\microsoft sql server\
                 mssql\data\testlog1.ldf',
      SIZE = 10MB,
      MAXSIZE = 100,
      FILEGROWTH = 20),
(NAME = Testlog2,
      FILENAME = 'c:\program files\microsoft sql server\
                 mssql\data\testlog2.ldf',
      SIZE = 10MB,
      MAXSIZE = 100,
      FILEGROWTH = 20)
```

In SQL Server, you can create a database for read-only purposes that can be distributed by way of removable media, such as CD-ROMs. To create a read-only database, you use the system stored procedure **sp_create_removable** instead of the **CREATE DATABASE** statement through Transact-SQL or Enterprise Manager.

Modifying Databases

After a database is built, you might need to change its definition. You might want to change the owner, expand or shrink the database's size, change configuration settings, add or remove files or filegroups, rename the database, or even move it. You cannot change a database if it is being backed up.

Changing the Database Owner and Permissions

The person who issues the **CREATE DATABASE** statement becomes the owner of the database. Because the **CREATE DATABASE** statement cannot specify an owner, you use the system stored procedure **sp_changedbowner** to change the database owner. This procedure is limited to the system administrator (**sysadmin**) role or the current database owner. The **dbo** (database owner) is a user who has implied permissions to perform all activities in the database.

The syntax of the **sp_changedbowner** stored procedure is as follows:

```
sp_changedbowner 'login'
    [ , remap_alias_flag ]
```

Following are the arguments for the **sp_changedbowner** stored procedure:

➤ *'login'*—The new owner. The user account must already exist in SQL Server. If this new user has access to the database through an alias, you must drop the alias before issuing the statement.

➤ *remap_alias_flag*—An alias remapping indicator. A **true** value (the default) maps aliases of the old database owner (**dbo**) to the new owner. A **false** value drops the old aliases.

The following example changes the owner to John and maps the aliases:

```
Exec sp_changedbowner 'John'
```

Note: You cannot change the owners of the system databases.

Renaming a Database

To rename a database, use the system stored procedure **sp_renamedb**. Before renaming a database, use the **ALTER DATABASE** statement (discussed later in this chapter) to set the database to single-user mode. Only members of the **sysadmin** and **dbcreator** fixed server roles can rename a database. The new name must adhere to the rules for identifiers.

The syntax of the **sp_renamedb** stored procedure is as follows:

```
sp_renamedb 'old_name' , 'new_name'
```

The following example changes the name of the **test** database to **employee**:

```
EXEC sp_renamedb 'test', 'employee'
```

Altering a Database

You use the **ALTER DATABASE** statement to perform such changes as increasing or decreasing the size of a database, adding or removing files or filegroups, or changing the size of files or filegroups. You also use the **ALTER DATABASE** statement to change database options.

 To change database options, you now use **ALTER DATABASE**. In previous versions of SQL Server, you used the **sp_dboption** stored procedure, which is still available but not recommended because it might not be available in future releases.

The syntax of the **ALTER DATABASE** statement is as follows (the highlighted areas are new features):

```
ALTER DATABASE database
{ADD FILE <filespec> [ ,...n ] [TO FILEGROUP filegroup_name]
| ADD LOG FILE < filespec > [ ,...n ]
| REMOVE FILE logical_file_name
| ADD FILEGROUP filegroup_name
| REMOVE FILEGROUP filegroup_name
| MODIFY FILE <filespec>
| MODIFY NAME = new_dbname
| MODIFY FILEGROUP filegroup_name {filegroup_property
    | NAME = new_filegroup_name }
| SET < optionspec > [ ,...n ] [ WITH < termination > ]
| COLLATE < collation_name >
}
```

The **ALTER DATABASE** statement includes the following arguments (this is not a complete list):

➤ **REMOVE FILE**—Deletes the physical file and the file description from the database's system tables. A file must be empty to be removed.

➤ **REMOVE FILEGROUP**—Removes the filegroup and all the files in the filegroup. The filegroup must be empty; that is, the data within the files must be deleted or moved.

➤ MODIFY FILE—Allows changes to a file. Changes include logical file name, size, **FILEGROWTH**, and **MAXSIZE**. Only one property can be changed at a time. Size can only be increased with this statement argument; to decrease a file's size, use the **DBCC SHRINKDATABASE** statement (described later in this chapter). The operating-system file name is changed only for files located in the **tempdb** database, and the change takes effect after SQL Server is restarted.

➤ MODIFY NAME—Allows you to rename the database.

Note: The recommended method for renaming a database is to use sp_renamedb.

➤ MODIFY FILEGROUP—In addition to specifying a new name, allows you to include the attributes **READONLY, READWRITE,** or **DEFAULT**. **READONLY** and **READWRITE** do not apply to the primary filegroup.

➤ WITH <termination>—Works with the **SET OPTION** clause and determines how to roll back transactions if a problem occurs when the state is changed. If the **termination** clause is omitted, transactions roll back or commit on their own.

Listing 3.3 creates a filegroup named **TestGroup** in the **Test** database, adds one 10MB file to the filegroup, and makes the new filegroup the default. Three **ALTER DATABASE** statements are needed to accomplish these tasks. (Normally, the file name and path would be on one line.)

Listing 3.3   A basic ALTER DATABASE statement working with a filegroup.

```
USE master
GO
ALTER DATABASE Test
ADD FILEGROUP TestGroup
GO

ALTER DATABASE Test
ADD FILE
( NAME = testdat2,
  FILENAME = 'c:\Program Files\Microsoft SQL Server\
              MSSQL\Data\testdat2.ndf',
  SIZE = 10MB,
  MAXSIZE = 100MB,
  FILEGROWTH = 5MB)
TO FILEGROUP TestGroup

ALTER DATABASE Test
MODIFY FILEGROUP TestGroup DEFAULT
GO
```

Database Options

The **ALTER DATABASE** statement now includes the settings for the database options. In previous versions of SQL Server, these options were changed by using the **sp_dboption** stored procedure. The database option commands are organized into five categories:

➤ *State options*—Control user access to the database, whether the database is online, and whether writes are allowed.

➤ *Cursor options*—Control cursor behavior and scope.

➤ *Auto options*—Control automatic behaviors.

➤ *SQL options*—Control the ANSI compliance options.

➤ *Recovery options*—Control the database recovery model.

These options are discussed in Tables 3.1 through 3.5.

Note: Several of the settings have different names or are new.

Table 3.1 Settings for the state options.	
Setting	**Description**
SINGLE_USER	Specifies that only one user can access the database at one time.
RESTRICTED_USER	Specifies that only users from the **db_owner**, **dbcreator**, or **sysadmin** roles can access the database. This setting was called **dbo use only** in earlier versions.
MULTI_USER	Specifies normal operation; all authorized users can access the database.
OFFLINE I ONLINE	Controls whether the database is available.
READ_ONLY I READ_WRITE	Specifies whether the database is in read-only mode. The database cannot be in use when you execute this change.

Table 3.2 Settings for the cursor options.	
Setting	**Description**
CURSOR_CLOSE_ON_COMMIT	**ON** indicates that a cursor is closed after a commit or rollback. **OFF** indicates that a cursor stays open after a commit, but closes after a rollback.
CURSOR_DEFAULT_LOCAL I GLOBAL	Specifies the default cursor scope: either **LOCAL** or **GLOBAL**.

Table 3.3   Settings for the auto options.

Setting	Description
AUTO_CLOSE	**ON** specifies that the database is shut down cleanly and its resources are freed after the last user exits. **OFF** specifies that the database remains open after the last user exits.
AUTO_CREATE_STATISTICS	**ON** specifies that any missing statistics needed by a query for optimization are automatically built during optimization.
AUTO_SHRINK	**ON** specifies that the database files are candidates for automatic periodic shrinking.
AUTO_UPDATE_STATISTICS	**ON** specifies that any out-of-date statistics required by a query for optimization are automatically built during optimization. **OFF** specifies that statistics must be updated manually.

Table 3.4   Settings for the SQL options.

Setting	Description
ANSI_NULL_DEFAULT	**ON** specifies that the **CREATE TABLE** statement follows SQL-92 rules to determine whether a column allows null values.
ANSI_NULLS	**ON** specifies that all comparisons to a null value evaluate to **UNKNOWN**. **OFF** specifies that comparisons of non-Unicode values to a null value evaluate to **TRUE** if both values are **NULL**.
ANSI_PADDING	**ON** specifies that strings are padded to the same length before comparisons or insertions; **OFF** specifies that there is no padding.
ANSI_WARNINGS	**ON** specifies that errors or warnings are issued when conditions such as divide-by-zero occur.
ARITHABORT	**ON** specifies that a query is terminated when an overflow or a divide-by-zero error occurs during query execution.
CONCAT_NULL_YIELDS_NULL	**ON** specifies that the result of a concatenation operation is **NULL** when either operand is **NULL**. **OFF** specifies that the null value is treated as an empty character string. The default is **OFF**.
QUOTED_IDENTIFIER	**ON** specifies that double quotation marks can be used to enclose delimited identifiers.
NUMERIC_ROUNDABORT	**ON** specifies that an error is generated when loss of precision occurs in an expression.
RECURSIVE_TRIGGERS	**ON** specifies that recursive firing of triggers is allowed. **OFF** is the default. To disable indirect recursion, use **sp_configure** to set the **nested triggers** server option to 0.

Table 3.5	Settings for the recovery options.
Setting	Description
FULL	Provides complete protection against media failure; you can restore all committed transactions.
BULK_LOGGED	Specifies that certain large-scale operations are not logged. These operations include **SELECT INTO**, bulk load operations (**bcp** and **BULK INSERT**), **CREATE INDEX**, and text and image operations (**WRITETEXT** and **UPDATETEXT**). In previous versions, this setting was called **SELECT INTO/BULKCOPY**.
SIMPLE	Provides a simple backup strategy that uses minimal log space. Log space can be reused automatically when it's no longer needed for server failure recovery; however, if the disk fails, you cannot recover the server data. In previous versions, this setting was called **Trunc. Log on Chkpt**.

 The recovery model replaces **SELECT INTO/BULKCOPY** (**BULK_LOGGED**) and **Trunc. Log on Chkpt** (**SIMPLE**). These options no longer appear in the Enterprise Manager.

The following example sets the database into restricted-user mode:

```
USE master
Go
ALTER DATABASE Test
SET RESTRICTED_USER
```

Shrinking a Database or File

You can manually shrink a database or individual files within a database by using the **DBCC SHRINKDATABASE** or **DBCC SHRINKFILE** statements, respectively. These statements remove unused pages. Permission defaults to members of the **sysadmin** fixed server role or the **db_owner** fixed database role; permission is not transferable.

With either function, you cannot make the database smaller than its original size, and the database cannot be smaller than the room required for the data contained in it. You can shrink individual files so they are smaller than their original size, depending on the amount of data in the file. You cannot shrink a database to be smaller than the size of the **model** database. You do not have to set the database to single-user or restricted-user mode to shrink either the database or a file within the database.

Shrinking the transaction log is different. A transaction file is made up of virtual log files; you cannot make a transaction log smaller than one of these log file boundaries. You should always truncate the log before shrinking it to reduce the size of the virtual log file.

Shrinking a Database

The syntax of the **SHRINK DATABASE** statement is as follows:

```
DBCC SHRINKDATABASE
    ( database_name [ , target_percent ]
        [ , { NOTRUNCATE | TRUNCATEONLY } ] )
```

The **SHRINK DATABASE** statement has the following arguments:

➤ *target_percent*—The amount of free space left in the database after it's shrunk.

➤ **NOTRUNCATE**—Retains the freed file space; otherwise, it is released to the operating system.

➤ **TRUNCATEONLY**—Releases unused space to the operating system by shrinking the file to the last allocated extent without moving any data. If this argument is specified, then *target_percent* is ignored.

The following example shrinks the **Test** database with 10 percent free space.

```
DBCC SHRINKDATABASE (Test, 10)
```

Shrinking a File

The syntax of the **SHRINK FILE** statement is as follows:

```
DBCC SHRINKFILE
    ( { file_name | file_id } { [ , target_size ]
        | [ , { EMPTYFILE | NOTRUNCATE | TRUNCATEONLY } ] } )
```

The **SHRINK FILE** statement has the following arguments:

➤ *file_name* or *file_id*—Specifies the logical file name or the identification number, respectively.

➤ *target_size*—Specifies the desired size in megabytes, expressed as an integer. If this argument is not specified, the **SHRINK FILE** statement reduces the size as much as possible.

➤ **EMPTYFILE**—Migrates all data to other files in the same filegroup.

The following example shrinks the **TestFile** file in the **Test** database to 5MB (after setting the active database):

```
USE Test
GO
DBCC SHRINKFILE (TestFile, 5)
```

Deleting a Database

You can delete user-created databases, but you cannot delete system databases. Deleting a database removes all database files and all references to the database. The only way to "undelete" is to restore a backup; therefore, it is highly recommended that you do a full backup before deleting a database. It's also recommended that you back up the **master** database after deleting a database.

If a database was part of replication, that database must be removed from replication before it can be deleted. A database cannot be in use when it's deleted. Permission defaults to the **dbo** (database owner), **sysadmin**, and **dbcreator** roles, and is not transferable. You can specify more than one database to be deleted with one statement.

The syntax of the **DROP DATABASE** statement is as follows:

```
DROP DATABASE database_name [ ,...n ]
```

Attaching and Detaching a Database

You can use the system stored procedures **sp_detach_db** and **sp_attach_db** to move the data and transaction log files from one server to another or even back to the same server. *Detaching* a database removes the database from SQL Server but leaves the database intact. When you *attach* the database, it is available in exactly the same state it was in when it was detached. You can use this technique when you want to increase the size of the disk that the database resides on rather than creating a secondary file. Only members of the **sysadmin** role can execute these procedures. It's recommended that you use **sp_attach_db** for attaching databases that were removed with the **sp_detach_db** stored procedure.

The sp_detach_db Stored Procedure

The syntax of this stored procedure is as follows:

```
sp_detach_db 'dbname' [, 'skipchecks' ]
```

The **sp_detach_db** stored procedure has the following arguments:

➤ *'dbname'*—Specifies the name of the database to be detached.

➤ *'skipchecks'*—Specifies whether to check statistics. A value of **true** does not run **UPDATE STATISTICS**; a value of **false** runs it. The default value is **NULL**.

The following example detaches the **pubs** database and skips the **UPDATE STATISTICS** function:

```
EXEC sp_detach_db 'pubs', 'true'
```

The sp_attach_db Stored Procedure

The syntax of this stored procedure is as follows:

```
sp_attach_db 'dbname' , 'filename_n' [ ,...16 ]
```

The **sp_attach_db** stored procedure has the following arguments:

➤ *'dbname'*—Specifies the name of the database to be attached. The name must be unique.

➤ *'filename_n'*—Specifies the physical name, including the path of a database file. A maximum of 16 file names can be specified. The list must include at least the primary file, which contains the system tables that point to other files in the database. The list must also include any files that were moved after the database was detached.

The following example attaches the **pubs** database, using the primary file and the transaction log file located in the data directory (the file name would normally be typed on one line):

```
EXEC sp_attach_db @dbname = N'pubs',
    @filename1 = N'c:\Program Files\Microsoft SQL Server\
            MSSQL\Data\pubs.mdf',
    @filename2 = N'c:\Program Files\Microsoft SQL Server\
            MSSQL\Data\pubs_log.ldf'
```

Viewing Database Information

In addition to using the Enterprise Manager to view database information, you can use several system procedures.

The DATABASEPROPERTYEX Function

This function displays the current value of the specified property in the specified database. In previous versions of SQL Server, this function was called **DATABASEPROPERTY**, which still exists for backward compatibility.

The syntax of the **DATABASEPROPERTYEX** function is as follows:

```
DATABASEPROPERTYEX( database , property )
```

The following example displays the collation property of the **Northwind** database.

```
SELECT DATABASEPROPERTYEX('Northwind', 'Collation')
```

The sp_helpdb Stored Procedure

The **sp_helpdb** stored procedure reports information about a specified database or all databases. Execute permission defaults to the **public** role. If the user executing the stored procedure does not have access permission to the database, an error message and only some of the data are displayed.

Database information includes the name, size, ID, date created, compatibility level, and status (options currently set). If you specify a database, then you also get information on each file in that database (name, ID, physical name, filegroup, size, maximum size, growth, and usage [data or log]).

The syntax of the **sp_helpdb** stored procedure is as follows:

```
sp_helpdb [ [ @dbname= ] 'name' ] or sp_helpdb ['name']
```

The following example reports information about the **test** database:

```
Exec sp_helpdb test
```

The sp_helpfile Stored Procedure

The **sp_helpfile** stored procedure returns information about a specified file or all files associated with the current database. This information includes the name, ID, physical name, filegroup, size, maximum size, growth, and usage (data or log). Execute permission defaults to the **public** role.

The syntax of the **sp_helpfile** stored procedure is as follows:

```
sp_helpfile [ [ @filename = ] 'name' ]
```

The following example activates the **test** database and returns information about all files associated with it:

```
Use test
Go
Exec sp_helpfile
```

The sp_help Stored Procedure

The **sp_help** stored procedure displays information about database objects that are associated with the **sysobjects** table. You can use **sp_help** instead of checking an object's information using the Properties dialog.

The syntax of the **sp_help** stored procedure is as follows:

```
sp_help < object name > 'name' ]

sp_help [Sales by Year]

Name           Type              Created_datetime
-------------------------------------------------------------
Sales by Year stored procedure 2000-08-06 01:34:13.060


Parameter_name  Type      Length  Prec  Scale  Param_order  Collation
---------------------------------------------------------------------
@Beginning_Date datetime 8        23    3      1            NULL
@Ending_Date    datetime 8        23    3      2            NULL
```

The sp_helpfilegroup Stored Procedure

The **sp_helpfilegroup** stored procedure returns information about a specified filegroup or all filegroups associated with the current database; there's one row for each filegroup. This information includes the name, ID, and number of files in the group. Execute permission defaults to the **public** role.

The syntax of the **sp_helpfilegroup** stored procedure is as follows:

```
sp_helpfilegroup [ 'name' ]
```

The following example activates the **test** database and returns information about all filegroups associated with it:

```
Use test
Go
Exec sp_helpfilegroup
```

The DBCC SQLPERF Statement

The **DBCC SQLPERF** statement provides statistics of transaction-log space in all databases. Use this information to monitor the amount of space so you can better determine when to back up or truncate the transaction log. Execute permission defaults to any user. There will be one row for each database on the server; each row includes the database name, log size, and percentage of log space used.

The syntax of the **DBCC SQLPERF** statement is as follows:

```
DBCC SQLPERF ( LOGSPACE )
```

The sp_spaceused Stored Procedure

The **sp_spaceused** stored procedure summarizes the disk space reserved and used by the database or an object (if specified). Execute permission defaults to the **public** role. The procedure provides the following information about databases: name, size, unallocated space, reserved space, total space used by data, space used by indexes, and unused space. The procedure provides the following information about tables: name, number of rows, reserved space, total space used by data, space used by indexes, and unused space.

The syntax of the **sp_spaceused** stored procedure is as follows:

```
sp_spaceused ['objname'] [,'updateusage']
```

The **sp_spaceused** stored procedure has the following arguments:

➤ *'objname'*—Displays information for the specified table only.

➤ *'updateusage'*—Specifies whether to update usage statistics. A value of **true** runs the **DBCC UPDATEUSAGE** function; a value of **false** is the default.

Changing the Active Database

When a new user account is created, a default database is specified; by default, this is the **master** database. When you log onto SQL Server, you are usually connected to your default database. To change the context of your session to another database, you issue the **USE** statement. You still must have access privileges to the database to gain access. The **USE** statement takes effect immediately. The following example activates the **Northwind** database:

```
USE Northwind
```

Practice Questions

Case Study

The MyCollectibles specialty store has decided to automate its processes. The owners want to keep track of their employees, customers, and supplies. MyCollectibles is a small store that specializes in just a few categories of collectibles (dolls and bears).

The Owner

I want a system that will keep track of everything easily and affordably. We need to get a handle on what types of collectibles sell well and which ones we should stop carrying. I would also like to keep notes about my employees.

The Accounting Personnel

I need a system that tracks inventory: who supplies what; who buys what; what is on hand; and when I should reorder. We have fewer than 10 employees, and we have fewer than 50 categories and suppliers, so we don't need a large system.

Store Manager

I need to understand my customers. I need to understand what is selling and who is buying. I want to be able to send out special fliers through the mail and through the Internet to let customers know that their favorite product is on sale.

Question 1

System tables exist in which databases? [Check all correct answers]

❑ a. **master**

❑ b. **model**

❑ c. **msdb**

❑ d. **tempdb**

❑ e. **Northwind**

All of the answers are correct. System tables exist in every database.

Question 2

> The **msdb** database contains data for what purpose?
>
> ○ a. Storing system-level data
>
> ○ b. Providing a template for creating new databases
>
> ○ c. Storing data required by the SQL Server Agent
>
> ○ d. Providing a temporary storage area

Answer c is correct. The **msdb** database stores data required by the SQL Server Agent. Answer a is incorrect because the **master** database stores system-level data. Answer b is incorrect because the **model** database provides a template for creating new databases. Answer d is incorrect because the **tempdb** database provides a temporary storage area.

Question 3

> Which system table stores information about who can log into the server?
>
> ○ a. **sysoledbusers**
>
> ○ b. **syslogins**
>
> ○ c. **sysmembers**
>
> ○ d. **sysoperators**
>
> ○ e. None of the above

Answer b is correct. The **syslogins** table stores information about who can log into the server. Answer a is incorrect because the **sysoledbusers** table stores information about users mapped to a linked server. Answer c is incorrect because the **sysmembers** table stores information about members in a specific database. Answer d is incorrect because the **sysoperators** table stores information about persons who are notified by SQL Server Agent tasks.

Question 4

Based on the case study, which files will you need and/or use? [Check all correct answers]

- ❏ a. Primary file
- ❏ b. Secondary file
- ❏ c. Transaction log
- ❏ d. System file
- ❏ e. All of the above

Answers a and c are correct. A database must have at least a primary file and a transaction log. Answer b is incorrect; a secondary file is optional and, for this small company, is most likely unnecessary. Answer d is incorrect because there is no such thing as a system file; system tables are usually contained in the primary file.

Question 5

Rearrange the following code segments to create the database for the case study. You want the primary file to grow by megabytes and the log to grow by percentage. Not all code segments need to be used.

```
(NAME = 'MyCollectibles_log',
(NAME = 'MyCollectibles',
CREATE DATABASE MyCollectibles
FILEGROWTH = 10
FILEGROWTH = 10%)
FILEGROWTH = 10)
FILENAME = 'c:\program files\microsoft sql server\
mssql\data\MyCollectibles.mdf',
FILENAME = 'c:\program files\microsoft sql server\
mssql\data\MyCollectibleslog.ldf',
LOG ON
MAXSIZE = 10MB,
MAXSIZE = 450,
MAXSIZE = 50,
NAME = 'MyCollectibles',
ON
SIZE = 10,
SIZE = 2MB,
SIZE = 90,
```

The correct answer is

```
CREATE DATABASE MyCollectibles
ON
(NAME = 'MyCollectibles',
  FILENAME = 'c:\program files\microsoft sql server\
  mssql\data\MyCollectibles.mdf',
  SIZE = 10,
  MAXSIZE = 50,
  FILEGROWTH = 10)
```

```
LOG ON
(NAME = 'MyCollectibles_log',
  FILENAME = 'c:\program files\microsoft sql server\
  mssql\data\MyCollectibleslog.ldf',
  SIZE = 2MB,
  MAXSIZE = 10MB,
  FILEGROWTH = 10%)
```

Because this is a small store, an initial size of 10MB and a maximum size of 50MB is probably sufficient. The transaction log is usually around 25 percent of the database size, so it would be set to 2MB. The requirements called for the primary file to grow by MB and the log to grow by a percentage.

Question 7

The manager has decided that he wants to make sales data over a month old be read-only. What are the necessary steps in the correct order?

Step A:

```
ALTER DATABASE MyCollectibles
ADD FILEGROUP HistoryGroup
```

Step B:

```
ALTER DATABASE MyCollectibles
MODIFY FILEGROUP READONLY
```

Step C:

```
ALTER DATABASE MyCollectibles
ADD FILE
    (NAME = 'History1',
    FILENAME = 'c:\Program Files\Microsoft SQL Server\
    MSSQL\DATA\History1.ndf',
    SIZE = 5MB,
TO FILEGROUP HistoryGroup
```

Step D:

```
ALTER DATABASE MyCollectibles
SET READ_ONLY
```

○ a. Step A, Step C, Step B, Step D

○ b. Step D

○ c. Step A, Step B, Step C

○ d. Step A, Step C, Step B

Answer d is correct. You first add a filegroup, then add a file to the filegroup, and finally, make that filegroup read-only. Answer b is incorrect because Step D makes the entire database, not just part of the database, read-only. Answer a is incorrect because it includes Step D. Answer c is incorrect because you need to add the file to the filegroup before making the filegroup read-only.

Question 8

One of your suppliers has sent you a file of products to import into your database. The first step is to make the database ready. How can this best be accomplished in SQL Server 2000?

○ a.
```
USE master
EXEC sp_dboption 'MyCollectibles',
'select into/bulkcopy', 'TRUE
```
○ b.
```
USE master
ALTER DATABASE MyCollectibles
SET BULK_LOGGED
```
○ c.
```
USE master
ALTER DATABASE MyCollectibles
SET RECOVERY select into/bulkcopy
```
○ d.
```
USE master
ALTER DATABASE MyCollectibles
SET RECOVERY BULK_LOGGED
```

Answer d is correct. To import data, you need to set the database property to allow bulk inserts. Answer d is the proper method of setting this property. Although answer a still works, it's not the recommended way. Answer b is incorrect because it is missing the option keyword **RECOVERY**. Answer c is incorrect because the **select into/bulkcopy** parameter does not exist.

Question 9

You want to determine all the files in **MyCollectibles**. How can you accomplish this?

○ a. Execute the command and parameter **sp_helpfile MyCollectibles**.

○ b. Execute the command and parameter **sp_spaceused MyCollectibles**.

○ c. Execute the command **sp_helpdb**.

○ d. Execute the command and parameter **sp_helpdb MyCollectibles**.

Answer d is correct. The **sp_helpdb** stored procedure with the database name parameter displays general information about the database and lists all of the files within the specified database. Answer a is incorrect; although you can use **sp_helpfile** to list all the files in a database, you do not include the database name. Answer b is incorrect because the **sp_spaceused** stored procedure displays space used by the specified database or one of its tables. Answer c is incorrect because the **sp_helpdb** stored procedure without the database parameter displays only general database information for each database on the server.

Question 10

How is the IAM different from the GAM and the SGAM?

○ a. The GAM and SGAM track allocation for a single object; the IAM tracks allocation for all objects.

○ b. The IAM tracks allocation for a single object; the GAM and SGAM track allocation for all objects.

○ c. The IAM tracks pages; the GAM and SGAM track extents.

○ d. The GAM and SGAM track pages; the IAM tracks extents.

Answer b is correct. The IAM tracks a specific table or index, and the GAM and SGAM track all extents. All three pages track extents, so answers c and d are incorrect.

Need to Know More?

 Iseminger, David. *SQL Server 2000 Reference Library*. Redmond, WA: Microsoft Press, 2000. ISBN 0-7356-1280-3. A selected collection of SQL Server 2000 Books Online; there are six volumes focused on key areas. Volume 2 deals with database creation.

 Microsoft SQL Server Books Online has a section on "Creating and Maintaining Databases."

 Search the TechNet CD or its online version through **www.microsoft.com/ technet/**. Keywords to search on would be "databases", "filegroups", and "transaction log".

 www.microsoft.com/sql/—Find up-to-date information about SQL Server at Microsoft's Web site.

4

Database Objects

. . . .

Terms you'll need to understand:

✓ Data type

✓ Data integrity

✓ Table

✓ Index

✓ Constraint

✓ Primary key

✓ Foreign key

✓ Referential integrity

✓ **IDENTITY** property

✓ **DEFAULT** constraint

✓ **UNIQUE** constraint

Techniques you'll need to master:

✓ Defining data types

✓ Creating tables

✓ Modifying tables

✓ Defining constraints

✓ Defining **DEFAULT** and **RULE** objects

✓ Scripting objects

In the previous two chapters, we began by developing various models for storing the data that organizations have available to them and logically showing how they later plan to use this data for business purposes. Then we looked at different ways of creating a database structure that fulfills an organization's business needs. In this chapter, we will look at the ways the data itself is stored within that database structure.

We've already said that Microsoft SQL Server 2000 is a relational database management system (RDBMS). Obviously, that means that something inside the database is related to something else. In fact, an RDBMS is composed of data stored in such a way as to indicate relationships between select pieces of that data. Columns and rows of data are thus combined to form those relationships, and this occurs in tables. Then, those tables are further linked by additional relationships stored in various ways that facilitate reliable data storage and rapid manipulation of the information.

We'll begin by looking at the data itself as we define several data types that become the building blocks of a database. Once you understand the different types of data that can be stored in databases, the next step will be creating those tables (with their resultant columns) for later use. *Tables* are just storage locations for pieces of data arranged in columnar format.

First, we'll take a look at creating and modifying database objects. Please note, however, that although indexes, views, stored procedures, triggers, and user-defined functions are all major database objects themselves, they will not be discussed in this chapter. Rather, they are the subjects of Chapters 6, 7, 8, 9, and 10, respectively. In this chapter, we'll focus on *data types* and how they declare what kind of information a variable will contain. We initially discussed data types in Chapter 2, but in this chapter, we will discuss declaring data types when you're creating tables. We will also define some of the constraints that get applied to the data stored in your tables.

Creating and Altering Database Objects

There are a few top-level objects in SQL Server that you will need to familiarize yourself with before taking the exam. These objects are:

➤ Tables

➤ Views

➤ Stored procedures

➤ Rules

➤ Defaults

➤ User-defined data types

➤ User-defined functions

These objects can be viewed in Enterprise Manager, and most of them contain other objects with which you should be familiar. For example, index objects are clearly related to tables, and you will find additional information under either topic in Enterprise Manager's online help.

SQL Server objects follow the same naming conventions that identifiers do (see Chapter 3). An identifier should not have any embedded spaces. If you create an identifier with embedded spaces, then you will need to delimit that object name with the square bracket symbols: [ ]. Following are some guidelines for naming objects:

Note: Using the square brackets to delimit identifiers always works. Using quotes works only if they are turned on with the **SET QUOTED_IDENTIFIER** *option.*

➤ Names should be meaningful but short. For example, **int_age_of_employee** is meaningful, with the prefix of **int** signifying an **integer** variable, but **int_age** is shorter and just as meaningful.

➤ Use a standard naming convention. It doesn't matter what naming convention you decide on as long as you follow some standard so all users have a clear understanding. Keep your naming convention simple and clear.

➤ Distinguish between types of objects. It's very helpful to know that an object is referring to a view versus a table, so using **view** in a view's name would be recommended.

➤ Avoid using the same name for different objects. For instance, if you have a role called **managers**, then use **tbl_manager** (instead of **managers**) for the name of the table.

➤ Avoid embedded spaces or reserved words in your identifiers so you do not need to delimit them.

Tables

Data is stored in rows within tables, and we have already explained that each row is one *instance* of an entity. A row, then, consists of one or more columns that contain an entity's attributes. Remember, entities and attributes are two database modeling terms discussed in Chapter 2. We also discussed the **CREATE TABLE** statement in Chapter 3. The **text, ntext,** and **image** data types are stored separately from the row and will be discussed in the following sections.

Row Structure

A row consists of five segments: header, fixed data, null block, variable block, and variable data, as shown in Figure 4.1. The row's *header*, which is composed of 4 bytes, contains information about the columns that, when combined, form the row of information stored about each instance of an entity. The row's *fixed data* portion contains all of the fixed-length data columns. Next is the row's *null block* segment, which is a variable-length set of bytes indicating the number of columns, plus a bitmap (consisting of one bit per column) indicating whether an individual column is null. The *variable block* exists only if the row has variable-length columns. The variable block consists of 2 bytes indicating the number of variable-length columns and then 2 bytes for each column, indicating the end of the column. The *variable data* is entered in the row.

Working with Data Types

When you design columns in your tables, you ultimately decide what types of values will be stored in them. Common SQL Server data types include:

➤ char

➤ int

➤ varchar

➤ datetime

➤ bit

➤ text

 The **int** data type is a 4-byte value that can store numbers between −2,147,483,648 and 2,147,483,648.

More data types are available; some are related to those just listed. For example, SQL Server 2000 has a new data type called **bigint**, which can store 8 bytes. The new **sql_variant** data type can contain **char**, **nchar**, **smallint**, and **float** values; however, it cannot contain larger data types such as **image** or **text**.

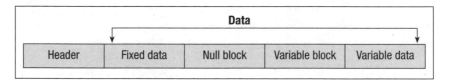

Figure 4.1 The structure of a row.

In addition to understanding column design, you should also have a basic understanding of row structure. Some data types, such as **text** and **image** types, can store large amounts of data. The data for these types is stored in something called a B-Tree structure. This structure allows operations performed on the data to run much faster than they would if the data were actually stored in a single continuous set of bytes.

If you do want SQL Server to store data as a continuous set of bytes, you can enable the **text in row** feature. A minimum of 24 bytes and a maximum of 7,000 bytes can be specified using this feature. Use the **sp_tableoption** system stored procedure to enable the **text in row** feature. The following example sets the **text in row** option for the **Customers** table to 2,000 bytes. If the data for the column is more than 2,000 bytes, then that column's data is stored in the B-Tree structure rather than in the column's row.

```
Exec sp_tableoption N'Customers', 'text in row', '2000'
```

*Note: If you're using the **text in row** feature, the maximum size for a row is still 8,060 bytes.*

The SQL Server exam will expect you to be very familiar with data types that store dates. Be sure you are comfortable using the **DATEDIFF** function, and understand how SQL Server stores dates internally. For example, the **datetime** data type is stored as two integers that are 4 bytes each in size. Within the **datetime** data type, a number of days after (or before) 1/1/1900 is the first integer value. The second integer value is the number of milliseconds following 12:00 A.M. The easiest way to remember this is to look at the **datetime** data type's name. The date is stored first, and the time is stored second—hence the name **datetime**.

Remember that the latest possible date that can be stored in the **datetime** data type is 12/31/9999, and the earliest date that can be stored is 1/1/1753.

The **CREATE TABLE** Statement

Tables are created using a Transact-SQL statement or Enterprise Manager. In the examples that follow, we'll use the Transact-SQL syntax.

Members of the **db_owner** and **db_ddladmin** roles can create tables by default. Members of the **db_owner** and **sysadmin** roles can assign **CREATE TABLE** permission to other users.

The basic **CREATE TABLE** statement must include the table name, the name of each column in the table, and the columns' data types. You should also specify **NULL** or **NOT NULL** for each column. Additionally, you can specify table constraints, column constraints, and a filegroup location for the **table, text, ntext,** and **image** data types. Table names must follow the rules for identifiers, and the *owner.table* name combination must be unique within the database. Column names must be unique for a specified table but not necessarily unique for the database.

Some points to consider:

➤ You can have a theoretical maximum of more than 2 billion objects (including tables) per database.

➤ The maximum number of columns is 1,024.

➤ A row can have a maximum of 8,060 bytes—excluding the **text, ntext,** and **image** data types—unless the **text in row** feature is specified.

➤ With this version of SQL, you now can store different collations within the same database.

Note: A collation specifies the bit patterns that represent each character and the rules by which characters are sorted and compared. In earlier versions of SQL Server, the collation was set at the server level. Now it can be set at the database level or even at the column level. The collation replaces code pages and sort orders. If a database is going to be part of replication, then you should keep collations the same between replicated servers.

➤ If you do not specify the table owner, then it defaults to the person issuing the **CREATE TABLE** statement. It's recommended that you specify the table owner as the database owner (**dbo**) to ensure a proper chain of ownership.

➤ A table can also have virtual columns, called *computed columns,* which are not physically stored in the table but are calculated. An example of a computed column is **cost = product * quantity.**

➤ Special planning needs to happen if your table is going to be involved in replication. Different collations between servers, **IDENTITY** property implementation, and different server versions have to be handled. Some of these will be discussed in the "Replication and Data Types" section later in this chapter.

The following example creates a table with a user-defined data type and a computed column:

```
CREATE TABLE dbo.employees
(
    emp_id  empid      -- user-defined data type
    fname   varchar(20)     NOT NULL,
```

```
minit    char(1) NULL,
lname    varchar(30)      NOT NULL,
hire_date        smalldatetime        NOT NULL,
citystate AS city + " " + state -- computed column
)
```

 If you use the **CREATE TABLE** statement followed by *Test1.Test2*, then *Test1* is the name of the database, and *Test2* is the name of the table (**CREATE TABLE** *Test1.Test2*).

Temporary Tables

You can create temporary tables the same way you create permanent tables. Temporary tables are created in the **tempdb** database. There are two types of temporary tables: local and global. Local tables have a single pound sign (#) as the first character of their names. Only the user who created the table can access it. Local temporary tables are deleted when the connection used to create the temporary table is closed. Global temporary tables have a double pound sign (##) as the first character of their names. Any user of the database can view them. Global temporary tables are deleted when all users accessing them have closed their connections.

Note: Temporary object names, including table names, are limited to 116 characters instead of the 128 characters allowed for regular names.

Modifying Tables

Once you've created a table, you can modify it. You can add or remove columns, add or drop constraints, or change data types. You use the **ALTER TABLE** statement to perform these actions. Permissions default to the table owner and to the **sysadmin, db_owner,** and **db_ddladmin** roles and are not transferable. Examples of altering a table for constraints are described under each constraint type later in the chapter. Following are examples of adding and dropping a column.

*Note: When you're changing the data type of a column, the old data type must be implicitly convertible to the new data type. The new type cannot be **timestamp**. If the old data type was an identity, then the new data type must be compatible.*

The following example adds an **Email** column to the **employees** table. The column uses the **varchar** data type (with a maximum size of 100 characters).

```
ALTER TABLE dbo.employees
    ADD Email varchar(100) NOT NULL
```

The following example drops the **Email** column from the **employees** table:

```
ALTER TABLE dbo.employees
    DROP COLUMN Email
```

 If you do not want existing data to be confirmed for a **CHECK** or **FOREIGN KEY** constraint, you should use the **WITH NOCHECK** argument in the **ALTER TABLE** command.

Deleting a Table

You can delete user-created tables, but you cannot delete system tables. Deleting a table removes all references to the table and removes all data within the table. In addition, the permission specification for the table is deleted. The only way to "undelete" is to restore a backup; therefore, you should do a full backup before deleting a table. You should also make sure that you delete all dependencies between the table and other objects. Use the **sp_depends** system stored procedure to view existing dependencies. You can drop more than one table at a time.

The syntax of the **DROP TABLE** statement is:

```
DROP TABLE table_name [,...n]
```

Defining Data Types

Remember that the columns in your tables began as attributes you defined when you created your system's model (see Chapter 2). That should have been the first indicator of what the stored data would look like. (For example: Will it be stored in the form of text, money, or numbers? If the data will be stored as a number, how many digits will be needed?) Therefore, specifying a data item's type defines what format and, sometimes, what range of values will be acceptable for entry into a particular storage location.

Data type definitions help determine what kind of information can be stored in items that are variable in nature. These *variables* are pieces of data whose values are not constant but rather are intended to change (sometimes frequently) over time. These include column values within a table, expression parameters where subsequent change is expected, or similar places where changing data is kept, such as the components of stored procedures, triggers, or transactions that allow differing value substitutions.

SQL Server provides many system-supplied data types. You can also create user-defined data types.

When defining data types, you can optimize performance and save space by choosing the type most appropriate for your data's intended use. Don't unnecessarily add precision to your data just because you can.

The following example illustrates the point that you should know which data types to use in given situations. The data type **datetime** takes 8 bytes, has a precision to 3.33 milliseconds, and can store dates back to 1/1/1753. The data type **smalldatetime** takes only 4 bytes, although it has a precision to only one minute and can store dates back to only 1/1/1900. If you are never going to need dates before 1900 or need times beyond a precision of one minute, then you can cut your data storage by 50 percent by selecting the most appropriate data type: **smalldatetime**.

System-Supplied Data Types

System-supplied data types include exact numeric (**decimal, numeric, integers, money, small money, bit**), approximate numeric (**float, real**), date and time (**datetime, smalldatetime**), character strings (**char, varchar, text**), Unicode character strings— strings with double byte characters—(**nchar, nvarchar, ntext**), binary strings (**binary, varbinary, image**), and several special data types, including **table, cursor, sql_variant, uniqueidentifier**, and **timestamp** (also called **rowversion**). The integers classification is further broken down into data types (**bigint, int, smallint, tinyint**).

SQL Server 2000 provides a few new system-supplied data types:

➤ **bigint**—An 8-byte integer with a value range of plus or minus 2^63.

➤ **sql_variant**—A data type that stores the values of various SQL-Server-supported data types, except for the **text, ntext, timestamp**, and **image** data types. The **sql_variant** data type is similar to the **variant** type in Visual Basic in that it can represent many different data types in different situations.

   Note: You should also be aware that when Microsoft lists the exclusions for these data types, sql_variant itself is listed as an excluded data type.

➤ **table**—A special data type used to store a result set for later processing. The **table** data type cannot be used in column definitions. It can be used only with local variables or return values.

User-Defined Data Types

User-defined data types are based on system data types. You can refine a system-supplied data type for your particular application. User-defined data types are particular to a database and are stored in the **systypes** system table.

Any user-defined data types defined in the **model** database are added to all databases created based on that model.

You can create or drop user-defined data types by using either Enterprise Manager or system stored procedures (**sp_addtype** or **sp_droptype**). The name for the user-defined data type must adhere to the rules for identifiers described in Chapter 3 and must be unique in each database.

Creating a User-Defined Data Type

Execute permission for creating data types defaults to the **public** role. The syntax for creating user-defined data types is as follows:

```
sp_addtype type, system_data_type
    [ , 'null_type' ]
    [ , 'owner_name' ]
```

The **sp_addtype** stored procedure has the following arguments:

➤ *type*—The name of the user-defined data type.

➤ *system_data_type*—The SQL-Server-supplied data type on which this new type is based.

➤ *null_type*—The default nullability. You can override this argument's default when you use the column definition portion of the **CREATE TABLE** statement.

➤ *owner_name*—The data type's owner. If you do not specify an owner, the default owner becomes the person creating the data type.

Following is an example of creating a data type named **city**, which cannot be null:

```
sp_addtype city, 'varchar(15)','NOT NULL', dbo
```

Note: Single quotes are used around items that contain punctuation, such as parentheses or spaces.

Dropping a User-Defined Data Type

Execute permission for dropping data types defaults to members of the **sysadmin**, **db_ddladmin**, and **db_owner** roles and to the owner of the object defined when it was created. The syntax for dropping a user-defined data type is as follows:

```
sp_droptype type
```

The following example drops a user-defined data type named **city**:

```
sp_droptype city
```

*Note: To retrieve a list of user-defined data types, execute the **sp_help** system stored procedure.*

Guidelines for Assigning Data Types

The following are some guidelines for assigning system-defined or user-defined data types to your columns:

➤ For variable-length columns, use variable types such as **varchar** instead of fixed-length types such as **char**. Fixed-length types will pad spaces to fill the field.

➤ Use the variable providing the least amount of precision that you need. For example, use **tinyint** instead of **int** if the largest value is 256, or use **smalldatetime** instead of **datetime**.

➤ Use **decimal** for numeric data types that require precision.

➤ For character types with less than 8,000 bytes, use **varchar**; otherwise, use **text** or **image**.

➤ To represent currency, use the **money** or **smallmoney** data types.

➤ Do not use the **float** or **real** data types for primary or foreign keys. Avoid these types in **WHERE** clauses.

➤ The **cursor** and **table** data types cannot be used in column definitions; these data types can be used only as variables in stored procedures or return values.

Designing Attribute Integrity

When creating the database model, you determined data integrity rules that later became the constraints on the data within your entities. You defined these constraints either when you created the table or, more commonly, after using the **ALTER TABLE** statement. Constraint types are **DEFAULT, CHECK, PRIMARY KEY, UNIQUE,** and **FOREIGN KEY** (with or without the **CASCADE REFERENTIAL** clause).

Defining Constraints

Constraints can be added even though a table already contains data. Constraints can be applied to a single column (column-level) or to multiple columns (table-level). When you add a constraint, SQL Server verifies the existing data before adding the constraint. You should provide names for your constraints rather than using the system-generated names.

You can view constraints by using the **sp_helpconstraint** or **sp_help** system stored procedures, or you can query the schema views **check_constraints**, **referential_constraints**, and **table_constraints**. Constraint definitions are stored in the **syscomments, sysreference,** and **sysconstraints** system tables.

The DEFAULT Constraint

A **DEFAULT** constraint enters a specified value if none is provided when the data is entered in the table. Some points to consider are as follows:

➤ A **DEFAULT** constraint applies only to the **INSERT** command.

➤ Each column can have only one default.

➤ A **DEFAULT** constraint cannot be used with the **IDENTITY** property or the **timestamp** data type.

➤ A **DEFAULT** constraint can use some system functions, such as **USER, CURRENT_USER, SESSION_USER, SYSTEM_USER,** or **CURRENT_TIMESTAMP.**

The following example alters the **Products** table and adds a **DEFAULT** constraint:

```
ALTER TABLE dbo.Products
    ADD CONSTRAINT df_ReorderLevel DEFAULT 0 for ReorderLevel
```

Remember that you can inhibit **NULL** values in columns by using the **NOT NULL** constraint.

The CHECK Constraint

A **CHECK** constraint is used to restrict the data that a user can enter in a field. Implicitly, the data type is a **CHECK** constraint. Consider the following points:

➤ Data is verified for each **INSERT** or **UPDATE** command.

➤ The formula can refer to other columns in the same table.

➤ A **CHECK** constraint cannot be placed on **timestamp** columns.

➤ A **CHECK** constraint cannot contain subqueries.

➤ The **DBCC CHECKCONSTRAINTS** statement lists all rows that fail the constraint.

The following example alters the **Products** table and adds a **CHECK** constraint:

```
ALTER TABLE dbo.Products
    ADD CONSTRAINT ck_salary
    CHECK (Salary > 10,000 and Salary < 100,000)
```

 Because a **CHECK** constraint can refer to other columns in the table, use a **CHECK** constraint rather than a trigger whenever possible. A **CHECK** constraint occurs before the **INSERT** or **UPDATE**, whereas a trigger happens afterward.

The PRIMARY KEY Constraint

The **PRIMARY KEY** constraint identifies each row with this designation as being unique. Some points to consider are as follows:

➤ Only one **PRIMARY KEY** constraint can be defined per table.

➤ Data values entered must be unique.

➤ The column cannot be **NULL**.

➤ A **PRIMARY KEY** constraint can be applied to one or more columns. If a single column does not identify a record uniquely, then you should choose a set of columns and designate them, combined, as the primary key.

➤ A unique index is created automatically. It is clustered by default.

➤ The index created cannot be dropped. You would have to drop the **PRIMARY KEY** constraint.

The following example alters the **Products** table and adds a **PRIMARY KEY** constraint with a nonclustered index:

```
ALTER TABLE dbo.Products
    ADD CONSTRAINT pk_ProductID
    PRIMARY KEY NONCLUSTERED (ProductID)
```

The UNIQUE Constraint

The **UNIQUE** constraint states that two rows within the table cannot have the same value in the column or columns specified. This constraint is used for columns (other than the primary key) that also must have unique values. Remember the following points:

➤ You can have multiple **UNIQUE** constraints in a table.

➤ The **UNIQUE** constraint allows one **NULL** value. It's recommended that you make the column **NOT NULL**.

➤ The **UNIQUE** constraint applies to one or more columns that are not the primary key.

➤ The system enforces the constraint by creating a unique index on the column or columns. The index is nonclustered by default.

The following example alters the **Employees** table and adds a unique clustered index to the **email** column:

```
ALTER TABLE dbo.Employees
ADD CONSTRAINT U_email UNIQUE CLUSTERED (email)
```

 Remember that SQL Server enforces unique constraints by creating nonclustered indexes that are unique. **UNIQUE** constraints cannot assign values.

The FOREIGN KEY Constraint

A *foreign key* is a column or set of columns used to enforce a link between the data in two tables. The **FOREIGN KEY** constraint defines this relationship. Remember the following points:

➤ The foreign key refers to a primary key or a unique key in the referenced (parent) table.

➤ A **FOREIGN KEY** constraint applies to one or more columns.

➤ The number and data type of the columns must match those in the referenced (parent) table.

➤ Indexes are not created automatically. However, it's recommended that to improve join performance, you create an index on the foreign key column(s).

➤ If the foreign key is referring to the same table, you can omit the **FOREIGN KEY** clause and use only the **REFERENCES** clause.

➤ Users modifying data must have **SELECT** or **REFERENCE** permission in the referenced (parent) table.

The following example adds a **FOREIGN KEY** constraint to the **Orders** table. The foreign key in the **Orders** table is the **CustomerID**, and it refers to the **CustomerID** column in the **Customers** table:

```
ALTER TABLE dbo.Orders
    ADD CONSTRAINT Fk_Orders_Customers
    FOREIGN KEY (CustomerID)
    REFERENCES dbo.Customers(CustomerID)
```

Remember that the order of constraints is:

1. Either the **UNIQUE** or **PRIMARY KEY** constraint
2. The **FOREIGN KEY** constraint

Cascading Referential Integrity

A new feature in SQL Server 2000 is the addition of the **CASCADE** clause for the **FOREIGN KEY** constraint. Any change to the **PRIMARY KEY** or **UNIQUE** constraints can automatically be propagated to the foreign key value. There are two types of **CASCADE** clauses: **ON DELETE** and **ON UPDATE**. They each can be either **CASCADE** or **NO ACTION**. Some points to consider are as follows:

➤ The default value is **NO ACTION** (the same as in previous SQL Server versions). **NO ACTION** means that if the delete or update would cause a referential integrity fault, then an error would be raised and the request would be rolled back.

➤ A series of cascades can occur when one table refers to another table, which in turn refers to another table. A **NO ACTION** value in any of these cascades will roll back the entire transaction.

➤ Cascading actions and **INSTEAD OF** triggers are mutually exclusive.

➤ A **CASCADE** clause cannot be placed on **timestamp** columns.

The following example shows a **FOREIGN KEY** constraint on the **Orders** table with cascading referential integrity for both **DELETE** and **UPDATE**:

```
ALTER TABLE dbo.Orders
    ADD CONSTRAINT Fk_Orders_Customers
    FOREIGN KEY (CustomerID)
    REFERENCES dbo.Customers(CustomerID)
    ON DELETE CASCADE
    ON UPDATE CASCADE
```

The use of the **CASCADE** clause propagates the delete to update to the referencing tables, rather than generating an error or requiring triggers or stored procedures to handle the propagation. Put simply, it causes a delete to be checked on each table that is subsequently referenced by any of the items being updated.

Disabling Constraints

You might want to temporarily disable a constraint in some situations, such as when you're importing large amounts of data or when you're adding the constraint and you know that your data meets the constraint. You can disable or re-enable the constraint by using the **ALTER TABLE** statement when you're initially adding the constraint to a table or when you want to change the state of an existing constraint. Some points to consider are as follows:

➤ You can disable only **CHECK** and **FOREIGN KEY** constraints. The other constraints must be dropped and then added again.

➤ To disable a constraint when you're creating it, add the **WITH NOCHECK** option to the **ALTER TABLE** statement.

➤ To disable or enable an existing constraint, you use the **ALTER TABLE** statement with the **NOCHECK** or **CHECK** option, respectively.

➤ If the table contains data that does not conform to the constraint, then when you later update a row, you will get a constraint error even if you're not updating the particular column that is indicating you have a constraint error.

➤ Disabling a constraint does not disable the constraints on any other tables to which it is related. In other words, if you disable constraints on the **Orders** table, the disabling does not affect the **Customers** table.

The following example adds a new **FOREIGN KEY** constraint to the **Orders** table without verifying (**WITH NOCHECK**) the existing data:

```
ALTER TABLE dbo.Orders
    WITH NOCHECK
    ADD CONSTRAINT Fk_Orders_Customers
    FOREIGN KEY (CustomerID)
    REFERENCES dbo.Customers(CustomerID)
```

The following example disables an existing constraint:

```
ALTER TABLE dbo.Orders
    NOCHECK
    CONSTRAINT Fk_Orders_Customers
```

 CHECK constraints are logical expressions that can prevent database users from entering invalid data into particular columns. Remember that all data in an existing table is validated with any **CHECK** constraints that you add.

Replication and Data Types

Replication involves storing the same pieces of information at numerous locations for subsequent use should the primary source of that information become unavailable. When your database is replicated to different servers, consider the following points:

➤ **timestamp** *columns*—The **timestamp** column behaves differently if a table is part of replication. For merge replication or transactional replication with the queued updating option, the **timestamp** column is replicated, but the literal **timestamp** values are regenerated rather than replicated. For snapshot and transactional publications, and for publications that allow immediate updating, the literal **timestamp** values are replicated, but the column's data type is changed to binary (8).

➤ **uniqueidentifier** *columns*—For merge replication, snapshot replication, or transactional replication with queued updating, SQL Server will add a **uniqueidentifier** column if one does not exist. It is created when the initial snapshot is created for merge replication and when the publication is created for all other types. When queued updating is used, a predefined **uniqueidentifier** column will be added for row versioning irrespective of the presence of a global **uniqueidentifier** column in the table. In addition, for merge replication, the **uniqueidentifier** column must have the **ROWGUIDCOL** property.

➤ *Columns with* **text** *or* **image** *data types*—Updates made at the Subscriber to replicated data with **text** or **image** data types are not supported for snapshot replication or for transactional replication with the immediate updating or queued updating options. Replicating and duplicating these columns are fully supported when you're not using updateable subscriptions. Publishing **text** and **image** data types is also supported in merge replication.

➤ *Collation*—You should choose the same collation schema and case sensitivity at both the Publisher sending the data and the Subscriber for items that are going to be replicated.

➤ *New data types in SQL Server 2000*—Be careful that you understand the data type mapping between the new data types when your replication occurs between different versions of SQL Server.

By implementing the **Immediate-Updating Subscribers** option, you can allow modification of data on Subscribers using transactional replication.

Generating Column Values

By using the **IDENTITY** property or the **uniqueidentifier** data type with the **NEWID** function, you can have SQL Server automatically generate column values. The **ROWGUIDCOL** property is used with the **uniqueidentifier** data type to generate sequential numbers across servers. The **IDENTITY** property is applied per table; if you need unique numbers within a database, use the **uniqueidentifier** data type.

 When column values in a database are valid, this validity is known as *domain integrity*.

The IDENTITY Property

SQL Server automatically generates a sequential value when the **IDENTITY** property is assigned. You can specify a starting value and an increment value. The **IDENTITY** property is often used as the primary key. Some points to consider:

➤ The **IDENTITY** property can be used only once in a table.

➤ The data type must be **integer, numeric,** or **decimal.** The **numeric** and **decimal** data types must have a scale of zero.

➤ A column with the **IDENTITY** property cannot be **NULL** or have a **DEFAULT** constraint.

➤ A column with the **IDENTITY** property cannot be updated.

➤ Uniqueness is not guaranteed; use the **UNIQUE INDEX** constraint.

➤ There are several functions that will display information (**IDENT_SEED, IDENT_INCR, SCOPE_IDENTITY,** and **IDENT_CURRENT**). You can use the **IDENTITYCOL** keyword in queries or use the **@@identity** global variable to return the last value inserted during a session. For example:

```
INSERT INTO guitars (description,model,price)
VALUES ('Starburst',25,499)
SELECT @@IDENTITY AS 'ID'
```

Note: Gaps can occur in the sequence because of deleted rows or incomplete transactions; the values are not reused.

The following example creates a **Products** table in which the **product_code** column contains the **IDENTITY** property with an initial value of 100 and an increment value of 2. This means that the first **product_code** is 100, the second is 102, and so on.

```
CREATE TABLE product (
    product_code int IDENTITY(100, 2) NOT NULL,
    name varchar (30),
    description varchar (300))
```

When a column in a table has the **IDENTITY** property, you can execute the **SET IDENTITY_INSERT ON** statement to enable particular values to be inserted into that column.

The IDENTITY Property and Replication

If the table with an IDENTITY column is going to be part of replication, and you're going to allow new rows at both the Publisher and the Subscriber, then you need to consider how to handle possible duplicates or replication failures because of duplicates. You should set the NOT FOR REPLICATION property for IDENTITY columns because on normal inserts into a table, the IDENTITY value is increased. After replication, the IDENTITY columns for the Subscriber and the Publisher will not be synchronized. If this happens, new rows that are inserted in each replica can have the same identity value for two different rows. Data cannot replicate if more than one row has the same identity and if the IDENTITY column is the primary key (or is defined with the UNIQUE constraint).

Keep in mind techniques for handling replication problems with the **IDENTITY** property.

The uniqueidentifier Data Type and the NEWID Function

The **uniqueidentifier** data type is used with the **NEWID** function. The **uniqueidentifier** data type consists of a 16-byte hexadecimal number that stores a globally unique identifier (GUID). The **NEWID** function creates the GUID value. Unlike the IDENTITY property, the **uniqueidentifier** data type does not automatically generate values; you set the default of the column to be the **NEWID** function.

The following example creates a table with a **product_code** that uses the **uniqueidentifier** data type and the **NEWID** function as the DEFAULT definition:

```
CREATE TABLE product (
    product_code uniqueidentifier NOT NULL DEFAULT NEWID(),
    name varchar (30),
    description varchar (300))
```

Creating DEFAULT and RULE Objects

In addition to using constraints, you can also create DEFAULT and RULE objects at the database level. These objects are then applied to a column or data type within the database. Similar to the way a global variable works, these objects allow you to define something once and use it many times. The preferred method, however, is to use the **DEFAULT** and **CHECK** constraints rather than these objects.

 For the exam, remember that the **RULE** objects are used primarily for backward compatibility. **CHECK** constraints are now the standard for attribute integrity.

The **DEFAULT** Object

You use the **CREATE DEFAULT** statement to create a default; you then use the **sp_bindefault** stored procedure to apply the default to a column or data type within the database. If the default is not compatible with the data type of the column, then SQL Server issues an error. If the value is too long for the column, the value is truncated. You use the **sp_unbindefault** stored procedure to remove the default from the column or data type, and you use the **DROP DEFAULT** statement to delete the object.

The following code snippets are examples of using a **DEFAULT** object. The first example creates the **DEFAULT**, the second example applies it to a column, the third example unbinds it from a column, and the last example deletes the **DEFAULT**:

```
/* Creates a DEFAULT */
USE MyDatabase
GO
CREATE DEFAULT numeric_default AS 0

/* Applies a DEFAULT to a column */
USE MyDatabase
EXEC sp_bindefault 'numeric_default', 'orders.quantity'

/* Removes a DEFAULT from a column */
USE MyDatabase
EXEC sp_unbindrule 'orders.quantity'

/* Deletes a DEFAULT */

USE MyDatabase
DROP DEFAULT 'numeric_default'
```

 As with **CHECK** constraints, by implementing **DEFAULT** definitions, you can effectively maintain domain integrity.

The RULE Object

You use the **CREATE RULE** statement to create a rule; you then use the **sp_bindrule** stored procedure to apply the rule to a column or data type. If the rule is not bound to a column, the rule might just as well not exist. When you bind a rule, it does not check existing data. You use the **sp_unbindrule** stored procedure to unbind the rule. You use the **sp_droprule** stored procedure to remove the rule from the database.

The following code snippets are examples of using a **RULE** object. The first example creates the **RULE**, the second example applies it to a column, the third example unbinds it from a column, and the last example deletes the **RULE**:

```
/* Creates a RULE */
USE MyDatabase
CREATE RULE
Salary_rule
   @Salary > = 10,000 and @Salary < 100,000)

/* Applies a RULE to a column */
USE MyDatabase
EXEC sp_bindrule 'Salary_rule', 'employees.Salary'

/* Removes a RULE from a column */
USE MyDatabase
EXEC sp_unbindrule 'employees.Salary'

/* Deletes a RULE */
USE MyDatabase
DROP RULE 'Salary_rule'
```

Scripting Objects

An important task is to save the definitions (called *schemas*) of database objects in a script file. These schemas can be used to re-create a database if it becomes totally corrupt, to create the database on another server, to serve as a template for other databases, or to serve as documentation. You use Enterprise Manager to generate these scripts. You can generate the entire database into one script file or several script files. You can script one, several, or all objects within a database.

Practice Questions

Case Study

The Be Happy Pet Supply Store has been functioning with paper and pencil. Staff members use ledgers and paper to keep track of their employees, customers, and supplies, but they have decided to transfer these operations to computers. You interview the various people.

The Owner

I want a system that will track everything easily and affordably. We need to get a handle on which types of pet supplies we sell well and which ones we should stop carrying. I would also like to keep notes about my employees.

The Accountant

I need a system that can track employees and their status. I need a system that tracks inventory: who supplies what; who buys what; what is on hand; and when I should reorder. We have fewer than 10 employees, and fewer than 50 categories and suppliers, so we don't need a large system.

The Store Manager

I want a system that lets me know who my customers are and what they are interested in, so I can stock those items. I also want to be able to send out special fliers to let customers know that their favorite products are on sale. I want a system that tells me if I have an item stored in the back room.

Question 1

For this case study, you feel that the primary keys of the **Employees**, **Categories**, and **Suppliers** tables can have similar data definitions. What should you do? [Check all correct answers]

- ❏ a. Create a user-defined data type, ID as **tinyint**, in the **model** database.
- ❏ b. Create a user-defined data type, ID as **tinyint**, in the **master** database.
- ❏ c. Create a user-defined data type, ID as **tinyint**, in each database individually.
- ❏ d. Create a user-defined data type, ID as **bigint**, in each database individually.

Answers a and c are correct. A user-defined data type must be defined in each database where it is to be used (answer c). Any user-defined data types created in the **model** database will be copied to newly created databases (answer a). Defining a data type in the **master** database would not work for your database. Therefore, answer b is incorrect. Answer d is incorrect because **bigint** is too large for this small company.

Question 2

> In the case study, you're defining the primary key for the **Employees** table. You want the system to automatically generate a number. What is the best syntax for the field definition?
>
> ○ a. **EmployeeNo tinyint IDENTITY (1, 1) NOT NULL**
>
> ○ b. **EmployeeNo int IDENTITY (1, 1) NOT NULL**
>
> ○ c. **EmployeeNo tinyint NOT NULL**
>
> ○ d. **EmployeeNo Char(10) IDENTITY (1, 1) NOT NULL**

Answer a is correct. To automatically generate numbers, you will use the **IDENTITY** property. It must have a numeric data type that can be represented as an integer (a whole number). Although answer b is correct, using the **int** data type for this customer is not optimizing performance. Answer c is incorrect because it's missing the **IDENTITY** property definition. Answer d is incorrect because it does not use a numeric data type.

Question 3

You want to ensure that quantities in the **OrderDetails** table can be used in calculations, but you don't want to require data entry. What is the correct syntax to solve your problem?

○ a.
```
ALTER TABLE dbo.OrderDetails
ADD CONSTRAINT CK_OrderDetails_Quantity
CHECK (Quantity =1)
```

○ b.
```
ALTER TABLE dbo.OrderDetails
ADD CONSTRAINT DF_Order_Details_Quantity
DEFAULT (1) FOR Quantity
```

○ c.
```
ALTER TABLE dbo.OrderDetails
ALTER COLUMN Quantity tinyint NOT NULL
```

○ d. Write a stored procedure.

Answer b is correct. Answers a and c are incorrect because they would require the user to enter a value. In addition, answer a is incorrect because it would allow the quantity to be 1, and nothing else. Answer d does not really solve the problem.

Question 4

Two of the tables in your database are:

Employees

Suppliers

Place the following fields under the appropriate tables. Items can be used more than once or never.

LastName	**FirstName**	**ContactName**
Company	**Address**	**City**
PostalCode	**OrderDate**	

The correct answer is:

Employees

> LastName
>
> FirstName
>
> Address
>
> City
>
> PostalCode

Suppliers

> ContactName
>
> Company
>
> Address
>
> City
>
> PostalCode

The **Employees** table should use the following fields: **LastName, FirstName, Address, City,** and **PostalCode.** The **Suppliers** table should use the following fields: **ContactName, Company, Address, City,** and **PostalCode.** For employees, you would want the first name and last name, but for suppliers, you would just use a contact name that included first and last names. You would not need **Company** in the **Employees** table because that would be unnecessary data. Both tables would require an address. **OrderDate** has nothing to do with either employees or suppliers; this field would be in the **Orders** table.

Question 5

What type of field definition would you use to fulfill the store owner's request for tracking notes on employees?

- ○ a. **varchar(2000)**
- ○ b. **char(2000)**
- ○ c. **text**
- ○ d. **bigint**
- ○ e. **image**

Answer a is correct for this company because it satisfies the owner's requirements for data storage with the least amount of overhead and storage space. Answer b is incorrect because it requires more additional space than needed. Answers c and e are incorrect because they use more overhead than necessary. Answer d is incorrect because the **bigint** data type holds only integers.

Question 6

Place the following tables and relationships together:

Customers

Products

Suppliers

Orders

OrderDetails

One-to-many

One-to-one

The correct answer is:

Customers one-to-many **Orders** one-to-many **OrderDetails**

OrderDetails one-to-many **Products**

Suppliers one-to-many **Products**

Categories one-to-many **Products**

Customers can have one or more orders, and orders are made up of one or more details (products). Suppliers can supply one or more products, and products can be in one or more categories.

Question 7

One of the suppliers for the Be Happy Pet Store has given you a **Products** table that you can import into the store's **Products** table. You want to disable the **CHECK** constraint on **UnitPrice**. What is the correct syntax?

○ a.
```
ALTER TABLE dbo.Products
WITH NOCHECK
CONSTRAINT ck_UnitPrice
```

○ b.
```
ALTER TABLE dbo.Products
NOCHECK
```

○ c.
```
ALTER TABLE dbo.Products
NOCHECK
ck_UnitPrice
```

○ d.
```
ALTER TABLE dbo.Products
NOCHECK
CONSTRAINT ck_UnitPrice
```

Answer d is correct. Answer a is incorrect; the **WITH NOCHECK** clause is used when you're adding a constraint and want to disable checking. Answer b is incorrect because it is missing the **CONSTRAINT** keyword and the column name. Answer c is incorrect because it is missing the **CONSTRAINT** keyword.

Question 8

Using the case study, you're creating a foreign key relationship between your **Customers** table and your **Orders** table. You want to ensure that when you delete a customer record, all of that customer's orders are also deleted. How would you accomplish this?

○ a. Create a trigger; SQL does not support cascading referential integrity.

○ b. Add **ON DELETE CASCADE** to the **FOREIGN KEY** constraint in the **Orders** table.

○ c. Add **ON DELETE CASCADE** to the **PRIMARY KEY** constraint in the **Customers** table.

○ d. Do nothing; **CASCADE ON DELETE** is the default for **FOREIGN KEY** constraints.

Answer b is correct. Answer a is incorrect because SQL Server 2000 now supports cascading referential integrity. Answer c is incorrect because you need to put the condition on the foreign key, not on the primary key. Answer d is incorrect because **NO ACTION** is the default, not **CASCADE**.

Question 9

You have a database with several tables that will be merged into one table. You want the system to generate a unique number to identify each row in each table, but these numbers should also be unique when the tables are combined. How would you accomplish this?

○ a. Add the following column definition to each table:

```
ALTER TABLE dbo.Be_Happy_Pet
   ADD rowid uniqueidentifier NOT NULL
       DEFAULT NEWID()
```

○ b. Add the following column definition to each table:

```
ALTER TABLE dbo.Be_Happy_Pet
    ADD rowid int IDENTITY(1, 1) NOT NULL
```

○ c. Add the following column definition to each table:

```
ALTER TABLE dbo.Be_Happy_Pet
   ADD rowid uniqueidentifier DEFAULT NEWID()
```

○ d. Add the following column definition to each table:

```
ALTER TABLE dbo.Be_Happy_Pet
    ADD rowid int NOT NULL DEFAULT NEWID()
```

Answer a is correct. Answer b is incorrect; the **IDENTITY** property is unique for a table only, and you need uniqueness for all tables in the database. Answer c is incorrect because it leaves out **NOT NULL**. Answer d is incorrect because the **NEWID** function can be used only with the **uniqueidentifier** data type.

Need to Know More?

 Iseminger, David. *SQL Server 2000 Reference Library*. Redmond, WA: Microsoft Press, 2000. ISBN 0-7356-1280-3. A selected collection of SQL Server 2000 Books Online; there are six volumes focused on key areas. Volume 2 deals with table creation.

 MS SQL Server Books Online has a section on creating and maintaining databases. MS SQL Server Books Online can be installed from the SQL Server CD or accessed online at **http://msdn.microsoft.com/ library/default.asp?URL=/library/psdk/sql/portal_7ap1.htm**.

 Search the TechNet CD or its online version through **www.microsoft.com**. Examples of keywords to search on are "table", "constraint", "cascading referential integrity", "**uniqueidentifier**", and "ROWGUIDCOL".

 www.microsoft.com/sql/ or **http://msdn.microsoft.com/sqlserver/ default.asp** are good places to find up-to-date information about SQL Server.

 www.sqlmag.com—Both the hard copy and the Web site for *SQL Magazine* have large amounts of information on SQL Server.

5

Retrieving and Modifying Data

Terms you'll need to understand:

- ✓ Transact-SQL
- ✓ Structured Query Language (SQL)
- ✓ Data Control Language (DCL)
- ✓ Data Definition Language (DDL)
- ✓ Data Manipulation Language (DML)
- ✓ Functions
- ✓ Collation
- ✓ **SELECT** statement
- ✓ Table joins
- ✓ Subquery
- ✓ **DELETE** statement
- ✓ **UPDATE** statement
- ✓ **INSERT** statement
- ✓ BCP (Bulk Copy Program) utility
- ✓ **BULK INSERT** statement
- ✓ Data Transformation Services (DTS)

Techniques you'll need to master:

- ✓ Defining objects
- ✓ Using built-in functions
- ✓ Retrieving data
- ✓ Modifying data
- ✓ Importing and exporting data with the BCP utility or the **BULK INSERT** statement
- ✓ Using Data Transformation Services (DTS)

You have your database built; you now need to populate the database and retrieve and modify the data. In this chapter, we'll discuss using Transact-SQL to retrieve and modify data. We'll also look at methods of doing bulk imports and exports of data.

Referring to a SQL Server Object

When referring to objects in SQL Server, you should qualify any objects that are not intrinsic. For example, if you are referring to the **Northwind** database from a **SELECT** statement within the **Pubs** database, you should use the following fully qualified syntax:

```
SELECT *
FROM Northwind.dbo.Customers
```

Thus, a fully qualified name includes the server, the database, the owner, and the object (table or view); for example, **ServerA.Northwind.dbo.Employees**. The qualifiers are separated by a dot (.). You can omit some or all of the qualifiers except for the object.

Note: You use a dot placeholder if you omit a qualifier in the middle.

If you omit a qualifier, it defaults as follows: The server defaults to the current local server instance; the database defaults to the current database; and the owner defaults to the user for the connection.

The following examples demonstrate referring to SQL Server objects:

```
-- a fully qualified object name
ServerA.Northwind.dbo.Employees -- server is the local server
Northwind.dbo.Employees -- current database and user on serverA
ServerA...Employees
```

Transact-SQL

Transact-SQL is SQL Server's implementation of the ANSI-standard Structured Query Language (with additional features included). Transact-SQL is divided into categories: Data Definition Language (DDL), Data Manipulation Language (DML), and Data Control Language (DCL). DDL statements include **CREATE, ALTER,** and **DROP** (which we discussed in Chapters 3 and 4). DML statements include **SELECT, INSERT, UPDATE,** and **DELETE.** DCL statements include **GRANT, DENY,** and **REVOKE** (we'll review this in Chapter 14 when we discuss security). Transact-SQL provides additional elements, including local variables, operators, functions, control-of-flow statements, and comments.

Functions

SQL Server includes several built-in functions. These functions retrieve system data or transform data by using the parameters you supply. With or without parameters, functions require parentheses after their names. Table 5.1 lists functions by category, and Table 5.2 shows where you can use functions.

Functions are either *deterministic* (always returns the same result with the same input) or *nondeterministic* (might not return the same result with the same input). SQL Server 2000, unlike its predecessors, has two limits in regard to nondeterministic functions:

➤ You cannot create an index on a computed column whose expression includes a nondeterministic function.

➤ You cannot create a clustered index on a view if the view refers to any nondeterministic functions.

 The exam can include any of SQL Server's built-in functions.

In Table 5.1, the parenthetical numbers in the Description column refer to function types; see the notes immediately following the table.

To avoid ambiguity, you should use the four-digit year value. If you use a two-digit year, you must understand the *two-digit year cutoff rule*. Years equal to or below the last two digits stay in the same century. Years greater than the last two digits are in the previous century. For example, if the two-digit year cutoff is 2049 (the default), the two-digit year 49 is interpreted as 2049, and the two-digit year 50 is interpreted as 1950.

Note: The default two-digit year cutoff for OLE automation objects is 2030.

 Microsoft expects that you know the date parts and understand the two-digit year cutoff rule.

In addition to the built-in functions, there are also Transact-SQL operators, such as the string concatenation (+) operator. These operators allow you to combine or transform columns within an expression such as the **SELECT** statement. For example, you can concatenate a **FirstName** field, a space, and a **LastName** field to get a full name: **FirstName** + " " + **LastName**.

Table 5.1	Function categories.
Category	**Description**
Aggregate functions	(2) Perform a calculation on a collection and return a single value. Examples are **AVG**, **MAX**, **MIN**, **SUM**, **COUNT**, **COUNT BIG**, and **GROUPING**. The **COUNT** and **COUNT BIG** functions are the same except that **COUNT** returns an **int** data type, and **COUNT BIG** returns a **bigint** data type. With the exception of the **COUNT** (*) statement, aggregate functions ignore null values.
Configuration functions	(1) (3) Return information about current configuration settings. Examples: **@@SERVERNAME**, **@@VERSION**, **@@NESTLEVEL**. Note that **@@** indicates a global variable. How the system increments **@@DBTS** has changed in SQL Server 2000; this variable is now incremented when a row that contains a **timestamp** column is modified.
Cursor functions	(1) (3) Return information about the status of a cursor. Examples: **@@CURSOR_ROWS**, **CURSOR_STATUS**, **@@FETCH_STATUS**.
Date and time functions	(1) (4) Manipulate **datetime** and **smalldatetime** values. Examples: **DATEADD**, **DATEDIFF**, **DATENAME**, **DATEPART**, **DAY**, **GETDATE**, **GETUTCDATE**, **MONTH**, **YEAR**.
Mathematical functions	(1) (2) Perform trigonometric, geometric, and other numeric operations. Examples: **ABS**, **SQUARE**, **POWER**.
Meta data functions	(1) (3) Return information on the attributes of database objects. Examples: **DB_NAME**, **FILE_NAME**, **COL_LENGTH**, **OBJECT_NAME**.
Rowset functions	(3) Return an object that can be used in the place of a table reference in a Transact-SQL statement. Examples: **CONTAINSTABLE**, **FREETEXTTABLE**, **OPENQUERY**, **OPENROWSET**, **OPENXML**. These are covered in Chapter 12.
Security functions	(1) (3) Return information about users and roles. Examples: **USER**, **USER_ID**, **IS_MEMBER**, **HAS_DBACCESS**.
String functions	(1) (2) Operate on a string input value (**char**, **varchar**, **nchar**, **nvarchar**, **binary**, and **varbinary**) and return a string or numeric value. Examples: **LEFT**, **RIGHT**, **LTRIM**, **RTRIM**, **LEN**, **SUBSTRING**.
System functions	(1) (4) Return information about values, objects, and settings in SQL Server. Examples: **CASE**, **CAST**, **CONVERT**, **CURRENT_USER**, **@@IDENTITY**, **ISNULL**.
System statistical functions	(1) (3) Return information about the performance of SQL Server. Examples: **@@CONNECTIONS**, **@@TOTAL_ERRORS**.
Text and image functions	(1) (3) Return information about **text** and **image** values. Examples: **PATINDEX**, **TEXTPTR**, **TEXTVALID**.

(1) Scalar functions—Operate on a single value and then return a single value.

(2) Deterministic functions—Always return the same result with the same input.

(3) Nondeterministic functions—Might not return the same result with the same input.

(4) Mixed functions—Contain a mix of some deterministic and some nondeterministic functions.

Table 5.2 Function scenarios.	
Use	**Example**
The **SELECT** statement of a query	**SELECT DB_NAME(), SELECT SUM(Price)**
A **WHERE** clause as a search condition	**SELECT x FROM y WHERE UPPER(LastName) = 'SMITH'**
A **WHERE** clause in a view to make it dynamic	**Create view x AS SELECT * FROM Employees where EmployeeID = SUSER_SID()**
Any expression	**SELECT DATENAME(month, GETDATE())**
A **CHECK** constraint or trigger	**Hiredate DATETIME CHECK Hiredate = > GETDATE()**
A **DEFAULT** constraint or trigger	**Created DATETIME DEFAULT GETDATE(),**

Other, more involved, functions are the **CASE** function and the **CONVERT** and **CAST** functions.

The CASE Function

The **CASE** scalar function evaluates a set of conditions and returns one of the choices. The **CASE** function has two types or formats. The simple **CASE** function compares an expression to another expression and returns a value. The searched **CASE** function evaluates Boolean expressions and determines the result.

Listing 5.1 provides the syntax and an example of the simple **CASE** function. Listing 5.2 provides the syntax and an example of the searched **CASE** function.

Listing 5.1 Syntax and example of a simple CASE function.

```
CASE input_expression
    WHEN when_expression THEN result_expression
        [ ...n ]
    [ ELSE else_result_expression ]
END
/* Simple CASE */
USE Northwind
SELECT   Category =
    CASE CategoryName
        WHEN 'Dairy Products' THEN 'Dairy'
        WHEN 'Grains/Cereals' THEN 'Grains'
        WHEN 'Meat/Poultry' THEN 'Meat-Chicken'
        WHEN 'Produce' THEN 'Vegetables'
        WHEN 'Seafood' THEN 'Fish'
        ELSE CategoryName
    END
From Categories
```

Listing 5.2   Syntax and example of a searched CASE function.

```
CASE
    WHEN Boolean_expression THEN result_expression
        [ ...n ]
    [ ELSE else_result_expression  ]
END
/* Searched CASE */
USE Northwind
SELECT ProductName, 'Product Class' =
CASE
    WHEN UnitPrice IS NULL THEN 'Not yet priced'
    WHEN UnitPrice <= 10 THEN 'Inexpensive'
    WHEN UnitPrice > 10 and UnitPrice <100 THEN 'Moderate Price'
    ELSE 'Expensive Product'
END
From Products
```

The CONVERT and CAST Functions

You can implicitly or explicitly convert an expression of one data type into another data type with some restrictions. To explicitly convert, you use either the **CONVERT** function or the **CAST** function. **CAST** is ANSI standard. **CONVERT** has a **style** property that can be used with the **datetime, numeric,** and **money** data types to further define the outcome.

Some data types cannot be converted into another data type, either implicitly or explicitly. For instance, you cannot convert the **uniqueidentifier** data type into any of the **numeric** data types.

When you convert an expression, remember to allow room for enough characters to display the converted value. SQL Server might issue an error or truncate the value and display an asterisk (*) if the field where the result will be displayed does not have enough characters for the full display. For example, if you have a **money** field that has value of 10,000, and you convert it to a **char(2)** field, you will get an asterisk instead of a value. For example, consider the following code:

```
USE pubs
SELECT CONVERT(char(3), ytd_sales)
FROM titles
WHERE pub_id = 0877
```

Because the previous code converts **ytd_sales** to a character value with a length of three, only **ytd_sales** values with three digits or fewer will be displayed. The rest of the **ytd_sales** values will be returned as asterisks, as shown in the following results.

```
*
NULL
375
375
*
*
```

```
(7 row(s) affected)
```

Listing 5.3 provides the syntax of the **CONVERT** and **CAST** functions, with an example of each.

Listing 5.3   Syntax and examples of the **CASE** and **CONVERT** functions.

```
This is the format for the CAST syntax:
CAST (expression AS data_type )
This is of the format for the CONVERT syntax:
CONVERT ( data_type [ ( length ) ] , expression [ , style ] )

This is an example of code using the CAST function:
-- Use CAST
USE Northwind
GO
SELECT ProductName, UnitPrice
FROM Products
WHERE LTRIM(CAST(UnitPrice AS char(20))) LIKE '2%'
GO
This is an example of code using the CONVERT function:
-- Use CONVERT
USE Northwind
GO
SELECT ProductName, UnitPrice
FROM Products
WHERE LTRIM(CONVERT(char(20), UnitPrice)) LIKE '2%'
GO
```

*Note: Converting the **money** data type to a character data type adds spaces to the left.*

Collation Precedence

In earlier versions of SQL Server, you specified the code page, the character sort order, and the Unicode collation separately at the server level only. In SQL Server 2000, you specify a *collation*, which includes all three items. You do this at the server level, which determines the default collation settings that you will use for any subsequent servers you install. At the database level, you can define a collation precedence that is different from that defined at the server, or you can let it default to the server's collation. You can even define a column-level collation that is different from the database-level collation. The collation name—such as **SQL_Latin1_General_CP1_CI_AI**—is defined as follows: **Latin1_General** is the language for dictionary sorting, **CP1** is the code page, **CI** means case insensitive, and **AI** means accent insensitive.

Defining a different collation-precedence order at the column level on multiple columns can cause problems when you are later doing collation comparisons between the data in those columns. The *collation precedence rules*, also known as the *collation coercion rules*, determine the following:

➤ The collation of the resulting expression if it evaluates to a character string

➤ The collation that is used by collation-sensitive operators such as **LIKE** and **IN**

The collation precedence rules apply only to the character string data types (**char, varchar, text, nchar, nvarchar,** and **ntext**).

> The exam will test your knowledge of the parameters for the **CONVERT** function (which are the output data type, the expression to convert, and the format style).
>
> It is especially important that you know the styles for **datetime** conversions (which you can find in SQL Server Books Online).
>
> Remember, too, that the default style that the **CONVERT** function uses is 0 or 100 (mon dd yyyy hh:miAM (or PM)).
>
> For **char** data types, the default implements a length of 30 if you do not specify a length argument.

Retrieving Data

To retrieve or view the data that you have stored in your database, you use the **SELECT** statement. The **SELECT** statement returns a *result set*, similar in structure to a table. The result set contains column headings, column data, and a row for each record that matches your criteria. A result set can be empty; in other words, it returns no data. A column heading can be blank. A simplified version follows. We will highlight key points and assume that you are familiar with basic SQL (Structured Query Language).

The Basic SELECT Statement

Following is the syntax of the SELECT statement:

```
SELECT [ ALL | DISTINCT ]
        [ { TOP integer | TOP integer PERCENT } [ WITH TIES ]
select_list
FROM table_source
[ WHERE search_condition ]
```

To return a result set, you need the FROM clause with at least one object, usually a table or a view. A SELECT statement without a FROM clause can only assign or return variables or include functions. Remember, if there are any embedded spaces or nonstandard identifiers, they must be enclosed in square brackets ([ ]) or double quotes (" ").

Remember that you can use the **OPENROWSET** and **OPENQUERY** functions within a **FROM** clause in lieu of table names. **OPENROWSET** is a function that lets you connect to a remote data source. **OPENQUERY** is a function that runs a query on a linked server.

The SELECT statement defines the columns and their order in the result set. The list can include column names, constants, expressions, the IDENTITYCOL keyword, the ROWGUIDCOL keyword, and column aliases. IDENTITYCOL is the keyword you use when representing the identity column of a given table. The ROWGUIDCOL is the keyword that specifies the column that makes each row unique in a table. Use this specification mainly for replication purposes when you require real-time data transfer. An asterisk (*) in a SELECT statement retrieves all columns in the order of the table definition. You can define a column alias by using either of the following methods:

➤ column_name AS alias

➤ alias = expression

Qualifying a column (**tableA.column1**) is optional unless there is a possibility of ambiguity; then qualifying a column is a requirement. When you're qualifying a column, if the table has an alias, then you must use the table alias and not the table name.

The **DISTINCT** keyword eliminates duplicate rows from the result set. Only unique rows will be returned. The **DISTINCT** clause applies to the entire SE-LECT statement as one unit. Null values are considered equal with **DISTINCT**.

The **TOP** clause limits the result set to the first *n* rows, where *n* rows can be a number or a percentage. If you don't have an **ORDER BY** clause, consistent results are not guaranteed. With an **ORDER BY** clause, you can use the **WITH TIES** clause, which might return additional rows.

The **FROM** clause in a **SELECT** statement can be specified as one or more tables or views, as a rowset function (such as **OPENXML**), or as a *derived table*, which is a nested **SELECT** statement that returns rows. When the table source includes an alias, it simplifies long names and helps prevent ambiguity. You always use an alias for a derived table.

 If you specify a table source alias, you must use it anywhere that you use the source objects, such as in the **SELECT** statement and the **WHERE** clause.

The following example code shows the syntax for using join operations in a **FROM** clause:

```
< table_source > < join_type > < table_source >
ON < search_condition >
< join_type > ::=
    [ INNER | { { LEFT | RIGHT | FULL } [ OUTER] } ] JOIN
```

 We recommend that you do not use the nonstandard *= and =* outer join operators in the **WHERE** clause. For example, you should *not* use the following syntax: **SELECT Table1.Column1, Table2.Column2 FROM Table1, Table2 WHERE Table1.id *=Table2.id**.

The **WHERE** clause specifies search conditions that narrow the result set. You cannot include aggregate functions in the **WHERE** clause.

Listings 5.4 through 5.7 are examples of the basic **SELECT** statement.

Listing 5.4   Selecting a table with a column alias and an expression.

```
FROM [Order Details]
WHERE quantity > 10
```

Listing 5.5   A WHERE clause that returns only last names starting with "S."

```
USE Northwind
SELECT LastName, Firstname
FROM Employees
WHERE LastName LIKE 'S%'
```

Listing 5.6   A table join with a qualified object.

```
SELECT OrderID, ProductName
FROM Northwind.dbo.[Order Details] ord
JOIN Northwind.dbo.Products
ON Ord.ProductID = Products.ProductID
```

Listing 5.7   Selecting a table with a TOP clause.

```
SELECT TOP 5 ProductName, UnitPrice
FROM dbo.Products
Order BY UnitPrice desc
```

Additional Clauses for the SELECT Statement

We have already discussed the **FROM** clause. Now we will focus on clauses that you can use when you organize data you want returned from a query.

The GROUP BY Clause

To group the result set, you use the **GROUP BY** clause. The syntax is:

```
GROUP BY group_by_expression [ WITH { CUBE | ROLLUP } ]
```

If your **SELECT** statement parameters include aggregate functions, then a summary value is included for each group, and individual rows are not included. Columns specified in the **SELECT** statement that are *not* part of the aggregate expression must also be included in the *group_by_expression* argument. You should always include an **ORDER BY** clause with a **GROUP BY** clause.

If you specify more than one column in an **ORDER BY** clause, the first column you specify takes precedence, then the second, third, fourth, and so on.

The *group_by_expression* argument cannot include columns with data types of **text**, **ntext**, or **image**. The size of columns and aggregates is limited by the row size of 8,060 bytes because of the intermediate tables required by the system. If you are using the **CUBE** or **ROLLUP** clause, then the limit is 10 grouping expressions.

The following snippet shows a **GROUP BY** clause with an aggregate. This example returns only the category name with the average price for the category.

```
Use Northwind
SELECT CategoryName, AVG(UnitPrice)AS 'Average'
FROM Categories cat JOIN Products pro
ON pro.CategoryID = cat.CategoryID
GROUP BY CategoryName
ORDER BY CategoryName
```

The following snippet shows a **GROUP BY** clause without an aggregate. This example returns a row for each of the categories. You will notice that although there are two beverages with a unit price of $14.00, you will see only one occurrence, rather than both.

```
Use Northwind
SELECT CategoryName, UnitPrice
FROM Categories cat JOIN Products pro
ON pro.CategoryID = cat.CategoryID
GROUP BY CategoryName, UnitPrice
ORDER BY CategoryName, UnitPrice
```

If you use a **UNION** operator when you join multiple **SELECT** statements, you must specify the **GROUP BY** clause for each **SELECT** statement independently. In other words, you cannot use a single **GROUP BY** clause when you organize data for multiple **SELECT** statements by using the **UNION** operator.

The WITH CUBE Clause

When you supply the **WITH CUBE** clause, you add summary rows for every possible combination of groups and subgroups in the result set. The **NULL** in the column indicates that you are using summary rows. The following snippet shows a **GROUP BY WITH CUBE** clause.

```
Use Northwind
SELECT CategoryName, ProductName,
      Avg(UnitsInStock)AS 'Average in Stock'
FROM Categories cat JOIN Products pro
ON pro.CategoryID = cat.CategoryID
WHERE ProductName LIKE 'G%'
GROUP BY CategoryName, ProductName WITH CUBE
```

The WITH ROLLUP Clause

Like the **WITH CUBE** clause, the **WITH ROLLUP** clause adds summary rows, but they are summarized in a hierarchical order from the lowest level in the group to the highest. The order in which you specify the grouping columns determines the group hierarchy. Therefore, changing the order of the grouping columns can affect the number of rows produced in the result set. The snippet that follows shows a **GROUP BY WITH ROLLUP** clause.

```
Use Northwind
SELECT CategoryName, ProductName,
Avg(UnitsInStock)AS 'Average in Stock'
FROM Categories cat JOIN Products pro
ON pro.CategoryID = cat.CategoryID
WHERE ProductName LIKE 'G%'
GROUP BY CategoryName, ProductName WITH ROLLUP
```

 Distinct aggregates—for example, **AVG(DISTINCT *column_name*)**— cannot be used with **CUBE** or **ROLLUP**. They will produce an error.

The HAVING Clause

The **HAVING** clause is to the **GROUP BY** clause as the **WHERE** clause is to the **SELECT** clause. The **HAVING** clause narrows the result set to those values that match the **HAVING** condition. First you process the data in the **SELECT** ... **GROUP BY** clause, and create an intermediate result set. Then you apply the **HAVING** clause conditions, and display the rows that match those conditions in the final result set. The **HAVING** clause has the following syntax:

```
HAVING search_condition
```

The snippet that follows shows the use of a **HAVING** clause that returns items with unit prices greater than the specified amount and orders them as directed:

```
Use Northwind
SELECT CategoryName, AVG(UnitPrice)AS 'Average'
FROM Categories cat JOIN Products pro
ON pro.CategoryID = cat.CategoryID
GROUP BY CategoryName
HAVING AVG(UnitPrice) > 21
ORDER BY CategoryName
```

Just as with the **GROUP BY** clause, you cannot apply the **HAVING** clause to multiple **SELECT** statements. For example, each **SELECT** statement you combine with **UNION** operators must have its own individual **HAVING** clause specified.

The following **SELECT** statements have their own **GROUP BY** and **HAVING** clauses. This is important to remember for the exam.

Also, it is important to note that you apply the **HAVING** clause condition after the **GROUP BY** clause, as shown in the example that follows:

```
USE Northwind
SELECT ProductName, AVG(UnitPrice)
FROM Products
GROUP BY ProductName
HAVING SUM(UnitPrice) > 10
UNION
SELECT CustomerID, AVG(Freight)
FROM Orders
GROUP BY CustomerID
HAVING SUM(Freight) > 10
```

The ORDER BY Clause

Use the **ORDER BY** clause to sort the result set for the **SELECT** statement. The **ORDER BY** clause has the following syntax:

```
[ ORDER BY order_expression [ ASC | DESC ] ]
```

The **ORDER BY** clause sorts the result set in either ascending order (**ASC**) or descending order (**DESC**) before displaying it. You create an intermediate result set that matches all the options of the **SELECT** clause; then you sort and display the result set. The *order_expression* argument cannot include columns with data types of **text**, **ntext**, or **image**. The size of columns in the *order_expression* argument is limited by the row size of 8,060 bytes because of the intermediate table required by the system. Null values are sorted as the least possibility.

The COMPUTE and COMPUTE BY Clauses

Use the **COMPUTE** and **COMPUTE BY** clauses to create multiple result sets for a **SELECT** statement. The **COMPUTE** clause has the following syntax:

```
[ COMPUTE
    { { AVG | COUNT | MAX | MIN | STDEV | STDEVP
      | VAR | VARP | SUM }
          ( expression ) } [ ,...n ]
    [ BY expression [ ,...n ] ]
]
```

Both the **COMPUTE** and **COMPUTE BY** clauses create multiple result sets. Whereas a **GROUP BY** clause summarizes for the group and returns only the group total, the **COMPUTE** and **COMPUTE BY** clauses include details and summary information.

The **COMPUTE** and **COMPUTE BY** clauses are not recommended; instead, you should use **CUBE, ROLLUP,** or the Microsoft SQL Server 2000 Analysis Services with OLE DB for Analysis Services. **CUBE** and **ROLLUP** are not ANSI standard.

The UNION Operator

The **UNION** operator allows you to combine two **SELECT** statements into one result set. The number of columns in each **SELECT** statement must match, and the data types must be compatible. The column names in the first **SELECT** statement determine the names in the result set. The **UNION** operator is used as follows:

```
SELECT statement1 UNION SELECT statement2
```

Be sure that you are comfortable using the **UNION** operator before you take the exam. Many questions will try to confuse you by showing incorrect syntax, such as the improper use of **GROUP BY** clauses in conjunction with the **UNION** operator.

The Subquery

A *subquery* is a **SELECT** query that returns a single value and is nested inside a **SELECT, INSERT, UPDATE,** or **DELETE** statement or inside another subquery. You can use a subquery anywhere the system allows an expression. Nesting of subqueries is limited by the available memory and by the complexity of the queries, but nesting cannot exceed 32 levels. Often, you can reword many subqueries as joins. Enclose all subqueries in parentheses.

Another name for a subquery is an *inner query* or *inner select*. The name for a statement containing a subquery is *outer query* or *outer select*.

Format the three basic types of subqueries as follows:

➤ WHERE *expression* [NOT] IN (*subquery*)

➤ WHERE *expression comparison_operator* [ANY | ALL] (*subquery*)

➤ WHERE [NOT] EXISTS (*subquery*)

Most subqueries are independent; that is, you can execute them independently of the outer query. The subquery is executed once, its value is replaced in the expression, and the outer query is then evaluated. A *correlated subquery* is different; it is dependent upon the outer query and is evaluated for each row that is selected by the outer query.

Listing 5.8 is an example of a subquery and its alternative join.

Listing 5.8   A subquery and its alternative join.

```
/* Uses a subquery to select only beverages */
USE Northwind
SELECT ProductName
FROM Products
WHERE CategoryID IN
  (SELECT CategoryID
   FROM Categories
   Where CategoryName = 'Beverages')
GO
/* Uses a join to select only beverages */
USE Northwind
SELECT ProductName
FROM Categories Join Products
ON Categories.CategoryID = Products.CategoryID
WHERE CategoryName = 'Beverages'
```

Modifying Data

Data within a database obviously goes through many changes. New records need adding, obsolete records need deleting, and existing data may otherwise need changing. This section discusses the Transact-SQL statements you use when modifying data.

Using the DELETE Statement to Delete Rows

The syntax for the **DELETE** statement is as follows:

```
DELETE table_or_view FROM table_sources WHERE search_condition
```

Use the **DELETE** statement when you're deleting one or more rows from a table. The table itself is not deleted even if you remove all rows; deleting a table requires the **DROP** statement. All rows that match the search condition of the **DELETE** statement's **WHERE** clause are deleted from the database. A **DELETE** statement without a **WHERE** clause deletes *all* rows in the table and records each deletion in the log. You should use the **TRUNCATE TABLE** statement instead of using a **DELETE** statement without a **WHERE** clause. The **TRUNCATE TABLE** statement is more efficient and uses fewer server resources.

*Note: If you omit the **WHERE** clause, then all rows in the table are deleted and logged.*

The **FROM** clause is optional; it further qualifies the criteria in the **WHERE** clause. Rows in tables listed in the **FROM** clause are not deleted. **DELETE** permissions default to members of the **sysadmin, db_owner,** and **db_datawriter** roles and to the table owner. All except the **db_datawriter** role can transfer permission.

Listing 5.9 shows a couple of examples. The first example is a simple **DELETE** statement without a **FROM** clause, and the second example shows how you use the **FROM** clause. A deletion can fail if referential integrity is broken; even if only one row fails, they all fail.

 If you want all the rows in a table deleted, the **TRUNCATE TABLE** statement is faster than the **DELETE** statement. **DELETE** physically removes rows one at a time and records each deleted row in the transaction log.

Listing 5.9   Examples of the DELETE statement.

```
USE Northwind
DELETE Suppliers
WHERE CompanyName = 'Bigfoot Breweries'
GO
DELETE Products
FROM Suppliers
WHERE Products.SupplierID = Suppliers.SupplierID
  AND Suppliers.CompanyName = 'Bigfoot Breweries'
```

Note: To prevent referential integrity problems, you would use the two DELETE statements in Listing 5.9 in the reverse order.

Using the UPDATE Statement to Modify Data

The syntax for the **UPDATE** statement is as follows:

```
UPDATE table_or_view
SET
  column_name = { expression | DEFAULT | NULL }
FROM table_sources WHERE search_condition
```

Use the **UPDATE** statement when you're modifying the data in a row or rows of a table. You can modify one or more columns within the same **UPDATE** statement. The new data must comply with any constraints or rules for the table, **NULL** settings, or data type. If it doesn't, an error is returned and the update is cancelled. If your update causes the row to exceed the maximum size (8,060 bytes), an error is returned and the update is cancelled. **UPDATE** permissions default to members of the **sysadmin, db_owner,** and **db_datawriter** roles and to the table owner. All of these (except the **db_datawriter** role) can transfer permission.

The **UPDATE** statement is logged. If your modification is for **text, ntext,** or **image** data types, you should consider using the **WRITETEXT** statement or the **UPDATETEXT** statement instead; these are not logged (by default).

All rows that match the **search_condition** argument of the **WHERE** clause are updated. The **FROM** clause is optional; it further qualifies the criteria in the **WHERE** clause. Rows in tables listed in the **FROM** clause are not modified.

Listing 5.10 shows some **UPDATE** examples. The first example updates every row in the table. The second example uses the **FROM** clause and updates only certain rows.

Listing 5.10 Examples of the UPDATE statement.

```
/* Update all prices by 10% */
USE Northwind
Update Products
Set UnitPrice = UnitPrice * 1.1
GO
/* Update all prices by 10% for Supplier 'Bigfoot Breweries' */
USE Northwind
Update Products
Set UnitPrice = UnitPrice * 1.1
From Suppliers, Products
WHERE Suppliers.SupplierID = Products.SupplierID
AND Suppliers.CompanyName = 'Bigfoot Breweries'
```

Updating and Inserting **text, ntext,** and **image** Data Types

Update or insert the rich text data types (**text, ntext,** and **image**) by using the **UPDATETEXT** and **WRITETEXT** statements, respectively. **WRITETEXT** replaces the entire data within the column.

Using the INSERT Statement to Add Rows

The syntax is:

```
INSERT table_or_view [ ( column_list ) ]
   { VALUES
       ( { DEFAULT | NULL | expression } [ ,....n] )
   }
   | DEFAULT VALUES
```

The basic **INSERT** statement adds only one row to your table. You provide values for each column in the table except for **IDENTITY** columns, **timestamp** data types, and columns with a default when you want the default. If all of your columns include the **IDENTITY** property or have defaults or allow null values, then you can use the **DEFAULT VALUES** keyword. This creates a new row with all defaults. **INSERT** permissions default to members of the **sysadmin, db_owner,** and **db_datawriter** roles and to the table owner. All except the **db_datawriter** role can transfer permission.

If any value violates a constraint or if a data type mismatch occurs, the **INSERT** is cancelled and an error message is generated. If the values are listed in the same order as the columns, then the **COLUMNS** clause can be omitted. Between the **INSERT** keyword and the table name, you can include the keyword **INTO,** but it is optional and is left out in the syntax and examples provided here.

Listing 5.11 shows two examples. You do not provide a value for the **CategoryID** column because it has an **IDENTITY** property. The **Description** column will appear as a reserved word in the SQL Query Analyzer unless it's enclosed in brackets ([]). Either way—with or without the brackets—is correct. The first example in Listing 5.11 uses the column names, and the second does not.

Listing 5.11   Examples of the **INSERT** statement.

```
/* Insert a new row in the Categories table */
USE Northwind
INSERT Categories
(CategoryName, [Description])
VALUES ('Test', 'This is a Test')

/* The same INSERT without the column names */
USE Northwind
INSERT Categories
VALUES ('Test', 'This is a Test')
```

Inserting Multiple Rows

You can insert more than one row in a table by using the **SELECT INTO** statement or the **INSERT...SELECT** statement.

The **SELECT INTO** statement creates a new table and populates it with the result set of the **SELECT** statement. Its syntax is:

```
SELECT <select_list> INTO new_table_name FROM source
```

The **INSERT...SELECT** statement adds one or more new rows to an existing table. Its syntax is:

```
INSERT INTO existing_tableA [ ( column_list ) ]
SELECT <select_list> FROM other_table WHERE condition
```

Bulk Copy Operations

The **BULK INSERT** Transact-SQL statement can be used when you're importing data into SQL Server but not when you're exporting data from SQL Server. The BCP command-line utility can both import and export data. Both the **BULK INSERT** Transact-SQL statement and the BCP utility can be used to insert data into a table or to view a table's data, depending on the format specified by the user.

 To import data into a table, remember that you need to alter the database and set the recovery option to **BULK_LOGGED**. When you indicate the **-E** parameter for the BCP utility, you enable specific values to be entered into an **IDENTITY** column. Using this parameter is the same as using the **SET IDENTITY INSERT ON** statement.

The BULK INSERT Statement

Here is the basic syntax for the **BULK INSERT** statement:

```
BULK INSERT [database_name.owner.] table_name FROM data_file
WITH ( [<parameter_list>] )
```

Some highlights about the **BULK INSERT** statement:

➤ The parentheses after **WITH** and at the end of the parameter list are required.

➤ The database or owner defaults to the current database or user, respectively. That user must have correct permissions.

➤ The *data_file* argument is the full path of the data file that contains data. If the file is remote to the SQL server, you need to use the Universal Naming Convention (UNC)—for example, *servername**sharename**path**filename*.

➤ Only members of the **sysadmin** and **bulkadmin** roles can execute the **BULK INSERT** statement.

➤ A format file should be included if you are not specifying all of the columns, if the columns are in a different order, or if column delimiters vary. The format file is created by the BCP utility.

The BCP Utility

The basic syntax for the BCP utility is shown here:

```
bcp [database_name.owner.]
source direction datafile
<parameters>
```

Note: Since version 7, the BCP utility has been written using the ODBC bulk API (application programming interface). Before version 7, it was written using the DB-Library bulk copy API.

Some highlights about the BCP utility:

➤ The database or owner defaults to the current database or user, respectively. That user must have correct permissions.

➤ The *source* can be a table, a view, or a query. If the query returns multiple result sets, only the first result set is copied to the data file; the others are ignored.

➤ The *direction* can be **in** (importing data into a table), **out** (exporting data), **queryout** (used when the source is a query), or **format** (creates a format file).

➤ The *data_file* argument is the full path of the data file that contains data. If the file is remote to the SQL server, you need to use the UNC—for example, *\\servername\sharename\path\filename*.

➤ SQL Server ignores **timestamp** values and regenerates them when the row is added.

➤ Nonstandard identifiers need to be enclosed in square brackets ([]).

➤ When you're bulk-copying data using the native or character format, the BCP utility, by default, converts character data to OEM code page characters for export and to ANSI/Microsoft Windows code page characters for import. To prevent the loss of extended or double-byte character set (DBCS) characters, you should use Unicode native data format (-**N**), Unicode character data format (-**w**), or a specific code page (-**C**).

➤ In SQL Server 2000, you can specify column-level collations for bulk copy operations.

Data Transformation Services

The Data Transformation Services (DTS) feature is another method of importing or exporting data introduced in SQL Server version 7. DTS is a set of graphical tools and programmable objects that allow you to extract, transform, and consolidate data from disparate sources into single or multiple destinations. DTS meets the very important business need of centralizing data from disparate data sources. DTS has several components: DTS packages, connections, DTS tasks, DTS transformations, and DTS workflows.

A *DTS package* is a structured collection of connections, DTS tasks, transformations, and workflow constraints that you can assemble by using one of the DTS tools or programmatically. You save a package in one of four formats: SQL Server

Meta Data Services, a SQL Server **msdb** database, a structured storage file (.dts), or a Visual Basic file.

Connections can be based on an OLE DB source, such as SQL Server, Oracle, Excel, Access, Visual FoxPro, text file, Microsoft Exchange, Microsoft Active Directory services, or any source that has an OLE DB interface.

A *DTS task* is a step, within the package, that performs a work unit that moves, transforms, or processes a job. These tasks include:

➤ Importing or exporting data between sources via OLE DB.

➤ Transforming data into different data types or values.

➤ Copying database objects with some restrictions (only between SQL 7 and SQL 2000 servers). Data objects include indexes, views, logins, stored procedures, triggers, rules, defaults, constraints, and user-defined data types.

➤ Sending and receiving messages between users and/or packages.

➤ Executing Transact-SQL statements or ActiveX scripts.

➤ Saving data to global variables to be used by other DTS tasks or packages.

You can include parameterized queries in a DTS task; the placeholder is a question mark (?). You can create custom DTS tasks in Visual Basic or C++.

A *DTS transformation* is one or more operations applied to the data before it reaches its destination. A transformation can include manipulating data types, applying functions written with ActiveX scripts, using built-in functions, or even calling a COM object.

A *DTS workflow* defines the sequence of steps, including different paths if a step succeeds or fails.

DTS also has a facility to save the metadata and data lineage information to the Meta Data Services. The DTS packages that Meta Data Services stores are used in data warehousing to track the history of the transformation.

Practice Questions

Case Study

The Big-T company sells office supplies to various stores around the country. The company has a database that includes the following tables: **Products, Categories, SalesTeam,** and **Sales.**

The Owner

I have all this data about sales and salespersons. I need to be able to generate reports that tell me who my best salespeople are and who needs some help. I also need to know which products sell well.

The Inventory Manager

I need reports that track inventory: who supplies what; who buys what; what is on hand; and when I should reorder.

The Sales Manager

I need reports that track my best-selling products and my least-selling products. I also need to know who the best and worst salespeople are. If I can understand who is doing poorly, I can get them training.

The Data Entry Manager

Most of our salespeople live in our local area, and I don't want to have to type the state and ZIP codes when entering records for new sales personnel.

Question 1

For this case study, the sales manager wants a simple report with one column that includes both the product name and the price. What is the code required to do this? [Check all correct answers]

☐ a.
```
SELECT ProductName + ' - '
    + CONVERT(CHAR(10), Price)
as 'Product and Price'
FROM dbo.Products
```

☐ b.
```
SELECT ProductName + ' - '
+ CONVERT(Price, CHAR(10))
as 'Product and Price'
FROM dbo.Products
```

☐ c.
```
SELECT ProductName + ' - '
+ CAST(Price AS CHAR(10))
as 'Product and Price'
FROM dbo.Products
```

☐ d.
```
SELECT ProductName + ' - '
+ CAST(Price, CHAR(10))
as 'Product and Price'
FROM dbo.Products
```

Answers a and c are correct. With the **CONVERT** function, you put the new data type first, followed by a comma and the column you are converting. With the **CAST** function, you put the column first, followed by the word **AS**, followed by the new data type.

Question 2

The owner is looking to downsize and needs to know who the five lowest-selling salespeople are. Place the following code lines in the correct order. Not all code needs to be used.

```
FROM Sales JOIN SalesTeam
FROM Sales LEFT OUTER JOIN SalesTeam
ON Sales.Salesperson_id =
SalesTeam.Salesperson_id
ORDER BY Sales
ORDER BY Sales, DESC
SELECT Top 5 WITH TIES SalesPersonName, Sales
SELECT Top 5 PERCENT WITH TIES
SalesPersonName, Sales
```

The correct answer is:

```
SELECT Top 5 WITH TIES SalesPersonName, Sales
FROM Sales JOIN SalesTeam
ON Sales.Salesperson_id =
SalesTeam.Salesperson_id
ORDER BY Sales
```

A **JOIN** clause without a predicate is the same as an inner join, which is what you want because you want only matches. Descending order would give you the top five salespeople, not the lowest five. Using 5 percent could give you more than five people, and the owner wanted only five people.

Question 3

The price of BuyMore pens has gone down by 5 percent, and the manager wants to pass the savings on to his customers. What is the correct code?

○ a.
```
UPDATE products
SET price = price * .95
FROM Suppliers, Products
WHERE Suppliers.SupplierID =
Products.SupplierID
AND Suppliers.CompanyName = 'BuyMore'
```

○ b.
```
UPDATE products
SET price = price * 1.05
FROM Suppliers, Products
WHERE Suppliers.SupplierID =
Products.SupplierID
AND Suppliers.CompanyName = 'BuyMore'
```

○ c.
```
UPDATE products
SET price = price * .95
WHERE ProductID = 'BuyMore'
```

○ d.
```
UPDATE products
price = price * .95
FROM Suppliers, Products
WHERE Suppliers.SupplierID =
Products.SupplierID
AND Suppliers.CompanyName = 'BuyMore'
```

Answer a is correct. Answer b is incorrect because it would increase the price by 5 percent instead of decreasing the price. Answer c is incorrect because it implies that the **Products** table contains the supplier name, and this is not good design. Answer d is incorrect because it is missing the **SET** keyword.

Question 4

Business has picked up, and the sales manager has acquired a new salesperson, located in the company headquarters' hometown. The salesperson is Mary Smith, who lives at 123 Ann Street, Cramtown, AZ. Her hire date is today. Which of the following code samples are correct? [Check all correct answers]

❑ a.
```
INSERT SalesTeam
(FirstName, LastName, Street, City, hiredate)
VALUES
('Smith', 'Mary', '123 Ann Street',
'Cramtown', GETDATE())
```

❑ b.
```
INSERT SalesTeam
(FirstName, LastName, Street, City, hiredate)
VALUES
('Mary', 'Smith', '123 Ann Street',
'Cramtown', Today())
```

❑ c.
```
INSERT SalesTeam
(FirstName, LastName, Street, City, State,
ZipCode, hiredate)
VALUES
('Mary', 'Smith', '123 Ann Street',
'Cramtown', 'AZ', '81111', GETDATE())
```

❑ d.
```
INSERT SalesTeam
(FirstName, LastName, Street, City, hiredate)
VALUES
('Mary', 'Smith', '123 Ann Street',
'Cramtown', GETDATE())
```

Answers c and d are correct. Because the data entry person indicated that she did not want to enter the state and ZIP code, you can safely assume that there are default constraints for these values, and so you can either include or not include them. Answer a is incorrect because the first and last names are in the incorrect order. Answer b is incorrect because there is no **TODAY** function.

Question 5

Tom Jones has retired and is being replaced by Marty Johnson. Place the following code lines in the correct order. Not all code needs to be used.

```
(SELECT Sales.Salesperson_id FROM SalesTeam
WHERE FirstName = 'Marty'
SELECT Sales.Salesperson_id FROM SalesTeam
WHERE FirstName = 'Marty'
(SELECT Sales.Salesperson_id FROM SalesTeam
WHERE FirstName = 'TOM'
AND LastName = 'Johnson')
AND LastName = 'Johnson'
AND LastName = 'Jones'
AND LastName = 'Jones')
DELETE SalesTeam
SET Sales.Salesperson_id =
UPDATE sales
WHERE FirstName = 'Tom'
GO
```

The correct answer is:

```
UPDATE sales
SET Sales.Salesperson_id =
(SELECT Sales.Salesperson_id FROM SalesTeam
WHERE FirstName = 'Marty'
AND LastName = 'Johnson')
WHERE Sales.Salesperson_id =
(SELECT Sales.Salesperson_id FROM SalesTeam
WHERE FirstName = 'Tom'
AND LastName = 'Jones')
GO
DELETE SalesTeam
WHERE FirstName = 'Tom' AND
LastName = 'Jones'
```

You need to update the **Sales** table with the new salesperson's ID first. You can use a subquery to get the correct salesperson ID. Remember that a subquery must be enclosed in parentheses.

Question 6

The manager wants to export the **Products** table, with no modifications, to send to a client. Which is the proper tool to use?

○ a. **BULK INSERT** statement

○ b. BCP utility

○ c. DTS

○ d. **COLLATE** statement

Answer b is correct. Answer a is incorrect because the **BULK INSERT** statement can do only imports, not exports. Answer c is incorrect because, although DTS would work, you do not have any transformations, so the BCP utility would be more appropriate. Answer d is incorrect because the **COLLATE** statement does not import or export; it changes the collation property.

Question 7

The owner wants you to build a similar database on the same server. The database will contain the **Products**, **Categories**, and **SalesTeam** tables with their associated data. The business owner wants to change some column definitions in the new database. Which is the proper tool to use?

○ a. **BULK INSERT** statement

○ b. BCP utility

○ c. DTS

○ d. SQL scripts

Answer c is correct. DTS allows you not only to copy the data, but also to copy the structures and to transform the column definitions in one package. Answer a is incorrect because the **BULK INSERT** statement will not help you; it imports only data and not objects. Answer b is incorrect because the BCP utility imports and exports only data, not objects, so you would have to create the objects. Answer d is incorrect because the SQL scripts will help you build the objects but not copy the data.

Need to Know More?

Iseminger, David. *SQL Server 2000 Reference Library*. Redmond, WA: Microsoft Press, 2000. ISBN 0-7356-1280-3. A selected collection of SQL Server 2000 Books Online; there are six volumes focused on key areas. Volume 5 contains all you want to know about Transact-SQL.

Vieira, Rob. *Professional SQL Server 7.0 Programming*. Chicago, IL: Wrox Press, Inc., 1999. ISBN 1861002319. This book covers SQL Server 7 programming, which will help you with Transact-SQL and other programming details, with the exception of new items for SQL Server 2000.

Microsoft SQL Server Books Online has sections on creating or maintaining databases. You can install this documentation from the SQL Server CD or access it online through **http://msdn.microsoft.com/library/default.asp/**.

Search the TechNet CD or its online version through **www.microsoft.com/technet**. Keywords you can search on are "FUNCTION", "COLLATION", "UPDATE", "BULK INSERT", and "DTS".

www.microsoft.com/sql/ or **http://msdn.microsoft.com/sqlserver/default.asp** are good places for finding up-to-date information about SQL Server.

www.sqlmag.com—*SQL Magazine*—both the hard copy and the Web site—has a large amount of information on SQL Server.

6

Implementing Indexes

Terms you'll need to understand:

✓ Clustered index

✓ Nonclustered index

✓ Simple index

✓ Primary key index

✓ Composite index

✓ **UPDATE STATISTICS**

Techniques you'll need to master:

✓ Adding indexes

✓ Renaming indexes

✓ Dropping indexes

✓ Implementing clustered and nonclustered indexes

An *index* is a database object that shows the order in which values of one or more columns are stored in a table. In relational databases, indexes are valuable because they provide the ability to quickly access records in a table. Although indexes are not necessary for the proper operation of SQL Server 2000, their value to the user or administrator rises rapidly as the amount of data stored in an indexed database increases. This quick access is achieved based on the values in a column or set of columns. The index provides pointers to column values in a table and then arranges them according to a specified sort order.

A table index is similar to a book's index in that it provides a precise location for content materials based on keywords (columns). For example, if you were repeatedly looking for specific hotel reservations to post changed arrival dates and you knew the customers' last names, an alphabetical index telling you the exact location of each reservation based upon the customers' last names would allow you to search (or query) that reservation information faster than you could if you had to search through every single reservation for each change.

Index Types

SQL Server 2000 provides two types of indexes: clustered and nonclustered. Clustered indexes are created using the specifications for how data in a table is physically stored within that table's structure. The data actually becomes part of the indexed storage. Searching clustered indexes involves traversing the storage path to the data rather than following a pointer, as in nonclustered indexes.

Because you are talking about the physical storage of data, each table can have only one clustered index. To create a clustered index, use the **CREATE** command with the **CLUSTERED** option:

```
CREATE [ CLUSTERED ] INDEX index_name ON table_name
```

Nonclustered indexes do use pointers that point to specific records in a table, but these indexes do not use the specifications for how those records are physically stored. That is, the data itself is not part of the index, as it is in clustered indexes. In addition, nonclustered indexes are actually separate database objects within a database.

The **TEMPDB** database is used as the sorting work area for nonclustered indexes. This work area is freed when the sort is finished. Because nonclustered indexes use pointers to data—and not actual data storage positioning, as clustered indexes do—you can create more than one nonclustered index for each database. Because of this ability to include multiple nonclustered indexes, this is the default index type when indexes are created. To create a nonclustered index, use the **CREATE** command with the **NONCLUSTERED** option:

```
CREATE [ NONCLUSTERED ] INDEX index_name ON table_name
```

When you're working with exam questions that deal with clustered and nonclustered indexes, remember that a table can contain only one clustered index. Additionally, you should always try to use nonclustered indexes on columns where few records are returned.

Nonclustered indexes work best on columns that contain a range of values such as **datetime** values. Remember that nonclustered indexes use the table's clustered index keys as pointers to the actual data.

In addition to the two kinds of indexes just discussed, two new kinds of indexes are available with SQL Server 2000: indexes based on computed columns, and indexes based on views. Both computed columns and views are temporary in nature and therefore have no physical location for their data. Both are recalculated each time their information is queried. Now, an indexing capability is available for these items.

Creating Indexes

For each index you create, you have to supply an index name and identify the table on which the index will be formed. You can base the index on one or more columns, and you can indicate whether the values allowed in the index will be unique or can be duplicated. Use the **CREATE** command with the **UNIQUE** option:

```
CREATE [ UNIQUE ] [ NONCLUSTERED ] INDEX index_name ON table_name
```

An index that applies to only a single column is called a *simple index*. Conversely, an index that applies to multiple columns is called a *composite index*. When you're creating indexes, the default search direction is ascending, but you can specify descending if necessary.

Simple and Composite Indexes

When you create a primary key for a table, SQL Server creates a new clustered index known as a *primary key index*. Because you can have only one clustered index per table, you can have only one primary key index per table. The following example creates a simple index on the **reservation_id** column of a **reservations** table:

```
USE hotel
CREATE INDEX reservation_id_ind
   ON reservations (reservation_id)
GO
```

 You can use the **DROP_EXISTING** option with the **CREATE INDEX** statement to drop and re-create all indexes.

Generally, you should create an index only if the data to be stored in the corresponding indexed column(s) will be queried often or frequently used as a means of identifying information stored in specific rows. However, frequent updates to indexed column data are slow operations. They require you to make tradeoff decisions between query speed and database maintenance efficiencies. Indexes can also take up valuable disk space, which is a significant system constraint in some organizations. Indexes also consume multiple pages of storage space because the values being indexed are replicated for each record. The overhead per clustered index row is approximately 8 bytes plus the number of variable-length (or nulls-allowed) fields per record. This is calculated as shown in the following formula:

row length = 8 + (length of data) + (number of variable-length fields)

For a nonclustered index row, the overhead is the same formula, substituting 12 bytes plus the number of variable-length fields per record, as shown in the following formula:

row length = 12 + (length of data) + (number of variable-length fields)

In most situations, the speed advantage you receive from using indexes for data retrieval overshadows the disadvantages.

Determining Which Columns to Index

Indexes can be created on one or more columns in a database, and multicolumn indexes allow you to differentiate records that contain the same value for a particular column. When deciding which columns to index for a table, you should consider the number of indexes already created, and remember that you should avoid putting too many indexes on a single table.

Now you know that you can create indexes based on a single column or on multiple columns in a database table. However, why should you use indexes based on multiple columns instead of indexes using only single columns? Multiple-column indexes enable you to distinguish between rows in which one column may have the same value used in another row within the same column. Single-column indexes do not allow this refinement. In addition, using indexes coupled with primary key indexes can be beneficial when you sort (or base queries) on two or more columns at a time. For example, if you frequently set a **WHERE** or **JOIN** clause for **first name** and **last name** columns in the same query, it makes sense to create a multicolumn index on those two columns.

Using the Create Index Wizard

SQL Server Enterprise Manager allows you to use visual tools in addition to Transact-SQL (T-SQL) to create indexes. For example, you can use the Table Designer or the Create Index Wizard.

To create an index with the Create Index Wizard, perform the following steps:

1. Open Enterprise Manager.

2. Select the **Pubs** database in the console tree. A list of objects is displayed in the details pane, as illustrated in Figure 6.1.

3. Choose Tools|Wizards.

4. Expand the Database node in the Select Wizard dialog box.

5. Select Create Index Wizard, and then choose OK.

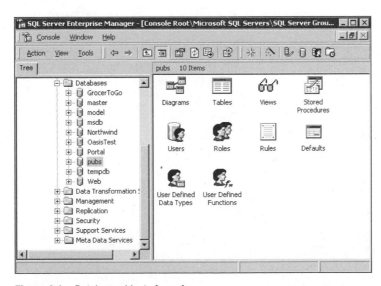

Figure 6.1   Database objects for **pubs**.

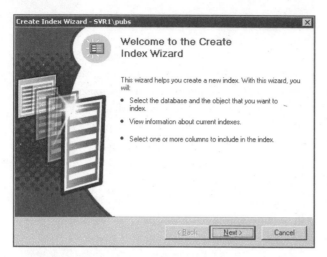

Figure 6.2 The Create Index Wizard.

6. When the Welcome page appears for the Create Index Wizard, as illustrated in Figure 6.2, choose Next.

7. On the Select Database And Table page of the wizard, select the **pubs** database and the **Authors** table; then choose Next.

8. The current index information is displayed. Choose Next.

9. On the Select Columns page of the wizard, select **au_lname** and the Sort Order (DESC) option, as illustrated in Figure 6.3. Choose Next to continue.

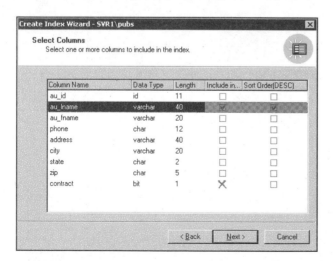

Figure 6.3 Indexing on the author's last name.

10. On the Specify Index Options page, select Optimal for the fill factor; then choose Next.

11. When the Completing Index Wizard page appears, change the index name to **authors_Index_lname**, and then choose Finish.

12. After the message box appears telling you that the index was created successfully, choose OK.

Examining Query Analyzer for Index Performance

Using SQL Query Analyzer, you can view performance statistics related to table indexes. This can be one of the best ways to determine where indexes should or should not be placed. To create an estimated execution plan:

1. Open SQL Query Analyzer.

2. When the Connect To SQL Server dialog appears, type in the server name and your login information; then choose OK.

3. Select the **Northwind** database from the database drop-down list, as illustrated in Figure 6.4.

4. In the query window, type the following SQL statement:

```
SELECT Customers.CompanyName,
       Orders.OrderDate,
       Products.ProductName,
       [Order Details].UnitPrice,
       [Order Details].Quantity
FROM Customers INNER JOIN Orders ON
       Customers.CustomerID = Orders.CustomerID
       INNER JOIN [Order Details] ON
       Orders.OrderID = [Order Details].OrderID
       INNER JOIN Products ON
[Order Details].ProductID = Products.ProductID
```

5. Press F5 to execute the query.

6. Click the Display Estimated Execution Plan button next to the database drop-down list, as illustrated in Figure 6.5.

7. When the execution plan is shown in the bottom window pane, hover your cursor over the **Products.ProductName** icon, as illustrated in Figure 6.6.

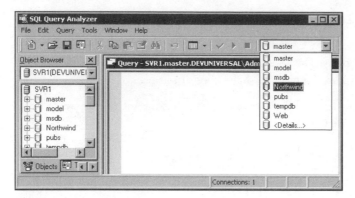

Figure 6.4 Selecting the **Northwind** database.

Figure 6.5 The Display Estimated Execution Plan button.

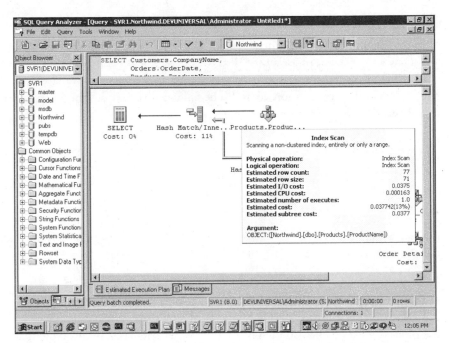

Figure 6.6   Results of the execution plan, showing nonclustered index statistics.

8. As you can see, the estimated row count and estimated cost statistics, among others, give you a better picture as to how the index helps your query. Using this kind of information, you can implement a solid physical database design.

 Remember that you *always* read the execution plan from right to left, top to bottom.

Dropping and Altering Indexes

Although the SQL 2000 exam will not deal with this topic per se, it is important to have a basic understanding of how to remove or update indexes in SQL Server 2000. You can also rebuild indexes and get statistics about the distribution of the key values in each index.

Dropping an Index

To remove an index, you can simply use the **DROP INDEX T-SQL** statement. In fact, it is a good idea to use a **DROP INDEX** statement before using a **CREATE INDEX** statement. If you look back earlier in the chapter, we created a simple index called **reservation_id_ind**. The following code drops this index if it already exists and then creates a new one:

```
SET NOCOUNT OFF
USE hotel
IF EXISTS (SELECT name FROM sysindexes
      WHERE name = 'reservation_id_ind')
   DROP INDEX reservations.reservation_id
GO
USE hotel
CREATE INDEX reservation_id_ind
   ON reservations (reservation_id)
GO
```

Once you execute a **DROP INDEX** statement, any space previously utilized by the index is released and can then be used for other database objects. Note that the **DROP INDEX** statement cannot be executed for indexes on system tables.

Altering an Index

You can alter an index by opening the Table Designer for a table and then clicking the Indexes/Keys button to open the Properties page, as illustrated in Figure 6.7.

Using the **DBCC DBREINDEX** Statement to Rebuild an Index

You can use the **DBCC DBREINDEX** statement to rebuild an index or multiple indexes for a table. The main advantage of using **DBCC DBREINDEX** is that you can use it to re-create one or more indexes without having to drop the table's primary key.

Normally, when you implement a clustered index for a primary key, you have to drop the primary key column before you can use the **DROP INDEX** statement to delete the clustered index.

Because nonclustered indexes use the table's clustered index keys as pointers, the index keys must be re-created when the clustered index is re-created.

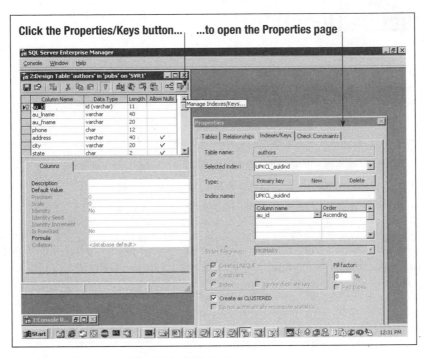

Figure 6.7   Altering indexes with the Table Designer.

Using the UPDATE STATISTICS Statement

SQL Server stores statistics about the distribution of the key values in each index. These statistics are used to establish which index or indexes to use to process queries. When a **CREATE INDEX** statement is issued, SQL Server automatically includes the option to update statistics for the index.

However, to optimize query performance, you should execute an **UPDATE STATISTICS** statement on indexes that have related key values that change frequently. In other words, if a large amount of data in an indexed column has been added, changed, or removed, **UPDATE STATISTICS** will update information about the distribution of key values in the indexed table or view. For example, to update all indexes in the **reservations** table, you can use the following Transact-SQL statement:

```
UPDATE STATISTICS reservations
```

You can also update a single index—in this case, **reservation_id_ind**—by using the following T-SQL statement:

```
UPDATE STATISTICS reservations reservation_id_ind
```

Practice Questions

Question 1

> Where should you create nonclustered indexes?
>
> ○ a. On columns used frequently in the **WHERE** clause of a query
>
> ○ b. On columns used frequently in the **FROM** clause of a query
>
> ○ c. On columns used frequently in the **SELECT** clause of a query
>
> ○ d. On columns used frequently in the **ORDER BY** clause of a query

Answer a is correct. Nonclustered indexes are best used to join or query by in a SELECT statement. In this case, the FROM, SELECT, and ORDER BY clauses do not benefit from the nonclustered index.

Question 2

> You are implementing a physical database design for a car insurance company, and you want to implement indexes on certain tables to improve query performance. Which of the following guidelines should you use to implement indexes on the insurance company's database?
>
> ○ a. You should create at least two nonclustered indexes per join table.
>
> ○ b. You should create at least two clustered indexes per join table.
>
> ○ c. You should create a single clustered index for columns most commonly used, and create nonclustered indexes for other columns that are commonly used.
>
> ○ d. You should create a single nonclustered index for columns most commonly used, and create clustered indexes for other columns that are commonly used.

Answer c is correct. You cannot have more than one clustered index per table. There is also no absolute number of nonclustered indexes you should implement for a table. If using two indexes provides the best optimization, then it is a good choice. However, using a single index could be the best choice for other scenarios. Answers b, c, and d are not appropriate for this scenario.

Question 3

Which of the following does SQL Server 2000 create automatically? [Check all correct answers]

❑ a. Distribution statistics for indexes

❑ b. Estimated execution plans for indexes

❑ c. Nonclustered indexes for primary keys

❑ d. Clustered indexes for primary keys

Answers a and d are correct. Clustered indexes are created automatically when you specify a primary key. In addition, SQL Server creates distribution statistics when it creates indexes. Answers b and c are incorrect; SQL Server 2000 does not automatically create these items.

Question 4

Which of the following are examples of possible candidates for a clustered index? [Check all correct answers]

❑ a. State

❑ b. Company branch

❑ c. Date of sale

❑ d. ZIP code

❑ e. Customer district

Answers a, b, c, d, and e are all correct. The key question to ask yourself when selecting the best column on which to base the clustered index is, "Will there be frequent queries that need to return a lot of records based on the order of this column?"

Question 5

> Your **Invoices** table contains an **invoice date** column, a **unique invoice number** column, and other invoice data. On a daily basis, 9,000 rows are inserted into this table. SQL queries often use this table to get all records for one week's worth of data. Additionally, many users need concurrent access to the **Invoices** table. The invoice number is currently indexed using a clustered index. Why is this a bad situation?
>
> ○ a. Invoice numbers are not unique.
>
> ○ b. There are too many users querying this table, and this causes concurrency problems.
>
> ○ c. The invoice numbers are not unique, and clustered indexes work best on non-unique data.
>
> ○ d. The invoice numbers are unique, and your users are not searching on ranges of invoice numbers.

Answer d is correct. The invoice number would not be a good candidate for the clustered index for a few reasons. The best reason is that the invoice numbers are unique and your users are not searching on ranges of invoice numbers. That being the case, placing invoice numbers in sequential order physically on disk is not likely to be helpful. This is because range scans will probably not be done on invoice numbers. Invoice numbers are unique; therefore answers a and c are incorrect. Answer b is not applicable to this situation.

Question 6

You have just created a new database called **Web**. You need to create a new table to store information that will be saved from an ASP application running in IIS. The table should contain the columns **ID**, **logtime**, **HTTP_USER_AGENT**, **AUTH_USER**, **LOGON_USER**, **REMOTE_ADDR**, **REMOTE_HOST**, and **ALL_HTTP**. The primary key will be the **ID** column, and you will be doing many join operations on the **LOGON_USER** column, so it needs to be indexed. You do not want to recompute statistics, and you want the fill factor set to 50 percent. Based on this information, place the following T-SQL script necessary for these needs into the correct order.

❏ a.
```
CREATE INDEX [IX_Weblog] ON [dbo].[Weblog]
([LOGON_USER]) WITH  FILLFACTOR = 1/2,
STATISTICS_RECOMPUTE = OFF ON [PRIMARY]
GO
```

❏ b.
```
CREATE  INDEX [IX_Weblog] ON [dbo].[Weblog]
([LOGON_USER]) WITH  FILLFACTOR = 50,
STATISTICS_NORECOMPUTE  ON [PRIMARY]
GO
```

❏ c.
```
if exists (select * from dbo.sysobjects
where
   id = object_id(N'[dbo].[Weblog]')
   and OBJECTPROPERTY(id, N'IsUserlable') = 1)
   drop table [dbo].[Weblog]
GO
```

❏ d.
```
ALTER TABLE [dbo].[Weblog] WITH NOCHECK ADD
    CONSTRAINT [PK_Weblog]
        PRIMARY KEY  CLUSTERED
    (
        [ID]
    )  ON [PRIMARY]
GO
```

(continued)

Question 6 *(continued)*

```
❏ e.
CREATE TABLE [dbo].[Weblog] (
    [ID] [int] IDENTITY (1, 1) NOT NULL ,
    [logtime] [datetime] NOT NULL ,
    [HTTP_USER_AGENT] [varchar] (500)
        COLLATE SQL_Latin1_General_CP1_CI_AS
        NULL ,
    [AUTH_USER] [varchar] (50) COLLATE
        SQL_Latin1_General_CP1_CI_AS NULL ,
    [LOGON_USER] [varchar] (50) COLLATE
        SQL_Latin1_General_CP1_CI_AS NULL ,
    [REMOTE_ADDR] [varchar] (50) COLLATE
        SQL_Latin1_General_CP1_CI_AS NULL ,
    [REMOTE_HOST] [varchar] (50) COLLATE
        SQL_Latin1_General_CP1_CI_AS NULL ,
    [ALL_HTTP] [varchar] (5000) COLLATE
        SQL_Latin1_General_CP1_CI_AS NULL
) ON [PRIMARY]
GO


❏ f.
CREATE INDEX [IX_Weblog] ON [dbo].[Weblog]
    ([LOGON_USER]) WITH  FILLFACTOR = 50%,
    STATISTICS_RECOMPUTE = OFF ON [PRIMARY]
GO
```

Answers e, d, and b are correct, in that order. Answer a is incorrect because
FILLFACTOR = 1/2 is invalid, as is **STATISTICS_RECOMPUTE = OFF**.
Although answer c is valid in order to drop the table in case it already existed, this
is not necessary, as the question specifies. Answer f is also incorrect because you
do not use the percent sign (%) when specifying the **FILLFACTOR**. **RECOM-
PUTE = OFF** is also invalid. Instead, use the **NORECOMPUTE** keyword.

Question 7

> Which of the following are types of indexes used in SQL Server? [Check all correct answers]
>
> ❑ a. Clustered
>
> ❑ b. Nonclustered
>
> ❑ c. Foreign key
>
> ❑ d. Unique
>
> ❑ e. Primary key

Answers a, b, and d are correct. Answers c and d are not valid index types in SQL Server.

Question 8

> Which of the following code snippets will create a new table named **Table1**, with a clustered index on the primary key?
>
> ○ a.
> ```
> CREATE TABLE [dbo].[Table1] (
>   [ID] [char] (10) NULL ,
>   [Firstname] [varchar] (50)  NULL ,
>   [Lastname] [char] (10)   NULL
> ) ON [PRIMARY]
> GO
> ```
>
> ○ b.
> ```
> CREATE TABLE [dbo].[Table1] (
>   [ID] [char] (10)   NOT NULL
>   CONSTRAINT [PK_Table1] PRIMARY KEY CLUSTERED,
>   [Firstname] [varchar] (50)   NULL ,
>   [Lastname] [char] (10)   NULL
> ) ON [PRIMARY]
> GO
> ```

(continued)

Question 8 *(continued)*

```
○ c.
CREATE TABLE [dbo].[Table1] (
  [ID] [char] (10)  NOT NULL ,
  [Firstname] [varchar] (50)  NULL ,
  [Lastname] [char] (10)  NULL
) ON CONSTRAINT [ID] PRIMARY KEY CLUSTERED
GO


○ d.
CREATE TABLE [dbo].[Table1] (
  [ID] [char] (10)  NOT NULL ,
  [Firstname] [varchar] (50)  NULL ,
  [Lastname] [char] (10)  NULL
) ON [PRIMARY]
GO


ALTER TABLE [dbo].[Table1] WITH NOCHECK ADD
  CONSTRAINT [PK_Table1]
    PRIMARY KEY CLUSTERED
  (
    [ID]
  )  ON [PRIMARY]
GO
```

Answer d is correct. Answer a is incorrect because there is no primary key information. Answers b and c are not using valid syntax.

Question 9

> Which of the following code snippets will create a unique index named **IX_JOINTS** on the column named **JOINTNUMBER** using an **int** data type?
>
> ○ a.
> ```
> CREATE UNIQUE INDEX [jointnumber] ON [dbo].
> [joint]([ IX_joints]) ON [PRIMARY]
> ```
>
> ○ b.
> ```
> CREATE UNIQUE INDEX [IX_joints] ON [dbo].
> [joints]([joinnumber2]) ON [PRIMARY]
> ```
>
> ○ c.
> ```
> CREATE UNIQUE INDEX ON [dbo].[jointnumber]
> ([IX_JOINTS]) ON [PRIMARY]
> ```
>
> ○ d.
> ```
> CREATE INDEX [IX_joints] ON [dbo].[joints]
> ([jointnumber4]) ON [PRIMARY]
> ```

Answer b is correct. Answers a, c, and d use incorrect syntax.

Question 10

> How many clustered and nonclustered indexes can you have in a table?
>
> ○ a. You can have only one clustered index per table, but you can have more than one nonclustered index.
>
> ○ b. You can have only one nonclustered index per table, but you can have more than one clustered index.
>
> ○ c. You can have more than one clustered index per table if a primary key is not implemented, but you can have only one nonclustered index.
>
> ○ d. You can have only one unique index per table, but you can have more than one clustered or nonclustered index.

Answer a is correct. Answers b, c, and d are incorrect because you are not limited to one clustered index, and the number of clustered indexes does not change based on whether or not a table has a primary key.

Need to Know More?

 Delaney, Kalen. *Inside Microsoft SQL Server 2000*. Redmond, WA: Microsoft Press, 2000. ISBN 0-7356-0998-5. Microsoft calls this "a guide to the architecture and internals" of SQL Server 2000.

 Iseminger, David. *SQL Server 2000 Reference Library*. Redmond, WA: Microsoft Press, 2000. ISBN 0-7356-1280-3. A selected collection of SQL Server 2000 Books Online; there are six volumes focused on key areas.

 SQL Server 2000 Resource Kit. Redmond, WA: Microsoft Press, 2000. ISBN 0-7356-1266-8. Extensive reference information on SQL Server 2000 core functionality and new features.

 Microsoft SQL Server Books Online has sections on stored procedures. This book set can be installed from the SQL Server 2000 CD or accessed online through **http://msdn.microsoft.com/library/ default.asp**. Search on the keyword "indexes".

 Search the TechNet CD or its online version through **www.microsoft.com/ technet/**. Search on the keyword "indexes". Additionally, navigate the product segment, and search through the SQL Server sections on "indexes" at **http://www.microsoft.com/technet/indexes/**.

 www.microsoft.com/indexes/default.asp—Find up-to-date information about Microsoft's latest information about indexes.

 www.microsoft.com/sql/ and **http://msdn.microsoft.com/sqlserver/ default.asp** are good places to find up-to-date information about SQL Server 2000.

 www.sqlmag.com—*SQL Magazine*—both the hard copy and the Web site—has a large amount of information on SQL Server 2000.

Views

Terms you'll need to understand:

✓ Views

✓ Partitioning

✓ Indexed view

✓ XML (Extensible Markup Language)

Techniques you'll need to master:

✓ Creating views

✓ Modifying views

✓ Deleting views

✓ Partitioning data

✓ Creating partitioned views

✓ Understanding indexed views

A view can be thought of as a virtual table or a stored query. You can only create views in the current database. Although it acts somewhat like a table, a view does not actually exist like tables do. The data accessible through a view is not stored in the database as a distinct object. However, the tables and views referenced by the new view can exist in other databases or even other servers if the view is defined using distributed queries. You store the query as an object in the database, but (except for indexed views) you do not store the table that results from the query. You re-create the table (or in this case, the view) each time you use it. Views are made up of tables (called *base tables*) or are created by combining two or more eligible objects such as tables, procedures, or views. You cannot create temporary views, and you cannot create views on temporary tables. With the release of SQL Server 2000, you can create *distributed views*, which link two databases on the same or different servers. The one exception to not storing a view in the database is the new indexed view, which you do store as an object. We will discuss this later in the chapter.

Why Use Views?

There are many advantages to using views. These advantages include restricting the data available to users. Some data can be accessible to users for query and modification, while the rest of the table or database remains invisible and inaccessible. Permission to access the subset of data in a view must be granted, denied, or revoked, regardless of the set of permissions in force on the underlying table(s). Views also provide a mechanism that allows developers to customize how users can logically view the data stored in base tables. Sometimes developers also use views to speed application performance. Simplifying command use many times is not an issue because end users are shielded from SQL syntax through GUI front ends. Therefore, one could say that the best reason to use views is to improve application-level performance.

SQL Server 2000 has a new feature called indexed views that you can use to create views that have their indexed results stored on a disk.

Focus or Customize Data

Views can vertically slice the data of a table or tables and display only certain columns, thereby focusing the end users on just what they need for their tasks at hand. The view eliminates unnecessary data, and it can even prevent a user from accessing sensitive data. Views let you control access and provide security.

You can also use views when customizing the data for a specific user or role. For instance, you can create a view such that an account manager can see data for just the customers whom he or she is responsible for monitoring. You can even link a view to a specific login ID.

Mask Complexity

Views can mask or simplify how a user sees the data. You can take complicated joins, projections, or queries and create a view that the user then accesses with a simple query. This technique can include accessing heterogeneous data across several servers. It is also great for remapping column names. For instance, if the underlying base table has a column called **usr**, in your view definition, you can rename this column as **UserName**. For security reasons, you can also hide design changes in your base tables. The information schema views to the system tables are an example of views that provide consistency while allowing the system to change the base tables in a subsequent release.

Increase Security

You can use views as part of your security plan. Rather than give users permission to access the underlying base tables, you create views of just the columns that you want users to access. You can grant permissions to the view without granting them to the underlying base table. A typical example is the **Employees** table. You may grant employees permission to view addresses but not salaries.

 Just because you log on to one SQL Server database successfully does not mean you have permission to access others. If you create a view that joins data from two different databases, make sure you have permissions granted for both of them.

Import and Export Data

Views simplify importing and exporting data (with some restrictions discussed later; see "Modifying a View"). An example is using Excel's Pivot feature to analyze sales data from two or more tables (or possibly even two or more databases). A pivot report is an interactive table that you can use to easily summarize data by rotating its rows adn columns to view different summaries of the source data. Using views when importing and exporting data can provide performance benefits.

Combine Partitioned Data

You can partition data across horizontal lines, such as creating a separate sales table for each region (east, west, north, and south). You then can join these tables by using a partitioned view so they appear as one table. You can also store the tables on the same or different servers.

Performance is the main reason for partitioning data across multiple tables or multiple servers. A query accessing only a piece of your data runs faster because the system ends up scanning less data. In addition, when tables reside on different servers (or on computers with multiple processors), parallel scanning can improve query performance.

Creating Views

Before describing the **CREATE VIEW** statement's syntax, we'll consider several guidelines for using views.

Guidelines for Creating Views

When creating a view, you must first have the proper **CREATE VIEW** permissions; you must also have proper access to the underlying tables or views that make up the new view. The **CREATE** permission defaults to **sysadmin, db_owner, db_ddladmin,** and other people who have been granted the **CREATE** permission. Although anyone who creates a view can be its owner, the usual recommendation is that you define the owner of a view as the **dbo** user. This prevents chain-of-ownership problems from occurring later.

 You should understand a view's chain of ownership. If the same person does not own both the view and its base objects, the system might deny permission even though you may have permission for the view.

When creating a view and entering it at the same time as a batch of other queries, you must enter the **CREATE VIEW** statement first.

Some additional guidelines:

➤ Although they may refer to tables from other databases, you can create views only in the current database.

➤ You can nest views up to 32 levels. In other words, a view can refer to a view, which can refer to another view, and so on. This can go on for 32 iterations.

➤ You cannot associate rules or **DEFAULT** definitions with a view. Nor can you use the **AFTER** trigger. You can, however, use the **INSTEAD OF** trigger. Underlying tables can have rules and can use defaults and **AFTER** triggers.

➤ The query defining the view cannot include the **ORDER BY** clause (unless accompanied by the **TOP** keyword in the **SELECT** statement), the **COMPUTE** or **COMPUTE BY** clauses, or the **INTO** keyword in the **SELECT** statement.

➤ Views cannot refer to temporary tables or use table variables.

➤ If you encrypt the view definition, not even the owner can view the definition. Make sure you retain a copy of the SQL code that you used to create the view.

➤ The maximum number of columns you can refer to in a view is 1,024.

➤ If you drop one of the underlying base tables, SQL Server produces an error message only when someone tries to use the view (except as noted in the **WITH SCHEMABINDING** option). You can re-create the dropped table if its schema is not changed and if the view will not need to be re-created. If you used the **WITH SCHEMABINDING** option when creating the view, then you cannot drop the underlying tables.

➤ Only the view's query tree is stored in the procedure cache. Each time you access a view, you must recompile its execution plan. The exception to this is an indexed view.

*Note: Before you create the view, you should verify your **SELECT** statement to make sure it returns the data that you want.*

The syntax of the **CREATE VIEW** statement is as follows:

```
CREATE VIEW [ < database_name > . ]
[ < owner > . ] view_name
[ ( column [ ,...n ] ) ]
 [ WITH < view_attribute > [ ,...n ] ]
AS
select_statement
 [ WITH CHECK OPTION ]
< view_attribute > ::=
{ ENCRYPTION | SCHEMABINDING | VIEW_METADATA }
```

Key Arguments
The **CREATE VIEW** statement has the following key arguments:

➤ *owner.view_name*—The *owner* portion is optional, but including it is usually a good idea to avoid chain-of-ownership problems. However, if you omit the owner's name, it defaults to **dbo**. A view's name, which you specify, must follow the same rules for identifiers described earlier (in Chapter 3). A view cannot have the same name as a table in the same database. The recommended name is a combination of the owner's name and the object's name. You should also have a standard identifier that distinguishes a view from a table (such as adding _vw to the end of the view name) unless you omit such an identifier as an added security measure to hide the fact that the view is not the underlying table.

➤ *(column [,...n])*—This argument names the aliases you use as names for the columns. You must provide names for columns when they do not have names (such as columns created as an aggregate), when they are derived columns (from expressions or functions), or when their names are duplicates of other columns' names. You can, however, rename any column, and the data type of the underlying column of data will remain the same. You can also specify the column names within the **SELECT** statement.

➤ *select_statement*—The **SELECT** statement is any valid SQL statement that actually specifies the view's components, subject to the restrictions listed earlier (first in batch, nested to 32 levels, and so on).

➤ **WITH CHECK OPTION**—This argument checks the **SELECT** statement and ensures that all data modification statements (**INSERT, UPDATE, DELETE**) applied to the view comply with the established criteria and get applied to the data that gets modified by the view. In other words, if the modification would result in the row not meeting the criteria of the *select_statement*, then the system denies the modification. If you do not include the **WITH CHECK OPTION** argument, then a view modification can hide data that was previously visible.

➤ **WITH ENCRYPTION**—This argument encrypts the **CREATE VIEW** statement definition that the system stores in the system table columns. (When not encrypted, this definition is in the **syscomments** table.) This option helps keep secret the tables that make up the view. Additionally, you cannot publish encrypted views as part of replication.

➤ **WITH SCHEMABINDING**—This argument binds the schema and the view together. You must use the optional **owner** portion of object names in the **SELECT** statement when invoking **WITH SCHEMABINDING**. You cannot modify or drop the underlying view or table without first dropping or modifying the view and removing the **SCHEMABINDING** argument.

➤ **WITH VIEW_METADATA**—This argument returns the view's metadata information (instead of the base table or tables) when you request browse-mode metadata from one of the DBLIB, ODBC, or OLE DB APIs. This makes a view's columns (except **timestamp**) updateable if it uses the **INSERT** or **UPDATE INSTEAD OF** triggers.

Let's look at some examples of the **CREATE VIEW** statement. In Listing 7.1, we create two views. The first example creates a simple view with one table and a subset of columns. The second example creates a view, supplies column names, and uses an aggregate as well as a simple join.

Listing 7.1 Two basic **CREATE VIEW** statements.

```
/* simple view with one table and subset of columns */
USE Northwind
CREATE VIEW Employee_Phone_View
AS
SELECT LastName, FirstName, Extension
FROM Employees
GO
/* A view with column names, an aggregate, and a join */
USE Northwind
CREATE VIEW Category_View (category, average_price)
AS
SELECT CategoryName, AVG(UnitPrice)
FROM Products JOIN Categories
ON Products.CategoryID = Categories.CategoryID
GROUP BY CategoryName
```

View Definition Information

A view's name gets filed away in the **INFORMATION_SCHEMA.TABLES** view (or **sysobjects** table). If you are looking for information about columns within a view, you can locate them in the **INFORMATION_SCHEMA.VIEW_ COLUMN_USAGE** view (or the **syscolumns** table). If you need information about objects that the view depends upon, this is in the **INFORMATION_ SCHEMA.VIEW_TABLE-USAGE** view (or **sysdepends** table). You can even find the entire text version of the **CREATE VIEW** statement in storage for later reference. It is in the **INFORMATION_SCHEMA.VIEWS** view (or the **syscomments** table). However, you can interpret none of the **CREATE VIEW** text (not even by the view's owner) if the **ENCRYPTION** clause was invoked when the view was created.

In addition to querying the views and tables, you can use the **sp_helptext** stored procedure when reading the view's definition (or, for that matter, any object's definition). The syntax is

```
sp_helptext objname
```

The **sp_depends** stored procedure displays all view dependencies. The syntax is

```
sp_depends objname
```

Modifying a View

Once you create a view, you can rename it, change its definition, or even delete it. Remember, if you change a view's definition or name, other objects referring to (or depending on) that view may also require changes to continue functioning properly. For instance, if you have a stored procedure that expects a view to contain a **last name** column and you drop that column from your view, the stored procedure will cause an error when it executes.

Altering a view saves any associated view permissions. If you drop and then re-create the view, you will need to grant permissions again.

If you create a view with a **SELECT** and you later add columns to the underlying table, then you must also alter the view before you see the new columns again. The system interprets the colum ns only when you're initially creating the view.

The syntax of the **ALTER VIEW** statement is as follows:

```
ALTER VIEW [ < database_name > . ]
[ < owner > . ] view_name
[ ( column [ ,...n ] ) ]
 [ WITH < view_attribute > [ ,...n ] ]
AS
select_statement
 [ WITH CHECK OPTION ]
< view_attribute > ::=
{ ENCRYPTION | SCHEMABINDING |
  VIEW_METADATA }
```

If you want to be able to update data in a view without causing records to disappear, you can specify the **WITH CHECK OPTION** argument in the **CREATE VIEW** statement.

Guidelines for Altering Views

You will notice that the syntax of the **ALTER VIEW** statement is the same as that of the **CREATE VIEW** statement. If you originally defined the view with an option such as **ENCRYPTION**, then to keep that option, you must include it in the **ALTER VIEW** statement. **ALTER VIEW** permissions default to the **db_owner** and **db_ddladmin** roles and to the view owner. They are not transferable.

In addition, the user issuing the **ALTER VIEW** statement must have **ALTER VIEW** permission and **SELECT** permission on the underlying base objects. To alter a view with **SCHEMABINDING**, the user must also have **REFERENCES** permission on each underlying object.

If you assign permissions to the view and later change the name of a column, the system transfers the permissions to the new column that you just named. If, however, you assign permissions to the individual columns within the view, and you change the column name, the system does not transfer these permissions.

If a view is in use when you issue the **ALTER VIEW** statement, the system places an exclusive lock on the view and makes the changes when all users release the view. The system also removes any copies from the procedure cache and recompiles it the next time anyone accesses the view.

In Listing 7.2, we alter the simple view that was created as the first example in Listing 7.1. Here, we'll add the employee's home phone number.

Listing 7.2   An **ALTER VIEW** statement.

```
USE Northwind
ALTER VIEW Employee_Phone_View
AS
SELECT LastName, FirstName, Extension, HomePhone
FROM Employees
```

Renaming a View

You rename a view by using the **sp_rename** system stored procedure. After renaming the view, you should flush the procedure cache (**DBCC FREEPROCCACHE**) and ensure that the system recompiles all dependent views. The syntax for renaming a view is as follows:

```
sp_rename old_name, new_name
```

Deleting a View

When you delete a view, you remove all of the information in the system tables we described in the "View Definition Information" section earlier in this chapter. You also drop all permissions. Dropping an underlying object does not delete the view; you must explicitly delete it. Deleting an indexed view drops all the indexes on the view. The syntax is shown below:

```
DROP VIEW { view } [ ,...n ]
```

You can drop one or more views at the same time. You must have the proper permission before you can delete a view. Before deleting a view, check all dependencies, and correct discrepancies.

Modifying Data through a View

You can modify data through a view (with some restrictions). There are three ways you can modify data with views. First, you can use the **INSTEAD OF** trigger with logic when using the **INSERT, DELETE,** or **UPDATE** statements. We will cover triggers in more detail in Chapter 9. Second, you can use updateable partitioned views. We discuss these later in this chapter. And third, you can use standard views.

Standard views operate with the following restrictions:

➤ The view cannot be based solely on an expression; it must contain at least one table in the **FROM** clause.

➤ No aggregate functions (**AVG, COUNT, SUM, MIN, MAX, GROUPING, STDEV, STDEVP, VAR, VARP**) or **GROUP BY, UNION, DISTINCT,** or **TOP** clauses are used in the select list. The **SELECT** statement can include a subquery with an aggregate function as long as you do not modify the derived values generated by the aggregate functions. One exception is the use of **UNION ALL** in an updateable partitioned view.

 Remember, you cannot use aggregate functions in a **WHERE** clause. Some SQL statements displayed in exam questions will contain aggregate functions such as **SUM**. Although the question might not have anything to do with using aggregate functions, be aware that they are invalid in a **WHERE** clause, and therefore your answer might not be correct.

➤ The columns in the select list must be simple references to underlying columns; no derived columns can be used.

➤ Data modified on views defined with the **WITH CHECK OPTION** clause cannot cause a row to fall out of the view scope.

➤ If there is more than one table in the select list, then only one underlying table at a time can be modified or deleted.

➤ In the underlying table, all columns that require values either are being updated or have **DEFAULT** definitions, or allow nulls.

➤ Modifications to columns must adhere to the rules set forth in the underlying tables, such as constraints, nullability, and foreign key constraints.

➤ You cannot use the **READTEXT** and **WRITETEXT** statements with **text, ntext,** or **image** columns in a view.

You will notice that, in the examples that follow, the **INSERT, UPDATE,** and **DELETE** statements are the same ones you saw in Chapter 4. These statements are the same whether you are referring to a table or a view. Listing 7.3 shows an example of adding data through a view. For this example, we define a table, a view, and an **INSERT** statement. You will notice that although the view does not include the **Employee ID** or **Birthdate** columns, the **INSERT** statement is still valid because the **Employee ID** column has an **IDENTITY** property (with the system providing its data), and the **Birthdate** column allows nulls.

Listing 7.3   Adding data through a view.

```
/* Create a table */
CREATE TABLE Employees
 (EmpID [tinyint] IDENTITY (1, 1) NOT NULL ,
 LastName nvarchar(20) NOT NULL ,
 FirstName nvarchar(10) NOT NULL ,
 BirthDate smalldatetime NULL)
GO
/* Create a view */
CREATE VIEW Employee_View
AS
SELECT LastName, FirstName
FROM Employees
GO
/* Add a new record */
INSERT INTO Employee_View
 VALUES ('Jones', 'Sam')
```

Next is an example of modifying data through a view. For this example, we will use the same table and view described in Listing 7.3.

```
UPDATE Employee_View
Set LastName = 'Smith'
WHERE LastName = 'Jones'
```

Finally, here is an example of deleting data through a view. For this example, we will use the same table and view described in Listing 7.3.

```
DELETE FROM Employee_View
WHERE LastName = 'Smith'
```

Using Partitioned Views

As stated earlier in this chapter (see the "Why Use Views?" section), a partitioned view joins data that was horizontally split. A *local* partitioned view has all underlying tables in the same instance of SQL Server. A *distributed* partitioned view has at least one of its underlying tables or views on another SQL server.

The first step in creating a partitioned view is partitioning the table. Replace the original table with smaller tables spliced horizontally; that is, each member table has some subset of the rows but the same number of columns as the sum of all participating objects. Each member table has the same number of columns, and the columns have the same attributes. A recommendation is that you should retain the same database name (although this is not a requirement) when you're distributing member tables on other servers. Base the splice on a range of key values contained in one of the columns. The values cannot overlap. One example requires an ID between 1 to 1,000 and between 1,001 and 2000, and so on.

Rules for Partitioning Views

The rules for the partitioning column are as follows:

➤ Each underlying base table must have a partitioning column defined with one (and only one) **CHECK** constraint so that any given value of the partitioning column maps to a single table. The **CHECK** constraints can use only these operators: **BETWEEN, AND, OR,** <, <=, >, >=, =.

➤ A partitioning column cannot allow nulls, must be part of the primary key, and cannot be made up of computed columns.

➤ A partitioning column must be in the same ordinal location in the select list of each **SELECT** statement in the view.

Distributed partitioned tables require that you set up linked servers (discussed in Chapter 12) and that you set the **lazy schema validation** option, using **sp_serveroption**.

Create a partitioned view in each database where the underlying partitioned table resides. Listing 7.4 shows the definition of a partitioned table split across two servers and shows the creation of its partitioned view. The view in this example ends up in each database.

Listing 7.4   Example of a partitioned table and view.

```
/* Create an employees table on Server 1 */
USE CompanyDatabase
CREATE TABLE Server1.dbo.Employees_1
(EmpID [tinyint] IDENTITY (100, 1) PRIMARY KEY
 CHECK (EmpID BETWEEN 100 AND 199),
LastName nvarchar(20) NOT NULL ,
FirstName nvarchar(10) NOT NULL ,
BirthDate smalldatetime NULL)
GO
/* Create an employees table on Server 2 */
USE CompanyDatabase
```

```
CREATE TABLE Server2.dbo.Employees_2
(EmpID [tinyint] IDENTITY (200, 1) PRIMARY KEY
 CHECK (EmpID BETWEEN 200 AND 299),
LastName nvarchar(20) NOT NULL ,
FirstName nvarchar(10) NOT NULL ,
BirthDate smalldatetime NULL)
Go
/* Create the view on each server */
CREATE VIEW Employees_View
AS
SELECT * FROM Server1.CompanyDatabase.dbo.Employees_1
UNION ALL
SELECT * FROM Server2.CompanyDatabase.dbo.Employees_2
```

Updateable Partitioned Views

A partitioned view can be updateable if the set of individual **SELECT** statements refers to one SQL Server base table and if you combine the statements
that use the **UNION ALL** statement. The table can be local or linked (using the
four-part name or one of the **REMOTE** statements described in Chapter 12).
You cannot use a pass-through query. The tables must reside on the server installed
with SQL Server 2000 Enterprise or Developer edition. A way you can ensure
atomicity is to start a distributed transaction across all tables affected by the update.

 Microsoft expects you to know about different types of partitioning.
Horizontal partitioning occurs when you split tables based on the
number of records (rows) it contains. Horizontal partitioning is best
used to partition a table that has many rows but only a few columns.
This will increase performance. Vertical partitioning occurs when you
split tables based on the number of columns it has. Vertical partitioning
is best used when only a few of the table's columns are used regularly.

Using Indexed Views

With SQL Server 2000, you now can index views. This helps you improve the
performance of joins and aggregations, and it lessens the decision support
workloads when the underlying data is updated infrequently. Microsoft does not
recommend using indexed views on databases with many updates or for queries
without joins or aggregations. Unlike a regular view, for which only the query is
stored in the database, with an indexed view, the database actually stores the
result set like a table. There are, however, many restrictions on views before an
index is created.

Restrictions on Indexed Views

Following are the restrictions on indexed views:

➤ The view can refer only to base tables, and the tables must be in the same database and have the same owner.

➤ You must use the **SCHEMABINDING** option.

➤ The **SELECT** statement must include the column names, cannot use the asterisk (*), can have no table joins or derived tables, and can't use **UNION**, **TOP, ORDER BY,** or aggregations (except **SUM**). In other words, it must be a simple **SELECT** statement.

➤ You cannot repeat the same column in the select list (for example, **Col_A, Col_B, Col_A**) except in simple expressions (for example, **Col_A + Col_B, Col_A**).

The first index you create on the view must be a clustered index. You can create additional nonclustered indexes. See Chapter 6 for information on creating indexes.

You gain the benefits of an indexed view when settings that affect Transact-SQL statements in the connection that creates the index are the same as the connections that query the view. You can change these settings with the **SET** option. These settings include **ANSI_NULLS, ANSI_PADDING, ANSI_WARNINGS, ARITHABORT, CONCAT_NULL_YIELDS_NULL,** and **QUOTED_ IDENTIFIER**. Also, you must set the **NUMERIC_ROUNDABORT** option to **OFF**.

 Should you encounter a question about using indexes on tables and the resulting performance of **INSERT**, **UPDATE**, and **DELETE** statements, remember that these types of statements run faster when there are fewer indexes on the table.

Using XML Views

Similar to creating views by using the **CREATE VIEW** statement and specifying SQL queries against the view, you can create Extensible Markup Language (XML) views of relational data by using XML-Data Reduced (XDR) schemas and querying them by using XPath queries. XDR schemas such as Document Type Definitions (DTDs) describe the structure of the data. Where DTD only uses characters, the XDR specifies the data type of the elements. Public XDR schemas can exist, such as Microsoft BizTalk, and you can access them by using the Transact-SQL **FOR XML** statement. Also, you can make, annotate, and access copies of public XDR schemas with an Xpath query. In the mapping schema, the table names and columns are case-sensitive. Listing 7.5 is an example of an XDR schema for the table shown in Listing 7.3.

Listing 7.5 XDR schema for an **Employee** table.

```
<?xml version="1.0" ?>
<Schema xmlns="urn:schemas-microsoft-com:xml-data"
  xmlns:dt="urn:schemas-microsoft-com:datatypes"
  xmlns:sql="urn:schemas-microsoft-com:xml-sql">

<ElementType name="Employee" sql:relation="Employees" >
 <AttributeType name="EmpID" />
 <AttributeType name="FName" />
 <AttributeType name="LName" />
 <AttributeType name="BDate" />

 <attribute type="EmpID" sql:field="EmpID" />
 <attribute type="FName" sql:field="FirstName" />
 <attribute type="LName" sql:field="LastName" />
 <attribute type="BDate" sql:field="BirthDate" />
</ElementType>
</Schema>
```

Practice Questions

Question 1

Your school wants to create an application that lets the students change their addresses and phone numbers but does not give them access to the other student-related fields. Which of the following shows the correct syntax?

○ a.
```
CREATE VIEW dbo.Student_address_view
AS
SELECT LastName, FirstName, Street,
City, State, Phone
FROM Students
```

○ b.
```
CREATE VIEW dbo.Students
AS
SELECT LastName, FirstName, Street,
City, State, Phone
FROM Students
```

○ c.
```
CREATE VIEW dbo.Student_address_view
AS
SELECT LastName, FirstName, Street,
City, State, Phone
FROM Students
ORDER BY LastName
```

○ d.
```
CREATE VIEW dbo.Student_address_view
(First, Last, Street, City, State)
AS
SELECT LastName, FirstName, Street,
City, State, Phone
FROM Students
```

Answer a is correct. A simple view includes a name and a **SELECT** statement. Answer b is incorrect because two objects cannot have the same name within the same database. Answer c is incorrect because you cannot use an **ORDER BY** clause in the **SELECT** statement of a view. Answer d is incorrect because the column names of the view are not in the order of the **SELECT** statement or are missing.

Question 2

What are some valid reasons for creating views? [Check all correct answers]

❑ a. You want users prevented from seeing certain fields in a table.

❑ b. You want simplified code.

❑ c. You want security enforced.

❑ d. You want partitioned data looked at as one entity.

❑ e. You want a customized view for a particular user ID.

Answers a, b, c, d, and e are all correct. You can use views when hiding fields, simplifying complex joins, and enforcing security by preventing users from accessing certain columns. You can use views when customizing other views for a particular user ID. You can join already partitioned data for optimization by using a view so that it gives the appearance that all the data resides in the same table on the same server.

Question 3

How would you design the student tables to accommodate a proposed plan for combining data storage from multiple schools (school A and school B) without giving either school access to the other's data? [Check all correct answers]

❑ a.

```
USE TarkDatabase
CREATE TABLE Server1.dbo.Student_a
(StudentID [smallint] IDENTITY (1, 1)
_PRIMARY KEY
 CHECK (StudentID BETWEEN 1 AND 10001),
LastName nvarchar(20) NOT NULL ,
FirstName nvarchar(10) NOT NULL ,
BirthDate smalldatetime NULL)
```

❑ b.

```
USE TarkDatabase
CREATE TABLE Server1.dbo.Student_a
(StudentID [smallint] IDENTITY (1, 1)
_PRIMARY KEY
 CHECK (StudentID BETWEEN 1 AND 10000),
LastName nvarchar(20) NOT NULL ,
FirstName nvarchar(10) NOT NULL ,
BirthDate smalldatetime NULL)
```

❑ c.

```
USE TarkDatabase
CREATE TABLE Server1.dbo.Student_b
(StudentID [smallint] IDENTITY (1, 1)
_PRIMARY KEY
 CHECK (StudentID BETWEEN 10001 AND 19999),
LastName nvarchar(20) NOT NULL ,
FirstName nvarchar(10) NOT NULL ,
BirthDate smalldatetime NULL)
```

(continued)

Question 3 *(continued)*

```
❑ d.
USE TarkDatabase
CREATE TABLE Server1.dbo.Student_b
(StudentID [smallint] IDENTITY (1, 1)
_PRIMARY KEY
 CHECK (StudentID BETWEEN 10000 AND 20000),
LastName nvarchar(20) NOT NULL ,
FirstName nvarchar(10) NOT NULL ,
BirthDate smalldatetime NULL)
```

Answers b and c are correct. You would want.to partition the tables based on the student ID. The student ID numbers cannot overlap. Answers b and c partition the table so that the student IDs do not overlap. Any other combination of answers would result in overlapping student IDs.

Question 4

What is the correct syntax for the view that would show all students enrolled in schools A and B of the previous question?

○ a.
```
CREATE VIEW dbo.Students_view
AS
SELECT StudentID, LastName, FirstName,
 _BirthDate
FROM tarkdatabase.dbo.Student_a
UNION ALL
CREATE VIEW dbo.Students_view
AS
SELECT LastName, FirstName, StudentID,
 _BirthDate
FROM tarkdatabase.dbo.Student_b
```

(continued)

Question 4 *(continued)*

○ b.
```
CREATE VIEW dbo.Students_view
AS
SELECT StudentID, LastName, FirstName
FROM Student_a
UNION ALL
SELECT StudentID, LastName, FirstName,
 _BirthDate
FROM Student_b
```

○ c.
```
CREATE VIEW dbo.Students_view
AS
SELECT StudentID, LastName, FirstName,
  BirthDate
FROM Student_a
UNION
SELECT StudentID, LastName, FirstName,
 _BirthDate
FROM Student_b
```

○ d.
```
CREATE VIEW dbo.Students_view
AS
SELECT StudentID, LastName, FirstName,
 _BirthDate
FROM Student_a
UNION ALL
SELECT StudentID, LastName, FirstName,
 _BirthDate
FROM Student_b
```

Answer d is correct. You combine partitioned tables in a view by creating a **SE-LECT** statement for each table and combining the statements by using the **UNION ALL** clause. Answer a is incorrect because it includes the **CREATE VIEW** statement twice; you should use it only once (first) and then combine the **SELECT** statements. Answer b is incorrect because you do not have the same number of columns in each **SELECT** statement. Answer c is incorrect because you must use the **UNION ALL** clause, not the **UNION** clause.

Question 5

You want to be able to modify data through your view. What are some considerations? [Check all correct answers]

- ❑ a. You cannot have table joins in the **SELECT** statement.
- ❑ b. You cannot use aggregates in the **SELECT** statement.
- ❑ c. You can modify only one of the base tables at a time.
- ❑ d. When you perform an **INSERT**, all columns must be available in the view, they must allow nulls, or they must have defaults.

Answers b, c, and d are correct. An updateable view cannot use aggregates or derived columns. The **SELECT** statement can be a table join, but the modification can affect only one of the tables at a time. With an **INSERT**, you must be able to provide data for all columns in the view (either by allowing nulls or by using defaults). Answer a is incorrect because you can have table joins in the **SELECT** statement.

Question 6

You have the following table. Which views are updateable? [Check all correct answers]

```
CREATE TABLE Courses
(CourseID [smallint] IDENTITY (1, 1)
_PRIMARY KEY
CourseCategory nvarchar(20) NOT NULL ,
CourseTitle nvarchar (100) NOT NULL)
GO
```

❑ a.
```
CREATE VIEW Course_View
AS
SELECT CourseCategory, CourseTitle
FROM Courses
```

❑ b.
```
CREATE VIEW Course_View
AS
SELECT CourseID, CourseCategory, CourseTitle
FROM Courses
```

❑ c.
```
CREATE VIEW Course_View
AS
SELECT CourseTitle
FROM Courses
```

❑ d.
```
CREATE VIEW Course_View
AS
SELECT CourseCategory
FROM Courses
```

Answers a and b are correct. An updateable view requires all columns listed unless they have defaults or all nulls. Although answer a does not include the **CourseID** column, the answer is still valid because the **CourseID** column has an **IDENTITY** property and is automatically calculated. Answers c and d are incorrect because they are missing one of the columns that does not allow nulls.

Question 7

> Put the following snippets of code together to create an indexed view that lets you see the definition in the **syscomments** table.
>
> ```
> SELECT *
> SELECT Col_A, Col_B, Col_C
> SELECT Col_A, Col_B, Col_A
> FROM Table_A
> FROM VIEW_A
> FROM Table_A join Table_B
> ON Table_A.Col_A = Table_B.ColA
> WITH ENCRYPTION
> WITH SCHEMABINDING
> ```

The correct answer is:

```
SELECT Col_A, Col_B, Col_C
FROM Table_A
WITH SCHEMABINDING
```

An indexed view must include the column names; it cannot use the asterisks. You cannot include table joins or other views in the **FROM** clause. You must also include the **WITH SCHEMABINDING** clause. The **ENCRYPTION** clause can be used with indexed views, but in this request, you wanted the definition to be visible.

Question 8

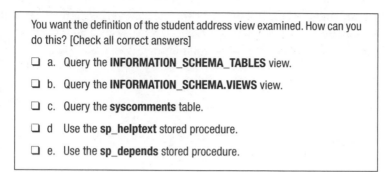

You want the definition of the student address view examined. How can you do this? [Check all correct answers]

❑ a. Query the **INFORMATION_SCHEMA_TABLES** view.

❑ b. Query the **INFORMATION_SCHEMA.VIEWS** view.

❑ c. Query the **syscomments** table.

❑ d Use the **sp_helptext** stored procedure.

❑ e. Use the **sp_depends** stored procedure.

Answers b, c, and d are correct. You can query the **syscomments** table or the **INFORMATION_SCHEMA.VIEWS** view, which is based on the **syscomments** table. You can also use the stored procedure **sp_helptext**. Answer a is incorrect because this view contains information on the view name, not its definition. Answer e is incorrect because the stored procedure **sp_depends** contains view dependencies, not its definition.

Need to Know More?

 Iseminger, David. *SQL Server 2000 Reference Library.* Redmond, WA: Microsoft Press, 2000. ISBN 0-7356-1280-3. A selected collection of SQL Server 2000 Books Online; there are six volumes focused on key areas. Volume 2 contains information on creating objects such as databases, views, and tables. Volume 1 contains information on XML views.

 MS SQL Server Books Online has sections on views, partitions, and XDR. You can install this collection from the SQL Server CD or access it online at **http://msdn.microsoft.com/library/default.asp?URL= /library/psdk/sql/portal_7ap1.htm.**

 Search the TechNet CD or its online version through **www.microsoft.com/ technet.** Keywords you can search on are "views", "index views", "partitions", and "XDR".

 www.microsoft.com/sql/ and **http://msdn.microsoft.com/sqlserver/ default.asp** are good places to find up-to-date information about SQL Server.

 www.sqlmag.com—*SQL Magazine*—both the hard copy and the Web site—has a lot of information on SQL Server.

Stored Procedures

. . . .

Terms you'll need to understand:

✓ Stored procedure

✓ Nested stored procedure

✓ **RAISERROR** statement

Techniques you'll need to master:

✓ Creating stored procedures

✓ Modifying stored procedures

✓ Executing stored procedures

✓ Including error handling within a stored procedure

A *stored procedure* is a series of SQL statements that are precompiled, named, and saved in SQL Server in order to be executed on a reusable basis. Stored procedures provide flexibility for application programs that help determine which procedure the server executes at runtime. Stored procedures can be *nested* (can call other stored procedures), and they can accept input parameters, return output parameters, or return status information. In this chapter, we will discuss designing, creating, modifying, and executing stored procedures.

Design Considerations

Using stored procedures provides a method of encapsulating tasks. Stored procedures offer several benefits over submitting straight Transact-SQL statements to the SQL Server:

➤ Stored procedures allow modular programming; you can create a procedure once and then use it many times. Stored procedures can be written by an experienced database person and used by developers who are less well versed in working with databases. Stored procedures reduce development overhead in that you write and test once but then can reuse the same procedure in numerous situations.

➤ Stored procedures improve performance in two ways. First, executing a stored procedure is faster than sending the Transact-SQL statements each time (because stored procedures are parsed, optimized, and stored in memory). Second, you can add conditional logic that becomes part of the single execution plan.

➤ Stored procedures can reduce network traffic in that a long Transact-SQL sequence does not have to be sent across the network each time; only the **execute** command goes across the network. In applications that use embedded SQL commands instead of stored procedures, every SQL statement is sent across the network for processing.

➤ Stored procedures can be part of your security plan. You can grant users access to execute a stored procedure without granting them access to the tables and views that are manipulated by the stored procedure.

 When stored procedures refer to database objects owned by a user other than the owner of the stored procedure, **EXECUTE** permissions must be checked for all objects including the stored procedure.

➤ A stored procedure should do only one task (the same way a module should do only a single task).

➤ You can reduce performance issues with system tables (located in **tempdb**) by minimizing the use of temporary stored procedures. Because SQL Server now saves execution plans in memory, you can use other tools (such as the **sp_executesql** system stored procedure), which do not have conflicts with system tables in the **tempdb** database.

There are several types of stored procedures:

➤ *System* stored procedures are stored in the **master** database. In most of the previous chapters, we have discussed (and frequently used) some of these procedures. Their names are prefaced with "sp_". System administrators and database designers use them as tools when they perform routine tasks in their database environment. System stored procedures can be executed in any database.

Before taking the exam, make sure you are familiar with the most common system stored procedures: **sp_monitor**, **sp_help**, **sp_helptext**, and **sp_lock**.

➤ *Local* stored procedures are created and stored in a user database. Execute them within the database where you first create them.

➤ *Temporary* stored procedures are stored in the **tempdb** database. Identify them with a single number sign (#) as the first character of their names if they are local to a user's connection, or with a double number sign (##) as the first character of their names if they are global to all users' connections.

➤ *Extended* stored procedures are stored in the **master** database. Preface their names with "xp_". They are dynamic link libraries (DLLs) that SQL Server dynamically loads and executes.

➤ *Remote* stored procedures execute stored procedures on remote servers, but you no longer need remote stored procedures because, for all practical purposes (back through version 6.0), distributed queries have replaced them.

Note: Remote stored procedures cannot participate in transactions, and you cannot roll back any changes you make on the remote server by using them.

Creating Stored Procedures

Create stored procedures in the current database (with the exception of temporary stored procedures, which are created in the **tempdb** database). You should individually test each of the Transact-SQL statements contained in your stored procedure to make sure that they do what you expect.

Guidelines for Creating Stored Procedures

CREATE permissions default to members of the **sysadmin**, **db_owner**, and **db_ddladmin** roles. Members of the **sysadmin** and **db_owner** roles can transfer **CREATE PROCEDURE** permissions to other users. **EXECUTE** permission defaults to the roles listed here and to the procedure owner, who can then assign this permission to other database users. Following are some guidelines for creating stored procedures:

➤ Stored procedures can refer to most SQL Server objects, such as tables, views, functions (both system and user-defined), and other stored procedures.

➤ A stored procedure can create a temporary table (which exists for the life of the stored procedure and then gets deleted).

➤ A stored procedure can include any number and type of Transact-SQL statements except for **CREATE DEFAULT**, **CREATE PROCEDURE**, **CREATE RULE**, **CREATE TRIGGER**, and **CREATE VIEW**. If you create other objects (such as tables), you should qualify them with the object owner.

➤ The maximum size of a stored procedure is 128MB (depending on available memory).

➤ You can nest stored procedures up to 32 levels. If an attempt to execute more than 32 levels occurs, the entire procedure is aborted. The nested stored procedure can access all objects of its parent procedure (that is, if A calls B, then B can access all of A's objects). You can also recursively nest stored procedures (that is, A calls B, which calls A).

➤ When you create a procedure, you should set the **dbo** as the owner.

Objects within a stored procedure are resolved at runtime and therefore should be qualified within the stored procedure.

➤ Objects referenced within a stored procedure should have their owner names qualified in the reference. If they're not, they default to the stored procedure's creator.

➤ Do not start your stored procedure's name with "sp_" because that indicates a system stored procedure. If you try to call a stored procedure that starts with "sp_", SQL Server will first search the MASTER database before searching the current database. If you do try to call a stored procedure that starts with a "sp_" identifier, SQL Server will first search the MASTER database before searching the current database."

> SET QUOTED_IDENTIFIER and SET ANSI_NULLS settings are saved when the stored procedure is created. The client ignores these settings. The other SET settings are not saved with the procedure.

SET QUOTED_IDENTIFIER and **SET ANSI_NULLS** are determined at creation time. All other settings are determined at execution time.

The syntax of the **CREATE PROCEDURE** statement is as follows:

```
CREATE PROCEDURE procedure_name [ ; number ]
    [ { @parameter data_type }
        [ VARYING ] [ = default ] [ OUTPUT ]
    ] [ ,...n ]
[ WITH
    { RECOMPILE | ENCRYPTION | RECOMPILE , ENCRYPTION } ]
[ FOR REPLICATION ]
AS sql_statement [ ...n ]
```

Although you can spell out "**PROCEDURE**", the statement is usually abbreviated as **CREATE PROC**.

Parameters

You create parameters in order to pass data to and from a stored procedure. There are two types of parameters: input and output. Input parameters, as their name suggests, are used to submit values as arguments to the stored procedure. Within the procedure itself, you can set input parameters to have default values in case the input parameter is not specified. Output parameters are values returned from a stored procedure. These values are local variables declared using the **OUTPUT** keyword.

Key Arguments

The **CREATE PROCEDURE** statement has the following key arguments:

> *procedure_name*—The procedure's name, which, like all names, must conform to the rules of identifiers (described in Chapter 3). You can create local and global procedures by prefacing the names with a single number sign (#) or double number sign (##), respectively.

➤ *; number*—An optional number you use when grouping similar procedures together. If you use this notation, you drop the entire group by specifying the name without a number.

➤ **WITH {RECOMPILE | ENCRYPTION | RECOMPILE, ENCRYP-TION} RECOMPILE**—Means that the stored procedure is not cached but is recompiled at runtime each time it gets executed. **ENCRYPTION** means that the definition is not readable, even by the creator. If you specify both, you separate them with a comma.

➤ **FOR REPLICATION**—Means that the stored procedure is used as a filter for replication and is executed only during replication. The procedure can never be executed on the Replication Subscriber. The **RECOMPILE** option and the **FOR REPLICATION** option are mutually exclusive.

➤ **AS** *sql_statement*—Allows you to include any number of Transact-SQL statements.

Stored procedures can specify input or output parameters. The maximum number of parameters is 2,100. When you specify a parameter, you indicate its data type and its direction, **OUTPUT**. You can optionally specify a default value. If no default value is specified, then the parameter must be supplied when you're executing the stored procedure. Following is a list of **OUTPUT** parameters:

➤ *@parameter*—The parameter name. The at sign (@) must be the first character of the parameter, indicating that it's local to the procedure. The parameter can represent constants but not database objects such as tables or column names. You can use global variables, indicated by the "double at" sign (@@).

➤ *data_type*—Indicates the type of data that the parameter (or variable) can hold. Any SQL data type is allowed with the exception of the **cursor** data type, which can be used only for output parameters and which must contain the **VARYING** keyword. In other words, if you specify **cursor**, you must also specify the **VARYING** and **OUTPUT** keywords. **VARYING** indicates that the contents are dynamic.

➤ *= default*—Indicates the default value of the parameter. Example, **@quantity = 0** would set the **quantity** parameter to zero. If no default is specified, and a parameter is not provided when the stored procedure is called, the system generates an error. To prevent this error, you can set the default equal to **NULL**.

Executing a stored procedure without required parameters that do not have associated defaults will generate an error.

➤ OUTPUT—Indicates that the stored procedure will return the specified parameter. If not specified, the parameter is an input to the stored procedure.

 You must also include the **OUTPUT** keyword both in the **CREATE** statement and in the **EXECUTE** statement.

➤ Stored procedures can also return a status or code. For this, you use the **RETURN** (value) statement within the stored procedure. The value is the **int** data type. When you execute the stored procedure, you set a variable equal to the stored procedure.

Listing 8.1 shows three examples of stored procedures. The first one is a simple procedure with no parameters. The second example has one input parameter with a default value assigned and one output parameter. The third example has one input parameter, one output parameter, and a return code. An explanation of each example precedes the applicable example.

Listing 8.1 Sample stored procedures.

```
/* This is a simple procedure with no parameters.
It finds the 5 least expensive products */
CREATE PROC FiveLeastExpensiveProducts
AS
SELECT TOP 5 ProductName, UnitPrice
    FROM Products
    ORDER BY UnitPrice asc


/* This is a simple procedure with one input
parameter and one outpul parameter.
It finds the quantity on hand for the product
 name that was passed. */
CREATE PROC GetStock
@ProdName nvarchar(40) = '%',
@InStock smallint OUTPUT
AS
SELECT @InStock = UnitsInStock
FROM Products
WHERE ProductName LIKE @ProdName


/* This is a simple procedure with one input parameter,
one output parameter, and a return code. */
CREATE PROC dbo.OrderCount
    @CustomerID nchar (5),
    @OrderCount int OUTPUT
```

```
AS
IF EXISTS
  (SELECT *
   FROM Orders
   WHERE CustomerID = @CustomerID
     AND
     ShippedDate IS Null)
  BEGIN
     SELECT @OrderCount=COUNT(*)
     FROM Orders
     WHERE CustomerID = @CustomerID
     RETURN (1)
  END
ELSE RETURN (0)
GO
```

You can specify the **TOP** keyword to return a certain number of records or a certain percentage of records. For example, **SELECT TOP 10 * FROM EMPLOYEES** returns the first 10 records in the **Employees** table, and **SELECT TOP 10 PERCENT * FROM EMPLOYEES** returns 10 percent of the records in the **Employees** table. Be very careful when you read SQL syntax statements such as these on the exam.

Modifying a Stored Procedure

Once you create a stored procedure, you can rename it, change its definition, or delete it. Remember that if you change its definition or its name, other objects referring to it might not function correctly. Altering a stored procedure saves any permissions associated with the stored procedure. If you drop and then re-create the stored procedure, you will need to grant permissions again.

The **ALTER PROCEDURE** statement looks identical to the **CREATE PROCEDURE** statement except that the word **CREATE** is replaced with **ALTER**. If you want to retain **ENCRYPTION** or **RECOMPILE**, you need to specify them again.

Renaming a Stored Procedure

You rename a stored procedure by using the **sp_rename** system stored procedure. After renaming the stored procedure, you should flush the procedure cache (**DBCC FREEPROCCACHE**) to ensure that the system recompiles all dependent stored procedures and views. The syntax for this is as follows:

```
sp_rename old_name, new_name
```

Deleting a Stored Procedure

When you delete a stored procedure, all of the information in the system tables describing the stored procedure is removed. All permissions are also dropped. Dropping an underlying object does not delete the stored procedure; it must explicitly be deleted. If you grouped stored procedures, then they must be dropped as a group; individual stored procedures within the group cannot be deleted. Below is the syntax:

```
DROP stored procedure { procedure} [ ,...n ]
```

You can drop one or more stored procedures at the same time. You must have the proper permission to delete a stored procedure. Before deleting a stored procedure, check all dependencies and correct them first.

Getting Information on a Stored Procedure

Several system stored procedures will help you obtain information about stored procedures or other objects. You can use **sp_helptext**, **sp_help**, **sp_depends**, and **sp_helpextendedproc**:

➤ The **sp_helptext** system stored procedure displays the definition of a stored procedure (with the exception that if you specify the **ENCRYPTION** option, the system cannot interpret the definition).

➤ The **sp_help** system stored procedure returns the stored procedure's name, owner, and creation date. In addition, for each parameter, this procedure shows the parameter name, data type, size, and order (such as 1, 2, 3, etc.).

➤ The **sp_depends** system stored procedure returns any dependencies on the specified object.

➤ The **sp_helpextendedproc** system stored procedure lists the extended stored procedure and the DLL that was called within the extended stored procedure.

Executing a Stored Procedure

To execute a stored procedure, you specify the stored procedure name followed by any necessary parameters. You can specify the parameters either by position or by name. If a stored procedure returns a return code, then you set the variable equal to the stored procedure name. When specifying output parameters, you must specify the **OUTPUT** keyword in the **EXECUTE** statement. If you specify the parameter's name, it must be spelled correctly. If you specify the parameters by position, you cannot skip any parameters in the middle, but you can omit the last one.

The syntax for executing a stored procedure is as follows:

```
[ [ EXECUTE
    {
        [ @return_status = ]
            { procedure_name [ ;number ] | @procedure_name_var
    }
    [ [ @parameter = ] { value | @variable [ OUTPUT ] | [ DEFAULT
] ]
        [ ,...n ]
[ WITH RECOMPILE ]
```

Key Arguments

The **EXECUTE** statement has the following key arguments:

➤ *@return_status* =—If a stored procedure can return a status code, then you define a local variable and set the procedure equal to it.

➤ *procedure_name*—You specify the procedure name, and if it has a number associated with it, you need to specify that number, too. You can use a variable (*@procedure_name_var*) that contains the stored procedure name.

➤ For each parameter, you either specify the values separated by a comma (in the same position they were defined inside the procedure), or set the parameter name = value. If a parameter is defined as **OUTPUT,** you must include the **OUTPUT** keyword in the **EXECUTE** statement.

➤ DEFAULT—Means that you want the defined default value to be used. If **DEFAULT** is used but one was not specified in the definition, then an error results.

➤ WITH RECOMPILE—Forces a new plan to be compiled.

Listing 8.2 shows how you execute the stored procedures shown in Listing 8.1. In the second example, notice that you have to declare a variable for use as the **OUTPUT** parameter. Also, note that the declared variable stores the value of the **OUTPUT** parameter. Before you can see it, you need to perform some action to display it or use it. Likewise, in the third example, you need to declare the variables before you use them. An explanation of each example precedes the example.

Listing 8.2   Examples of executing stored procedures.

```
/* This is a simple procedure with no parameters.
It finds the 5 least expensive products */
EXEC FiveLeastExpensiveProducts

/* This is a simple procedure with
one input and one output parameter.
```

```
It finds the quantity on hand for
the product 'Chocolade' .
Note: You need to declare the output
parameter and display it. */
Declare @InStock smallint
EXEC getstock 'Chocolade', @InStock OUTPUT
Select @InStock -- Displays the output value

/* This is a simple procedure with one input parameter,
one output parameter, and a return code.
Note: You need to declare the variables,
including the return code.
You also need to print or display to see the results. */
DECLARE
 @CustomerID   nchar (5),
 @ReturnCode    int,
 @NumberOrders  int

SET @CustomerID = 'BLAUS'

EXEC @ReturnCode = OrderCount @CustomerID, @NumberOrders OUTPUT
IF @ReturnCode = 1
BEGIN
Print 'No Orders'
END
ELSE
BEGIN
Print 'Orders are ' + CONVERT(varchar(6), @NumberOrders)
END
```

Nested Stored Procedures

As we mentioned earlier, a stored procedure can call another stored procedure. This is called a *nested stored procedure*. Nesting is limited to 32 levels; however, there is no limit on the number of other stored procedures that a particular stored procedure can call, as long as the number of nesting layers is kept under 32. You can also use the **RETURN** statement within the internal stored procedure, and the calling stored procedure can determine what course of action to take. The **@@NESTLEVEL** function indicates the current nesting level.

Recompiling a Stored Procedure

Databases and their data evolve or change over time. Because of this fact, you may need to recompile the stored procedures to re-optimize them. You can recompile stored procedures in three ways. We have seen earlier (when discussing the **CREATE STORED PROCEDURE** statement) that we can include the **WITH RECOMPILE** option. This means that the stored procedure is recompiled every time it is executed. This is not used often because it defeats one of the main purposes of a stored procedure—saving compile time. We also saw earlier that you can include the **WITH RECOMPILE** option with the **EXECUTE** statement and that the combination forces a recompile. The third way is to execute the **sp_recompile** system stored procedure, which forces a recompile of a stored procedure the next time it is run. If this system stored procedure is executed without an object, then it sets recompiling for every stored procedure in the database. You can specify a table to recompile all stored procedures dependent on that table.

It is important that you understand that if objects referenced by a stored procedure change (such as when you're adding indexes or importing a large amount of data), you should force a recompile of the stored procedure.

Error Handling within a Stored Procedure

A stored procedure can be thought of as a small program; as such, it can include error handling techniques as well as flow control. You can use the **RETURN** statement to exit a procedure before it ends. We saw this in the third example in Listing 8.1. A return value of zero (0) usually indicates success.

When an error occurs, the system returns the error number in the **@@ERROR** function. This value is reset with each statement, so your system should check that value after each applicable statement. A value of zero indicates success.

You can use the **RAISERROR** statement so that it returns an error message and notifies the system when an error occurs. This statement stores the error number in the **@@ERROR** system function. The **PRINT** statement also displays an error message but does not store the error in the **@@ERROR** function. The syntax of the **RAISERROR** statement is as follows:

```
RAISERROR ( { msg_id | msg_str } { , severity , state }
```

You can either include a system or user-defined message ID (*msg_id*) or specify the text of the message. You must include the error's *severity* and *state*. The *severity* indicates the level of seriousness. A value of 20 through 25 indicates a fatal error and terminates the client's connection. Usually you use a value from 0 through 18, with 16 being a standard value. Any number above 18 requires the user to be in the **sysadmin** server role. The *state* is an arbitrary integer (1 to 127) that can be used by the user to further clarify the error. This argument is required, and the default value is usually set to 1.

 It is important to understand how you can add error handling in stored procedures and how **@@ERROR** can be utilized.

Listing 8.3 contains an example of a stored procedure that includes error handling and flow control.

Listing 8.3   Stored procedure with error handling.

```
/* Update employee's home phone number */
/* with error checking */

USE Northwind
GO
CREATE PROC UpdateEmployeHomePhone
@EmpID int = NULL,
@Phone nvarchar(24) = NULL
AS
IF @EmpID is NULL
BEGIN
    PRINT 'You must supply a valid Employee ID'
    RETURN
END
/* Ensure that it is a valid employee */
IF NOT EXISTS
    (SELECT * FROM dbo.Employees WHERE EmployeeID = @EmpID)
BEGIN
    RAISERROR ('Employee not found', 16, 1)
    RETURN
END
BEGIN TRANSACTION
    UPDATE dbo.Employees
    SET HomePhone = @Phone
    WHERE EmployeeID = @EmpID
COMMIT TRANSACTION
/* Display success to caller */
SELECT 'The Phone Number for ' +
    CAST(@EmpID AS VarChar(5)) +
    ' has been changed to ' +
    @Phone
```

Practice Questions

Question 1

You have added 10,000 records to the **Employees** table, which is accessed by several stored procedures. After importing the data, what should you do to make sure your stored procedures are properly optimized?

○ a. Execute each stored procedure once.

○ b. Execute **sp_recompile Employees**.

○ c. Alter all the stored procedures and add **WITH RECOMPILE** to their definitions.

○ d. Execute **sp_recompile UpdatePhone**.

Answer b is correct. Executing the **sp_recompile** system stored procedure against the table will set all the stored procedures and triggers to be recompiled the next time they are run. Answer a is incorrect because you did not specify the **WITH RECOMPILE** option with the **EXECUTE** statement. Answer c is incorrect because altering the stored procedures and adding the **WITH RECOMPILE** option would mean that they would be recompiled every time you ran them, thus losing the efficiency of using stored procedures. Answer d is incorrect because it would recompile the **UpdatePhone** stored procedure but not all the others that access the table.

Question 2

You want to create a stored procedure that will update employees' salaries for a given department. The **Employees** table is described in Exhibit 1. Select and place the code snippets in the correct order. Not all code snippets need to be used.

Exhibit 1:

```
CREATE TABLE dbo.Employees (
    EmployeeID int IDENTITY (1, 1) NOT NULL ,
    LastName nvarchar (20)  NOT NULL ,
    FirstName nvarchar (10)  NOT NULL ,
    Department nvarchar (30)  NULL ,
    Salary money NULL)
```

Select and place:

```
@Dept nvarchar(30) = NULL,
@SalIncr Decimal(2,2) = 0.0

AS

BEGIN
    PRINT 'You must supply a valid Department'
    RETURN
END

BEGIN TRANSACTION

COMMIT TRANSACTION

CREATE PROCEDURE UpdateSalaryByDept
Declare @newSal Decimal(3,2)
SET @newSal = 1. + @SalIncr

GO

IF @Dept is NULL

UPDATE dbo.Employees
SET Salary = Salary * @newSal
WHERE Department = @Dept
```

The correct sequence is:

```
    CREATE PROCEDURE UpdateSalaryByDept
    @Dept nvarchar(30) = NULL,
    @SalIncr Decimal(2,2) = 0.0
    AS
    IF @Dept is NULL
BEGIN
    PRINT 'You must supply a valid Department'
    RETURN
END
Declare @newSal Decimal(3,2)
SET @newSal = 1. + @SalIncr
BEGIN TRANSACTION
    UPDATE dbo.Employees1
    SET Salary = Salary * @newSal
    WHERE Department = @Dept
COMMIT TRANSACTION
GO
```

You first issue the **CREATE PROC** statement, followed by any parameters and then the **AS** keyword, followed by the Transact-SQL statements. You would test for the input parameters first before starting the logic. You should start the transaction just before it is needed, which is when you do the data modification.

Question 3

You are the DBA of Toyshop. The database has the **Orders** and **LineItem** tables as shown in Exhibit 1. You want to create a stored procedure that retrieves all orders for a specific customer. Select and place the code snippets in the correct order. Not all code snippets need to be used.

Exhibit 1:

```
CREATE TABLE dbo.Orders (
OrderID int IDENTITY (1, 1) NOT NULL,
CustomerID int NOT NULL,
OrderDate datetime NOT NULL)
GO
CREATE TABLE LineItem (
OrderID int NOT NULL,
ProductID int NOT NULL,
Quantity int NOT NULL)
```

Select and place:

```
@Custno int = NULL
@Orders OUTPUT


AS


BEGIN
    PRINT 'You must supply a
    valid Customer No.'
    RETURN
END


CREATE PROCEDURE GetLineItems


IF @Custno is NULL


SELECT li.OrderID, ProductID, quantity
FROM dbo.LineItem li INNER JOIN
     dbo.Orders ord
ON li.OrderID = ord.OrderID
WHERE ord.customerid = @custno


GO
```

The correct sequence is:

```
CREATE PROCEDURE GetLineItems
@Custno int = NULL
AS
IF @Custno is NULL
BEGIN
    PRINT 'You must supply a
     valid Customer No.'
    RETURN
END
SELECT li.OrderID, ProductID, quantity
FROM dbo.LineItem li INNER JOIN
     dbo.Orders ord
ON li.OrderID = ord.OrderID
WHERE ord.customerid = @custno
GO
```

You define the **CREATE PROCEDURE** statement by declaring its name, followed by any parameters, the **AS** keyword, then the test for the parameters, and the **SELECT** statement.

Question 4

You have the following stored procedure shown in Exhibit 1. You want to execute the stored procedure for the table shown in Exhibit 2. What are the correct statements? Choose two that make a complete solution.

Exhibit 1:

```
CREATE PROC GetPhone
@CustNo int,
@PhoneNo nvarchar(15) OUTPUT
AS
SELECT Phone
FROM Customer
WHERE CustID = @CustNo
```

Exhibit 2:

```
CREATE TABLE dbo.Customer (
    CustID int IDENTITY (1, 1) NOT NULL ,
    LastName nvarchar (20)  NOT NULL ,
    FirstName nvarchar (10)  NOT NULL ,
    Phone nvarchar (10) NULL)
```

❑ a.

```
Declare @CustNo int
Declare @Phone nvarchar (15)
SET @CustNo = 1
```

❑ b.

```
SET @CustNo int = 1
SET @Phone nvarchar (15)= NULL
```

❑ c.

```
Exec GetPhone @CustNo, @Phone OUTPUT
```

❑ d.

```
Exec GetPhone @CustNo
```

Answers a and c are correct. First, you need to declare the variables and set them accordingly. Then you issue the **EXECUTE** statement, specifying the input and output parameters; you must include the **OUTPUT** keyword in the **EXECUTE** statement. Answer b is incorrect because you cannot declare and set a variable with the **SET** keyword. Answer d is incorrect because it left out the **OUTPUT** parameter.

Question 5

You have the following stored procedure. You are getting an error message when you try to execute the **CREATE PROC** statement. What line is causing the error?

```
1. CREATE PROC NewView
2. @Name VARCHAR (20) = NULL
3. AS
4. CREATE VIEW @Name
5. AS
6. SELECT * FROM Employees
```

○ a. 1
○ b. 2
○ c. 4
○ d. 5
○ e. 6

Answer c is correct. You cannot include the **CREATE VIEW** statement inside a stored procedure. You can issue a **CREATE TABLE** statement, but not a **CREATE VIEW** statement. The other statements would not create an error by themselves.

Question 6

You are the DBA of the Jones Bookstore. You have created a stored procedure, shown in Exhibit 1, that works against the table shown in Exhibit 2. What is the result of executing the following statement?

```
EXECUTE sp_helptext MyBook
```

Exhibit 1:
```
CREATE PROC sp_helptext
@Tit char(4) = NULL
AS
SELECT title, Price
FROM titles
WHERE title = @Tit
```

Exhibit 2:
```
CREATE TABLE titles (
title_id int IDENTITY NOT NULL,
title varchar(80)NOT NULL,
Pub_ID char(4) Null,
Price Money Null)
```

○ a. **MyBook $20.00**

○ b. The definition of the stored procedure shown in Exhibit 1

○ c. No results

○ d. An error message: "The object 'MyBook' does not exist in database 'Test'."

Answer d is correct. If you define a stored procedure with the same name as a system stored procedure, the system stored procedure will always execute first, and the user-defined stored procedure will never execute. Answer a is incorrect because the stored procedure will not run and therefore will not retrieve the title. Answer b is incorrect because the code in Exhibit 1 does not contain errors. If there were an object, such as a table or stored procedure, with the name **MyBook**, then answer b could be correct. Answer c is incorrect because you will get either the definition of the object, if it exists, or an error message.

Question 7

You are the DBA of your company. You have a payroll table, shown in Exhibit 1. You want to permit all users to select and update on all fields except **Salary**. You do not want users to have access to the table itself. What can you do? [Select all correct ansers]

Exhibit 1:

```
CREATE TABLE payroll (
Employee_id int IDENTITY NOT NULL,
LastName Varchar(30),
FirstName VarChar (30),
HireDate datetime,
Salary Money
   DEFAULT 0)
```

❑ a.
```
CREATE VIEW Payroll_View
AS
SELECT Employee_id, LastName, FirstName, HireDate
FROM payroll
```

❑ b.
```
CREATE PROC GetPayrollData
AS
SELECT Employee_id, LastName, FirstName, HireDate
FROM payroll
```

❑ c.
```
CREATE PROC NewPayrollData
@Last Varchar(30),
@First VarChar (30),
@Hire datetime,
AS
INSERT payroll
(LastName, FirstName, HireDate)
VALUES
(@Last, @First, @Hire)
```

(continued)

Question 7 *(continued)*

```
❑ d.
CREATE PROC GetPayrollData
@Empid int,
@Last Varchar(30),
@First VarChar (30),
@Hire datetime,
AS
SELECT Employee_id, LastName, FirstName, HireDate
FROM payroll
GO
INSERT payroll
(Employee_id, LastName, FirstName, HireDate)
VALUES
(@EmpID, @Last, @First, @Hire)
GO
```

Answers a, b, and c are correct. You can create either a view or a stored procedure. You would need two stored procedures: one for the **SELECT** statement and one for the **INSERT** statement. Answer d is incorrect because it tries to do both **INSERT** and **SELECT**. If you wanted to execute the **SELECT** statement, you would get an error because you did not provide the parameters. In addition, because the **EmployeeID** is an **IDENTITY column**, you would not provide a value. Instead, SQL Server would provide the value automatically.

Question 8

You have a stored procedure, shown in Exhibit 1, using the table shown in Exhibit 2. You want to ensure that your procedure handles errors. What would you put in line 5? Choose two answers to make a complete answer.

Exhibit 1:

```
1. CREATE PROC AddCustomer
@Custid int = NULL,
@Last varchar(20) = NULL,
@First varchar (10)= NULL,
@Phone varchar (10)= NULL
2.  AS
3. BEGIN TRANS
4. INSERT Customer
   VALUES
  (@CustID, @Last, @First, @Phone)
5. ?
6. COMMIT TRAN
```

Exhibit 2:

```
CREATE TABLE dbo.Customer (
    CustomerID int IDENTITY (1, 1) NOT NULL ,
    LastName varchar (20)  NOT NULL ,
    FirstName varchar (10)  NOT NULL ,
    Phone varchar (10) NULL)
```

❏ a.
```
IF @@ERROR = 0
```

❏ b.
```
IF @@ERROR <> 0
```

❏ c.
```
BEGIN
  ROLLBACK TRAN
  RETURN
END
```

❏ d.
```
BEGIN
  ROLLBACK TRAN
END
```

Answers b and c are correct. You should test for errors. If **@@ERROR** is zero, then there are no errors; if it is not zero, then there are errors, and you'll want to roll back the transaction. Answer a is incorrect because you would roll back if there were no errors. Answer d is incorrect because without the **RETURN** statement, you would fall through and execute the **COMMIT TRAN** statement.

Need to Know More?

Iseminger, David. *SQL Server 2000 Reference Library*. Redmond, WA: Microsoft Press, 2000. ISBN 0-7356-1280-3. A selected collection of SQL Server 2000 Books Online; there are six volumes focused on key areas. Volume 2 contains information on creating objects such as stored procedures. Volume 6 contains information on stored procedures and replication stored procedures.

Microsoft SQL Server Books Online has sections on stored procedures. This book series can be installed from the SQL Server CD or accessed online through **http://msdn.microsoft.com/library/default.asp**.

Search the TechNet CD or its online version through **www.microsoft.com/technet**. Keywords to search on are "stored procedures", "replication stored procedures", and "execute".

www.microsoft.com/sql/ and **http://msdn.microsoft.com/sqlserver/default.asp** are good places to find up-to-date information about SQL Server.

www.sqlmag.com—*SQL Magazine*—both the hard copy and the Web site—has a large amount of information on SQL Server.

Triggers

Terms you'll need to understand:

✓ Triggers
✓ **AFTER** trigger
✓ **INSTEAD OF** trigger
✓ Referential actions
✓ **ON DELETE CASCADE**
✓ **sp_rename**
✓ **DROP** trigger
✓ **sp_settriggerorder**
✓ **DISABLE** trigger

Techniques you'll need to master:

✓ Creating triggers
✓ Using **INSTEAD OF** triggers
✓ Modifying triggers
✓ Activating triggers
✓ Implementing referential actions

SQL Server provides two ways to enforce business rules and data integrity. In Chapter 4, we looked at constraints. In this chapter, we will look at triggers. Triggers are special stored procedures that are automatically executed after a modification event (**INSERT, DELETE,** or **UPDATE**) occurs.

Why Use Triggers?

Constraints and data types allow you to enforce simple business rules on a particular column; for example, you can specify that an employee number must be numeric, or a ZIP code must be five digits plus a dash plus four digits. Triggers allow you to enforce complex business rules. A trigger and the statement causing it to fire are one transaction and can roll back the modification. Triggers have several purposes:

➤ Triggers can cascade changes through related tables. This need has been replaced in SQL Server 2000 with the more efficient cascading referential integrity, which we discussed in Chapter 4.

➤ Triggers can handle more complex logic than a **CHECK** constraint can. This logic includes referring to other tables or even other databases.

➤ You can use triggers to evaluate the state of a table before and after the modification, and you can save this data in another table.

➤ You can assign multiple triggers of the same type on the same table to take different actions.

➤ Triggers allow you to communicate errors in a more meaningful way than the system-generated messages that constraints must rely upon.

➤ Triggers allow you to propagate changes to denormalized tables.

 For simple business rules, constraints are the preferred method.

When deciding whether to use a constraint or a trigger, you should always use the least overhead to get the job done. Constraints should be used unless the logic requires a trigger. The **INSTEAD OF** trigger is a new kind of stored procedure that executes tasks based on **INSERT, UPDATE,** or **DELETE** statements. The code in a normal trigger is executed only after constraints have been processed and any transactions created by the trigger have been committed. However, the **INSTEAD OF** trigger is executed *before* constraint processing and so can prevent actions such as insertions, updates, or deletions. For example, an **INSTEAD OF** trigger attached to a **Customers** table can prevent customer data from being modified; you'd do this by replacing the **INSERT, UPDATE,** or **DELETE** statement with a **RAISERROR** statement.

 You can use the **WITH LOG** option with the **RAISERROR** statement to write the error to the Windows NT (or 2000) application event log. The error message you specify can optionally reside in the **SYSMESSAGES** table. There is one specific error number to remember for the exam. Error 1205 specifies that a deadlock has occurred, and a severity level of 13 is applied.

The sequence of operation is: **INSTEAD OF** trigger, constraint, **AFTER** or **FOR** trigger. If a constraint fails, the **INSTEAD OF** trigger is rolled back and the **AFTER** trigger never happens. The **INSTEAD OF** trigger is new to SQL Server 2000. Prior versions had only the **AFTER** trigger, which was also called the **FOR** trigger. It can be confusing, but the **AFTER** and **FOR** triggers are the same thing, and the operation of the **AFTER** triggers is the same as the operation of the **FOR** triggers.

 The sequence of events is: **INSTEAD OF** trigger, constraints, **AFTER** triggers. Any failure rolls back the modification.

Design Considerations

There are two types of triggers. The most common type is the **AFTER** (or **FOR**) trigger. This is executed after the action of the modification statement. The second type is new to SQL Server 2000 and is called the **INSTEAD OF** trigger. It gets executed in place of the modification action. Another way to think about it is: The **INSTEAD OF** trigger is invoked instead of the actual command that caused the trigger to execute. The **INSTEAD OF** trigger can also be used with views to extend the types of updates allowed. Table 9.1 compares the two types of triggers.

INSTEAD OF triggers are not recursive. If they execute a statement on the same table, then the normal constraints and **AFTER** triggers are processed.

Trigger performance overhead is usually low. Both the **inserted** and **deleted** logical tables created by the trigger process are in memory. So the only overhead comes from accessing other tables that might not be in memory. Cursors have a negative impact on performance; therefore, it is recommended that you use rowset-based logic rather than cursors in triggers that affect multiple rows.

Table 9.1 AFTER and INSTEAD OF triggers compared.		
Function	AFTER Trigger	INSTEAD OF Trigger
Can be used with	Tables	Tables and views
How many per table or view	Multiple triggers per triggering action (**UPDATE**, **DELETE**, and **INSERT**)	One trigger per triggering action (**UPDATE**, **DELETE**, and **INSERT**)
Cascading references	No restrictions apply	Are not allowed on tables that have a foreign key constraint with the **ON DELETE** or **ON UPDATE** option
Execution	Occurs after the following: constraint processing; declarative referential actions; creation of **Inserted** and **Deleted** tables; the triggering action	Occurs before constraint processing; in place of the triggering action; after creation of inserted and deleted tables
Order of execution	First and last execution can be specified	Not applicable
text, **ntext**, and **image** column references in inserted and deleted tables	Not allowed	Allowed

INSTEAD OF triggers permit you to update views that are normally not updateable, either because they trap for columns that shouldn't be included or because they propagate changes to multiple underlying tables.

Two advantages of **INSTEAD OF** triggers are that they allow updates on views that would ordinarily not be updateable, and they allow you to process part of a batch or take alternative actions within the batch. A *batch* is a collection of SQL statements submitted together and executed as a group.

Trigger Activation with Implicit or Explicit **NULL** or **DEFAULT** Values

When a column allows **NULL** values or does not allow **NULL** values but has a **DEFAULT** value, a trigger can be activated in certain situations. These are:

➤ The **FOR INSERT** and **FOR UPDATE** triggers are activated if you supply a value for the column that is defined as **NULL** or has a **DEFAULT**.

➤ If you insert a row that has a **FOR INSERT** trigger and you do not supply a value for the **NULL** or **DEFAULT** column, then the trigger is still activated. The column is still inserted and therefore activates the trigger.

➤ If you update a row that has a **FOR UPDATE** trigger and you do not supply a value for the **NULL** or **DEFAULT** column, then the trigger is not activated. With an update, only the columns that are changed fire the trigger.

Creating Triggers

Triggers are created in the current database. You should test each of a trigger's Transact-SQL statements individually to make sure that they do what you expect. **CREATE** permissions default to members of the **sysadmin, db_owner,** and **db_ddladmin** roles and to the table owner, and permissions are not transferable. For an **INSTEAD OF** trigger on a view, the owner of the view must also own the underlying base tables and any tables referenced by the trigger.

Note: AFTER and FOR triggers are the same things. Therefore, references to AFTER triggers are the same as references to FOR triggers.

The following are some guidelines for creating triggers:

➤ Triggers can refer to objects in multiple databases.

➤ You cannot create a trigger on a temporary table or a system table. You can refer to a temporary table. You should refer to system views and not tables.

 It is important to understand that cascading referential integrity should be used rather than triggers in SQL Server 2000.

➤ **INSTEAD OF DELETE** and **INSTEAD OF UPDATE** triggers cannot be defined on a table that has a foreign key defined with an **ON DELETE** or **ON UPDATE** action.

➤ The **TRUNCATE TABLE** statement does not fire any triggers. Part of the reason for this is that **TRUNCATE TABLE** is not logged.

➤ The **WRITETEXT** statement does not fire any triggers, whether or not it is logged.

➤ The same trigger can be activated by more than one action, such as **UPDATE** and **INSERT**.

➤ You can define multiple **AFTER** triggers on the same table for the same action (**INSERT, UPDATE,** or **DELETE**). For each action, you can have only one **INSTEAD OF** trigger per table or view. You can have a view that contains a view, and both views can have **INSTEAD OF** triggers.

➤ **AFTER** triggers happen only if all constraints and referential cascade operations succeed.

➤ INSTEAD OF triggers are not allowed on an updateable view with the WITH CHECK OPTION clause. You must alter the view to remove this clause if you want to use an INSTEAD OF trigger.

➤ The deleted and inserted tables are logical (conceptual) tables created in memory. They are an image of the table with the trigger, and they hold either the deleted record or the inserted record. If an UPDATE trigger is issued, you get both the deleted and inserted tables.

➤ Only the INSTEAD OF trigger can refer to text, ntext, and image columns.

➤ Multiple AFTER triggers on the same table are executed randomly. New in SQL Server 2000, you can specify the first and last AFTER trigger. You use the sp_settriggerorder stored procedure to define these.

➤ Triggers should not return results. Therefore, you should not use SELECT statements that return results or variable assignments.

➤ The following Transact-SQL statements cannot be used within a trigger: AL-TER DATABASE, CREATE DATABASE, DROP DATABASE, RECONFIGURE, RESTORE DATABASE, and RESTORE LOG. Also, the following commands that are supported for backward compatibility are not allowed: DISK INIT, DISK RESIZE, LOAD DATABASE, LOAD LOG.

➤ Triggers can be nested to a maximum of 32 levels. If a trigger changes a table on which there is another trigger, the second trigger is activated and can then call a third trigger, and so on. Exceeding the limit rolls back all triggers and the modification that fired the trigger.

➤ If you execute a batch that causes a trigger to be fired, and the trigger issues a ROLLBACK TRANSACTION statement, then the remaining batch is cancelled and any actions within the batch are rolled back.

You cannot use CREATE or DROP statements in triggers. In addition, you might see a trick question about using a SELECT INTO statement within a trigger. Using SELECT INTO is also invalid because that would create a table just as the CREATE TABLE statement would.

Listing 9.1 shows two examples of AFTER triggers. The first example uses the Northwind database. When an order is placed, the quantity on hand in the Products table must be reduced appropriately. The second example records history whenever an employee changes data in the employees table. The trigger assumes that you have two identical tables: employees and employeehist.

*Note: In an update, the old record is written to the **deleted** table, and the new record is written to the **inserted** table.*

An example of an **INSTEAD OF** trigger is shown in Listing 9.2, later in the chapter.

Listing 9.1   Two examples of **AFTER** triggers.

```
/* Update the quantity available in the Products table
when an order is placed */
CREATE TRIGGER Stock_Insert
ON [Order Details]
AFTER INSERT
AS
UPDATE Prod SET
UnitsInStock = (Prod.UnitsInStock - I.Quantity)
FROM Products AS Prod INNER JOIN Inserted AS I
ON Prod.ProductID = I.ProductID
GO
/* When an employee changes any data in the employee record,
record the old data in a history table. */
CREATE TRIGGER Employee_History_Update
ON [Employees]
AFTER UPDATE
AS
  INSERT INTO employeehist
  (emp_id,
   LastName,
   FirstName,
     HomePhone)
   SELECT  del.emp_id,
           del.LastName,
           del.FirstName,
           del.HomePhone
   FROM deleted del
GO
```

Using Triggers to Implement Referential Actions

Most of the time, people use the primary and foreign keys of tables to enforce referential integrity. However, you can manage rules about the relationships between tables by using trigger integrity. This is because any statement that causes the trigger to execute and the Transact-SQL statements within the trigger itself are all part of one transaction. In other words, either they all run successfully, or they are all rolled back as if nothing ever happened. If constraints do not provide you with the functionality you need, then triggers are very useful. Although using trigger integrity allows you to leverage complex processing logic using Transact-SQL, cascading referential integrity constraints are generally more efficient.

> Cascading referential integrity constraints are new to SQL Server 2000. For the exam, it is important to remember that the **ON DELETE CASCADE** statement will cause child table records to be deleted when their corresponding parent records are deleted, not the other way around. For example, if you delete from the **Customers** table a record with a **CustomerID** of 99, all records with a **CustomerID** (foreign key) of 99 in the **Orders** table will also be deleted.
>
> If the **ON DELETE NO ACTION** statement were used in this same scenario, the record in the **Customers** table would not be deleted, and an error would be raised because child records exist in the **Orders** table.

How INSTEAD OF Triggers Work

In addition to using triggers for integrity, you can now also use them to replace **INSERT, UPDATE,** and **DELETE** commands. You can do this with **INSTEAD OF** triggers. **INSTEAD OF** triggers override the normal modification action and are executed in place of the **INSERT, UPDATE,** or **DELETE** statement. These triggers are used to validate information before performing the modification and either rolling back the request or providing alternative actions. The other main purpose is to extend modification to views that ordinarily would not allow changes. You can modify multiple base tables or modify views that contain the following types of columns: **timestamp** data type, computed columns, or **IDENTITY** columns.

If a view includes all the columns just mentioned, then the user needs to supply entries for all the columns (even ones for these special types) and will receive an error if they are not included. The **INSTEAD OF** trigger traps the modification and makes the necessary changes on the base table (or tables) rather than on the view.

When you update **text, ntext,** and **image** columns, the contents of the columns are stored in the **inserted** and **deleted** tables. Because these tables are contained in memory, statements that modify many rows with large **text, ntext,** or **image** values take considerable memory.

An **INSTEAD OF** trigger can have logic that builds column data from values sent to it or from a combination of values sent plus lookups from other base tables. Listing 9.2 contains a table that has three columns: **ID, Last Name,** and **First Name.** This table has a view with two columns: **ID** and the full name, where the full name is **First Name** concatenated with a space and then followed by the **Last Name.** The **INSTEAD OF** trigger is applied to this view to update the underlying table.

Listing 9.2 Modifying a table through a view when a column is a combined column.

```
/* Person Table */
CREATE TABLE PersonTable
    (
     ID      int,
     FirstName varchar(20),
     LastName  varchar(30)
    )
GO
/* Person View */
CREATE VIEW FullNameView
AS
SELECT ID, FirstName + ' ' + LastName AS FullName
FROM PersonTable
GO
/* Trigger to insert data using the view. */
CREATE TRIGGER InsteadName on FullNameView
INSTEAD OF INSERT
AS
BEGIN
    INSERT INTO PersonTable
        SELECT ID,
            -- Pull out the first name string.
            SUBSTRING(
                FullName,
                1,
                (CHARINDEX(' ', FullName) - 1)
                ),
            -- Pull out the last name string.
            SUBSTRING(
                FullName,
                (CHARINDEX(' ', FullName) + 1),
                DATALENGTH(CombinedName)
                )
        FROM inserted
END
```

Modifying a Trigger

Once you create a trigger, you can rename it, change its definition, or even delete it.

The **ALTER TRIGGER** statement is identical to the **CREATE TRIGGER** statement except that the word **CREATE** is replaced with **ALTER**. If you want to retain **ENCRYPTION**, you need to specify it again. If an **ALTER TRIGGER** statement changes a first or last trigger, the order value must be reset with the **sp_settriggerorder** stored procedure.

Renaming a Trigger

You rename a trigger by using the **sp_rename** system stored procedure. When you rename a trigger, the name of the trigger in the text of the trigger definition does not change. To change the name of the trigger in the definition, you must modify the trigger directly. The syntax is:

```
sp_rename old_name, new_name
```

Deleting a Trigger

When you delete a trigger, all of the information in the system tables describing the trigger is removed. Dropping the table that has the associated trigger also drops the trigger. To drop a trigger named **tgi_employee**, for example, you would use the following syntax:

```
DROP TRIGGER tgi_employee
```

You can drop one or more triggers at the same time. You must have the proper permission to delete a trigger. Before deleting a trigger, check all dependencies and correct them.

 Triggers for the same modification execute in random order. You can now set the first and last trigger.

Setting the First or Last Trigger

If you have multiple **AFTER** triggers on a table for the same modification, they will execute in random order. You can, however, specify that a particular trigger will execute first and a different one will execute last; the remaining triggers will execute in random order. You can set first and last triggers for each modification. If a trigger is used for more than one modification, you must set its first/last status for each type of modification. You cannot have the same trigger for the same modification be both the first and the last trigger.

The syntax for ordering an **UPDATE** trigger named **tgupd_customers** to run first would be:

```
sp_settriggerorder[@triggername = ] 'tgupd_customers'
    , [@order = ] 'first'
    , [@stmttype = ] 'udpate'
```

You can omit the parameter labels and just include the parameter values as shown in the previous example. The **sp_settriggerorder** stored procedure has the following key arguments:

➤ **triggername**—Is the name of the trigger you are setting.

➤ **value**—Is the word **first, last,** or **none**, indicating the order. **None** places it back in random order.

➤ **statement_type**—Specifies the modification that fires the trigger. The values can be **INSERT, DELETE,** or **UPDATE**.

The exam questions might not be about triggers specifically but might be about the T-SQL code within them. You can use cursors to loop through the deleted and inserted logical tables. For example, **SELECT * FROM DELETED** would provide you with data that was deleted, causing your trigger to execute. Remember that any T-SQL code can call global cursors within the current connection. All cursors are set to global by default. Fast forward cursors are optimized for sequential fetching of records, but they cannot be used with the **FOR UPDATE** clause because they are read-only.

Disabling or Enabling a Trigger

You can disable a trigger on a table without deleting it. You use the **ALTER TABLE** statement. You can then re-enable the disabled trigger with the same **ALTER TABLE** statement. You can disable all triggers on a table or disable one or several triggers. This process is similar to enabling and disabling constraints, as discussed in Chapter 4. The **ALL** keyword disables all triggers on the table, or you can specify one or more triggers by name.

The following syntax will disable the **tgupd_customers** trigger on the **Customers** table:

```
ALTER TABLE Customers DISABLE TRIGGER tgupd_customers
```

Practice Questions

Question 1

You have a **Categories** table and a **Products** table shown in Exhibit 1. When a category is deleted, you want to mark the products associated with the category as discontinued rather than deleting them. How can you accomplish this?

Exhibit 1:

```
CREATE TABLE dbo.Categories (
    CategoryID int IDENTITY (1, 1) NOT NULL ,
    CategoryName nvarchar (15) NOT NULL ,
    Description ntext NULL )
CREATE TABLE dbo.Products (
    ProductID int IDENTITY (1, 1) NOT NULL ,
    ProductName nvarchar (40)  NOT NULL ,
    Discontinued bit NOT NULL )
```

○ a.

```
CREATE TRIGGER Discontinue_Product
 ON Categories AFTER DELETE
AS
    UPDATE Products
    SET Discontinued = 1
    FROM Products AS Prod INNER JOIN
    Deleted AS Del
    ON Prod.CategoryID = Del.CategoryID
```

○ b.

```
CREATE TRIGGER Discontinue_Product
ON Categories AFTER DELETE
AS
    UPDATE Prod
    SET Discontinued = 1
    FROM Products AS Prod INNER JOIN
    Deleted AS Del
    ON Prod.CategoryID = Del.CategoryID
```

(continued)

Question 1 *(continued)*

```
O c.
CREATE TRIGGER Discontinue_Product
 ON Products AFTER DELETE
AS
    UPDATE Prod
    SET Discontinued = 1
    FROM Products AS Prod INNER JOIN
    Deleted AS Del
    ON Prod.CategoryID = Del.CategoryID


O d.
CREATE TRIGGER Discontinue_Product
 ON Categories INSTEAD OF DELETE
AS
    UPDATE Prod
    SET Discontinued = 1
    FROM Products AS Prod INNER JOIN
    Deleted AS Del
    ON Prod.CategoryID = Del.CategoryID
```

Answer b is correct. You put the trigger on the **Categories** table and use the **AFTER DELETE** option. Answer a is incorrect because, if you have a table alias (**Prod**), you must use it in the **UPDATE** statement; you cannot use the table name (**Products**). Answer c is incorrect because you do not put the trigger on the **Products** table; you put the trigger where the **DELETE** is going to occur, which is the **Categories** table. Answer d is incorrect because an **INSTEAD OF** trigger would fire instead of deleting the record in the **Categories** table.

Question 2

You have a **Products** table and an **OrderDetails** table, shown in Exhibit 1. If an order has a history, then rather than deleting it, you want to set its **Discontinued** column. If it has no history, then you want to delete it. Each answer supplies a complete solution. [Select all correct answers]

Exhibit 1:

```
CREATE TABLE dbo.Products (
    ProductID int IDENTITY (1, 1) NOT NULL ,
    ProductName nvarchar (40)  NOT NULL ,
    Discontinued bit NOT NULL )
CREATE TABLE dbo.OrderDetails (
    OrderID int NOT NULL ,
    ProductID int NOT NULL ,
    UnitPrice money NOT NULL)
```

❏ a.

```
CREATE TRIGGER Product_Delete
 ON Product INSTEAD OF DELETE
AS
 IF (Select Count (*)
    FROM OrderDetails INNER JOIN deleted
    ON OrderDetails.ProductID =
    deleted.ProductID
    ) > 0
```

❏ b.

```
CREATE TRIGGER Product_Delete
 ON Product FOR DELETE
AS
 IF (Select Count (*)
    FROM OrderDetails INNER JOIN deleted
    ON OrderDetails.ProductID =
    deleted.ProductID
    ) > 0
```

(continued)

Question 2 *(continued)*

```
❑ c.
BEGIN
    UPDATE Products
    SET Discontinued = 1
    FROM Products INNER JOIN deleted
    ON Products.ProductID = deleted.ProductID
END
ELSE


❑ d.
BEGIN
    UPDATE Products
    SET Discontinued = 1
    FROM Products INNER JOIN deleted
    ON Products.ProductID = deleted.ProductID
END


❑ e.
BEGIN
    DELETE Products
    FROM Products INNER JOIN deleted
    ON Products.ProductID = deleted.ProductID
END


❑ f.
BEGIN
    DELETE Products
    FROM Products INNER JOIN deleted
    ON Products.ProductID = deleted.ProductID
END
ELSE
```

Answers a, c, and e are correct. You would use an **INSTEAD OF** trigger because you want a different action than that provided by the **DELETE** statement. You test for whether there are orders in the **OrderDetails** table; if there are, you update; otherwise, you delete. Answer b is incorrect because it uses a **FOR** trigger. Answers d and f are incorrect because they would do the opposite of what you want. The **ELSE** statement is in the wrong place.

Question 3

When an order is placed, you want to update the quantity on hand. The **Products** and **OrderDetails** tables are listed in Exhibit 1. Select and place the code snippets to accomplish this task.

Exhibit 1:

```
CREATE TABLE dbo.Products (
    ProductID int IDENTITY (1, 1) NOT NULL ,
    ProductName nvarchar (40)  NOT NULL ,
    QuantityOnHand int NOT NULL )
CREATE TABLE dbo.OrderDetails (
    OrderID int NOT NULL ,
    ProductID int NOT NULL ,
    Quantity int NOT NULL,
    UnitPrice money NOT NULL)
```

Select and Place:

```
AS
CREATE TRIGGER Stock_Insert
FOR INSERT
FOR UPDATE
FROM Products INNER JOIN Inserted
ON OrderDetails
ON Products
ON Products.ProductID = Inserted.ProductID
SET
QuantityOnHand = (Products.QuantityOnHand -
Inserted.Quantity)
UPDATE Products
```

The correct answer is

```
CREATE TRIGGER Stock_Insert
ON OrderDetails
FOR INSERT
AS
UPDATE Products
SET
QuantityOnHand = (Products.QuantityOnHand -
Inserted.Quantity)
FROM Products INNER JOIN Inserted
ON Products.ProductID = Inserted.ProductID
```

On the **OrderDetails** table, you define a **FOR INSERT** trigger that updates the **Products** table and decrements the **QuantityOnHand** by the **Quantity** ordered in the **OrderDetails** table. This quantity is stored in the **inserted** table created by SQL Server when the **INSERT** statement is executed.

Question 4

You have three **AFTER** triggers specified for **INSERT**. The triggers are called **Trigger1**, **Trigger2**, and **Trigger3**. You want to ensure that **Trigger1** fires first and **Trigger2** next and **Trigger3** last. What do you need to do? [Choose two answers. Both are required for a complete response]

❑ a. **sp_settriggerorder 'MyTrigger1', 'first', 'INSERT'**

❑ b. **sp_settriggerorder 'MyTrigger2', 'second', 'INSERT'**

❑ c. **sp_settriggerorder 'MyTrigger3', 'last', 'INSERT'**

❑ d. **sp_settriggerorder 'MyTrigger3', 'third', 'INSERT'**

Answers a and c are correct. The only two options for setting the trigger order is specify the first and last triggers; all other triggers fire in random order. Answers b and d are incorrect because there is no option named "second" or "third."

Question 5

When an **AFTER UPDATE** trigger is firing, what are the contents of the special tables created by the system?

○ a. The deleted table contains the old records.

○ b. The inserted table contains the updated records.

○ c. The updated table contains the updated records.

○ d. Both a and b.

○ e. None of the above.

Answer d is correct. For an **UPDATE** trigger, the old image of the row is copied to the **deleted** table, and the new image of the row is copied to the inserted table. Answer c is incorrect because there is no such table as the "updated" table. Answer a or b alone is incorrect because you get both tables. Answer e is incorrect because a and b together are correct.

Question 6

You are a DBA in charge of the **Library** database. You want to ensure that if a person has overdue fines, such fines cannot be deleted from the system. You have a **Persons** table and a **Fines** table shown in Exhibit 1. In Exhibit 2 is a partially completed trigger. What code best completes your task?

Exhibit 1:

```
CREATE TABLE dbo.Persons (
    PersonID int IDENTITY (1, 1) NOT NULL ,
    LastName nvarchar (40)  NOT NULL ,
    FirstName nvarchar (40)  NOT NULL)
CREATE TABLE dbo.Fines (
    FineID int NOT NULL ,
    PersonID int NOT NULL ,
    Quantity int NOT NULL)
```

(continued)

Question 6 (continued)

```
Exhibit 2:
CREATE TRIGGER Person_Delete
 ON Person FOR DELETE
AS
 IF (Select Count (*)
    FROM Fines INNER JOIN deleted
    ON Fines.PersonID = deleted.PersonID
    ) > 0
```

○ a.
```
BEGIN
   RAISERROR('Person has outstanding
   fines.', 16, 1)
   ROLLBACK TRANSACTION
END
   COMMIT TRANSACTION
```

○ b.
```
BEGIN
   RAISERROR('Person has outstanding
   fines.', 16, 1)
END
```

○ c.
```
BEGIN
   ROLLBACK TRANSACTION
END
```

○ d.
```
BEGIN
   RAISERROR('Person has outstanding
   fines.', 16, 1)
   ROLLBACK TRANSACTION
END
```

Answer d is correct. You need to raise an error to the calling program to tell it that the transaction failed and indicate why; then you roll back the transaction. Answer a is incorrect because the trigger will continue falling through the code and will commit the transaction. Answer b is incorrect because, although you notify the calling program, you never issue the rollback, so the operation will be committed. Answer c is incorrect because you do the rollback, but you never notify the calling program that there was an error.

Question 7

You are the DBA of your company. You want to allow users the ability to update all items in the **Employees** table except for the **EmployeeID**. The **Employees** table is shown in Exhibit 1. Select and place the code snippets in the correct order.

Exhibit 1:
```
CREATE TABLE dbo.Employees (
    EmployeeID int NOT NULL ,
    LastName nvarchar (40)  NOT NULL ,
    FirstName nvarchar (40)  NOT NULL)
```

Select and Place:
```
AFTER UPDATE
AS
BEGIN
BEGIN
CREATE TRIGGER Update_Employee
ELSE
END
    FirstName = inserted.FirstName
FROM Employees INNER JOIN inserted
IF UPDATE(EmployeeID)
ON EMPLOYEES
ON Employees.EmployeeID = inserted.EmployeeID
RAISERROR ('You cannot update
   the Employee ID', 16, 1)
ROLLBACK TRANSACTION
SET LastName = inserted.LastName,
UPDATE Employees
```

The correct answer is:

```
CREATE TRIGGER Update_Employee
ON EMPLOYEES
AFTER UPDATE
AS
IF UPDATE(EmployeeID)
BEGIN
RAISERROR ('You cannot update the
   Employee ID', 16, 1)
ROLLBACK TRANSACTION
END
```

You create an **AFTER UPDATE** trigger on the **Employees** table with the **IF UPDATE** clause. If the **UPDATE** statement includes the **EmployeeID** column, then the operation is rolled back. Otherwise, it is completed. You do not have to do the update, it is already done; you just have to roll it back if there are errors.

Question 8

You are the DBA of your company. You have a table that contains an **IDENTITY** property and a computed column. You create a view that contains all the columns in the table. You want to make this view updateable. What can you do? The table and view are shown in Exhibit 1.

Exhibit 1:

```
CREATE TABLE CardTable
  (PrimaryKey      int IDENTITY(1,1),
   CardType            varchar(10) NOT NULL,
   CardNumber          varchar(10) NOT NULL,
   TypeNumber AS (CardType + CardNumber)
  )
GO
CREATE VIEW CardView
AS SELECT PrimaryKey, CardType, CardNumber,
  TypeNumber
FROM CardTable
GO
```

○ a.
```
CREATE TRIGGER Insert_Trigger
ON CardView
INSTEAD OF INSERT
AS
BEGIN
  INSERT INTO CardTable
      SELECT PrimaryKey, CardType, CardNumber,
      TypeNumber
      FROM inserted
END
```

(continued)

Question 8 *(continued)*

```
○ b.
CREATE TRIGGER Insert_Trigger
ON CardView
INSTEAD OF INSERT
AS
BEGIN
  INSERT INTO CardTable
       SELECT CardType, CardNumber
       FROM inserted
END


○ c.
CREATE TRIGGER Insert_Trigger
ON CardView
INSTEAD OF INSERT
AS
BEGIN
  INSERT INTO CardTable
       SELECT PrimaryKey, CardType,
       CardNumber
       FROM inserted
END


○ d.
CREATE TRIGGER Insert_Trigger
ON CardView
INSTEAD OF INSERT
AS
BEGIN
  INSERT INTO CardTable
       SELECT CardType, CardNumber,
       TypeNumber
       FROM inserted
END
```

Answer b is correct. You must supply all the columns in the **INSERT** statement on the view, but you cannot supply the **PrimaryKey** and **TypeNumber** columns for the underlying table. You use an **INSTEAD OF** trigger that ignores these two columns and does the **INSERT** with just the other two columns. Answer a is incorrect because it includes all the columns, because **PrimaryKey** has an **IDEN-TITY** property and cannot be inserted, and because **TypeNumber** is a computed column and likewise cannot be inserted. Answers c and d each have one or the other column that cannot be inserted.

Need to Know More?

 Iseminger, David. *SQL Server 2000 Reference Library*. Redmond, WA: Microsoft Press, 2000. ISBN 0-7356-1280-3. A selected collection of SQL Server 2000 Books Online; there are six volumes focused on key areas. Volume 2 contains information on creating objects such as triggers. Volume 6 contains information on stored procedures, which you may find interesting because triggers are special stored procedures.

 MS SQL Server Books Online has sections on triggers. This collection can be installed from the SQL Server CD or accessed online at **http://msdn.microsoft.com/library/default.asp?URL=/library/psdk/sql/portal_7ap1.htm**.

 Search the TechNet CD or its online version through **www.microsoft.com/technet**. Keywords to search on would be "triggers", "replication", and "constraints".

 www.microsoft.com/sql/ and **http://msdn.microsoft.com/sqlserver/default.asp** are good places to find up-to-date information about SQL Server.

 www.sqlmag.com—*SQL Magazine*—both the hard copy and the Web site—has a large amount of information on SQL Server.

User-Defined Functions

Terms you'll need to understand:

✓ Functions

✓ User-defined function (UDF)

✓ Scalar-valued UDF

✓ Table-valued UDF

✓ Inline table-valued UDF

✓ Multistatement table-valued UDF

✓ System scalar-valued UDF

✓ System table-valued UDF

Techniques you'll need to master:

✓ Understanding functions

✓ Defining UDFs

✓ Invoking scalar-valued UDFs

✓ Invoking table-valued UDFs

✓ Invoking system scalar-valued UDFs

✓ Invoking system table-valued UDFs

In Chapter 8, you saw that SQL Server 2000 has a set of statements—called *stored procedures*—that you can design, create, modify, and execute. You also saw how useful stored procedures can be when you want your application programs to have procedure execution flexibility decision points that do not have to be determined until runtime. We also discussed how you can nest stored procedures and configure them to accept input parameters, return output parameters, or simply return status information about your data.

Much like stored procedures, user-defined functions (UDFs) can also consist of a set of precompiled, named, and saved statements, and they can perform many of the same features you have already learned when working with stored procedures. Even with the limits placed upon the use of user-defined functions, other powerful enhancements are available when you can design your own functions.

Functions

Similar to the general use of the programming term "function," Transact-SQL functions are precompiled sets of computer programming steps that can be repeatedly invoked. The most compelling reason for using functions stems from the fact that the logical flow of the steps has to be developed and tested only once, but they can be called into operation repeatedly without further design consideration.

Using UDFs will affect the performance of queries. The extent of the performance impact depends upon how and where you use a user-defined function. This is also true of built-in functions. However, UDFs have the potential for more dramatic performance hits than built-in functions. You should exercise caution when implementing functions in your queries and perform benchmarking tests to ensure that the benefits of using your functions exceed the performance costs of using them.

Such Transact-SQL functions can consist of those system functions that are built in and rigidly invoked, or they can be the more flexible, reusable coded steps that administrators can create for later use and store in the form of subroutines that specifically fit an organization's needs. This latter type of function is called a *user-defined function*.

User-Defined Functions

New with this version of SQL Server, UDFs give you the programming-like ability to group your own sets of frequently used steps into reusable subroutines that you can recall at will, just like you do when inserting system-defined functions in your database design. Microsoft even includes sample UDFs (much like the sample databases installed with SQL Server 2000), which you can install during a custom installation. Selecting Code Samples installs them to the following default location:

C:\Program Files\Microsoft SQL Server\80\Tools\Devtools\Samples\Misc\Udf

In addition, like their programming counterparts, the functions, UDFs are important because the routines they perform, when eventually called into use, can represent predetermined logic with multiple applications, rules that are invoked in varied locations, or any set of complex coded statements that can be used repeatedly wherever necessary. When a UDF is called for any of these reasons, it returns a single value as its result after performing the required logic and incorporating any input parameters you specify.

There are three types of UDFs. The first two, scalar-valued and table-valued, act as described previously; they allow you to group your own programming steps into subroutines. Later, when you need those programming steps repeated, you simply call the UDF. It then performs those same predetermined steps and reliably returns a value for your continued use elsewhere in your sequential data manipulation. Scalar-valued UDFs return any valid SQL Server 2000 scalar data type. Table-valued UDFs go one step further and can have an entire table as their single returned value.

Scalar-valued user-defined functions can be used as check constraints for columns in table definitions. As long as an argument to the function is a constant or built-in function or an argument is the column being checked, the function may be used to validate the column's value. These UDF check constraints make it possible to use logic that is more complex for determining acceptable column values than what Boolean expressions or **LIKE** patterns would allow. You can also use scalar-valued functions to compute column values in table definitions. Arguments to computed column functions must be table columns, constants, or built-in functions.

Table-valued functions (or Rowset functions that return tables) can be used as alternatives to read-only views. Since views are limited to a single select statement, user-defined functions can provide greater functionality than a view. Powerful logic can be used when determining the records returned, which is not possible within a view. Another advantage of table-valued functions over views is that views cannot accept parameters—a separate view must be created if the **WHERE** clause must change for different search criteria. You can also use rowset functions as alternatives to temporary tables. For example, if you wished to find authors in the **Pubs** database who sold no books in a particular state, you could create a couple of functions that would generate the desired resultset.

The third type of UDF is actually a refinement of the scalar-valued or the table-valued UDF in that it is defined by the system. This type, called *system scalar-valued* UDFs or *system table-valued* UDFs, can return either a scalar data item or a table, depending on which of these two types is used. Each acts like a UDF, however, and returns either a scalar object or a table value when invoked at runtime.

Following is the syntax for creating UDFs:

```
CREATE FUNCTION [owner_name.] function_name
  ( [ @parameter_name <scalar data type>
  [ = default value ] [,....n] ] )
RETURNS { scalar type | TABLE }
  [WITH {ENCRYPTION | SCHEMABINDING | } ]
AS
BEGIN
  [ function statements ]
  {RETURN <type as defined
    in RETURNS clause> | RETURN
    ( SELECT statement ) }
END
```

As we have already stated, UDFs are used much like stored procedures in that predetermined coded steps are simply called into use wherever needed. In addition, when you're using either UDFs or stored procedures, parameters can be inserted and values are returned as a result. However, there are some noteworthy differences between the two.

Parameters used within stored procedures let you pass values as input and receive others passed back to you as output. However, the outward flowing parameter cannot be used as data elsewhere in your logic. Rather, it simply indicates either the success or the failure of the called procedure.

UDFs, on the other hand, might only allow parameters to pass inward, but the output they produce (although not actually passed as parameters) can be much more useful than merely indicating success or failure. Unlike a stored procedure, a UDF must have a **RETURN** statement specified, but the value it produces after it operates can actually be used as data in subsequent operational steps.

These features may make UDFs much more attractive in your design than stored procedures. Their attractiveness depends on your programming needs and on what you intend to do with the output returned after invoking necessary functions. Furthermore, as you will see in the following sections, the values that UDFs return can be scalar values or even complete tables, and these returns are determined by your ensuing data manipulation needs.

Scalar-Valued UDFs

The first type of UDF returns a scalar value as the result after it performs its coded logic. Wherever your Transact-SQL statements allow you to insert values, you can substitute scalar-valued UDFs. Any data-type value is allowable except for tables, cursors, binary large objects, and timestamps (commonly called rowversions). The returned value can be the derived value that is the result of the function's operation, or it can include additional computations on that resulting derived value.

> User-defined functions that return scalar values can be substituted in queries wherever a column name can be used.

Although scalar-valued UDFs do not produce output parameters, you can specify up to 1,024 input parameters in the **CREATE FUNCTION** statement when you're building the function. In addition, unlike its optional use in stored procedures, the dbo must be specified when you invoke scalar-valued UDFs.

The following is the syntax for using the **SELECT** statement to invoke a scalar-valued UDF:

```
SELECT dbo.function_name ( @parameter_name )
```

The following is the syntax for using the **EXECUTE** keyword to invoke a scalar-valued UDF:

```
EXECUTE @procedure_name = dbo.function_name @parameter_name
```

> Remember that you must use a two-part name when calling scalar-valued UDFs.

Scalar-valued UDFs return data of the type specified in the **CREATE FUNC-TION** statement. Any valid scalar type is allowed. User-defined data types and non-scalar types (such as **TABLE**) are not allowed. The type returned as a result of the **RETURNS** clause of the **CREATE FUNCTION** statement can include any valid data type except the following:

➤ **text**

➤ **ntext**

➤ **image**

➤ **timestamp**

➤ **cursor**

Table-Valued UDFs

Another type of UDF is one that, after running the programmed steps, returns a table as its resulting value. This type is referred to as a table-valued UDF. You create it by using the **TABLE** keyword in the **CREATE FUNCTION** statement. The resulting UDF can be either an *inline* or a *multistatement* table-valued UDF, depending on how it will later be used when you're working with your data.

 User-defined functions that return table values can be substituted for only the **FROM** portion of a query.

When you're building table-valued UDFs, as with scalar-valued UDFs, you can specify up to 1,024 input parameters in the **CREATE FUNCTION** statement. Unlike its required use in scalar-valued UDFs, the **dbo** designation is optional when you're invoking table-valued UDFs.

 You should be aware that table-valued UDFs have the **text in row** option automatically set to an unchangeable 256 characters per row for all returned tables.

Unlike the usual table manipulations allowed in SQL Server 2000, tables returned after you invoke table-valued UDFs do not allow all data operations on the information contained in the table's columns. For instance, you cannot manipulate any **text** or **ntext** columns (returned by the UDF) with the **UPDATETEXT, WRITETEXT,** or **READTEXT** statements.

Furthermore, you cannot update existing tables by invoking table-valued UDFs, and they cannot be used to create additional database objects. Effectively, you should not expect these UDFs (as with any function) to change anything in your current database.

However, you can still perform some of the data manipulations that are allowable on other tables. These include using the **JOIN** statement, in which you combine tables, as well as applying the **WHERE** condition clause.

Table-valued UDFs also give you a powerful alternative to using views. Table-valued UDFs allow multiple statements that contain your predetermined coded steps, whereas views allow only one **SELECT** statement when they are used to obtain information.

Inline Table-Valued UDFs

If, when you create your UDF, you use the **TABLE** designation in the **RETURNS** clause of the **CREATE FUNCTION** statement, but you define no variables, then an inline table-valued UDF will result.

Multistatement Table-Valued UDFs

If, when you create your UDF, you use the **TABLE** designation in the **RETURNS** clause of the **CREATE FUNCTION** statement, and you furnish variable table names, then a multistatement table-valued UDF will result.

System Scalar-Valued or Table-Valued UDFs

SQL Server 2000 also provides system built-in functions that simply act as UDFs because they wait until runtime before being invoked and they can be called from any database.

The following are examples of system UDFs:

➤ ::fn_helpcollations

➤ ::fn_servershareddrives

➤ ::fn_trace_geteventinfo

➤ ::fn_trace_getfileterinfo

➤ ::fn_trace_getinfo

➤ ::fn_trace_gettable

➤ ::fn_listextendedproperty

Remember the following about system UDFs:

➤ The distinguishing features of a table-valued UDF name are its use of the double leading colon (::) and its one-part name without either the database name or the dbo specified.

➤ The name of a scalar-valued UDF is simply a one-part name without the double leading colon; neither the database name nor the dbo can be specified.

System Functions

SQL Server 2000 also allows you to create your own system functions. Major benefits of creating such functions are that they can be invoked in any database without further qualification, and they operate as though they were created and invoked in the current database. Following are the rules for creating a system function:

➤ Create it in the **master** database.

➤ Do *not* use the double colon (::) designator.

➤ Precede the function name with the identifier **fn_**.

➤ Use the **changeobjectowner** stored procedure to set the function's owner to **system_function_schema**.

Some SQL Server 2000 built-in functions return different data each time they are called. Examples include **GETDATE**, **NEWID**, and **RAND**. These built-in functions are not allowed in UDFs.

Getting Information About Your UDFs

Should you need information about your UDFs, you have various methods of getting specific details. You can use either catalog objects or schema views to gather your needed information. You can also use the **OBJECTPROPERTY** function to get additional information.

Catalog Object Utilities

The first method for retrieving information involves using stored procedures as utilities to catalog objects. The following two stored procedures can furnish you with many of the specifics you need concerning your UDFs (like your functions' definitions):

➤ **sp_helptext**

➤ **sp_help**

Schema Views

The next method for retrieving information about your UDFs involves using schema views. Three information schema views are typically used for obtaining the same type of information for UDFs and stored procedures. These views are:

➤ ROUTINES

➤ ROUTINE_COLUMNS

➤ PARAMETERS

Much of the information you seek is available using either the stored procedures or the schema views just mentioned. However, information about built-in functions and many system table-valued functions is hidden, available only with the **ROUTINES** view, and available only when you're viewing those functions in the **master** database. Even then, many functions still provide only portions of their information set because the majority of their descriptions are hidden in code. Such functions are available, but their access is beyond the scope of this book.

 You should be aware that the only way you can get information about system table-valued UDF definitions is to use the **ROUTINES** view on the **master** database.

The OBJECTPROPERTY Function

The final method we'll discuss for retrieving information involves using the OBJECTPROPERTY function. The following OBJECTPROPERTY arguments are some of the ones that can furnish you with additional pieces of information about your UDFs:

➤ IsScalarFunction

➤ IsInlineFunction

➤ IsTableFunction

When you use the OBJECTPROPERTY function and specify any of the allowable arguments, such as those just listed, a single value will be returned. That value (and its interpretation) will be any one of the following:

➤ 0, which translates to **FALSE** and indicates that the object is *not* that type

➤ 1, which translates to **TRUE** and indicates that the object is that type

➤ NULL, which indicates that the information you entered contained an error

Practice Questions

Question 1

Which of the following is not a compelling reason for using functions?

○ a. Using functions can minimize testing requirements.

○ b. Functions facilitate use of tailored reusable coded programming steps.

○ c. Functions offer all the features of stored procedures plus the benefit of receiving usable data as output.

○ d. Using functions helps minimize database design considerations.

Answer c is correct. Functions do not offer all the features of stored procedures, and only UDFs provide usable data as output. Answer a is incorrect because functions can help minimize testing requirements; you develop and test code only one time, but you can use it repeatedly. Likewise, answer d is incorrect because functions do help minimize database design considerations; you develop the code only once but reuse it under different circumstances. Answer b is incorrect because functions do allow the use of tailored reusable coded programming steps.

Question 2

Which of the following types of UDFs requires the dbo to be specified?

○ a. Scalar-valued UDFs

○ b. Table-valued UDFs

○ c. Inline table-valued UDFs

○ d. Multistatement table-valued UDFs

○ e. System scalar-valued UDFs

○ f. System table-valued UDFs

○ g. System functions (user specified)

Answer a is correct. You must specify the dbo when creating or invoking scalar-valued UDFs. Answers b, c, d, e, and f are all incorrect because they all are table-valued UDFs, so specifying the dbo is optional. Answer g is incorrect because you are not allowed to specify the dbo when creating a system function.

Question 3

> Which of the following represents the number of inputs that you can specify when creating UDFs by using the **CREATE FUNCTION** statement?
>
> ○ a. 256
>
> ○ b. Unlimited
>
> ○ c. Any number between −256 and +1,024
>
> ○ d. 1,024

Answer d is correct. You can specify up to 1,024 input parameters in the **CREATE FUNCTION** statement when building UDFs. Answer a represents the number of characters automatically set in the **text in row** option for all tables returned by table-valued UDFs. Answer b is incorrect because there is a limit of 1,024. Answer c is incorrect because it is just a made-up range.

Question 4

Rearrange the following code snippets in the correct order to show the proper syntax for creating UDFs. Not all items need to be used.

```
FUNCTION
   ( [ @parameter_name <scalar data type>
FROM
N'SQL Server'
BEGIN
function_name
RETURNS { scalar type | TABLE }
CREATE FUNCTION [owner_name.] function_name
     in RETURNS clause> | RETURN
'SELECT name, id FROM function_name)
   [WITH {ENCRYPTION | SCHEMABINDING | } ]
END
   {RETURN <type as defined
     ( SELECT statement ) }
   [ = default value ] [,...n] ] )
sp_addlinkedserver
   [ function statements ]
CREATE
AS
GO
```

The correct answer is:

```
CREATE FUNCTION [owner_name.] function_name
   ( [ @parameter_name <scalar data type>
   [ = default value ] [,...n] ] )
RETURNS { scalar type | TABLE }
   [WITH {ENCRYPTION | SCHEMABINDING | } ]
AS
BEGIN
```

```
    [ function statements ]
    {RETURN <type as defined
      in RETURNS clause> | RETURN
      ( SELECT statement ) }
END
```

Remember that the **RETURNS** clause is required, and you must use the **END** statement.

Question 5

Which of the following represents the proper syntax for using the **EXECUTE** keyword to invoke a scalar-valued UDF?

○ a.
```
EXECUTE @procedure_name = dbo.function_name
@parameter_name
```

○ b.
```
EXECUTE @procedure_name = dbo.function_name
( @parameter_name )
```

○ c.
```
EXECUTE @procedure_name = function_name
@parameter_name
```

○ d.
```
EXECUTE @procedure_name = function_name
( @parameter_name )
```

Answer a is correct. It shows the proper syntax. Answer b improperly adds parentheses around the parameter. Answer c improperly omits the dbo. Answer d has the incorrect answers supplied in both b and c.

Question 6

Which of the following represents the proper syntax for using the **SELECT** keyword to invoke a scalar-valued UDF?

○ a.

```
SELECT function_name @parameter_name
```

○ b.

```
SELECT function_name ( @parameter_name )
```

○ c.

```
SELECT dbo.function_name @parameter_name
```

○ d.

```
SELECT dbo.function_name ( @parameter_name )
```

Answer d is correct. It shows the proper syntax. Answer b improperly omits the dbo. Answer c improperly omits parentheses around the parameter. Answer a has the incorrect answers supplied in both b and c.

Question 7

Which of the following represent properly formatted system UDFs? [Check all correct answers]

❏ a. **::fn_servershareddrives**

❏ b. **::fn_trace_gettable**

❏ c. **:fn_trace_getfileterinfo**

❏ d. **::fn_trace_eventinfo**

Answers a and b are correct. Both a and b use the proper format and include the correct UDF description. Answer c is incorrect; it does not use the double colon, so it is improperly formatted. Answer d is incorrect because it is properly formatted but does not use a correct system UDF.

Question 8

Which of the following data manipulation operations can you perform upon **text** or **ntext** columns of data returned as a result of calling a table-valued UDF? [Check all correct answers]

❑ a. **UPDATETEXT**

❑ b. **READTEXT**

❑ c. **WHERE**

❑ d. **WRITETEXT**

❑ e. **JOIN**

Answers c and e are correct. The **JOIN** statement and the **WHERE** clause are allowable statements and can thus be performed in this instance. Answers a, b, and d are all incorrect because none of these statements are allowed on returned table-valued UDF columns.

Question 9

If the **CREATE FUNCTION** statement used to create your UDF has multiple variables named in the **RETURNS** clause, which of the following UDF types probably is not being described?

○ a. Scalar-valued UDFs

○ b. Table-valued UDFs

○ c. Inline table-valued UDFs

○ d. Multistatement table-valued UDFs

○ e. System scalar-valued UDFs

○ f. System table-valued UDFs

Answer c is correct. Of the choices, only the inline table-valued UDF definitely does not have multiple variables. Answers a, b, d, e, and f are all incorrect because none of these statements clearly eliminates the possibility of using multiple variables in the **RETURNS** clause.

Question 10

Put the following items in the correct prioritized order of positive importance (most required) relative to creating your own system functions:

- The identifier **fn_**
- **System_function_schema**
- The double colon (::) designator
- The **master** database
- **GETDATE**, **NEWID**, and **RAND**
- The **changeobjectowner** stored procedure

The correct answer is:

- The **master** database
- The identifier **fn_**
- The **changeobjectowner** stored procedure
- **System_function_schema**
- The double colon (::) designator
- **GETDATE, NEWID,** and **RAND**

When creating your own system functions, remember:

- Create them in the **master** database—this is most important item.

- Precede the function name with the identifier **fn_**—this is the second most important item.

- Use the **changeobjectowner** stored procedure—this is third most important item.

- Set the function's owner to **system_function_schema**—this is the fourth most important item.

- Do not use the double colon (::) designator—this is the next to the least important item.

- The **GETDATE, NEWID,** and **RAND** functions return different data each time they are used and are not used in UDFs—this is, therefore, the least important item.

Need to Know More?

 Iseminger, David. *SQL Server 2000 Reference Library*. Redmond, WA: Microsoft Press, 2000. ISBN 0-7356-1280-3. A selected collection of SQL Server 2000 Books Online; there are six volumes focused on key areas. Volume 2 contains information on creating objects such as stored procedures and UDFs. Volume 6 contains information on invoking objects such as stored procedures and UDFs.

 MS SQL Server Books Online has sections on stored procedures. This book set can be installed from the SQL Server CD or accessed online through **http://msdn.microsoft.com/library/default.asp**.

 Search the TechNet CD or its online version through **www.microsoft.com/ technet**. Keywords to search on are "stored procedures", "user-defined function", and "create function".

 www.microsoft.com/sql/ and **http://msdn.microsoft.com/sqlserver/ default.asp** are good places to find up-to-date information about SQL Server.

 www.sqlmag.com—*SQL Magazine*—both the hard copy and the Web site—has a large amount of information on SQL Server.

Transactions, Cursors, and Locks

Terms you'll need to understand:

✓ Transaction

✓ Deadlock

✓ Cursor

✓ System stored procedure

✓ SQL Profiler

Techniques you'll need to master:

✓ Using cursors to loop through result sets

✓ Avoiding deadlocks

✓ Setting isolation levels for transactions

Transactions, cursors, and locks are database concepts that you will need to understand before you attempt to take the exam. In this chapter, we will look at how transactions are used in database applications, how cursors assist in fetching records from a result set, and how locks can be both useful and detrimental. In addition, we'll discuss various types of locking and transaction isolation levels.

Transactions

A *transaction* is a set of procedures that are executed as a single logical unit of work. A transaction in a database is much like a transaction in a bank. Imagine that you want to deposit a $100 check. This involves two main procedures:

1. The amount is withdrawn from the payer's account.

2. The amount is deposited into your account.

Although this process can take a long time to complete, if any portion of the operation fails, the entire bank transaction is voided, like a bounced check. Now, imagine that you have a database operation that requires a deduction from one customer's credit account, and the amount deducted will be placed in another customer's account. What would happen if you deducted the amount from the first customer's account and then the power to your database server was suddenly shut off? The first customer would have his credit amount deducted, but the second customer would not be given any credit. Therefore, you should wrap both of these operations into a single unit of work: a transaction.

Using Transactions in SQL Server

Although SQL Server can automatically implement transactions, programmers are responsible for initializing and terminating transactions in applications that implement the logical consistency of data. Programmers do this by defining the order of data manipulations that ensures the data's consistent state (according to business rules). These modifications can be wrapped into a transaction, and SQL Server will enforce the physical integrity of the operations.

SQL Server has the following three transaction types:

➤ *Autocommit* transactions, in which every statement runs in its own transaction

➤ *Explicit* transactions, which are started with **BEGIN TRANSACTION** statements and then completed with **COMMIT** or **ROLLBACK** statements

➤ *Implicit* transactions, which originate when a previous transaction is completed and which are explicitly ended with **COMMIT** or **ROLLBACK** statements

Remember, SQL Server 2000 autocommits transactions by default. This means that each individual SQL statement is a separate transaction that is committed automatically upon completion.

Transactions consist of four properties, commonly referred to as the ACID properties. ACID is an acronym for: atomicity, consistency, isolation, and durability.

Atomicity

A transaction is a unit of work which consists of a series of operations with a beginning and an end in an application. A transaction executes exactly once and is therefore considered atomic. This means that either all the work is done, or none of it is.

Actions connected to a transaction share a mutual function and are mutually supporting. This means that performing only part of the transaction's operations would defeat the purpose of the entire transaction. By being atomic, the transaction eliminates any chance of processing only a subset of the intended complete operation. This is an important concept and bears some elaboration. A locking mechanism can use two kinds of locks: local locks, which ensure the atomicity of transaction steps, and global locks, which guarantee that the interleaving between transactions does not violate semantic consistency. In effect, two different transactions could interfere with each other because the intent for each transaction is contrary to the other.

Consistency

You can think of a transaction as a unit of integrity because it preserves data consistency regardless of how the data's state changes during the operation. In other words, the transaction will leave all data involved in the transaction in a consistent state because data bound by a transaction will be semantically preserved.

Some of the responsibility for maintaining consistency falls to the SQL Server application developer, who must ensure that integrity constraints are enforced by the application. To illustrate this point by using our banking example, if you're developing a money-transfer application, you can't be held accountable when your code is correct but someone just makes a mistake using it. For example, it is the bank teller's responsibility to avoid misplacing decimal points during the transfer, and your application does not have to account for all possible mistakes that can be made.

Isolation

Concurrent transactions behave as if each one is the only one executing in the database. This means that they are isolated from each other. Any changes that are made during one transaction (which is running simultaneously with others) are completely separate from any other changes made elsewhere. Hence, every transaction appears to be the only one manipulating data in the database, even if other transactions are actually running at the same time. Furthermore, one transaction will not see any intermediate changes made by any other transactions. Later in this chapter, we will discuss the various isolation levels you can utilize in SQL Server for better throughput and consistency.

Durability

A transaction is also a unit of recovery because when a transaction is committed, SQL Server guarantees that its changes will be preserved. If the power to your computer is shut off in the middle of an operation, the operation will be rolled back. However, if the computer is shut down immediately after the commit, the operations performed in the transaction will be implemented. By utilizing transaction logging, SQL Server allows the system's restart procedure to complete unfinished operations, making the transaction durable.

 2PC is an abbreviation used to describe a synchronous transaction. 2PC means "two-phase commit."

The Transaction Log

SQL Server writes to a transaction log sequentially to ensure transaction durability. In the event of a power or system failure, the transaction logs can be used upon restart to automatically undo uncommitted data modifications made since the transaction started.

You can back up and restore data by using the transaction log in addition to performing full database backups and differential backups. Each transaction log is associated with a database, and the log fills up until it is backed up or truncated. If the transaction log expands too frequently or takes a long time to expand, performance can be affected. Set your transaction log to autogrow with the goal of sizing it so it should not need to grow. You should base the optimal size on the amount of logged activity in the database and the amount of time between backups.

For the active transaction log to be backed up, the log file and the primary data file must be accessible.

Transaction Isolation Levels

Transaction isolation levels in SQL Server control the degree to which transactions are isolated from each other.

One of the main functionalities of a database management system (DBMS) is to keep users from reading and writing to inconsistent data in the database. This inconsistency is due to current changes being applied and not yet committed. Without some sort of consistency management, users would end up inadvertently overwriting each other's updated data. To prevent this from happening, SQL Server implements four transaction isolation levels: **READ UNCOMMITTED**, **READ COMMITTED**, **REPEATABLE READ**, and **SERIALIZABLE**.

You can use the **SET** command as follows to change a transaction's isolation level:

```
SET TRANSACTION ISOLATION LEVEL
{READ COMMITTED | READ UNCOMMITTED |
REPEATABLE READ | SERIALIZABLE}
```

READ UNCOMMITTED

The **READ UNCOMMITTED** isolation level, also called *isolation level 0*, is the least restrictive isolation level used by SQL Server. **READ UNCOMMITTED** uses something called *dirty reads*: having one transaction read another transaction's uncommitted changes. At this level, data values can be changed, causing records to appear or disappear in the result set before the end of the transaction. This option has the same effect as setting **NOLOCK** on all tables in all **SELECT** statements in a transaction.

READ COMMITTED

This is the SQL Server default isolation level. At the **READ COMMITTED** level, SQL Server issues shared locks while reading data and respecting exclusive locks. You cannot read uncommitted data (do a dirty read) in this state, and any outstanding exclusive locks block you.

REPEATABLE READ

A transaction executing at the **REPEATABLE READ** isolation level holds all locks for the duration of the transaction. This isolation level guarantees that other transactions cannot change any records read in the transaction. In other words, repeating a **SELECT** statement forces SQL Server to return the same, unaltered records every time the operation is issued within the transaction. **REPEATABLE READ** protects a range of data from changes by other transactions, but it doesn't prohibit new rows (called *phantoms*) from being inserted into the protected result set.

SERIALIZABLE

SERIALIZABLE isolation is the most restrictive isolation level because it provides a simulated single-user environment within a multiuser database. The **SERIALIZABLE** level holds all its locks for a transaction's duration, just as **REPEATABLE READ** does, and it implements key-range locks to prohibit other transactions from inserting new records (phantoms) into that range. Although you can ensure better data consistency by using a more restrictive isolation level, it comes at the cost of concurrency because locks are held for a longer amount of time, increasing the possibility of blocking other operations.

You can use table-level locking hints to override a transaction isolation level. For example, the following code uses the table-level locking hint **NOLOCK**:

```
SET TRANSACTION ISOLATION LEVEL SERIALIZABLE
BEGIN TRANSACTION
SELECT browser_type FROM weblog WITH (NOLOCK)
```

 For the exam, it will be important to understand how to use table-locking hints to override a transaction isolation level.

Cursors

When your database applications use queries, the data returned is a *query result set* based on the SQL query statements. You can think of a cursor as another way of referring to a result set in terms of a "row by row" concept. A cursor works with one record at a time within a set of records (the result set).

Cursors are used in database operations by performing the following sequence of steps:

1. Relating a cursor to a result set (defined by a **SELECT** statement)

2. Defining the characteristics of the cursor (forward-only, scrollable, and so on)

54. At the **READ COMMITTED** level, SQL Server issues shared locks while reading data and respects exclusive locks. This is the SQL Server default isolation level. You cannot read uncommitted data in this state, and any outstanding exclusive locks block you.

55. A transaction executing at the **REPEATABLE READ** isolation level holds all locks for the duration of the transaction. This isolation level guarantees that other transactions cannot change any records read in the transaction. **REPEATABLE READ** protects a range of data from changes by other transactions, but it doesn't prohibit new rows (phantoms) from being inserted into the protected result set.

56. Serializable isolation is the most restrictive isolation level because it provides a simulated single-user environment within a multi-user database. The **SERIALIZABLE** level holds all its locks for a transaction's duration, just as **REPEATABLE READ**, and it implements key-range locks to prohibit other transactions from inserting new records (phantoms) into that range. Although you can ensure better data consistency by using a more restrictive isolation level, it comes at the cost of concurrency because locks are held longer, increasing the possibility of blocking other operations.

57. You can use table-level locking hints to override a transaction isolation level.

58. The SQL Server syntax for declaring a cursor is as follows:

```
DECLARE MyCursorName CURSOR
[ LOCAL | GLOBAL ]
[ FORWARD_ONLY | SCROLL ]
[ STATIC | KEYSET | DYNAMIC |
FAST_FORWARD ]
[ READ_ONLY | SCROLL_LOCKS | OPTI
MISTIC ]
FOR SELECT · FROM MyTableName
[ FOR UPDATE [ OF myColumnName] ]
```

59. To avoid locking issues, keep your transactions as short as possible.

60. SQL Server stores information about all unresolved locks in the **Syslocksinfo** system table.

REMOTE DATA ACCESS AND XML

61. The **FOR XML** clause has the following syntax:

```
SELECT statement
FOR XML { RAW | AUTO | EXPLICIT }
[ , XMLDATA ]
[ , ELEMENTS ]
[ , BINARY BASE64 ]
```

62. The **FOR XML** clause is *not* valid in:
- Subselections, which include nested **SELECT** statements, **SELECT INTO** statements, and assignments
- **COMPUTE BY** or **FOR BROWSE** clauses
- **GROUP BY** clauses with aggregate functions
- **SELECT** statements used in view definitions
- User-defined functions that return a rowset
- Stored procedures called within an **INSERT** statement

TUNING AND OPTIMIZING DATA ACCESS

63. *Physical Disk: Avg Disk Queue Length*—A high number on this counter means that disk requests are delayed because the disk cannot keep up with requests. If this number is consistently high, consider adjusting the disk configuration or reorganizing its data.

64. *Physical Disk: % Disk Time*—A number greater than 90 percent on any disk means that the disk is too busy; consider adjusting the disk configuration or reorganizing its data.

65. *Processor: % Processor Time*—A percentage of more than 90 is too high. Upgrade your processor, or terminate applications other than SQL Server to ensure better throughput.

66. **UPDATE STATISTICS** causes a shared table lock to be placed on the table from which statistical information is being retrieved. This will prevent **UPDATE**, **DELETE**, and **INSERT** statements from being executed. **SELECT** statements will execute normally.

CORIOLIS™
Certification Insider Press

The MCSE™ SQL Server™ 2000 Database Design Cram Sheet

This Cram Sheet contains the distilled, key facts about the MCSE SQL Server 2000 Database Design exam. Review this information last thing before entering the test room, paying special attention to those areas where you feel you need the most review. You can transfer any of these facts onto a blank sheet of paper before beginning the exam.

DATA MODELING

1. A *primary key* is composed of one or more attributes (columns) that uniquely identify an instance of the entity (a row in the table). In a relational database, every entity (table) should have a primary key.

2. Primary keys must adhere to certain rules:
   - The value must be unique for each instance of the entity.
   - The value must not be null.
   - The value cannot change or become null during the life of the instance.

3. A foreign key is an attribute or composite attribute that completes the relationship between two entities. This key, then, relates one entity to its parent entity. Foreign keys can relate to a primary key or to an alternate key in another entity. If a foreign key points to a primary key, then the foreign key must be non-null. Otherwise, it can be null. Foreign keys are used to maintain data integrity (referential integrity).

4. *Normalization* is a refinement process that occurs after you have identified all of the data objects. Normalization creates a set of relational entities or tables that are free of duplicate data and that can be modified correctly and consistently.

5. An entity is in *first normal form (1NF)* if there are no repeating attributes or groups of attributes and if the columns present atomic information.

6. A relational table is in *second normal form (2NF)* if it is in 1NF *and* every non-key attribute is fully dependent on the primary key. Second normal form has no redundant data.

7. *Third normal form (3NF)*—the most common form—removes data that is not dependent on the primary key. An entity is in third normal form if it is in 2NF *and* if no non-key attributes are transitively dependent on their primary keys.

8. The *referential integrity* rule states that every foreign key value must match a primary key value in an associated table. Referential integrity ensures that data stays consistent between the two tables after you use an **INSERT**, **DELETE**, or **UPDATE** command.

Note: *Although normalizing tables is effective for queries, to improve inserts, updates, and deletes (online transaction processing), you should, in some cases, denormalize and use fewer indexes on tables.*

DATABASE OBJECTS

9. Common SQL Server data types include **char**, **int**, **varchar**, **datetime**, **bit**, and **text**.

10. The **int** data type is a 4-byte value that can store numbers between $-2{,}147{,}483{,}648$ and $2{,}147{,}483{,}648$.

11. More data types are available; some are related to those just listed. For example, SQL Server 2000 has a new data type called **bigint**, which can store 8 bytes.

The new **sql_variant** data type can contain **char**, **nchar**, **smallint**, and **float** values; however, it cannot contain larger data types such as **image** or **text**.

12. The latest possible date that can stored in the **datetime** data type is 12/31/9999, and the earliest date that can be stored is 1/1/1753.

13. If you do not want existing data to be confirmed for a **CHECK** or **FOREIGN KEY** constraint, you should use the **WITH NOCHECK** argument in the **ALTER TABLE** command.

14. SQL Server 2000 provides a few new system-supplied data types:

   • **bigint**—An 8-byte integer with a value range of plus or minus 2^{63}.

   • **sql_variant**—Stores the values of various SQL-Server-supported data types, except for **text**, **ntext**, **timestamp**, and **image**. The **sql_variant** data type is similar to the **variant** type in Visual Basic in that it can represent many data types in different situations.

Note: *When Microsoft lists the exclusions for these data types, sql_variant itself is listed as an excluded data type.*

   • **table**—Stores a result set for later processing. The **table** data type cannot be used in column definitions. It can be used only with local variables or return values.

15. You can inhibit **NULL** values in columns by using the **NOT NULL** constraint.

16. Because a **CHECK** constraint can refer to other columns in the table, use a **CHECK** constraint rather than a trigger whenever possible. A **CHECK** constraint occurs before the **INSERT** or **UPDATE** statement, whereas a trigger happens afterward.

17. The **PRIMARY KEY** constraint identifies each row with this designation as being unique. Remember:

   • Only one **PRIMARY KEY** constraint can be defined per table.

   • A **PRIMARY KEY** constraint can be applied to one or more columns. If a single column does not identify a record uniquely, then choose a set of columns and designate them, combined, as the primary key.

   • A unique index is created automatically. It is clustered by default.

   • The index created cannot be dropped. You would have to drop the **PRIMARY KEY** constraint.

18. SQL Server enforces **UNIQUE** constraints by creating nonclustered indexes that are unique. **UNIQUE** constraints cannot assign values.

19. The order of constraints is:

   a. The **UNIQUE** or the **PRIMARY KEY** constraint

   b. The **FOREIGN KEY** constraint

20. The **CASCADE** clause propagates a deletion to the referencing tables, rather than generating an error or requiring triggers or stored procedures to handle the propagation.

21. **CHECK** constraints are logical expressions that can prevent database users from entering invalid data into particular columns. All data in a table is validated with any **CHECK** constraints that you add.

22. By implementing the **Immediate-Updating Subscribers** option, you can use transactional replication to modify data on computers subscribing to that service.

23. When column values in a database are valid, this validity is called *domain integrity*.

24. The **IDENTITY** property can be used only once in a table.

25. The **IDENTITY** property data type must be **integer**, **numeric**, or **decimal**. The **numeric** and **decimal** data types must have a scale of zero.

26. A column with the **IDENTITY** property cannot be **NULL** or have a **DEFAULT** constraint.

27. A column with the **IDENTITY** property cannot be updated.

28. Uniqueness with the **IDENTITY** property is not guaranteed; use the **UNIQUE INDEX** constraint.

29. When a column in a table has the **IDENTITY** property, you can execute the **SET IDENTITY_INSERT ON** statement to enable particular values to be inserted into that column.

30. The **RULE** objects are used primarily for backward compatibility. **CHECK** constraints are now the standard for attribute integrity.

31. As with **CHECK** constraints, by implementing **DEFAULT** definitions, you can effectively maintain domain integrity.

RETRIEVING AND MODIFYING DATA

32. SQL Server 2000, unlike its predecessors, has two limits for nondeterministic functions:

   • You cannot create an index on a computed column whose expression includes a nondeterministic function.

   • You cannot create a clustered index on a view if the view refers to any nondeterministic functions.

IMPLEMENTING INDEXES

33. A table can contain only one clustered index. Always try to use nonclustered indexes on columns where few records are returned.

34. Nonclustered indexes work best on columns that contain a range of values such as **datetime** values. Nonclustered indexes use the table's clustered index keys as pointers to the actual data.

35. You can use the **DROP_EXISTING** option with the **CREATE INDEX** statement to drop and re-create all indexes.

36. Generally, create an index only if the data to be stored in the corresponding indexed column(s) will often be queried or used to identify information stored in specific rows.

37. You *always* read the execution plan from right to left, top to bottom.

VIEWS

38. If you create a view that joins data from two databases, make sure you have permissions granted for both of them.

39. If you want to be able to update data in a view without causing records to disappear, you can specify the **WITH CHECK OPTION** argument in the **CREATE VIEW** statement.

40. The rules for the partitioning column are as follows:

- Each underlying base table must have a partitioning column defined with one (and only one) **CHECK** constraint so that any given value of the partitioning column maps to a single table. The **CHECK** constraints can use only these operators: **BETWEEN**, **AND**, **OR**, <, <=, >, >=, =.

- A partitioning column cannot allow nulls, must be part of the primary key, and cannot be made up of computed columns.

- A partitioning column must be in the same ordinal location in the select list of each **SELECT** statement in the view.

41. **INSERT**, **UPDATE**, and **DELETE** statements run faster when there are fewer indexes on a table.

STORED PROCEDURES

42. When stored procedures refer to database objects owned by a user other than the owner of the stored procedure, **EXECUTE** permissions must be checked for all objects, including the stored procedure.

43. Objects within a stored procedure are resolved at runtime and therefore should be qualified within the stored procedure.

44. **SET QUOTED_IDENTIFIER** and **SET ANSI_NULLS** are determined at database creation time. All other settings are determined at database execution time.

45. Executing a stored procedure without required parameters that do not have defaults will generate an error.

46. You must include the **OUTPUT** keyword both in the **CREATE** statement and in the **EXECUTE** statement.

47. If objects referenced by a stored procedure change (such as when you're adding indexes or importing a large amount of data), you should force a recompile of the stored procedure.

TRIGGERS

48. The sequence of events is: **INSTEAD OF** trigger, constraints, **AFTER** triggers. Any failure rolls back the modification.

49. **INSTEAD OF** triggers are not allowed on an updatable view with the **WITH CHECK OPTION** clause. You must alter the view to remove this clause if you want to use an **INSTEAD OF** trigger.

50. Cascading referential integrity constraints are new to SQL Server 2000. The **ON DELETE CASCADE** statement deletes child table records when their corresponding parent records are deleted, not the other way around. If you delete from the **Customers** table a record with a **CustomerID** of 99, all records with a **CustomerID** (foreign key) of 99 in the **Orders** table will also be deleted.

TRANSACTIONS, CURSORS, AND LOCKS

51. SQL Server 2000 autocommits transactions by default. Each individual SQL statement is a separate transaction that is committed automatically upon completion.

52. You can use the **SET** command as follows to change a transaction's isolation level:

```
SET TRANSACTION ISOLATION LEVEL
{READ COMMITTED | READ UNCOMMITTED |
REPEATABLE READ | SERIALIZABLE}
```

53. The **READ UNCOMMITTED** isolation level (isolation level 0) is the least restrictive isolation level used by SQL Server. **READ UNCOMMITTED** uses dirty reads: Your transaction can read another transaction's uncommitted changes. Data values could be changed, causing records to appear or disappear in the result set before the end of the transaction. This option has the same effect as setting **NOLOCK** on all tables in all **SELECT** statements in a transaction.

3. Executing a Transact-SQL statement that fills the cursor with data

4. Retrieving one or more rows with the cursor

5. Performing update or delete operations on the data in the cursor

6. Closing the cursor

Cursor Types

Cursors can be either *updateable* or *non-updateable*. If you need only to query data and not update it, you should use a non-updateable cursor to improve performance. *Scrollable* cursors, which are also updateable or non-updateable, allow you to navigate arbitrarily through a result set.

Dynamic and static cursors determine which data is available in the cursor at any point in time. A *static cursor* always contains records from a result set in the same state it was in when the cursor was opened. In other words, newly inserted records and updated records are not reflected in the result set. *Dynamic cursors*, however, show any available new records that have been added to the result set.

Keyset cursors are controlled through a set of unique identifiers called a *keyset*. The keys are built from a set of columns that uniquely identify the rows in the result set. The keyset includes all key values for records in the result set when the cursor was opened. Changes to data values made by either the keyset owner or other processes are visible when you're navigating through the result set. Inserts made outside the cursor by other processes are visible only if the cursor is closed and reopened. However, inserts made from inside the cursor are visible at the end of the result set.

Additionally, SQL Server 2000 implements a type of cursor called a *fast forward-only cursor* for performance optimization. A forward-only cursor is used to fetch rows sequentially from the beginning of the result set to the end. These rows are read-only, which means that you cannot use them with a FOR UPDATE clause. A fast forward-only cursor is optimized for faster sequential fetching. Scrollable cursors allow you to fetch records in any sequence.

Cursors are global by default. Global cursors can be used in any Transact-SQL code within a given connection; however, local cursors can be used only within their defined object (a stored procedure or trigger).

The SQL Server syntax for declaring a cursor is as follows:

```
DECLARE MyCursorName CURSOR
[ LOCAL | GLOBAL ]
[ FORWARD_ONLY | SCROLL ]
[ STATIC | KEYSET | DYNAMIC | FAST_FORWARD ]
[ READ_ONLY | SCROLL_LOCKS | OPTIMISTIC ]
FOR SELECT * FROM MyTableName
[ FOR UPDATE [ OF myColumnName] ]
```

Transact-SQL cursors are used mainly in stored procedures, triggers, and Transact-SQL scripts in which the cursors make the contents of a result set available to other Transact-SQL statements. In Listing 11.1, the Transact-SQL code uses a cursor named **weblog_cursor** to produce a loop through a Web database table named **Weblog**.

Listing 11.1   A Transact-SQL statement using a cursor to navigate through a Web database table.

```
USE Web
GO
DECLARE weblog_cursor CURSOR FOR
SELECT logtime, HTTP_USER_AGENT FROM Weblog
WHERE logtime > '5/26/2001'

OPEN weblog_cursor

-- Perform the first fetch
FETCH NEXT FROM weblog_cursor

-- Check to see if there are any more rows
WHILE @@FETCH_STATUS = 0
BEGIN
    -- if the previous fetch succeeds, then
    -- get another row.
    FETCH NEXT FROM weblog_cursor
END

CLOSE weblog_cursor
DEALLOCATE weblog_cursor
GO
```

The **Weblog** table, created using the code in Listing 11.1, stores Internet activity on a Web site. Anyone who connects to the Web site has his or her Internet browser application (such as Internet Explorer) and the date and time saved to the **Weblog** table. The results are illustrated in Figure 11.1.

Figure 11.1 Fetching results.

Locks

SQL Server can lock databases, tables, records, indexes, data pages, and index pages. Although SQL Server can automatically lock resources at an appropriate level for each command it is given, concurrency and data consistency must be balanced depending on the type of database applications you are running. The more locking is implemented, the more expensive it is in terms of concurrency because locking restricts access to data by other transactions. On the other hand, locking can prevent data inconsistency by ensuring that only one transaction at a time can update specific data.

 One of the best things you can do to avoid locking issues to begin with is simply to keep your transactions as short as possible. The exam will present you with questions that relate to this concept.

SQL Server sets exclusive locks on objects automatically when a user modifies them by using **INSERT, UPDATE,** or **DELETE** statements. Only one transaction at a time can hold an exclusive lock on a resource, and no other locks can be placed on that resource at the same time. Locking conflicts occur when a transaction holds a lock on a resource and another transaction attempts to place an incompatible lock on the same resource.

Deadlocks

A deadlock occurs when two transactions lock separate resources and then each transaction attempts to set a lock on the other transaction's resource. For example, one transaction opens an exclusive lock on the **Employees** table and then tries to set an exclusive lock on the **Orders** table. Simultaneously, another transaction acquires an exclusive lock on the **Orders** table and attempts to open an exclusive lock on the **Employees** table. In this situation, both of the transactions block each other and are stuck waiting for the object they want to be released.

When SQL Server detects a deadlock, it selects one of the transactions and performs a rollback, thereby releasing all locks that the transaction was applying.

You can minimize deadlocks by following a few simple rules:

➤ Consistently access shared resources in the same order.

➤ Keep transactions as short as possible.

➤ Use a low transaction isolation level.

➤ Use a clustered index on every table to ensure explicit record ordering.

 SQL Server stores information about all unresolved locks in the **Syslocksinfo** system table.

Resolving Deadlocks Manually

You can use SQL Profiler to monitor locks in addition to obtaining a list of long-running queries. In addition, one of the best ways to detect and remove locks is to use the **sp_who** stored procedure to retrieve system process ID (SPID) values. For example, the following are results from running **sp_who**:

```
spid    ecid    status      loginame cmd
------  ------  ----------  -------- ---
51      0       runnable    schase
```

In this example, after obtaining the SPID of 51 from running **sp_who**, you can terminate this process if it is monopolizing all of the server resources. You can terminate the process by typing the following command:

```
kill 51
```

Practice Questions

Question 1

> Which of the following transaction levels provides the lowest concurrency?
>
> ○ a. **SERIALIZABLE**
>
> ○ b. **READ COMMITTED**
>
> ○ c. **READ UNCOMMITTED**
>
> ○ d. **NON-CONCURRENT**

Answer a is correct. **SERIALIZABLE** provides the lowest concurrency. Answer b is incorrect because **READ COMMITTED** does not provide the lowest concurrency, although dirty reads and phantoms are possible. Answer c is incorrect because **READ UNCOMMITTED** is the least restrictive of all transaction isolation levels; therefore, it provides the best concurrency. Finally, answer d is incorrect because **NON-CONCURRENT** is not a valid isolation level.

Question 2

> You have recently implemented SQL Server 2000, and your data has been imported into your database. You want to validate the most important data because some of the dates could be invalid in the application from which the data was imported. You want to review the values from all **smalldatetime** columns to ensure that each year is four digits; however, each table contains a substantial amount of data. Therefore, you will need to use server-side processes to hold the data from each result set. Which of the following cursor types should you use?
>
> ○ a. Scrollable cursor
>
> ○ b. Client cursor
>
> ○ c. Forward-only cursor
>
> ○ d. Keyset cursor

Answer c is correct. Returning an entire result set would place too much strain on the client. Therefore, a cursor needs to be used to analyze the data in each record on a case-by-case basis. A forward-only cursor works best in this case because there is no reason to fetch a row more than once after it has been validated.

Answer a is incorrect because a scrollable cursor would be too much overhead for this scenario. Answer b is incorrect because it is not the best answer. Although you could use a client cursor, the best answer is a forward-only cursor. Answer d is incorrect because a keyset cursor would not be as fast as a forward-only cursor.

Question 3

Your company sells food products, and you want to design a SQL Server application for managing inventory. When an employee wants to see information about a particular product, your application will use the following query:

```
SELECT pr.ProductID , pr.ProductName ,
pr.UnitsInStock , cat.Description
FROM Products pr
INNER JOIN Categories cat
        ON pr.CategoryID = cat.CategoryID
WHERE pr.UnitsInStock < 10
```

This query will help the employee to determine when inventory needs to be refilled. The information will then be used to write a purchase order, and an **UPDATE** statement will be issued to update the inventory before the merchandise arrives in the warehouse. Many employees will use your application simultaneously, and other employees could be using another application to create new product records for new inventory items. You want to avoid locking problems while ensuring data integrity. What isolation level should you assign to the database connection that your application's transaction uses?

- ○ a. **SERIALIZABLE**
- ○ b. **READ COMMITTED**
- ○ c. **READ UNCOMMITTED**
- ○ d. **REPEATABLE READ**

Answer d is correct. You would use a **REPEATABLE READ** in this instance. Answer a is incorrect because although **SERIALIZABLE** could work, it is not the best option because concurrency would be affected too much. Answer b is incorrect because the **READ COMMITTED** level will prevent **SELECT** statements from reading dirty data; however, this level allows other transactions to add, change, or delete data before the transaction is complete. Answer c is incorrect because **READ UNCOMMITTED** allows dirty reads, which are not appropriate in this case.

Question 4

Which transaction isolation level allows uncommitted transaction data to be read by other transactions?

○ a. **SERIALIZABLE**

○ b. **READ COMMITTED**

○ c. **READ UNCOMMITTED**

○ d. **REPEATABLE READ**

Answer c is correct. The **READ UNCOMMITTED** level allows uncommitted transaction data to be read by other transactions. Answers a and d are incorrect because **SERIALIZABLE** and **REPEATABLE READ** do not allow reading of dirty data. Answer b is incorrect because the SQL Server default isolation level of **READ COMMITTED** does not allow dirty reads.

Question 5

Which of the following techniques minimize deadlocks? [Check all correct answers]

❑ a. Not using a **FOR UPDATE** clause with a fast forward only cursor.

❑ b. Using a **FOR UPDATE** clause with a fast forward-only cursor.

❑ c. Using fast forward-only cursors as updatable objects.

❑ d. Using fast forward-only cursors as read-only objects.

Answers a and d are correct. Answer b is incorrect because you cannot use a **FOR UPDATE** clause with a fast forward-only cursor. Answer c is incorrect because fast forward-only cursors are not updatable.

Question 6

> Which of the following statements about cursors are not true? [Check all correct answers]
>
> ❑ a. Cursors consistently access shared resources in the same order.
>
> ❑ b. Cursors use a single extensive transaction in place of multiple short transactions.
>
> ❑ c. Cursors use a low transaction isolation level.
>
> ❑ d. Cursors use a high transaction isolation level.

Answers a and c are correct. You should always keep transactions as short as possible. In addition, you should use a low transaction isolation level; therefore, answers b and d are incorrect.

Question 7

> Which of the following objects can SQL Server lock? [Check all correct answers]
>
> ❑ a. Databases
>
> ❑ b. Tables
>
> ❑ c. Records
>
> ❑ d. Indexes
>
> ❑ e. Data pages

Answers a, b, c, d, and e are all correct. SQL Server can lock all of these objects.

Question 8

> Which of the following ACID properties states that either all the work in a transaction is done or none of it is?
>
> ○ a. Atomicity
>
> ○ b. Consistency
>
> ○ c. Isolation
>
> ○ d. Durability

Answer a is correct. Atomicity means that either all the work in a transaction is done or none of it is. Answer b is incorrect because consistency means that a transaction preserves data regardless of how the data's state changes during the operation. Answer c is incorrect because isolation means that each transaction behaves as if each is the only one executing in the database. Finally, answer d is incorrect because durability means that SQL Server guarantees that a transaction's changes will be preserved if successful or rolled back if incomplete.

Question 9

Which of the following code snippets creates a local cursor named **MyCursor** that is updatable?

○ a.
```
DECLARE CURSOR FOR
SELECT logtime, HTTP_USER_AGENT FROM Weblog
WHERE logtime > '5/26/2001' AS MyCursor
```

○ b.
```
DECLARE CURSOR MyCursor FOR
SELECT logtime, HTTP_USER_AGENT FROM Weblog
WHERE logtime > '5/26/2001'
```

○ c.
```
DECLARE myCursor FOR
SELECT logtime, HTTP_USER_AGENT FROM Weblog
WHERE logtime > '5/26/2001' AS CURSOR
```

○ d.
```
DECLARE weblog_cursor CURSOR FOR
SELECT logtime, HTTP_USER_AGENT FROM Weblog
WHERE logtime > '5/26/2001'
```

Answer d is correct. Answers a, b, and c use incorrect syntax.

Question 10

When does SQL Server automatically set exclusive locks on objects? [Check all correct answers]

❑ a. When a user modifies the objects by using an **INSERT** statement

❑ b. When a user modifies the objects by using an **UPDATE** statement

❑ c. When a user modifies the objects by using a **DELETE** statement

❑ d. When a user modifies the objects by using a **SELECT** statement

Answers a, b, and c are correct. Answer d is incorrect because **SELECT** statements do not modify data unless a cursor is used to fetch data appropriately.

Need to Know More?

Iseminger, David. *SQL Server 2000 Reference Library*. Redmond, WA: Microsoft Press, 2000. ISBN 0-7356-1280-3. A selected collection of SQL Server 2000 Books Online; there are six volumes focused on key areas. Volume 1 contains information on transactions and locks. Volume 5 contains all you want to know about Transact-SQL, including transactions, cursors, and locks.

MS SQL Server Books Online has sections on stored procedures. This book set can be installed from the SQL Server CD or accessed online through **http://msdn.microsoft.com/library/default.asp**.

Search the TechNet CD or its online version through **www.microsoft.com/ technet**. Keywords to search on include "transactions," "cursors," and "locks."

http://msdn.microsoft.com/transactions/default.asp—Find up-to-date information about using transactions in SQL Server.

www.microsoft.com/sql/ and **http://msdn.microsoft.com/sqlserver/ default.asp** are good places to find up-to-date information about SQL Server.

www.sqlmag.com—*SQL Magazine*—both the hard copy and the Web site—has a large amount of information on SQL Server.

Remote Data Access and XML

Terms you'll need to understand:

✓ Rowset

✓ Linked server

✓ **OPENROWSET** function

✓ **OPENDATASOURCE** function

✓ **OPENQUERY** function

✓ Extensible Markup Language (XML)

✓ **OPENXML** statement

Techniques you'll need to master:

✓ Using linked servers

✓ Creating ad hoc queries using the **OPENROWSET** or **OPENDATASOURCE** functions

✓ Using pass-through queries with the **OPENQUERY** statement

✓ Retrieving data in XML format

✓ Parsing XML data with **OPENXML** statement

Data in an organization is usually heterogeneous; in other words the data might be on various SQL servers or in other types of databases. This chapter reviews techniques for accessing this heterogeneous data. We'll look at linked servers, ad hoc queries, and pass-through queries. In addition, with the Web being at the forefront of technology these days and with the creation of Extensible Markup Language (XML), SQL Server has added the ability to retrieve and write data by using XML. Additionally, you can replicate data between heterogeneous data sources. In other words, SQL Server can push data to non-SQL Server sources and can receive data from non-SQL servers.

Linked Servers

OLE DB providers expose data in tabular objects called *rowsets*. SQL Server allows rowsets from OLE DB providers to be referenced in Transact-SQL statements as if they were stored in a SQL Server table. A *linked server* is a configuration setting used to manage an OLE DB connection between the local SQL server and an OLE DB data source. The source can be another SQL Server database, an Oracle database, a Microsoft Access database, or any source that has an OLE DB provider.

You can use either the Enterprise Manager or the system stored procedure **sp_addlinkedserver** to create a linked server. The syntax for the **sp_addlinkedserver** stored procedure is as follows (the parameters, such as [**@server** =], can be omitted, as seen in some of the examples that follow):

```
EXEC sp_addlinkedserver
    @server = 'SVR1',
    @provider = 'Microsoft.Jet.OLEDB.4.0',
    @srvproduct = 'OLE DB Provider for Jet',
    @datasrc = 'C:\Program Files\Microsoft
     Visual Studio\VB98\NWIND.MDB'
GO
```

After establishing the linked server, you access data from that server by qualifying the name in the **SELECT** clause. In Transact-SQL statements, you refer to data objects in a linked server by using a four-part name in the form *linked_server_name.catalog.schema.object_name*. Separate each part by a dot (.). Table 12.1 describes the four-part name further. You pass the *catalog*, *schema*, and *object_name* parameters to the OLE DB provider to identify a specific data object. Therefore, these parameters depend on the OLE DB provider's required syntax.

Table 12.1 The four-part name of a linked server.	
Part Name	Description
linked_server_name	The name of the server referring to the OLE DB data source.
catalog	The catalog in the OLE DB data source that contains the object; in SQL Server, this is the database.
schema	The schema in the catalog that contains the object; in SQL Server, this is the owner ID.
object_name	The data object in the schema; in SQL Server, this is the table or view.

 A query without a schema (i.e., the owner) will generate an error because there is no way to resolve the owner; that is, there is no default.

The following code snippet creates a link to a second SQL Server computer and then retrieves all columns from the **Employees** table in the **Northwind** database on that second server:

```
EXEC sp_addlinkedserver 'OtherServer', N'SQL Server'
GO
SELECT *
FROM OtherServer.Northwind.dbo.Employees
```

The following code snippet creates a linked server connected to a Microsoft Access database and then retrieves all columns from the **Employees** table in the **Northwind** database in Access:

```
EXEC sp_addlinkedserver 'EMS', 'Access 2000',
    'Microsoft.Jet.OLEDB.4.0',
     'D:\Dev\ISAM\Trans_service.mdb'
GO
SELECT *
FROM EMS...Ancillary
```

Some considerations when you're working with Microsoft Access links are as follows:

➤ The Access database file must reside on the server; the path must be valid on the server.

➤ Access databases do not have catalog and schema names. You still need the dot placeholders as shown in the example.

The following code snippet creates a link to a Microsoft Excel spreadsheet (**In-voices**) and then retrieves all columns from the associated range:

```
sp_addlinkedserver N'Excel', N'Jet 4.0',
                   N'Microsoft.Jet.OLEDB.4.0',
                   N'd:\Dev\Invoices.xls',
                   NULL, N'Excel 5.0'
GO
SELECT *
FROM EXCEL...InvoiceData
```

Some considerations when you're working with Microsoft Excel links are as follows:

➤ Associate a range of cells with a name in Excel.

➤ The named range becomes the table name (**InvoiceData** in the previous example).

➤ When you insert a row into a named range of cells, the row will be added after the last row that is part of the named range.

The following code snippet creates a linked server connected to an Oracle data-base and then retrieves all columns from the **Manufacturing** database:

```
sp_addlinkedserver
     'OracleSvr', 'Oracle 7.3', 'MSDAORA', 'OracleDB'
GO
SELECT *
FROM OracleSvr..Samuel.Manufacturing
```

Some considerations when you're working with Oracle links are as follows:

➤ Ensure that the Oracle client software on the SQL server is at the correct level for the provider. The Microsoft OLE DB provider for Oracle requires Oracle Client Software Support File version 7.3.3.4.0 or later and SQL*Net version 2.3.3.0.4.

➤ On the SQL server, create a SQL*Net alias name (**OracleSvr** is the value assigned as the alias name in the previous example) that points to an Oracle database instance.

➤ Each Oracle database instance has only one catalog with an empty name.

➤ To refer to a table, you must use a four-part name of the form *OracleLinked ServerName..OwnerUserName.TableName*.

➤ For table and column names that were created in Oracle without quoted iden-tifiers, use all uppercase names.

➤ For table and column names that were created in Oracle with quoted identifiers, use the same case that was used in Oracle.

➤ INSERT statements should supply values for all columns in a table even if certain columns in the table can be NULL or have default values.

Ad Hoc Queries

When you need to refer to another server infrequently, instead of creating a linked server, you can use an *ad hoc* name within the query. You use the OPENROWSET and OPENDATASOURCE rowset functions to provide an ad hoc name to the query. However, these functions do not provide all of the functionality available from a linked server, such as managing login mappings, querying the linked server's metadata, and configuring various connection settings (such as time-out values).

The arguments of OPENROWSET and OPENDATASOURCE must be string-literals. They do not support variables. Similar to the linked server, both these functions provide ad hoc connection information to OLE DB providers. The functions cannot be used interchangeably.

The OPENROWSET Function

The OPENROWSET function provides all the connection information necessary to access remote data from an OLE DB provider. The OPENROWSET function can be used in place of the table name in the FROM clause of a query. If the OLE DB provider permits, the OPENROWSET function can also be used as the target table for INSERT, UPDATE, and DELETE statements. If a query returns multiple result sets, only the first set is returned by the OPENROWSET function.

If the OLE DB provider supports multiple catalogs and schemas, then the catalog and schema names are required; otherwise, they are optional. If the provider supports only schema names, then a two-part name of the form *schema.object* must be specified. If the provider supports only catalog names, then a three-part name of the form *catalog.schema.object* must be specified.

The OPENROWSET function has the following syntax:

```
OPENROWSET ( 'provider_name'
    , { 'datasource' ; 'user_id' ; 'password'
      | 'provider_string' }
    , { [ catalog. ] [ schema. ] object
      | 'query' }
    )
```

The **OPENROWSET** function has the following parameters:

➤ *'provider_name'*—The friendly name of the OLE DB provider as specified in the Registry.

➤ *'datasource'*—Usually the database.

➤ *'user_id'* ; *'password'*—A user and password combination that has permission to access the database on the remote server.

➤ *'provider_string'*—A provider-specific connection string, which usually encapsulates all the connection information (*provider_name, datasource,* and *user_id*) needed to initialize the provider.

➤ [*catalog.*] [*schema.*] *object*—The catalog or database, the owner, and the object name (table).

➤ *'query'*—A string constant that's sent to and executed by the provider, not SQL Server. The *'query'* parameter can be used in place of *catalog.schema.object.* You can use the query because the OLE DB source does not expose its data as tabular data through table names, but rather exposes its data only through a command language accessed using this query. This parameter can also be used as a pass-through query (discussed in more detail later in this chapter).

*Note: The OLE DB source must support the OLE DB **Command** object and its mandatory interfaces.*

The following code snippet provides two examples of using the **OPENROWSET** function to connect to another SQL server. The first example uses the *catalog.schema.object* syntax to retrieve all columns from the **Products** table in the **Northwind** database on that server. The second example passes a query to the other SQL server to retrieve all columns in the **Products** table that were ordered by **ProductName**:

```
/* Openrowset with a catalog.schema.object */
SELECT a.*
FROM OPENROWSET('SQLOLEDB','otherserver';'sa';'MyPass',
    'Northwind.dbo.products') AS a
GO
/* Openrowset with a query */
SELECT a.*
FROM OPENROWSET('SQLOLEDB','otherserver';'sa';'MyPass',
    'SELECT * FROM Northwind.dbo.products order
    by ProductName') AS a
```

The following code snippet provides an example of using the **OPENROWSET** function to connect to a Microsoft Access database. The example selects all columns in the **Orders** table of the **Northwind** database:

```
SELECT a.*
FROM OPENROWSET('Microsoft.Jet.OLEDB.4.0',
   'c:\MSOffice\Access\Samples\northwind.mdb';
      'admin';'mypwd', Orders)
   AS a
```

The following code snippet uses a table join to select all data from the **Employees** table in the local SQL Server **Northwind** database and from the **Orders** table in the Access **Northwind** database stored on the same computer:

```
SELECT emp.*, ord.*
FROM Northwind.dbo.employees AS emp INNER JOIN
   OPENROWSET('Microsoft.Jet.OLEDB.4.0',
   'c:\MSOffice\Access\Samples\northwind.mdb';
      'admin';'mypwd', Orders)
   AS ord
   ON emp.EmployeeID = ord.EmployeeID
```

The **OPENDATASOURCE** Function

The **OPENDATASOURCE** function provides connection information as part of a four-part object name (*server.catalog.schema.object*); this function takes the place of the server name. The **OPENDATASOURCE** function can be used in the same Transact-SQL syntax locations as a linked server name. The **OPENDATASOURCE** function can be used in a **SELECT, INSERT, UPDATE,** or **DELETE** statement. This function can also be used to call a remote stored procedure in an **EXECUTE** statement when the other server is SQL Server.

The **OPENDATASOURCE** function has the following syntax:

```
OPENDATASOURCE (provider_name, init_string)
```

The **OPENDATASOURCE** function has the following parameters:

➤ **provider_name**—The name registered as the **PROGID** of the OLE DB provider.

➤ **init_string**—The connection string passed to the provider. The string is written as keyword-value pairs separated by semicolons: **keyword1=value; keyword2=value.**

The following code snippet uses the **OPENROWSET** function to select all columns from the **Northwind** database on another SQL server:

```
SELECT   *
FROM     OPENDATASOURCE(
         'SQLOLEDB',
         'Data Source=ServerName;User ID=MyUID;Password=MyPass'
         ).Northwind.dbo.Products
```

The following code snippet uses the **OPENDATASOURCE** function and the OLE DB provider for Jet to select all data from an Excel spreadsheet:

```
SELECT *
FROM OpenDataSource(
'Microsoft.Jet.OLEDB.4.0',
'Data Source="c:\Manufacture\CompanySheet.xls";
   User ID=Admin;Password=;
Extended properties=Excel 5.0')...xactions
```

Pass-Through Queries

SQL Server sends a pass-through query as a query string to an OLE DB data source without processing the query on the SQL server. The query must be in the correct syntax for the OLE DB data source. A Transact-SQL statement on the SQL server uses the result of the pass-through query as though it were a regular table reference. The pass-through query string does not have to be a SQL statement; it is whatever the OLE DB provider requires. In other words, SQL Server does not care what the string contains as long as it returns a rowset back to SQL Server.

We already saw one example of a pass-through query that used the **OPENROWSET** function. You can also use the **OPENQUERY** function's syntax with a linked server. The **OPENQUERY** function can be used in place of the table name in the **FROM** clause of a query. If the OLE DB provider permits, the **OPENQUERY** function can also be used as the target table for **INSERT, UPDATE,** and **DELETE** statements. If a query returns multiple result sets, only the first is returned by the **OPENQUERY** function. The arguments of **OPENQUERY** must be string-literals; it does not support variables.

The following code snippet passes a query to another SQL server to retrieve first and last names from the **Employees** table in the **Northwind** database. This example uses the linked server **OtherServer,** created in an example provided earlier in this chapter:

```
SELECT *
FROM OPENQUERY(OtherServer, 'Select LastName, FirstName
from Employees Order by LastName')
```

The following code snippet passes a query to a Microsoft Access database to retrieve first and last names from the **Employees** table in the **Northwind** database. This example uses the linked server **Nwind**, created in an example provided earlier in this chapter:

```
SELECT *
FROM OPENQUERY(Nwind, 'SELECT LastName,
    FirstName from Employees Order by LastName')
```

The following code snippet passes a query to an Oracle server to retrieve a name and ID from the **Manufacturing** database. This example uses the linked server **OracleSvr**, created in an example provided earlier in this chapter:

```
SELECT *
FROM OPENQUERY(OracleSvr, 'SELECT name,
    id FROM Samuel.Manufacturing')
```

XML

Standard Generalized Markup Language (SGML) is a robust, complex language that was designed to set standards for publishing printed documents. Two subsets of SGML are Hypertext Markup Language (HTML), used in Web pages, and Extensible Markup Language (XML), used to describe the data and how the data is formatted. We'll assume that you are familiar with XML-Data language.

XML is now integrated and supported in SQL Server 2000. These integrated features include:

➤ The ability to access SQL Server by using Hypertext Transport Protocol (HTTP). For example: **http://IISServer/nwind?sql=SELECT+*+FROM+Customers+FOR+XML+AUTO&root=root**

➤ The ability to create XML views called *XML Data Reduced (XDR)* schemas and to use *XML Path Language (XPath)* queries to retrieve data from the XDR schema. Creating XML views is covered in Chapter 7.

➤ The ability to retrieve data by using the **SELECT** statement and the **FOR XML** clause or XPath queries.

➤ The ability to write data by using the **OPENXML** Transact-SQL statement.

The FOR XML Clause

SQL Server 2000 gives you the ability to return XML results from queries instead of returning typical result sets. To do this, you must set up Internet Information Services (IIS) to use SQL Server.

1. In Windows, choose Start|Programs|Microsoft SQL Server| Configure SQL XML Support In IIS.

2. Expand the server tree, and then right-click on your Web site name.

3. From the context menu, choose New|Virtual Directory, as illustrated in Figure 12.1.

4. On the General tab, set the name of the virtual directory to "pubs" as illustrated in Figure 12.2.

5. Select the Data Source tab, and then set the SQL Server and database to be used as the data source. In this case, you will want to set the database to **Pubs**.

6. On the Settings tab, enable the checkboxes next to Allow URL Queries, Allow Template Queries, and Allow XPath.

7. Choose OK to close the dialog box.

8. Now you are ready to open a browser window and issue a query that will return XML. Type the following URL into your browser, replacing **SVR1** with your SQL server name:

```
http://localhost/pubs?sql=SELECT+*+FROM
+Authors+FOR+XML+RAW&root=ROOT
```

9. Results similar to the illustration in Figure 12.3 will appear.

There are three modes for using the **FOR XML** clause: **AUTO**, **RAW**, and **EXPLICIT**. The **FOR XML** clause has three additional arguments: **XMLDATA**, **ELEMENTS**, and **BINARY BASE64**.

The **FOR XML** clause has the following syntax:

```
SELECT statement
FOR XML { RAW | AUTO | EXPLICIT }
    [ , XMLDATA ]
    [ , ELEMENTS ]
    [ , BINARY BASE64 ]
```

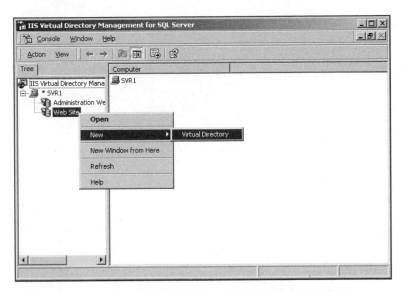

Figure 12.1   Creating a new virtual directory in Internet Information Services.

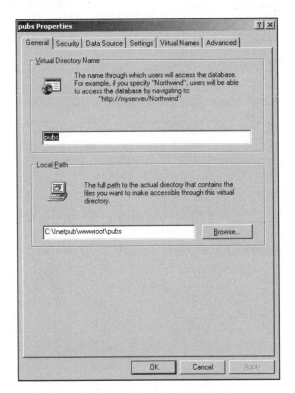

Figure 12.2   Setting up the pubs virtual directory.

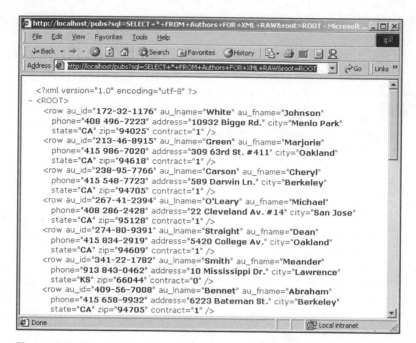

Figure 12.3 Using the **FOR XML RAW** clause in an HTTP query.

The **FOR XML** clause has the following modes and arguments:

➤ **AUTO** mode displays results as an XML hierarchy based upon the **FROM** clause.

➤ In **RAW** mode, each record is separated into XML row elements, and each non-**NULL** value is mapped to its corresponding column. This is illustrated in Figure 12.3.

➤ **EXPLICIT** mode allows you to specify the format of the XML returned from the query. The results are vertically partitioned in groups that become XML elements.

There are some restrictions to using the **FOR XML** clause. It is *not* valid in:

➤ Subselections, which include nested **SELECT** statements, **SELECT INTO** statements, and assignments

➤ **COMPUTE BY** or **FOR BROWSE** clauses

➤ **GROUP BY** clauses with aggregate functions

➤ **SELECT** statements used in view definitions

➤ User-defined functions that return a rowset

➤ Stored procedures called within an **INSERT** statement

Listing 12.1 contains a **SELECT** statement and several **FOR XML** clauses. Listing 12.2 provides the results of this **SELECT** statement without the **FOR XML** clause. Listing 12.3 provides the results of this **SELECT** statement with the **FOR XML AUTO** clause. Listing 12.4 provides the results of this **SELECT** statement with the **FOR XML RAW** clause.

Listing 12.1   A **SELECT** statement with and without various **FOR XML** clauses.

```
USE Northwind
SELECT Customers.CustomerID,
       Orders.OrderID,
       Shippers.CompanyName
From Customers JOIN Orders
On Customers.CustomerID = Orders.CustomerID
JOIN Shippers
ON Orders.ShipVia = Shippers.ShipperID
WHERE  Customers.CustomerID - 'BOLID'
OR Customers.CustomerID = 'CONSH'
ORDER BY Customers.CustomerID, Orders.OrderID
-- FOR XML AUTO
-- FOR XML RAW
-- FOR XML AUTO, XMLDATA
-- FOR XML RAW, ELEMENTS
```

Listing 12.2   Results of executing the statement in Listing 12.1 without the **FOR XML** clause.

```
CustomerID    OrderID    Shipper
----------    -------    --------------

BOLID         10326      United Package
BOLID         10801      United Package
BOLID         10970      Speedy Express
CONSH         10435      United Package
CONSH         10462      Speedy Express
CONSH         10848      United Package
```

Listing 12.3   Results of executing the statement in Listing 12.1 with the **FOR XML AUTO** clause.

```
<Customers CustomerID="BOLID">
   <Orders OrderID="10326">
      <Shippers CompanyName="United Package"/>
   </Orders>
   <Orders OrderID="10801">
      <Shippers CompanyName="United Package"/>
   </Orders>
   <Orders OrderID="10970">
      <Shippers CompanyName="Speedy Express"/>
```

```
    </Orders>
</Customers><Customers CustomerID="CONSH">
    <Orders OrderID="10435">
        <Shippers CompanyName="United Package"/>
    </Orders>
    <Orders OrderID="10462">
        <Shippers CompanyName="Speedy Express"/>
    </Orders>
    <Orders OrderID="10848">
        <Shippers CompanyName="United Package"/>
    </Orders>
</Customers>
```

Note: The results in Listing 12.3 would be one string; we have formatted them for readability.

Listing 12.4 Results of executing the statement in Listing 12.1 with the **FOR XML RAW** clause.

```
<row CustomerID="BOLID" OrderID="10326"
     CompanyName="United Package"/>
<row CustomerID="BOLID" OrderID="10801"
     CompanyName="United Package"/>
<row CustomerID="BOLID" OrderID="10970"
     CompanyName="Speedy Express"/>
<row CustomerID="CONSH" OrderID="10435"
     CompanyName="United Package"/>
<row CustomerID="CONSH" OrderID="10462"
     CompanyName="Speedy Express"/>
<row CustomerID="CONSH" OrderID="10848"
     CompanyName="United Package"/>
```

Note: The results in Listing 12.4 would be one string; we have formatted them for readability.

Listing 12.5 is a **SELECT** statement with a **FOR XML EXPLICIT** clause. It is the same **SELECT** statement shown in Listing 12.1 with the additional code necessary for the **EXPLICIT** option. Listing 12.6 provides the results of this **SELECT** statement.

Listing 12.5 A **SELECT** statement with the **FOR XML EXPLICIT** clause.

```
SELECT 1                   as Tag,
    NULL                   as Parent,
    Customers.CustomerID   as [Customer!1!CustomerID],
    NULL                   as [Order!2!OrderID],
    NULL                   as [Order!2!Shipper]
```

```
FROM Customers
WHERE  Customers.CustomerID = 'BOLID'
OR Customers.CustomerID = 'CONSH'
UNION ALL
SELECT 2,
       1,
       Customers.CustomerID,
       Orders.OrderID,
       Shippers.CompanyName
FROM Customers Join Orders
ON Customers.CustomerID = Orders.CustomerID
Join Shippers
ON Orders.ShipVia = Shippers.ShipperID
WHERE  Customers.CustomerID = 'BOLID'
OR Customers.CustomerID = 'CONSH'
ORDER BY [Customer!1!CustomerID], [Order!2!OrderID]
FOR XML EXPLICIT
```

Listing 12.6 provides the results of executing the statement in Listing 12.5 with
the **FOR XML EXPLICIT** clause. This is a partial result set. The results would
be one string; we have formatted them for readability.

**Listing 12.6   Results of executing the statement in Listing 12.5 with the FOR
XML EXPLICIT clause.**

```
<Customer CustomerID="BOLID">
    <Order OrderID="10326" Shipper="United Package"/>
    <Order OrderID="10801" Shipper="United Package"/>
    <Order OrderID="10970" Shipper="Speedy Express"/>
</Customer>
<Customer CustomerID="CONSH">
    <Order OrderID="10435" Shipper="United Package"/>
    <Order OrderID="10462" Shipper="Speedy Express"/>
    <Order OrderID="10848" Shipper="United Package"/>
</Customer>
```

Listing 12.7 shows the result of adding the **XMLDATA** parameter to the **FOR
XML AUTO** clause. Listing 12.7 uses the same **SELECT** statement shown in
Listing 12.1 with the additional clause.

**Listing 12.7   Results of executing the statement in Listing 12.1 with the FOR
XML RAW, XMLDATA clause.**

```
<Schema name="Schema1"
xmlns="urn:schemas-microsoft-com:xml-data"
xmlns:dt="urn:schemas-microsoft-com:datatypes">
<ElementType name="Customers" content="eltOnly"
```

```
model="closed" order="many">
<element type="Orders" maxOccurs="*"/>
<AttributeType name="CustomerID" dt:type="string"/>
<attribute type="CustomerID"/>
</ElementType>
<ElementType name="Orders" content="eltOnly"
model="closed" order="many">
<element type="Shippers" maxOccurs="*"/>
<AttributeType name="OrderID" dt:type="i4"/>
<attribute type="OrderID"/>
</ElementType>
<ElementType name="Shippers" content="empty"
model="closed">
<AttributeType name="CompanyName" dt:type="string"/>
<attribute type="CompanyName"/>
</ElementType>
</Schema>
<Customers xmlns="x-schema:#Schema1"
CustomerID="BOLID">
<Orders OrderID="10326">
<Shippers CompanyName="United Package"/>
</Orders>
<Orders OrderID="10801">
<Shippers CompanyName="United Package"/>
</Orders>
<Orders OrderID="10970">
<Shippers CompanyName="Speedy Express"/>
</Orders>
</Customers>
<Customers xmlns="x-schema:#Schema1"
CustomerID="CONSH">
<Orders OrderID="10435">
<Shippers CompanyName="United Package"/>
</Orders>
<Orders OrderID="10462">
<Shippers CompanyName="Speedy Express"/>
</Orders>
<Orders OrderID="10848">
<Shippers CompanyName="United Package"/>
</Orders>
</Customers>
```

Listing 12.8 shows the result of adding the **ELEMENTS** parameter to the **FOR XML RAW** clause. Listing 12.8 uses the same **SELECT** statement shown in Listing 12.1 with the additional clause.

Listing 12.8   Results of executing the statement in Listing 12.1 with the FOR XML RAW, ELEMENTS clause.

```
<Customers>
<CustomerID>BOLID</CustomerID>
<Orders>
<OrderID>10326</OrderID>
<Shippers>
<CompanyName>United Package</CompanyName>
</Shippers>
</Orders>
<Orders>
<OrderID>10801</OrderID>
<Shippers>
<CompanyName>United Package</CompanyName>
</Shippers>
</Orders>
<Orders>
<OrderID>10970</OrderID>
<Shippers><CompanyName>Speedy Express</CompanyName>
</Shippers>
</Orders>
</Customers>
<Customers>
<CustomerID>CONSH</CustomerID>
<Orders>
<OrderID>10435</OrderID>
<Shippers><CompanyName>United Package</CompanyName>
</Shippers>
</Orders>
<Orders>
<OrderID>10462</OrderID>
<Shippers><CompanyName>Speedy Express</CompanyName>
</Shippers>
</Orders><Orders>
<OrderID>10848</OrderID>
<Shippers><CompanyName>United Package</CompanyName>
</Shippers>
</Orders>
</Customers>
```

The OPENXML Statement

OPENXML is a rowset provider similar to a table or a view. It is a Transact-SQL keyword. OPENXML parses out an XML document and provides a rowset view of the XML data.

The **OPENXML** statement has the following syntax:

```
OPENXML(idoc,rowpattern,[flags])
[WITH (SchemaDeclaration | TableName)]
```

The **OPENXML** statement has the following parameters:

➤ **idoc**—The XML document handle, which is retrieved using the system stored procedure **sp_xml_preparedocument**. The **idoc** argument is an integer (**int**) data type. After the processing is complete, you execute the system stored procedure **sp_xml_removedocument** to remove the internal representation of the document.

➤ **rowpattern**—The Xpath; its data type is **nvarchar**.

➤ **flags**—Determines the mapping of rowset columns to the XML nodes. This argument uses the **byte** data type. This argument specifies the mapping that should be used—either attribute-centric mapping (default) or element-centric mapping—and specifies how the spillover column should be filled.

➤ **WITH**—A clause that formats the results (generated rowset) using the **SchemaDeclaration** argument or an existing table format. If the **WITH** clause is omitted, the *edge table* format is used. The edge table format is a fine-grained XML document structure (specifying such items as element and attribute names, the document hierarchy, and the namespaces) contained in a single table. The columns include the document node ID, its parent ID, the node type, the local name of the element, the namespace, the namespace URI (Uniform Resource Identifier), the data type of the element or attribute, the previous sibling element, and the attribute value. Some columns may be **NULL**. You get a row for each element in the XML document.

Listing 12.9 is an example of the **OPENXML** statement. You declare a variable (**DocHandle**) to hold the document ID that is retrieved from the system stored procedure **sp_xml_preparedocument**, and you declare another variable to contain the XML document, which is also passed to the stored procedure. You can then use the **OPENXML** statement to retrieve data from this document. Listing 12.10 provides the results of executing this **OPENXML** statement. Both the results and the Transact-SQL are illustrated in Figure 12.4.

You should be familiar with the **OPENXML** statement and the returns it generates.

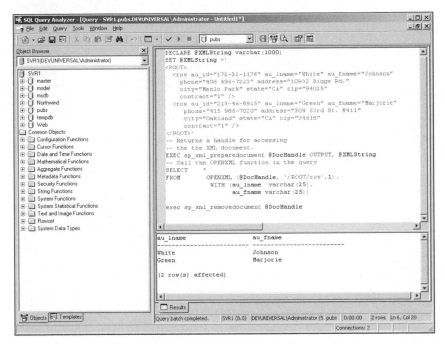

Figure 12.4 Query Analyzer containing Transact-SQL and results.

Listing 12.9 A sample **OPENXML** statement.

```
DECLARE @DocHandle int
DECLARE @XMLString varchar(1000)
SET @XMLString ='
<ROOT>
  <row au_id="172-32-1176" au_lname="White" au_fname="Johnson"
    phone="408 496-7223" address="10932 Bigge Rd."
    city="Menlo Park" state="CA" zip="94025"
    contract="1" />
  <row au_id="213-46-8915" au_lname="Green" au_fname="Marjorie"
    phone="415 986-7020" address="309 63rd St. #411"
    city="Oakland" state="CA" zip="94618"
    contract="1" />
</ROOT>'
-- Returns a handle for accessing
-- the the XML document.
EXEC sp_xml_preparedocument @DocHandle OUTPUT, @XMLString
-- Call the OPENXML function in the query
```

```
SELECT     *
FROM       OPENXML (@DocHandle, '/ROOT/row',1)
             WITH (au_lname  varchar(25),
                   au_fname varchar(25))

exec sp_xml_removedocument @DocHandle
```

Listing 12.10   The results of the OPENXML SELECT statement.

```
au_lname                      au_fname
------------------------      ------------------------
White                         Johnson
Green                         Marjorie

(2 row(s) affected)
```

Practice Questions

Case Study

The Ellie Company is a book publishing company. It has offices in New York and California. It has just acquired a small publishing company with an office in Dallas. This acquired company used Oracle for its database management system. The Ellie Company uses Microsoft SQL Server 2000.

Current Situation

The databases in the California and New York offices are both called **ElliePubs**. The database in Dallas is called **AllPubs** and is an Oracle database.

Proposed Situation

The company wants to keep the data in the Dallas office in Oracle and keep the data in the other offices in SQL Server. The company wants to be able to query data from all sources in the home office in New York.

Sales Manager

I am going to need sales reports that include data from all three sites. I don't want to have to get three separate reports and compare them manually.

Question 1

For this case study, how should the New York office access the California database? [Check all correct answers]

❑ a.

```
EXEC sp_addlinkedserver 'CAServer',
     N'SQL Server'
```

❑ b.

```
EXEC sp_addlinkedserver @server= 'CAServer',
@srvproduct = 'SQL Server', @provider ='SQLOLEDB',
@datasrc='CAServer',
@location = 'California',
@Catalog = 'ElliePubs'
```

❑ c.

```
EXEC sp_addlinkedserver @server= 'CAServer',
@srvproduct = 'SQL Server', @provider ='SQLOLEDB',
    @datasrc='CAServer',
@Catalog = 'ElliePubs'
```

❑ d.

```
EXEC sp_addlinkedserver @srvproduct = 'SQL Server',
@provider ='SQLOLEDB', @datasrc='CAServer', @Cata-
    log = 'ElliePubs'
```

Answers a and c are correct. In this case, when you're connecting to another SQL server, you need only the server name and the product. But you can include all the parameters if you wish. Answer b is incorrect because you would not define a location. Answer d is incorrect because you are missing the server name, and this is required.

Question 2

For this case study, the sales manager finds out that the Dallas office has an Access database that contains local customers. He wants to be able to query just this one time. What steps should he take?

○ a.   Create a linked server connected to the Access database, and then query for the data.

○ b.   Use an **OPENROWSET** command like this:

```
SELECT a.*
FROM OPENROWSET('Microsoft.Jet.OLEDB.4.0',
    'c:\Customers\customers.mdb';'admin';'mypwd',
    Customers)
    AS a
```

○ c.   Use an **OPENROWSET** command like this:

```
SELECT a.*
FROM
    OPENROWSET('SQLOLEDB','DallasServer';'sa';'MyPass',
    'Customers.dbo.Customers') AS a
```

○ d.   Use an **OPENQUERY** statement like this:

```
SELECT *
FROM OPENQUERY(DallasServer,
'Select * from Customers Order by LastName')
```

Answer b is correct. You would use an **OPENROWSET** command when you needed to access the data infrequently. Answer a would work, but because the sales manager wants to query only once, using a linked server is excessive. Answer c is an **OPENROWSET** statement used to access a SQL Server, not an Access database. Answer d is a pass-through query that requires a linked server (**DallasServer**) to have been previously established.

Question 3

For this case study, John works in the California office and wants to query the database in New York. What is the correct code?

○ a.
```
SELECT    *
FROM      OPENDATASOURCE(
          'OracleSvr',
          'Data Source=NYName;User ID=John;Password=JohnPass'
          ).NYData.dbo.Sales
```

○ b.
```
SELECT    *
FROM      OPENDATASOURCE(
          'SQLOLEDB',
          'Data Source:NYName;User ID:John;Password:JohnPass'
          ).NYData.dbo.Sales
```

○ c.
```
SELECT    *
FROM      OPENDATASOURCE(
          'SQLOLEDB',
          'Data Source=NYName;User ID=John;Password=JohnPass'
          ).NYData.dbo.Sales
```

○ d.
```
SELECT    *
FROM      OPENDATASOURCE(
          'SQLOLEDB',
          'Data Source=NYName,User ID=John,Password=JohnPass'
          ).NYData.dbo.Sales
```

Answer c is correct. You can use the **OPENDATASOURCE** function in place of the four-part object name. You specify the provider name and a set of keyword/value pairs separated by a semicolon. Answer a is incorrect because it is pointing to an Oracle server, and the New York office has SQL Server, not Oracle. Answer b is incorrect because it has colons instead of equal signs in the keyword/value pair. Answer d is incorrect because it has a comma instead of a semicolon separating the keyword/value pairs.

Question 4

For this case study, Tim works in the New York office and wants to query the database in Dallas. Rearrange the following code snippets in the correct order to accomplish this task. Not all items need to be used.

```
DallasSvr,
'DallasSvr',
FROM
FROM OPENQUERY
FROM OPENQUERY(
'MSDAORA', 'OracleDB'
N'SQL Server'
'Oracle 7.3',
'SELECT name, id FROM Mark.Sales')
SELECT name, id FROM Mark.Sales
sp_addlinkedserver
GO
```

The correct answer is:

```
sp_addlinkedserver 'DallasSvr', 'Oracle 7.3',
    'MSDAORA', 'OracleDB'
GO
SELECT *
FROM OPENQUERY(DallasSvr, SELECT * 'SELECT name, id
    FROM Mark.Sales')
```

Because the Dallas server uses Oracle, you need to use the Oracle provider information. The pass-through query uses the **OPENQUERY** statement, which requires the open parenthesis after the **OPENQUERY** keyword, followed by the name of the linked server and then the **SELECT** statement. The query must be enclosed in single quotes, and you need the closing parenthesis.

Question 5

> What are the three modes of the **FOR XML** clause? [Check all correct answers]
>
> ❑ a. **XMLDATA**
>
> ❑ b. **RAW**
>
> ❑ c. **BINARY BASE64**
>
> ❑ d. **AUTO**
>
> ❑ e. **ELEMENTS**
>
> ❑ f. **EXPLICIT**

Answers b, d, and f are correct. The **FOR XML** clause can use the **RAW**, **AUTO**, and **EXPLICIT** modes. The **XMLDATA**, **BINARY BASE64**, and **ELEMENTS** arguments are optional parameters that further define the format of the results.

Question 6

> The **FOR XML** clause cannot be used where? [Check all correct answers]
>
> ❑ a. **GROUP BY** clauses
>
> ❑ b. **COMPUTE BY** clauses
>
> ❑ c. View definitions
>
> ❑ d. Simple **SELECT** statements

Answers a, b, and c are correct. The **FOR XML** clause cannot be used in **SELECT** statements that have **GROUP BY** clauses or **COMPUTE BY** clauses or that are used to define views. Answer d is incorrect because the **FOR XML** clause can be used in a simple **SELECT** statement. (The clause cannot, however, be used in a nested **SELECT** statement.)

Question 7

John has written the following **SELECT** statement. What is the correct output?

```
USE Northwind
SELECT Customers.CustomerID,
       Orders.OrderID
From Customers JOIN Orders
On Customers.CustomerID = Orders.CustomerID
WHERE OrderID <10250
FOR XML AUTO
```

O a. (Typed on one line)

```
<Customers CustomerID="VINET"><Orders
    OrderID="10248"/>
</Customers><Customers CustomerID="TOMSP">
<Orders OrderID="10249"/></Customers>
```

O b. (Typed on one line)

```
<row CustomerID="VINET" OrderID="10248"/>
<row CustomerID="TOMSP" OrderID="10249"/>
```

O c.

```
VINET    10248
TOMSP    10249
```

O d. No output; you cannot use the **FOR XML** clause in this **SELECT** clause.

Answer a is correct. The **AUTO** parameter of the **FOR XML** clause formats the results in a simple, nested XML tree. Answer b is incorrect; it would be correct for the **RAW** mode of the **FOR XML** clause, but it isn't correct for the **AUTO** mode. Answer c is incorrect; it would be the result if you did not have a **FOR XML** clause or an **XMLDATA** argument with the proper **WITH** clause. Answer d is incorrect because the **FOR XML** clause is valid.

Question 8

Which of the following parameters of the **OPENXML** statement does the **sp_xml_preparedocument** stored procedure return?

○ a. **ROW PATTERN**

○ b. **idoc**

○ c. Mapping of rowset to columns

○ d. **BINARY BASE64**

Answer b is correct. The **sp_xml_preparedocument** stored procedure returns a pointer to the XML document. The pointer is then used in the **OPENXML** statement. Answer a is incorrect because Row Pattern XPath in the XML document is improper. Answer c is incorrect because the **flags** parameter is used to determine the output. Answer d is incorrect because **BINARY BASE64** is a parameter for the **FOR XML** clause.

Need to Know More?

 Iseminger, David. *SQL Server 2000 Reference Library*. Redmond, WA: Microsoft Press, 2000. ISBN 0-7356-1280-3. A selected collection of SQL Server 2000 Books Online; there are six volumes focused on key areas. Volume 1 contains information on XML and Internet support. Volume 5 contains all you want to know about Transact-SQL, including accessing heterogeneous data.

 MS SQL Server Books Online has sections on stored procedures. This collection can be installed from the SQL Server CD or accessed online through **http://msdn.microsoft.com/library/default.asp**.

 Search the TechNet CD or its online version through **www.microsoft.com/technet**. Keywords to search on are "stored procedures", "replication stored procedures", and "execute".

 http://msdn.microsoft.com/xml/default.asp—Find up-to-date information about XML development in SQL Server.

 www.microsoft.com/sql/ and **http://msdn.microsoft.com/sqlserver/default.asp** are good places to find up-to-date information about SQL Server.

 www.sqlmag.com—*SQL Magazine*—both the hard copy and the Web site—has a large amount of information on SQL Server.

Tuning and Optimizing Data Access

Terms you'll need to understand:

✓ RAID

✓ Thread

✓ Process

✓ RAM

✓ Paging

✓ Transaction

Techniques you'll need to master:

✓ Choosing an appropriate RAID level

✓ Using System Monitor

✓ Configuring SQL Server memory utilization

✓ Using SQL Profiler

✓ Using **DBCC SHOWCONTIG** to reduce disk fragmentation

✓ Using the **UPDATE STATISTICS** statement

After a database application is developed and implemented, steps must be taken to ensure that the application runs as efficiently as possible. The database needs to be monitored and optimized for efficiency. Data access and retrieval are often the most challenging performance areas for database developers. Many of the scalability and performance concerns that arise deal with data access features. As your database applications change over time, they must handle more users, heavier transaction workloads, and more complex functionality. Data access throughput becomes a major concern because increased workloads require more computer and network resources.

The foundation of high-performance data access includes high-quality architectural design, sufficient hardware resources, and optimized database-retrieval algorithms. Large database servers should have anywhere from 500 MB to 2 GB of RAM. Implementing two or more processors can also be very helpful. In this chapter, we will discuss these issues.

The Importance of Monitoring Performance

It's important to tune your database so that you maximize throughput while minimizing query response time. You also have to balance tuning for limiting network traffic and for keeping disk usage and CPU time to a minimum.

Performance issues should be considered before and during the design and development of your database, not after. After the database has been designed and filled with data, rearranging its structure can be very difficult. See Chapter 1 for more information

There are several ways to monitor database performance. To most effectively optimize the performance of SQL Server, you must determine which features will provide the biggest performance increase for the most widely used objects. For example, as you've learned from previous chapters, indexes allow SQL Server to locate data more efficiently—but only if they are used properly. You can use Query Analyzer to create visual plans in SQL Server so you can see how your indexes are being used in your queries.

To execute SQL statements in Query Analyzer:

1. Click Start|Programs|Microsoft SQL Server|Query Analyzer.

2. When the Connect To SQL Server dialog box appears, type the name of the computer running SQL Server, select either Windows Authentication or SQL Server authentication, and then click OK. You can type "localhost" for the SQL Server if you are running Query Analyzer on the same computer on which SQL Server is installed.

3. When Query Analyzer opens, type the following SQL statement as a test:

```
USE pubs
SELECT * FROM authors
```

4. To execute the query, press F5.

You can also monitor and tune SQL Server itself, in addition to Transact-SQL statements, indexes, and table joins in queries. We will also focus on optimizing Windows 2000 Server and using System Monitor and SQL Profiler.

Configuring Windows 2000 Server

Generally, Windows 2000 Server is configured optimally by using default settings; however, you can tweak a few settings to improve performance. For example, you can place the operating system's paging file on a different drive from the files used by SQL Server to improve throughput for paging. This will allow the operating system to write to the paging file while reading from another drive simultaneously.

Using RAID

In a RAID (redundant array of independent disks) hardware solution, the controller interface handles creating and regenerating redundant information. In Windows, the software can perform this activity. In either case, data is stored across an array of disks.

RAID utilizes multiple disk drives coordinated by a controller card, allowing individual data files to be written to more than one disk. There are two main ways to configure RAID drives: for performance or reliability. Various RAID levels are available; some offer better performance, and some offer better reliability:

➤ *RAID 0*—RAID 0 is striping, which provides high speed and low fault tolerance. RAID 0 provides the best performance but does not provide fault tolerance.

➤ *RAID 1*—RAID 1 is mirroring, which provides medium speed and high fault tolerance. RAID 1 provides the best fault tolerance but does not provide the best performance (due to writing data to one disk, as opposed to multiple disks concurrently).

➤ *RAID 5*—RAID 5 is striping with parity, which provides redundancy of all data on a disk array. This level allows a single disk to fail and be replaced while avoiding system downtime. Although RAID 5 offers lower performance than RAID 0 or RAID 1, it providers higher reliability and faster recovery.

To achieve optimal performance, you can combine RAID 1 and RAID 0 by mirroring a set of striped disks. The purpose of RAID 1 and RAID 5 is to guard against the loss of data in the event of a catastrophic hard disk failure. For all intents and purposes, the server will continue to operate as if no disk failure had occurred (albeit at a slower response rate) as will network load balancing and the load-balanced applications. However, there is no fault tolerance until the fault is repaired. Few RAID implementations can withstand two simultaneous failures.

When the failed disk is replaced, the data can be regenerated from the redundant information. Data regeneration occurs without bringing in backup tapes or performing manual update operations to cover transactions that took place since the last backup. When data regeneration is complete, all data is current and is again protected against disk failure. The ability to provide cost-effective high data availability is the key advantage of disk arrays.

Using System Monitor

The Windows 2000 Performance tool—the Performance console—is composed of two parts: System Monitor, and Performance Logs And Alerts. With System Monitor, you can collect and view real-time information about memory, disk, processor, and network activity (among others) in graph, histogram, or report form. You can configure logs to record performance data, and you can set system alerts to notify you when a specified counter's value is above or below a defined threshold. For more information about using System Monitor, see Windows NT/2000 Help.

To open the Performance console, perform the following steps:

1. Choose Start|Settings|Control Panel.

2. Double-click Administrative Tools.

3. Double-click Performance.

You can then add a performance counter by clicking the Add button on the console's toolbar. Once a counter has been added, corresponding information will be displayed in the status pane, as illustrated in Figure 13.1.

Use System Monitor to establish a performance baseline and to constantly monitor system performance. To analyze performance trends, you can compare current performance against the baseline.

The following lists of counters and events provide a starting point for monitoring SQL Server. Database administrators should create a custom monitoring system for individual servers, databases, and applications.

Performance Objects

Windows 2000 retrieves performance data from components in your computer. As a system component does its work, it generates performance data. That kind of data is called a *performance object* and is typically named for the component

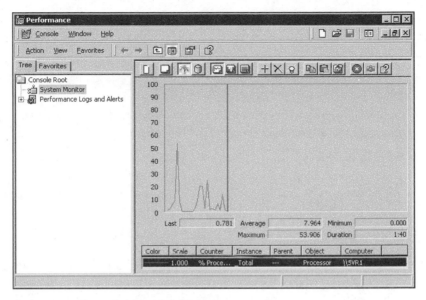

Figure 13.1   The status pane in the Performance console.

generating the data. For example, the Processor object is a collection of performance data about processors in your system.

Each performance object provides counters that represent data on specific aspects of a system or service. For example, the Pages/Sec counter provided by the Memory object tracks the rate of memory paging.

Although your system may typically make available many more objects, the default objects you'll use most frequently to monitor system components include the following:

➤ Disk usage counters:

  ➤ *Logical Disk: % Free Space*—You should ensure that the disk has plenty of free space for data and log file growth. You can set an alert when free space becomes low (about 10 percent) depending on database size and growth rate.

  ➤ *Physical Disk: Avg. Disk Queue Length*—This counter tells you the number of disk requests that are delayed because the disk cannot keep up with requests. If this number is consistently high, consider adjusting the disk configuration or reorganizing its data.

  ➤ *Physical Disk: % Disk Time*—A number greater than 90 percent on any disk means the disk is too busy, and you should consider adjusting the disk configuration or reorganizing its data.

➤ Memory counters:

　➤ *Process: Page Faults/Sec: sqlservr*—This counter tells you how many times SQL Server had to read from the disk for results rather than from memory. Normally, this number should be near zero, and you can use the Memory: Pages/Sec and Memory: Page Faults/Sec counters to analyze total system memory. If these counters are over 20, another process may be using too much memory. Another possibility is that you need to add more RAM to the server.

　➤ *SQL Server: Buffer Manager: Buffer Cache Hit Ratio*—This counter tells you how much requested data is coming from memory instead of from the hard drive. The counter should be 90 percent or greater. If not, you should consider adding more memory to the server.

➤ Processor counters:

　➤ *System: Processor Queue Length*—This counter tells you how many threads are waiting for the processor. If the queue length is zero, then CPU usage is low, and the disk subsystem could have a performance bottleneck.

　➤ *Processor: % Processor Time*—A number over 90 percent is too high. Consider upgrading your processor, or terminate applications other than SQL Server to ensure better throughput.

　➤ *Process: % Processor Time: sqlservr*—This counter indicates the percentage of processor time that all threads of the sqlservr process are using to execute instructions. Compare this to % Processor Time, which includes time used by threads running in other processes. If other processes are consuming too much time, terminate unneeded processes.

➤ SQL Server and database counters:

　➤ *SQL Server: General Statistics: User Connections*—Once you set user connections to the maximum expected number of concurrent users, use this counter to track the number of user connections. Set an alert to notify you when the number of current user connections reaches the maximum.

　➤ *SQL Server Locks: Number of Deadlocks/Sec*—This counter should be very low, if not zero. You can use the **sp_who** system stored procedure to see who might be locking the database.

　➤ *SQL Server: Databases: Transactions/Sec*—This counter shows how many transactions per second the specified database is supporting. This counter can be used for trend analysis.

　➤ *SQL Server: Databases: Percent Log Used*—This counter tells you how much of the transaction log is used for a database. You can create a log backup job and send a notification when the job runs successfully, or send an alert when the job fails.

➤ *SQL Server: Databases: Data File(s) Size (KB)*—This counter tells you the size of the data files for a database. The **tempdb** database is re-created each time SQL Server initializes, and if the **tempdb** data files are too small, the overall performance could be affected by **tempdb** autogrow operations.

Configuring SQL Server 2000

The goals of optimizing database performance are to minimize the response time for each query and to maximize the throughput of the entire database server by minimizing network traffic, disk I/O, and CPU time. Understanding how to design the logical and physical structure of the data, how to tune queries, and how to configure Microsoft SQL Server 2000 and the operating system can help you optimize database performance.

You can use Enterprise Manager to set the minimum and maximum amount of memory used for SQL Server 2000. To open the Memory properties, use the following procedure:

1. Right-click your server name in Enterprise Manager, and choose Properties from the context menu.

2. When the Properties dialog box appears, click the Memory tab (as illustrated in Figure 13.2).

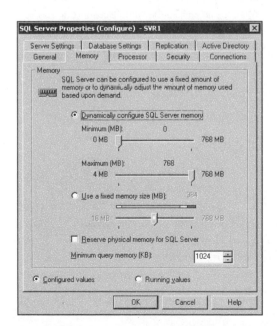

Figure 13.2 The Memory tab of the SQL Server Properties dialog box.

On the Memory tab, use the slider bars to set the minimum and maximum memory utilization. The maximum memory you can set is limited to the physical memory in your server. You can also set a fixed amount of memory, which is the same as setting the minimum and maximum amounts to the same value.

Using SQL Profiler

Although you can use System Monitor to evaluate performance, the effect might not be evident in your analysis. You can then use SQL Profiler to analyze the database's poor performance. You can use SQL Profiler to:

➤ List all long-running queries.

➤ Count all table scans, which are an indication that indexes are not being used.

➤ Analyze the queries that are creating deadlocks.

➤ Analyze the activity of a specific database user.

➤ Create a complete sample of database activity for the Index Tuning Wizard.

You can use SQL Profiler and System Monitor simultaneously on the same system to gather more detailed, time-related information on the interaction between hardware and software. For more information about System Monitor counters and interpreting them, see System Monitor's online help.

 As with other monitoring tools, SQL Profiler takes up system resources. Be sure to limit the number of traces as well as the complexity of your traces.

To run SQL Profiler:

1. Choose Start|Programs|Microsoft SQL Server|Enterprise Manager.

2. From the Tools menu, click SQL Profiler.

You must register the SQL server you want to profile after you start SQL Profiler. Then you connect to your SQL server as a member of the sysadmin role, such as the SA account. Once you register the SQL server, you can use the Create Trace Wizard or simply create a new trace. Every trace that gets executed contains information about what is being profiled along with information about how you want the results to be presented and the data you want the trace to include. This trace information describes what a SQL Profiler trace captures. To save trace results to a table, use the following procedure:

1. From the File menu, point to New, and then click Trace.

2. When the Connect To SQL Server dialog box appears, select the server to connect to and set the connection properties.

3. Enter a name for the trace in the Trace Name field of the Connect To SQL Server dialog box, and then click Save To Table.

4. When the Destination Table dialog box appears, select the destination database, and then enter or select the table name for the trace results.

5. Select the Set Maximum Rows (In Thousands) checkbox to specify the maximum number of records to save, as illustrated in Figure 13.3.

In the event you do not want to record the trace information on all items in a trace template, you can filter events using the following procedure:

1. From the File menu, point to Open, then click Trace Template.

2. Select the trace file to open.

3. In the Trace Template Properties dialog box, click the Filters tab.

4. In the Trace event list, click a criterion.

5. Enter a value in the field that appears beneath the trace event criterion.

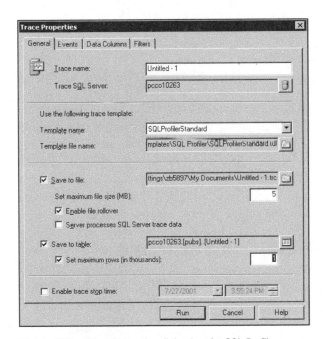

Figure 13.3   Trace Properties dialog box for SQL Profiler.

Reducing Disk Fragmentation

Rebuilding indexes is a useful way to remove fragmentation from the database. Fragmentation can have a large impact on I/O performance, so you should monitor fragmentation and remove it periodically. Use the **DBCC SHOWCONTIG** command to monitor how contiguous the pages are on a given index (this measurement is commonly referred to as scan density).

You can use the **TABLERESULTS** keyword with the **DBCC SHOWCONTIG** command to display the outcome as a result set. Results are displayed as a rowset. For example, the following code snippet defragments all indexes in the **Web** database.

```
USE Web
DBCC SHOWCONTIG WITH TABLERESULTS, ALL_INDEXES
```

Optimizing Transact-SQL Statements

Although you can check system-level server processes for performance problems, most of the time problems have to do with indexing or poorly optimized Transact-SQL (T-SQL) statements. You should consistently analyze any queries, inserts, updates, and deletes that the application is executing on the database. Queries that take too long to execute can be caused by the following problems:

➤ Bad network connections or distortion

➤ Bad RAM or not enough physical memory

➤ Missing or outdated statistics

➤ Improperly implemented indexes

You can usually improve performance for queries by adding pre-aggregated data to columns. The main thing to remember is this: For databases that are used mostly for data updates, low normalization causes poor performance because more data needs to be updated. On the other hand, low normalization for decision support (mostly **SELECT** statements) can usually help performance because of the low number of joins. For your databases, you will have to balance database performance needs in your design according to your business needs.

Using the UPDATE STATISTICS Statement

The **UPDATE STATISTICS** statement creates (or updates) information about the distribution of the key values for indexes to help SQL Server determine which indexes to use when processing queries. **UDPDATE STATISTICS** should be used when a large amount of data in an indexed column has been added, changed, or deleted.

UPDATE STATISTICS causes a shared table lock to be placed on the table from which statistical information is being retrieved. This lock will prevent **UPDATE**, **DELETE**, and **INSERT** statements from being executed. **SELECT** statements will execute normally.

The following is the syntax for **UPDATE STATISTICS**:

```
UPDATE STATISTICS MyTable
[MyIndex]
[WITH
[FULLSCAN] [SAMPLE] [PERCENT or ROWS]
[ALL | COLUMNS | INDEX]
[NORECOMPUTE]
```

Practice Questions

Question 1

System Monitor provides various types of counters, which you can use to monitor such things as the following:

Bottlenecked processor resources

Memory usage

Memory bottlenecks or leaks

Match the following definitions and statements with the counter types just listed (some items may be used more than once):

Memory\ Available Bytes

Processor\ Interrupts/sec

Memory\ Page Reads/Sec

System\ Processor Queue Length

Memory\ Pages/Sec

Processor\ % Processor Time

Memory\ Cache Bytes

Memory\ Transition Faults/Sec

Memory\ Pool Nonpaged Bytes

Paging File\ % Usage Object (all instances)

Cache\ Data Map Hits %

Server\ Pool Paged Bytes and Server\Pool Nonpaged Bytes

Process(process)\ % Processor Time

Memory\ Pool Paged Bytes

The correct answer is:

Bottlenecked processor resources

Processor\ Interrupts/Sec

Processor\ % Processor Time

Process(process)\ % Processor Time

System\ Processor Queue Length

Memory usage

Memory\ Available Bytes

Memory\ Cache Bytes

Memory bottlenecks or leaks

Memory\ Pages/Sec

Memory\ Page Reads/Sec

Memory\ Transition Faults/Sec

Memory\ Pool Paged Bytes

Memory\ Pool Nonpaged Bytes

Paging File\ % Usage Object (all instances)

Cache\ Data Map Hits %

Server\ Pool Paged Bytes and Server\Pool Nonpaged Bytes

Question 2

Which of the following RAID categories is known as disk mirroring?

- a. RAID 0
- b. RAID 1
- c. RAID 2
- d. RAID 3
- e. RAID 4
- f. RAID 5

Answer b is correct. RAID 1 (also called disk mirroring) uses two drives that store identical information. Answer a is incorrect because RAID 0 is disk striping with no fault tolerance protection. RAID 0 has the highest performance, but if one disk fails, all the data on the stripe set becomes inaccessible. Answer c is incorrect because RAID 2 is disk striping with error-correcting code (ECC), which is not as efficient as other RAID levels and is not generally used. Answer d is incorrect because RAID 3 is disk striping with ECC stored as parity. RAID 3 uses a single redundant check disk for each group of drives. Answer e is incorrect because RAID 4 is disk striping in large blocks or sector striping on the data on the drives. Answer f is incorrect because RAID 5 is disk striping with parity across three or more physical disks. RAID 5 volumes have better read performance than do mirrored volumes.

Question 3

Which of the following RAID categories is known as disk striping with parity?

- ○ a. RAID 0
- ○ b. RAID 1
- ○ c. RAID 2
- ○ d. RAID 3
- ○ e. RAID 4
- ○ f. RAID 5

Answer f is correct. RAID 5 is disk striping with parity across three or more physical disks. RAID 5 volumes have better read performance than do mirrored volumes. Answer a is incorrect because RAID 0 is disk striping with no fault tolerance protection. It has the highest performance, but if one disk fails, all the data on the stripe set becomes inaccessible. Answer b is incorrect because RAID 1 (disk mirroring) uses two drives that store identical information. Answer c is incorrect because RAID 2 is disk striping with error correction code (ECC), which uses extra check disks, with data bits striped across the data and check disks. Answer d is incorrect because RAID 3 is disk striping with ECC stored as parity. RAID 3 uses a single redundant check disk for each group of drives. Answer e is incorrect because RAID 4 is disk striping in large blocks or sector striping on the data on the drives.

Question 4

> You are running a data-intensive operation on SQL Server over the network. You need to assess the server and log its status. Before you start to monitor the Windows 2000 server that SQL Server is running on, which two objects most likely have the most usage? [Check all correct answers]
>
> ❑ a. Network
>
> ❑ b. Processor
>
> ❑ c. Disk
>
> ❑ d. Memory

Answers b and d are correct. Answer c is incorrect because nothing in this scenario indicates disk performance problems. Those would be indicated by % Disk Time. Answer a is incorrect because a network failure would probably prevent the query from taking place, and the network would not have the most usage.

Question 5

> You are running a data-intensive operation on SQL Server over the network. You need to assess the server and log its status. Upon monitoring the server, you notice that there is a low rate of page-read operations and high values for % Disk Time and Avg. Disk Queue Length. What is most likely causing the problem?
>
> ○ a. Network
>
> ○ b. Processor
>
> ○ c. Disk
>
> ○ d. Memory

Answer c is correct. If a low rate of page-read operations coincides with high values for % Disk Time and Avg. Disk Queue Length, there could be a disk bottleneck. Answer a is incorrect because a network failure would probably prevent the query from taking place and would not have caused a high value for % Disk Time. Answer b is incorrect because you were not given any processor information. Answer d is incorrect because a memory problem would not cause a decrease in page reads.

Question 6

> You are running a data-intensive operation on SQL Server over the network. You need to assess the server and log its status. Upon monitoring the server, you notice that there is an increase in disk queue length. You suspect a disk problem, and you find that the increase in disk queue length is not accompanied by a decrease in the page-read rate. What is most likely causing the problem?
>
> ○ a. Network
>
> ○ b. Processor
>
> ○ c. Disk
>
> ○ d. Memory

Answer d is correct. Answer a is incorrect because a network failure would probably prevent the query from taking place and would not have caused a high value for % Disk Time. Answer b is incorrect because you were not given any processor information. Answer c is incorrect because a low rate of page-read operations with high values for % Disk Time and Avg. Disk Queue Length indicates a disk bottleneck.

Question 7

> Which of the following statements about indexes are true? [Check all correct answers]
>
> ❑ a. The performance of **INSERT** statements is improved as the number of indexes per table increases.
>
> ❑ b. The performance of **INSERT** statements is improved when there are fewer indexes per table.
>
> ❑ c. The performance of **UPDATE** statements is improved when there are more indexes per table.
>
> ❑ d. The performance of **INSERT** statements is improved when there are fewer indexes per table.

Answers b and d are correct. The performance of **INSERT, UPDATE,** and **DELETE** statements is improved when there are fewer indexes per table.

Question 8

You want to improve database performance for **SELECT** statements. What can you do to achieve this? [Check all correct answers]

❏ a. Make the database highly normalized.

❏ b. Denormalize the database.

❏ c. Remove columns that contain pre-aggregated data.

❏ d. Implement new columns that contain pre-aggregated data.

Answers b and d are correct. Answer a is incorrect because highly normalized databases require more joins, thereby hindering performance. Answer c is incorrect because pre-aggregated data returns results faster.

Question 9

You are developing a physical design for your company's database. One of the other database administrators is using the Database Maintenance Plan Wizard to perform system administration tasks. One day he notices that adding an index or updating statistics does not update the schema and does not force a new execution plan. Based on this information, where should you place the transaction log?

○ a. On its own disk set

○ b. On a disk set used by other databases on another server

○ c. On a disk set used by other databases on the same server

○ d. On a mirrored disk set

Answer a is the best answer in this case. Answers b, c, and d are incorrect because optimally, the transaction log should be on its own disk set for best performance. Be sure to consider only the necessary question text when evaluating your answers. Also, remember to choose the *best* answer.

Question 10

What tool can you use to find long-running queries that have been issued from an instance of Query Analyzer?

○ a. System Monitor

○ b. The Performance console

○ c. Query Analyzer

○ d. SQL Server Profiler

Answer d is correct. Answers a and b are incorrect because System Monitor and the Performance console get information about operating-system-level objects only. Answer c is incorrect because Query Analyzer is used to execute Transact-SQL statements and to view their results, not to identify long-running queries.

Need to Know More?

 Iseminger, David. *SQL Server 2000 Reference Library*. Redmond, WA: Microsoft Press, 2000. ISBN 0-7356-1280-3. A selected collection of SQL Server 2000 Books Online; there are six volumes focused on key areas. Volume 1 contains information on database support. Volume 5 contains all you want to know about Transact-SQL, including tuning and optimizing data.

 MS SQL Server Books Online has sections on tuning and optimizing. This book set can be installed from the SQL Server CD or accessed online through: **http://msdn.microsoft.com/library/default.asp**.

 Search the TechNet CD or its online version through **www.microsoft.com/ technet**. Keywords to search on include "tuning", "optimizing", and "data access".

 http://msdn.microsoft.com/tuning/default.asp—Find up-to-date information about tuning SQL Server.

 www.microsoft.com/sql/ and **http://msdn.microsoft.com/sqlserver/ default.asp** are good places to find up-to-date information about SQL Server.

 www.sqlmag.com—*SQL Magazine*—both the hard copy and the Web site—has a large amount of information on SQL Server.

Database Security Plan

Terms you'll need to understand:

- ✓ Login authentication
- ✓ Permissions
- ✓ User accounts
- ✓ Fixed server role
- ✓ Fixed database role
- ✓ Public role
- ✓ User-defined database role
- ✓ Application role
- ✓ **ENCRYPT N** option
- ✓ **GRANT** statement
- ✓ **DENY** statement
- ✓ **REVOKE** statement
- ✓ Windows authentication mode
- ✓ Mixed mode
- ✓ Database security plan
- ✓ Ownership chains

Techniques you'll need to master:

- ✓ Restricting user accounts
- ✓ Controlling data access
- ✓ Applying ownership chains
- ✓ Implementing row-level security
- ✓ Restricting direct access to tables
- ✓ Designing a database security plan

No matter what form your database design takes, your principal concern should be securing its data for continued authorized use. This involves protecting the database from intended actions as well as from accidental ones that would negatively affect its continued operation as a valid source of data for your users.

Before we discuss how the pieces come together, it will help considerably if we discuss some basic security concepts that you will need to incorporate into your SQL Server 2000 database security plan. Because most of the decisions surrounding databases and their security are at the database administrator level, this chapter is written with the assumption that you are the database administrator. However, this information is just as important if you are designing a database and someone else will later be the database administrator.

Login Authentication

Before SQL Server allows a user to access data, SQL Server validates that particular user's identity and confirms that the user (or a group to which the user belongs) has already obtained approval for the access being attempted. As part of the login process, SQL Server verifies a user's identity by comparing the user-provided name and password (entered at login) with the same information previously stored on the server. To accomplish this, SQL Server first confirms that proper authorization for granting such access has previously been obtained by the user. That means that someone with access-granting authority has already approved this user's access and loaded both the username and a password into the server.

If the username and password supplied by the user match those stored in the server, the user passes the login authentication check and the server will let the user continue. If not, the login attempt fails.

The idea behind this login authentication is much the same as that used when network users attempt access to Windows 2000 objects through its security model. In fact, as you will later see, the Windows 2000 login procedure can actually facilitate a user's logging into SQL Server.

Permissions

Simply verifying users' identities does not necessarily mean that they have permission (or the right) to go where they want to go or do what they want to do. Users have to be given permission to perform such actions. Having permission to accomplish a task indicates that a user has already obtained proper authorization (from someone who has been granted permission to subsequently allow others) to perform such actions on the requested resources. So, as another part of a secure login process, the server checks for any applicable restrictions that might prevent a user's access to the data even though the user's identity has already been confirmed.

In SQL Server, a user must first obtain permission before accessing a SQL database or its data. After the user gains that initial access, SQL Server repeatedly uses permissions (user or group) when it determines whether specific user actions on the data or resources have already been allowed. In other words, after SQL Server's authentication process recognizes the user and confirms that prior access approval has been granted, it must next rule out the presence of any restrictions placed on the user's access that would negate the approval being requested. Such restrictions could prohibit this user (or any of the groups he belongs to) from logging in at the specific time he is attempting access, or it could limit his access to particular resources (or prevent access entirely).

Database User Accounts

One of the ways of tracking information about a user is through database user accounts. SQL Server 2000 treats user accounts much like the Windows 2000 security model does.

In fact, one of the possible SQL Server security modes (discussed later in this section) involves the direct use of Windows 2000 users and groups. In this case, SQL Server interprets a user account (or a group account) as consisting of all the information that defines it on a network. This information includes the username and password required for the user to log on, the groups to which the user account belongs, and the rights and permissions the user has for using the system and accessing its resources.

 If you delete and re-create a user account in Windows 2000, you must also delete the account from SQL Server's user database so the security identifier (SID) that SQL Server relies upon for its security is reset.

Another SQL Server security mode option (also discussed later in this section) is available. In this mode, rather than using Windows 2000 users and groups, you can grant data access after verifying authorization information (similar to that used with Windows 2000 security) in SQL Server's own database user accounts.

Note: Remember that in either case, SQL Server database user accounts are independently established for each separate database.

For the exam, be aware that any of the following can be used as a valid security account in SQL Server 2000:

➤ A Windows 2000 user

➤ A Windows 2000 group

➤ A SQL Server 2000 user

➤ An application role

➤ A user-defined role

Roles

A further refinement of SQL Server's user accounts is the concept of roles. Roles provide a means for grouping and applying centralized permissions to any number of user accounts when those users perform similar functions (or roles) in an organization. Resembling the way a Windows 2000 group consolidates multiple users into one location (where a single applicable permission can affect the entire group), SQL Server roles consolidate multiple permissions, which you can then grant to multiple users who perform similar tasks. There are several types of roles: fixed server roles, fixed database roles, the public role, user-defined database roles, and application roles.

SQL Server user accounts can have multiple roles assigned.

You can either use the predefined roles that are included with SQL Server or define your own roles. The predefined roles include *fixed server roles* (sometimes referred to simply as *server roles*) or *fixed database roles* (sometimes referred to simply as *database roles*). You determine which type of role to use based upon the level at which your database user needs access via that role.

The term "fixed" indicates that the list of these roles cannot be changed; you cannot add or remove predefined server or database roles. That is where *user-defined database roles* come in. This user-defined group can be tailored to include permissions to carry out any company task that will be performed by one or more individuals.

The *public role* can be considered a special case in the list of fixed database roles. A user's minimum set of permissions comes from the public role. It is different from the other roles in that users cannot be added to or removed from the public role.

The final type of role is an *application role*. It, like the public role, is special in that users cannot be added to or removed from this role. The application role, as we will explain, is much different from any of the other roles. Database administrators use an application role when they want to have the application determine the restrictions on a user's data access.

Fixed Server Role

The predefined list of permissions included in the fixed server role deals primarily with tasks performed at the server level and can be seen as potentially applying to all databases contained therein. These roles are typically used for assigning system maintenance tasks. Table 14.1 lists the SQL Server 2000 fixed server roles and their inherent permissions.

Fixed Database Role

The predefined list of permissions included in the fixed database role deals primarily with tasks performed only at the database level and involves tasks affecting only the specified databases where their definitions exist. Table 14.2 lists the SQL Server 2000 fixed database roles and their inherent permissions.

Public Role

Not usually listed as a fixed database role, the public role can be found in all databases (including the system databases that are installed automatically when creating your SQL server). Everyone accessing the database is automatically a member of the public role by default, and it is through this role that database administrators assign a minimum set of permissions to all database users. The

Table 14.1 Fixed server roles and permissions.	
Role	Permission(s)
dbcreator	Create or change
sysadmin	All
serveradmin	Configure servers
securityadmin	Configure server security
processadmin	Configure processes
setupadmin	Manage or install replication
bulkadmin	Perform **BULK INSERT**
diskadmin	Configure disks

Table 14.2 Fixed database roles and permissions.	
Role	**Permission(s)**
db_owner	All
db_securityadmin	Manage security
db_accessadmin	Manage access
db_backupoperator	Perform backups
db_datareader	Read table data
db_datawriter	Change table data
db_ddladmin	Change database objects
db_denydatawriter	Cannot change database objects
db_denydatareader	Cannot read table data

public role, therefore, can be seen as applicable at the database level and could easily be listed as one with special features.

Note: All database users are automatically members of the public role, and their presence there is protected because you cannot add or delete users from the public role.

User-Defined Database Role

In addition to using the predefined permission lists (included in the fixed database and server roles), you can design your own sets of permissions by creating user-defined database roles. These roles typically deal with tasks (other than those discussed earlier) that multiple workers perform in an organization. A database administrator tailor-makes the role, adding all the permissions she wants authorized for a non-specified user. Later she can add specific users to the role without having to create sets of permissions for each user.

For example, if 20 workers need the same set of permissions (because they perform similar job functions), a database administrator would have to create that set of permissions only once, and then she could simply add users or remove them from the role whenever she wanted to grant or revoke those permissions. Roles, therefore, ease the administrative burden of placing and removing permissions at the individual user level.

If an existing Windows 2000 (or Windows NT) group or fixed role does not exist, you can implement a user-defined database role to grant database-level permissions to a group of users.

The user-defined database role is the most widely used role. Fixed server and database roles can be viewed as having been added for your convenience when you first create your database. Both fixed methods provide generalized roles whose intent should not be construed as being sufficient for all instances. For the most part, tailored user-defined database roles should be created so that they furnish database users with only those permissions that they actually need.

To create a new user-defined role (i.e., **NewRoleName**), use the **sp_addrole** system stored procedure:

```
EXEC sp_addrole 'NewRoleName'
```

To add a user (in this example, **rmcmahon**) to your new user-defined role (**NewRoleName**), use the **sp_addrolemember** system stored procedure:

```
EXEC sp_addrolemember NewRoleName, [ rmcmahon ]
```

To drop a user (**rmcmahon**) from your user-defined role (**NewRoleName**), use the **sp_droprolemember** system stored procedure:

```
EXEC sp_droprolemember NewRoleName, [ rmcmahon ]
```

To drop a user-defined role (**NewRoleName**), use the **sp_droprole** system stored procedure:

```
EXEC sp_droprole NewRoleName
```

Application Role

Finally, there is one additional type of role: the application role. Using the application role, database administrators can shift the access-granting decision (when a user attempts a SQL Server connection) to the application in use by the user at the time of the attempted access.

To create a new application role (i.e., **NewAppRoleName**) with an access password (i.e., **SecureAccess**), use the **sp_addapprole** system stored procedure:

```
EXEC sp_addapprole 'NewAppRoleName' , 'SecureAccess'
```

Should you want to add encryption to the previous example, use the **sp_addapprole** system stored procedure with the **ENCRYPT N** option:

```
EXEC sp_addapprole 'NewAppRoleName' , {ENCRYPT N 'SecureAccess'}
```

Note: The previous encryption option is available only with ODBC and OLE DB clients and is not available with DB-Lib. With data sources for which encryption is not available, use encrypting protocols for network communication.

Now that you have (using either of the previous examples) created your new application role (**NewAppRoleName**), use the **GRANT** statement to add the specific rights (such as **ALL**) on the desired table (such as **Writers**):

```
GRANT ALL ON Writers TO NewAppRoleName
```

Note: When assigning rights to a table, you can specify the column where these rights apply. Otherwise, they apply to the whole table.

Conversely, should you have to remove rights from your application role (**NewAppRoleName**), use the **DENY** statement to remove the specific rights (**ALL**) from the desired table (**Writers**):

```
DENY ALL ON Writers TO NewAppRoleName
```

However, if you should want to reverse a rights assignment from your application role (**NewAppRoleName**) put in place by either of the previous two **GRANT** or **DENY** statements, use the **REVOKE** statement to reverse the previous action you took relative to specific rights (**ALL**) on the desired table (**Writers**):

```
REVOKE ALL ON Writers TO NewAppRoleName
```

 Application roles can have applications assigned to them; however, user and group accounts cannot be assigned (or mapped) to them.

Authentication Modes

Before granting users access to your secured data, you must determine which optional authentication mode—Windows 2000 or SQL Server 2000—will perform the required authentication check. In the latest two software releases (SQL Server 7 and SQL Server 2000), SQL Server secures its user accounts in one of only two alternative security modes: Windows authentication mode or mixed mode. Both login options currently available minimally involve the Windows 2000 (or Windows NT 4) security model instead of, as with earlier versions, relying solely on SQL Server for authentication.

Note: The SQL Server standard security mode is not an available option in SQL Server 2000.

Windows Authentication Mode

As shown in Figure 14.1, the default setup for SQL Server's authentication is Windows authentication mode. It is the default because this setting provides the highest security level of the choices available and indicates that Microsoft suggests that you should impose the highest security level possible on your data's access.

This authentication mode relies on the strength of the security identifier (SID) features that control network objects' access within the Windows 2000 authentication process. When you select this mode, your users' connections to SQL Server become trusted connections, so users will be required to first log into a Windows 2000 network. Actually, either Windows NT 4 or Windows 2000 will work when this mode is used. In both cases, the account representing the network user object (or any group object the user belongs to) can be the location where you, as the database administrator, assign the right for your user (or group) to log into SQL Server. What's more, because your users log into Windows 2000 and SQL Server at the same time (assuming they have had the right of access granted to them) and with the same password, the database administrator has less password maintenance to do, and users have fewer passwords to remember.

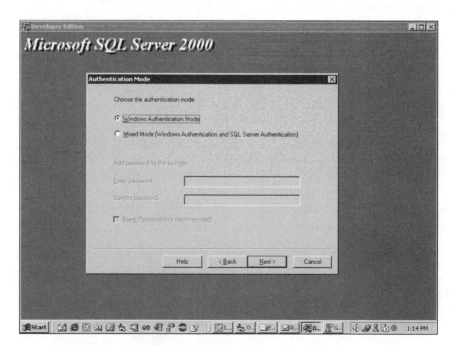

Figure 14.1   SQL Server 2000's authentication mode selection window.

Mixed Mode

As shown in Figure 14.1, the other setup choice for SQL Server's authentication option is mixed mode. This mode provides a somewhat lower security level for your data than the default Windows authentication mode, but it trades heightened security for backward compatibility and lets users access SQL Server from operating systems (like Windows 98 or Windows ME) that cannot support Windows authentication mode.

In mixed mode, Windows can still authenticate users whenever the client and server are both able to perform such authentication. However, in the absence of this ability, SQL Server requests a username and password in a procedure similar to that used for Windows 2000 logins. Rather than compare the username and password with the Windows 2000 stored information, SQL Server has its own information stored for the comparison and does its own authentication.

Because it cannot supply the same security check as Windows 2000, SQL Server cannot furnish users with access to trusted connections based on its own lower-level security mode. Rather, users connected using only SQL Server authentication are considered to be operating over non-trusted connections.

Should you decide to use mixed mode, you will have to enter and confirm an **sa** (system administrator) password or check (and later verify) the box and leave the password blank. These items can be seen in Figure 14.1.

Note: You are strongly urged never to leave your sa password blank.

Now that we have reviewed many of SQL Server's security features, let's look at how they all come together as interconnected pieces of your overall security plan.

The Database Security Plan

Your database security plan represents the way you protect your database's information by using many of the components discussed previously. We should start by explaining the difference between a security plan and a security policy. A *security policy* identifies the rules that will be followed to maintain security in a system, while a *security plan* details how those rules will be implemented. A security policy is generally included within a security plan.

 You should reexamine your security plan on a regular basis to ensure its currency.

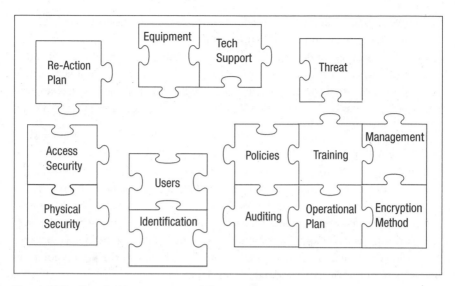

Figure 14.2   Security plan components fitting together.

As shown in Figure 14.2, the components of a security plan are similar to pieces of a large puzzle.[1] When the plan works properly, the pieces all fit snugly and lock seamlessly together, forming a secure framework that protects your information. However, when the plan does not work, even one faulty piece can weaken the whole plan and cause its total collapse.

Authentication Mode

The level of security your database security plan can maintain is determined by the authentication mode you select when you first install SQL Server. Therefore, before you begin your installation, you should already have determined your plan for authenticating users and granting them access to your data. That being said, your first priority obviously has to be your choice of authentication modes.

As we said earlier, two authentication modes are available—Windows authentication mode and mixed mode. Whichever you choose, limitations will be imposed on both you and your users. Either your login requirements will be stringent and will result in heightened security, or your login requirements will be less stringent and will result in lower levels of security.

---

[1] Reprinted from Richard McMahon and Glen Bicking, *Windows 2000 Security Design Exam Prep* (Scottsdale, AZ: The Coriolis Group, 2000), p. 53.

When Windows authentication mode is used, users must meet the login restrictions placed on them from the Windows NT/2000 server. This is the more stringent authentication mode, but it is the one normally recommended. Although this mode takes more effort to configure properly, your users will be able to access resources over trusted connections, and users will need only one user account and password to access both their networked resources and their data in SQL Server.

The easier mode for a database administrator to configure—mixed mode—does not provide users with access to resources over trusted connections. Their access is provided over non-trusted connections. Using Enterprise Manager to add SQL-Server-authenticated users is initially easier than going through the process of adding them through the Windows 2000 security procedures. If your environment includes (as most do) more than a few database servers, using SQL-Server-authenticated users can quickly become more work in the long run. This is because SQL-Server-authenticated users are local to the server, and the permissions you assign them apply only at the database level.

Users and Groups

Although your first database security priority might be your selection of which authentication mode to use, your network's implementation of user accounts (and its subsequent use of groups) will definitely affect how you create your database users. After you have your Windows 2000 user accounts, or you create your SQL Server 2000 user accounts, you should consider putting users who need the same levels of access together and creating groups to reduce the number of times you have to grant permissions. When you assign permissions to a group, granting one of those permissions to a user involves simply adding that user to the group. Taking the permission away simply means removing that user from the group with that permission. You can also deny users or groups permissions by using similar tactics.

This ability to add or remove users' permissions by managing group memberships becomes more important because you can assign multiple permissions to a single group when members of that group all require the same permissions. You can also deny multiple permissions to a single group when members of that group all require denial of the same permissions.

Database Access

No matter which authentication mode you selected and no matter where you created your user accounts, your single most powerful security decision is whether to grant a user access to the database at all. If you don't grant database access, users will not be granted access. You should, therefore, weigh carefully the user's need for such access and not grant it without a demonstrated need. On the other hand, because users typically require access to the database when performing many of their main job functions, you should not make obtaining permission for such access unnecessarily difficult. Remember, too, that the use of SQL Server's **guest** account is optional and not available unless you invoke the option.

At this point, you can also create a database role that permits access to your database. This role can then be used for users gaining access to your database through either of the authentication modes available. This is possible because, as we discussed, you can assign a SQL-Server-authenticated user to database roles. Because this gives you a single point where you can allow or deny access, it simplifies later access determination.

Permission Assignment

Once you give users access to the data, you can begin using the database roles (discussed earlier in this chapter) for assigning permissions. Using roles allows a more closely database-aligned definition of the groupings where you grant permissions for users to perform similar tasks. You can do this by using the Windows groups already formed on your network, but you might be able to create more applicable names for the groupings if you create roles and give them names that clearly describe those users needing to perform those roles.

An additional reason for using database roles to form groups is that these roles are part of your database; therefore, you can add your SQL-Server-authenticated users as well as your Windows-authenticated users. Roles clearly provide you with a single location where you can assign permissions one time and then invoke those permissions by using any of the methods previously described for grouping users (users, local groups, global groups, SQL Server logins, and so on).

After you have your roles created, you use the **GRANT, DENY,** and **REVOKE** statements that we discussed earlier in the chapter. Remember, permissions applied to the applicable roles by using these statements are passed on to the users assigned to those roles. However, it is also important to note that any instance of a **DENY** anywhere in a user's assigned roles removes any permissions applied through any other permission-granting mechanism.

Ownership Chains

Implicit in the previous permissions discussion is an understanding of the concept of ownership chains. The person creating an object is considered that object's owner. If a person creates an initial object and then creates subsequent objects using that initial object, the ownership chain is maintained. Permissions are checked only once—at the beginning of the chain. As long as the ownership chain is not broken, permission is assumed to be granted.

On the other hand, if one person creates an object and grants someone the right to use it when creating the subsequent objects, the ownership chain is broken when those subsequent objects are created. When access to those subsequent objects is later attempted, SQL Server notes the broken ownership chain and verifies whether the creator has granted access rights to the second person. If the rights were granted, SQL Server allows the second person to have access.

Going one step further, if the second person created a second object using the creator's initial object, SQL Server's use of the ownership chain would determine subsequent data use. If the second person tried granting permission for a third person to access his new object, SQL Server would deny the third person access to the second object. That is, it would deny access unless the creator of the first object explicitly granted access to his initial object to the third person as well as to the second person. Otherwise, SQL Server would allow the access that the creator had intended.

With a table or a view, the owner can determine who can later be granted access to his data. For example, when the owner of a table creates a view, he can grant an additional user permission to view the data without worrying about that user's further granting viewing rights to additional users. If the second user attempts to grant such rights, SQL Server's check of the ownership chain shows that the second user was not the creator of the data that forms the basis for the view; SQL Server therefore denies the second person the right to grant the permission, and this denial denies access to the additional users.

 Stored procedures are a valuable part of database security because stored procedures can access tables to which the user does not have rights. In addition, setting the access permissions via stored procedures this way provides more granular security on the underlying tables because the procedures can allow modifications on a row or column basis without using views or column-level permissions.

Practice Questions

Case Study

The Ellie Company is a book-publishing company. It has offices in New York and California. It has just acquired a small publishing company with an office in Dallas. This acquired company uses Oracle for its database management system. The Ellie Company uses Microsoft SQL Server 2000.

Current Situation

The databases in the California and New York offices are both called **EliePubs**. The database in Dallas is called **AllPubs** and is an Oracle database.

Proposed Situation

The company wants to keep the data in the Dallas office in Oracle and keep the data in the other offices in SQL Server. The company wants to be able to query data from all sources in the home office in New York.

Sales Manager

I am going to need sales reports that include data from all three sites. I don't want to have to get three separate reports and compare them manually.

Question 1

The New York database administrator wants to add a new user (Mike Lindsey: username **mlindsey**) from the recently acquired company in Dallas and wants this user to have only the permissions necessary to manage processes running on the New York SQL server. Which of the following options shows the most correct statement that will allow this?

○ a.
```
EXEC sp_addsrvrrolemember
'NEWYORK\mlindsey', 'processadmin'
```

○ b.
```
GRANT sp_addsrvrrolemember
'NEWYORK\mlindsey', 'processadmin'
```

○ c.
```
EXEC sp_addsrvrrolemember
'NEWYORK\mlindsey', 'syssadmin'
```

○ d.
```
GRANT sp_adddbrolemember
'NEWYORK\mlindsey', 'syssadmin'
```

Answer a is correct. It uses the correct syntax and grants only enough permission to perform the required task. Answers b and d are incorrect because **GRANT** is the wrong statement to effect this change. Additionally, answer d does not use the correct stored procedure to add a new user to a fixed server role. Answer c, though it would indeed allow this user to perform this function, is incorrect because the database administrator would be granting far too much authority to this user.

Question 2

Which of the following is not a type of user rights associated with permissions within databases?

○ a. **DELETE**

○ b. **REFER**

○ c. **INSERT**

○ d. **SELECT**

○ e. **EXECUTE**

○ f. **UPDATE**

Answer b is correct. The correct type is **REFERENCES** instead of **REFER**. Answers a, c, d, e, and f are all correct types of user rights for assigning permissions.

Question 3

For this case study, the California office's database administrator wants to allow server-wide login execution privileges (to her database's **Writers** table) for anyone filling the **serveradmin** role. Which of the following shows the correct code to allow these privileges?

○ a.
```
GRANT EXECUTE ON Writers TO serveradmin
```

○ b.
```
EXECUTE GRANT ON Writers TO serveradmin
```

○ c.
```
GRANT TO serveradmin EXECUTE ON Writers
```

○ d.
```
GRANT TO Writers EXECUTE ON serveradmin
```

Answer a is correct. This shows the correct syntax for the required rights assignment. Answers b, c, and d contain the same information, but they all use incorrect syntax.

. . . .

Question 4

For this case study, Alex Bitoun works in the new Dallas office and wants to create a new
application role. Rearrange the following code snippets in the correct order to accomplish this
task. Not all items need to be used, but use all that are appropriate for this role's creation.

```
USE DallasSvr,
'DallasSvr',
FROM
USE ElliePubs
'Dallasapp2',
,'odbc'
N
sp_addapprole
'secureword'
USE ALLPubs
SELECT name,
DB-LIB
sp_addlinkedserver
ENCRYPT
GO
```

The correct answer is:

```
USE ALLPubs
EXEC sp_addapprole 'Dallasapp2',
 {ENCRYPT N 'secureword'),'odbc'
GO
```

This answer uses all applicable items for creating the desired role.

Question 5

For this case study, the California office's database administrator wants to allow server-wide login execution privileges (to her database's **Writers** table) for anyone filling the **serveradmin** role. Until this morning, when your user account was deleted and re-created to increase your security access, your Windows 2000 user account was a member of that **serveradmin** role. Which of the following shows the correct code to allow these privileges with no further actions?

○ a.
```
GRANT EXECUTE ON Writers TO serveradmin
```

○ b.
```
EXECUTE GRANT ON Writers TO serveradmin
```

○ c.
```
GRANT TO serveradmin EXECUTE ON Writers
```

○ d. None of the above

Answer d is correct. An additional step is required for the database administrator to delete and re-create your database user account to reset the Windows 2000 security identifier that SQL Server uses. Answer a shows the correct syntax for the required rights assignment, but it assumes that the database administrator has already deleted and re-created your SQL Server database user account. Answers b and c contain the same information as answer a, but they both use incorrect syntax and are missing the step requiring the database administrator to delete your database user account.

Question 6

Which of the following is the true statement regarding the use of SQL Server's **guest** account?

○ a. The use of the guest account is optional.

○ b. When a user logs into SQL Server, he always assumes the identity of the guest account.

○ c. All users can assume the identity of the guest account to log into SQL Server.

○ d. You can add the guest account to and delete it from all databases.

Answer a is correct. Using a guest account on a database is an administrator's decision. Answers b, c, and d are all false statements. Answer b is incorrect because the identity can be assumed only if a guest account exists, and it will be assumed only if the user does not otherwise have access. Answer c is incorrect because users who have been denied access cannot log in as a guest. Answer d is incorrect because the guest account can be neither added to nor deleted from the **master** or **tempdb** databases.

Question 7

Which of the following are the correct names for the authentication modes available when you're installing SQL Server 2000? [Check all correct answers]

- ❑ a. SQL Server security mode
- ❑ b. Windows authentication mode
- ❑ c. Secure mode
- ❑ d. Standard security mode
- ❑ e. Enhanced security mode
- ❑ f. Mixed mode

Answers b and f are correct. The authentication modes available in SQL Server 2000 are Windows authentication mode and mixed mode. Answers a and d both refer to the same mode of security that was available until the release of SQL 7, but that is not an option in SQL Server 2000. Answers c and e are made-up names.

Question 8

Which of the following is the true statement regarding the use of application roles?

- ○ a. The use of passwords is optional.
- ○ b. To use the application role, your database user must be added to the member list.
- ○ c. Users assuming the application role inherit role permissions from all databases assigned.
- ○ d. The only current database role permissions retained by a user are those assigned to the public role.

Answer d is correct. Users lose all existing permissions in the current database except those assigned to the public role. Answers a, b, and c are all false statements. Answer a is incorrect because a password is required. Answer b is incorrect because application roles do not have members. Answer c is incorrect because users assuming the application role inherit permissions from only the current database.

Question 9

Which of the following is the correct name for the authentication mode you should use when installing SQL Server 2000 on a network where clients will be accessing data from both Windows 2000 and Unix?

○ a. SQL Server security mode

○ b. Windows authentication mode

○ c. Secure mode

○ d. Standard security mode

○ e. Enhanced security mode

○ f. Mixed mode

Answer f is correct. Mixed mode supports Windows authentication for the Windows 2000 users and SQL Server authentication for the Unix users. Answer b does not allow access to the Unix users. Answers a and d both refer to the same mode of security that was available until the release of SQL 7, but that is not an option in SQL Server 2000. Answers c and e are made-up names.

Question 10

Which of the following is not a true statement regarding the **sp_setapprole** system stored procedure?

○ a. The password can be encrypted.

○ b. The current application must provide the password.

○ c. The scope of an application role is server wide.

○ d. Users with no specified role assume the guest account's access permissions.

Answer c is correct. The scope of an application role is only the current database. Answers a, b, and d are all true statements.

Need to Know More?

 Delaney, Kalen. *Inside Microsoft SQL Server 2000.* Redmond, WA: Microsoft Press, 2000. ISBN 0-7356-0998-5. Microsoft calls this "a guide to the architecture and internals" of SQL Server 2000.

 Iseminger, David. *SQL Server 2000 Reference Library.* Redmond, WA: Microsoft Press, 2000. ISBN 0-7356-1280-3. A selected collection of SQL Server 2000 Books Online; there are six volumes focused on key areas.

 McMahon, Richard and Glen Bicking. *Windows 2000 Security Design Exam Prep.* Scottsdale, AZ: The Coriolis Group, 2000. ISBN 1-57610-707-8. Provides detailed coverage of Windows 2000 security issues relative to SQL Server 2000.

 SQL Server 2000 Resource Kit. Redmond, WA: Microsoft Press, 2000. ISBN 0-7356-1266-8. Extensive reference information on SQL Server 2000 core functionality and new features.

 MS SQL Server Books Online has sections on stored procedures. This book set can be installed from the SQL Server 2000 CD or accessed online through **http://msdn.microsoft.com/library/default.asp**. Search on the keyword "security."

 Search the TechNet CD or its online version through **www.microsoft.com/technet**. Search on the keyword "security". Additionally, navigate the product segment and search through the SQL Server sections on security at **http://www.microsoft.com/technet/security/**.

 www.microsoft.com/security/default.asp—Find up-to-date information about Microsoft's latest security measures.

 www.microsoft.com/sql/ and **http://msdn.microsoft.com/sqlserver/default.asp** are good places to find up-to-date information about SQL Server 2000.

 www.sqlmag.com—*SQL Magazine*—both the hard copy and the Web site—has a large amount of information on SQL Server 2000.

Sample Test

Question 1

Which of the following would benefit the most from denormalization?

○ a. Decision support systems that use multiple nonclustered indexes

○ b. Decision support systems that use multiple table joins

○ c. Transaction processing systems that use multijoin updates

○ d. Transaction processing systems that use multiple nonclustered indexes

Question 2

Which of the following would benefit the most from normalization?

○ a. Decision support systems that use multiple nonclustered indexes

○ b. Decision support systems that use multiple table joins

○ c. Transaction processing systems that use multijoin updates

○ d. Transaction processing systems that use multiple nonclustered indexes

Question 3

You are a SQL Server 2000 database administrator for a company that utilizes applications in a multi-user environment. You need to discover why users are having problems updating data in various tables. Which of the following has the most negative impact on concurrency?

- ○ a. Optimistic locking
- ○ b. Implementing **IDENTITY** columns
- ○ c. Implementing a primary key constraint
- ○ d. Processing nested transactions

Question 4

You are a SQL Server 2000 database administrator for a company that utilizes applications in a multi-user environment. You want to normalize the company's Web database to better maintain the data and to reduce the storage space required. Which of the following is a rule of normalization?

- ○ a. A table cannot contain repeating groups or multi-value columns.
- ○ b. A table must contain repeating groups or multi-value columns.
- ○ c. A non-key column cannot depend on a primary key.
- ○ d. Non-key columns must depend on other non-key columns.

Question 5

As the new database administrator for XYZ Company, you are considering database design factors. Currently, table records aren't stored in any particular order, so finding data in them requires a full table scan, which can be lengthy. You want to use the **Social Security Number** field to provide faster access to customer data. Which of the following should you do?

- ○ a. Denormalize the database.
- ○ b. Normalize the database.
- ○ c. Implement a primary key to avoid full table scans.
- ○ d. Implement an index to avoid full table scans.

Question 6

You are the database administrator for XYZ Company. Application users are complaining that database processes are taking longer and longer to execute during the day. Some processes are not being completed at all. What is most likely the problem?

○ a. The database server does not have enough memory.

○ b. The network does not have TCP/IP installed.

○ c. Virtual memory has become corrupted.

○ d. There is insufficient disk space.

Question 7

You are using System Monitor to check why your server has been paging excessively. You discover that a low rate of page-read operations coincides with high values for % Disk Time and Avg. Disk Queue Length. What is most likely the problem?

○ a. A memory shortage exists.

○ b. A disk bottleneck exists.

○ c. The disk is damaged.

○ d. The disk is low on space.

Question 8

Which of the following RAID categories is known as disk striping with parity?

○ a. RAID 0

○ b. RAID 1

○ c. RAID 2

○ d. RAID 3

○ e. RAID 4

○ f. RAID 5

Question 9

There are various types of counters in System Monitor:

> Bottlenecked processor resources
>
> Memory usage
>
> Memory bottlenecks or leaks

Match the following definitions and statements with the counter types (some items may be used more than once):

Definitions and Statements:

> Bottlenecked processor resources
>
> Memory usage
>
> Memory bottlenecks or leaks

Counter Types:

> Memory\ Available Bytes
>
> Processor\ Interrupts/Sec
>
> Memory\ Page Reads/Sec
>
> System\ Processor Queue Length
>
> Memory\ Pages/Sec
>
> Processor\ % Processor Time
>
> Memory\ Cache Bytes
>
> Memory\ Transition Faults/Sec
>
> Memory\ Pool Nonpaged Bytes
>
> Paging File\ % Usage Object (all instances)
>
> Cache\ Data Map Hits %
>
> Server\ Pool Paged Bytes and Server\Pool Nonpaged Bytes
>
> Process(process)\ % Processor Time
>
> Memory\ Pool Paged Bytes

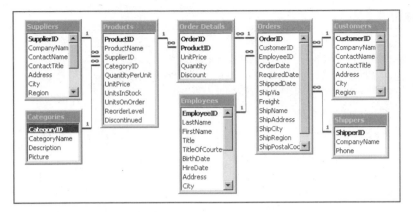

Exhibit 15.1   Relationship diagram.

Question 10

The XYZ Company has an order-tracking database application. In Exhibit 15.1, what kind of constraint can be described as, "Each order must contain one or more order details"?

○ a. Primary key constraint

○ b. Domain constraint

○ c. Translational constraint

○ d. Relational constraint

Question 11

The XYZ Company has an order-tracking database application. In Exhibit 15.1, what kind of constraint can be described as "Product ID 2 is Chang"?

○ a. Primary key constraint

○ b. Domain constraint

○ c. Translational constraint

○ d. Relational constraint

Question 12

The XYZ Company has an order-tracking database application. In Exhibit 15.1, what kind of constraint can be described as "The **SupplierID** field in the **Products** table must contain a numeric value"?

○ a. Primary key constraint

○ b. Domain constraint

○ c. Translational constraint

○ d. Relational constraint

Question 13

You are a SQL Server 2000 database administrator for a company that utilizes applications in a multi-user environment. You want to update an installation of SQL Server 2000. Which of the following options are available during Setup? [Check all correct answers]

❏ a. Add components to your existing installation.

❏ b. Uninstall your existing installation.

❏ c. Upgrade your existing installation.

❏ d. Update your server licenses.

Question 14

You are a SQL Server 2000 database administrator for a company that utilizes Internet database applications. You want to configure SQL XML Support in IIS. The IIS object that you will create is called "Web." Which of the following statements is true regarding this process?

○ a. Before you create the Web virtual directory, you must create a physical directory associated with the Web virtual directory.

○ b. Before you create the Web physical directory, you must create a virtual directory associated with the Web physical directory.

○ c. You must create a physical directory associated with the Web virtual directory immediately after you create the Web virtual directory.

○ d. You must create a virtual directory associated with the Web physical directory immediately after you create the Web physical directory.

Question 15

You are a SQL Server 2000 database administrator for a company that utilizes Internet database applications. Your network servers run Windows 2000, and most of the clients run Windows NT 4 Workstation. Security is a major concern, and each database user belongs to a group called Marketing; however, the marketing manager belongs to a group called Strategic. You know that SQL Server 2000 can operate in different authentication modes. Which of the following types of authentication could you use? [Check all correct answers]

❑ a. Windows authentication mode security

❑ b. Mixed mode security

❑ c. Windows authentication and SQL Server authentication combined

❑ d. Windows authentication and NTFS security combined

Question 16

Which of the following keywords are reserved in SQL Server 2000?

○ a. **AVG**

○ b. **COMMITTED**

○ c. **CONFIRM**

○ d. **SELECT**

Question 17

You are a SQL Server 2000 database administrator for the XYZ Company, which utilizes applications in a multi-user environment. The XYZ Company has an order-tracking database application. You have the following table definition in your SQL Server database:

```
CREATE TABLE OrderReport
  (key      int IDENTITY(1,1)
   cost   int NOT NULL,
   quantity        nvarchar(10) NOT NULL,
   amount_calc AS (cost  + quantity)
  )
```

In addition, you have a view based on the **OrderReport** table that contains all of the columns:

```
CREATE VIEW v_substitute
AS SELECT key, cost, quantity, amount_calc
FROM BaseTable
```

On the **v_substitute** view, you want to create a trigger that will construct an **INSERT** statement ignoring the primary key and computed columns. Which of the following code snippets should you use?

○ a.
```
CREATE TRIGGER my_trigger on v_substitute
INSERT INSTEAD OF
AS
BEGIN
  INSERT INTO OrderReport
       SELECT cost, quantity
       FROM inserted
END
GO
```

(continued)

Question 17 *(continued)*

```
○ b.
CREATE TRIGGER my_trigger on v_substitute
INSTEAD OF INSERT
AS
BEGIN
   INSERT INTO OrderReport
         SELECT cost, quantity
         FROM inserted
END
GO


○ c.
CREATE TRIGGER my_trigger on v_substitue
AFTER INSERT
AS
BEGIN
   INSERT INTO OrderReport
         SELECT cost, quantity
         FROM inserted
END
GO


○ d.
CREATE TRIGGER my_trigger on v_substitue
INSERT AFTER
AS
BEGIN
   INSERT INTO OrderReport
         SELECT cost, quantity
         FROM inserted
END
GO
```

Question 18

You are a SQL Server 2000 database administrator for a company that uses partitioned views to divide data across multiple servers. This system was designed to provide performance benefits, just as the company uses clustered servers to support the processing needs of its Web site. Which of the following statements can be used to modify multiple member tables referenced by the partitioned view? [Check all correct answers]

☐ a. **INSERT**

☐ b. **UPDATE**

☐ c. **DELETE**

☐ d. Partitioned views do not support **INSERT**, **UDPATE**, and **DELETE** statements

Question 19

Constraints allow you to automatically enforce the integrity of a database in SQL Server. Which of the following are constraints? [Check all correct answers]

☐ a. **part_number int PRIMARY KEY**

☐ b. **custom_check CHECK (quantity BETWEEN 0 and 10000)**

☐ c. **RULE id_chk AS @quantity BETWEEN 0 and 10000**

☐ d. **my_date datetime DEFAULT getdate()**

Question 20

Which of the following joins returns only records from two tables that meet the criteria defined in the **ON** clause?

○ a. Left join

○ b. Right join

○ c. Inner join

○ d. Outer join

Question 21

You are a SQL Server 2000 database administrator for a software development company that uses SQL Server internally. Due to the large number of tables in the company's document-management database, you are considering normalizing existing tables. Which of the following statements describes the first normal form?

○ a. Columns do not define similar attributes and do not contain multiple values in a single row.

○ b. Each column that does not compose the primary key should depend on all columns that make a composite key, not just on a subset of the columns that make up the composite key.

○ c. Columns that are not covered by the primary key should not depend on each other.

○ d. Primary keys are not indexed but are unique.

Question 22

You are a SQL Server 2000 database administrator for a software development company, and you are responsible for writing stored procedures. You want to involve two tables in a query within a stored procedure. You want to avoid producing a Cartesian product. What types of join should you use? [Check all correct answers]

❑ a. Left join

❑ b. Outer join

❑ c. Cross join

❑ d. Right join

Question 23

You are a SQL Server 2000 database administrator for a software development company that uses SQL Server internally. Due to the large number of tables in the company's document-management database, you are considering normalizing existing tables. Your application is targeted toward data warehousing. Which of the following correctly describes applicable considerations? [Check all correct answers]

❏ a. Complex joins are costly to processing.

❏ b. Normalization assists database reads.

❏ c. Complex joins assist database reads.

❏ d. Normalization assists database updates.

Question 24

You are a SQL Server 2000 database administrator for a small CAD company that uses SQL Server for its GIS databases. You are responsible for implementing stored procedures and triggers in many of the databases. Identify the correct order of SQL commands.

○ a. **SELECT** > **FROM** > **WHERE** > **GROUP** > **HAVING** > **ORDER BY** > **COMPUTE BY**

○ b. **SELECT** > **FROM** > **WHERE** > **GROUP** > **COMPUTE BY** > **HAVING** > **ORDER BY**

○ c. **SELECT** > **FROM** > **WHERE** > **GROUP** > **HAVING** > **COMPUTE BY** > **ORDER BY**

○ d. **SELECT** > **FROM** > **WHERE** > **GROUP** > **ORDER BY** > **HAVING** > **COMPUTE BY**

Question 25

You are a SQL Server 2000 database administrator for a small CAD company that uses SQL Server for its GIS databases. You are responsible for implementing stored procedures and triggers in many of the databases. You have concerns about the types of joins being used in some of the stored procedures. Which of the following correctly describes a cross join?

○ a. A cross join uses a comparison operator to match rows from two columns based on the values in the common columns. It then returns the rows that match.

○ b. A cross join returns all rows from both tables.

○ c. A cross join returns **NULL** values for the right table when there is no match.

○ d. All rows in the left table are matched with all rows in the right table.

Question 26

You are a SQL Server 2000 database administrator for a software development company that uses SQL Server internally. Due to the large number of tables in the company's document-management database, you are considering normalizing existing tables. Which of the following describes the third normal form?

○ a. Columns do not define similar attributes and do not contain multiple values in a single row.

○ b. No table has columns that define similar attributes, and no column contains multiple values in a single row.

○ c. Columns that are not covered by the primary key should not depend on each other.

○ d. Primary keys are not indexed but are unique.

Question 27

You are a SQL Server 2000 database administrator for a small CAD company that uses SQL Server for its GIS databases. You are responsible for implementing stored procedures and triggers in many of the databases. You have concerns about the types of joins being used in some of the stored procedures. You want to combine the result sets from two or more **SELECT** statements into one result set. What SQL constructs can you use? [Check all correct answers]

❑ a. **COMPUTE BY**

❑ b. **SUM**

❑ c. **UNION**

❑ d. **SELECT**

Question 28

You are a SQL Server 2000 database administrator for a small CAD company that uses SQL Server for its GIS databases. You are responsible for implementing stored procedures and triggers in many of the databases. You have concerns about the types of joins being used in some of the stored procedures. You want to combine the result sets from two or more **SELECT** statements into one result set. What is a prerequisite for doing this? [Check all correct answers]

❑ a. You must implement a **GROUP BY** clause.

❑ b. Result sets of each query must have the same number of columns with compatible data types.

❑ c. You must implement a **UNION** clause.

❑ d. Result sets of each query must have a different number of columns with compatible data types.

Question 29

You are a SQL Server 2000 database administrator for a small CAD company that uses SQL Server for its GIS databases. You are responsible for implementing stored procedures and triggers in many of the databases. You plan to use the **sql_variant** data type in a stored procedure. To work with a **sql_variant** data type, you need to cast the variant. Which of the following statements are valid? [Check all correct answers]

☐ a. **SET @xyz_chr = CAST@(xyz_var AS VARCHAR(12))**

☐ b. **SET @xyz_chr = CAST(@xyz_var AS VARCHAR(12))**

☐ c. **SET @abc_chr = CAST(@xyz_var AS VARCHAR(8))**

☐ d. **SET @abc_chr = CAST(!xyz_var AS VARCHAR(8))**

Question 30

You are a SQL Server 2000 database administrator for a small CAD company that uses SQL Server for its GIS databases. You are responsible for implementing stored procedures and triggers in many of the databases. You plan to use the **bigint** datatype in a stored procedure. Which of the following functions support **bigint**? [Check all correct answers]

☐ a. **ROWCOUNT_ BIG**

☐ b. **COUNT_BIG**

☐ c. **COUNT_B**

☐ d. **BIG_ROWCOUNT**

☐ e. **BIG_COUNT**

Question 31

You are a SQL Server 2000 database administrator for a small CAD company that uses SQL Server for its GIS databases. You are responsible for implementing stored procedures and triggers in many of the databases. You want to use the new SQL Server 2000 **table** data type. What is the correct syntax for defining a **table** data type?

○ a. **DECLARE @*local_variable* <*table_definition*>**

○ b. **DECLARE @*local_variable* TABLE <*table_definition*>**

○ c. **!DECLARE @*local_variable* <*table_definition*>**

○ d. **!DECLARE !*local_variable* TABLE <*table_definition*>**

Question 32

You are a SQL Server 2000 database administrator for a small CAD company that uses SQL Server for its GIS databases. You are responsible for implementing stored procedures and triggers in many of the databases. You want to use the new SQL Server 2000 **table** data type. Which of the following are practical reasons to use the **table** data type? [Check all correct answers]

❏ a. Disk space is used more efficiently than when you use the **tempdb** database.

❏ b. It is an alternative to storing temporary tables in the **tempdb** database.

❏ c. Table variables used in stored procedures result in faster and more frequent recompilations of the stored procedures than when temporary tables are used.

❏ d. It is managed in memory instead of on a physical drive.

❏ e. It is managed on a physical drive instead of in memory.

Question 33

Which of the following code segments makes proper use of a return value from a function?

○ a.
```
CREATE FUNCTION dbo.MyProductsTable ()
AS
RETURN SELECT TOP 5
ProductName AS MyProducts, UnitPrice
FROM Products
ORDER BY Products.UnitPrice
```

○ b.
```
CREATE FUNCTION dbo.MyProductsTable ()
RETURNS TABLE
RETURNS SELECT TOP 5
ProductName AS MyProducts, UnitPrice
FROM Products
ORDER BY Products.UnitPrice
```

○ c.
```
CREATE FUNCTION dbo.MyProductsTable ()
RETURNS TABLE
AS
SELECT TOP 5
ProductName AS MyProducts, UnitPrice
FROM Products
ORDER BY Products.UnitPrice
```

○ d.
```
CREATE FUNCTION dbo.MyProductsTable ()
RETURNS TABLE
AS
RETURN SELECT TOP 5
ProductName AS MyProducts, UnitPrice
FROM Products
ORDER BY Products.UnitPrice
```

Question 34

Which of the following statements are true of user-defined functions? [Check all correct answers]

- ❏ a. They can zero to many input parameters.
- ❏ b. They can return an **int** data type.
- ❏ c. They cannot return a **sql_variant** data type.
- ❏ d. They cannot return a **bigint** data type.

Question 35

Which of the following statements are true of using the **ON UPDATE CASCADE** constraint? [Check all correct answers]

- ❏ a. Delete operations can be cascaded from the referencing table to the referred table. Update operations cannot be cascaded from the referencing table to the referred table.
- ❏ b. Update operations can be cascaded from the referencing table to the referred table. Delete operations cannot be cascaded from the referencing table to the referred table.
- ❏ c. Delete operations can be cascaded from the referencing table to the referred table.
- ❏ d. Update operations can be cascaded from the referencing table to the referred table.

Question 36

You are a SQL Server 2000 database administrator for a small sales company that uses SQL Server for its databases. Employees use the **Sales** table in the **db_prod** database to save transactions and produce reports; however, performance has decreased suddenly. What can you do to make things run faster?

- ○ a. Add join hints to views for the **Sales** table.
- ○ b. Drop all indexes on the **Sales** table.
- ○ c. Disable the Auto Update Statistics option.
- ○ d. Normalize the data structure, and create necessary indexes.

Question 37

You are a SQL Server 2000 database administrator for a small sales company that uses SQL Server for its databases. Which of the following code fragments demonstrates the effect of preventing data on a referenced table from being deleted or updated if corresponding records exist on the referring table?

○ a.
```
CONSTRAINT FK_myOrder_Details FOREIGN KEY
(OrderID) REFERENCES dbo.myOrders(OrderID)
ON UPDATE ACTION
ON DELETE ACTION
```

○ b.
```
CONSTRAINT FK_myOrder_Details FOREIGN KEY
(OrderID) REFERENCES dbo.myOrders(OrderID)
ON UPDATE NO CASCADE
ON DELETE ACTION
```

○ c.
```
CONSTRAINT FK_myOrder_Details FOREIGN KEY
(OrderID) REFERENCES dbo.myOrders(OrderID)
ON UPDATE NO ACTION
ON DELETE NO ACTION
```

○ d.
```
CONSTRAINT FK_myOrder_Details FOREIGN KEY
(OrderID) REFERENCES dbo.myOrders(OrderID)
ON UPDATE
ON DELETE CASCADE
```

Question 38

You are a SQL Server 2000 database administrator for a small sales company that uses SQL Server for its databases. You are responsible for writing stored procedures and triggers. What variable can **SCOPE_IDENTITY** be used with?

○ a. the **!IDENTITY** global variable

○ b. the **@@IDENTITY** local variable

○ c. the **@@IDENTITY** global variable

○ d. the **@@ID** global variable

Question 39

Which of the following specifies which **AFTER** triggers associated with a table will be executed first or last?

○ a. **sp_settriggerorder**

○ b. **sp_settriggersort**

○ c. **sp_settriggerpriority**

○ d. **sp_settriggers**

Question 40

Which of the following provides a set of tools that lets you extract, alter, and consolidate data from dissimilar sources into one or more destinations?

○ a. XML

○ b. DTS

○ c. T-SQL

○ d. Meta Data Services

Answer Key

For the asterisked item, please see the textual representation of the answer on the appropriate page within this chapter.

1. b	15. a, b, c	29. b, c
2. c	16. d	30. a, b
3. d	17. b	31. b
4. a	18. a, b, c	32. a, b, d
5. d	19. a, b	33. d
6. d	20. c	34. a, b
7. b	21. a	35. c, d
8. f	22. a, b, d	36. d
9. *	23. a, d	37. c
10. d	24. a	38. c
11. c	25. d	39. a
12. b	26. c	40. b
13. a, b, c	27. c, d	
14. a	28. b, c	

Question 1

Answer b is correct because denormalization limits the number of joins performed. Although answer a could be true, it is not the best answer. Answers c and d are incorrect because denormalization requires the same data to be updated multiple times.

Question 2

Answer c is correct because normalization limits the amount of redundant data that must be updated. Answers a and b are incorrect because table joins actually hinder the performance of queries. Although a is a possible answer, it is not the best answer. Answer d is incorrect because multiple indexes hinder the performance of updates, even though indexes can help query processing performance.

Question 3

Answer d is correct. When you use transactions, locks are implemented on data, making it inaccessible to other users until the transaction is committed or rolled back. Answer a is incorrect because it can actually help concurrency in a database. Answers b and c are incorrect because identities and primary keys do not affect concurrency enough to be considered.

Question 4

Answer a is correct. The first normal form (1NF) specifies that a table cannot contain groups or columns containing multiple values. For example, the **Items** table cannot contain columns such as **Item1, Item2, Item3, Item4,** etc. Because answer a is correct, answer b is incorrect. Answers c and d are incorrect because 2NF requires that non-key columns depend on a primary key.

Question 5

Answer d is correct. Databases use indexes to store ordered lists of key values that are stored in fields or combinations of fields (such as a **Social Security Number** field). The index provides a way to access the list in order, so finding the key value is much faster than searching the table. Answers a and b are incorrect because normalization does not affect this scenario. Although implementing a primary key, as suggested in answer c, is a valid answer, it is not the best answer.

Question 6

Answer d is correct. The most common hardware problem affecting database performance is insufficient disk space. Servers use disk space for application storage, Registry data, database files, and temporary storage. In addition, servers use disk space to create virtual memory for the operating system. Answer a is incorrect because although insufficient memory can cause delays, it should not cause the database to fail completely. Answer b is incorrect because these symptoms are not caused by not having TCP/IP installed. Answer c is incorrect because virtual memory is a combination of RAM and disk space, which is more than the correct answer of just the disk space.

Question 7

Answer b is correct. A low rate of page-read operations coinciding with high values for % Disk Time and Avg. Disk Queue Length usually means that a disk bottleneck exists. Answer a is incorrect because a memory problem would not cause a decrease in page reads. Answer c is incorrect because you were not given any information stating that the disk was inactive. Answer d is incorrect because low disk space would not cause excessive paging.

Question 8

Answer f is correct. RAID 5 is disk striping with parity across three or more physical disks. RAID 5 volumes have better read performance than do mirrored volumes. Answer a is incorrect because RAID 0 is disk striping with no fault tolerance protection. It offers the best performance, but if one disk fails, all the data on the stripe set becomes inaccessible. Answer b is incorrect because RAID 1 (disk mirroring) uses two drives that store identical information. Answer c is incorrect because RAID 2 is disk striping with error-correcting code (ECC); this uses extra check disks, with data bits striped across the data and check disks. Answer d is incorrect because RAID 3 is disk striping with ECC stored as parity. RAID 3 uses a single redundant check disk for each group of drives. Answer e is incorrect because RAID 4 is disk striping in large blocks or sector striping on the data within the drives.

Question 9

The correct answer is:

Bottlenecked processor resources

Processor\ Interrupts/Sec

Processor\ % Processor Time

Process(process)\ % Processor Time

System\ Processor Queue Length

Memory usage

Memory\ Available Bytes

Memory\ Cache Bytes

Memory bottlenecks or leaks

Memory\ Pages/Sec

Memory\ Page Reads/Sec

Memory\ Transition Faults/Sec

Memory\ Pool Paged Bytes

Memory\ Pool Nonpaged Bytes

Paging File\ % Usage object (all instances)

Cache\ Data Map Hits %

Server\ Pool Paged Bytes and Server\Pool Nonpaged Bytes

Question 10

Answer d is correct. Relational constraints are used to enforce referential integrity. These kinds of constraints require the condition, "If A, then B." Answer a is incorrect because a primary key constraint is used to make a row (or record) unique. Answer b is incorrect because domain constraints are column constraints. Answer c is incorrect because translational constraints force values to be modified into a standard format.

Question 11

Answer c is correct. It is a translational constraint because it forces values to be modified into a standard format. Answer a is incorrect because a primary key constraint is used to make a row (or record) unique. Answer b is incorrect because domain constraints are column constraints. Answer d is incorrect because relational constraints are used to enforce referential integrity.

Question 12

Answer b is correct. It is a domain constraint because it imposes a column constraint. Answer a is incorrect because a primary key constraint is used to make a row (or record) unique. Answer c is incorrect because translational constraints force values to be modified into a standard format. Answer d is incorrect because relational constraints are used to enforce referential integrity.

Question 13

Answers a, b, and c are correct. Answer d is incorrect because you cannot update your server licenses during SQL Server 2000 Setup.

Question 14

Answer a is correct. Before you create a virtual directory, you must create a physical directory such as C:\Inetpub\wwwroot\Web. Answers b and c are incorrect because you don't create a physical directory in IIS. Answer d is incorrect because you create a virtual directory after you create a physical directory.

Question 15

Answers a, b, and c are correct. This is a trick question. SQL Server can operate in two modes: Windows authentication mode and mixed mode. Therefore, answers a and b are correct. Mixed mode security is a combination of Windows authentication and SQL Server authentication; therefore, answer c is also correct. Answer d is incorrect because NTFS security is not a type of SQL Server authentication.

Question 16

Answer d is correct. The **SELECT** keyword is reserved in SQL Server 2000. Answers a, b, and c are incorrect because **AVG, COMMITTED,** and **CON-FIRM** are no longer reserved keywords in SQL Server.

Question 17

Answer b is correct. It results in the desired outcome using the correctly format-ted syntax. Answer a is incorrect because the keyword **INSERT** is listed before **INSTEAD OF.** Answer c is incorrect because an **INSTEAD OF** trigger should be used to ignore other values presented from the original **INSERT** statement that might cause the trigger to fire. An **AFTER** trigger will not do that. Answer d is incorrect both logically and in syntax. The keyword **AFTER** should come before **INSERT**, and an **INSTEAD OF** trigger should be used in this case.

Question 18

Answers a, b, and c are correct. Partitioned views in SQL Server 2000 support **INSERT, UDPATE,** and **DELETE** statements. Therefore, answer d is incorrect.

Question 19

Answers a and b are correct. Answer a is a primary key constraint. Answer b is a **CHECK** constraint. Answer c is incorrect because it is a rule. Answer d is incor-rect because it is a default.

Question 20

Answer c is correct. It is the only choice that returns only records from two tables that meet the criteria defined in the **ON** clause. Answer a is incorrect because a left join includes all the records from the left table specified in the **ON** clause. Answer b is incorrect because a right join is the opposite of a left join. Answer d is incorrect because a full outer join returns all records in both the left and right tables specified in the **ON** clause.

Question 21

Answer a is correct. Normalized tables do not contain repeating columns or multiple values in a single column. Answers b and c are incorrect because they are not rules for first normal form. Answer d is incorrect because primary keys can be indexed.

Question 22

Answers a, b, and d are correct. A Cartesian product can be defined as being possible combinations of rows in tables. For example, if you join two tables without any kind of qualification or join type, the result is a Cartesian product. This is especially bad if tables contain thousands of rows. You should avoid creating Cartesian products by always qualifying your joins. Answer c is incorrect because a cross join does not prevent a Cartesian product from being produced.

Question 23

Answers a and d are correct. Complex joins require more processing because of the operation involved. Normalization improves the performance of database **UPDATE** commands because redundant data is reduced, thereby reducing the amount of data that has to be updated. Answer b is incorrect because more joins occur in a normalized database. Answer c is incorrect because joins actually hinder database read operations.

Question 24

Answer a is correct. The correct order for a **SELECT** statement is **SELECT, FROM, WHERE, GROUP, HAVING, ORDER BY, COMPUTE BY**. Answers b, c, and d are incorrect because they list commands in the incorrect order.

Question 25

Answer d is correct. In a cross join, all rows in the left table are matched with the rows in the right table. This result is the same as a Cartesian product. Answer a is incorrect because a **WHERE** clause (comparison operator) is not used to match rows. Answer b is incorrect because a cross join returns more than the sum of all rows in both tables. Answer c is incorrect because **NULL** values are not returned for non-matching criteria.

Question 26

Answer c is correct. This is a rule of third normal form. Answer a is incorrect because it is a rule of first normal form. Answer b is incorrect because it is not a rule of third normal form. Answer d is not technically correct because most primary keys are indexed, and this has no effect on normalization.

Question 27

Answers c and d are correct. **SELECT** and **UNION** statements both allow you to combine result sets. Answers a and b are incorrect because they are used to aggregate data.

Question 28

Answers b and c are correct. These two prerequisites must be fulfilled before you can combine the result sets from two or more **SELECT** statements into one result set. Answer a is incorrect because a **GROUP BY** clause does not join two result sets. Answer d is incorrect because **UNION** statements require compatible data types and the same number of columns.

Question 29

Answers b and c are correct. They both use the correct format. Answer a is incorrect because the @ sign is in the wrong place. Answer d is incorrect because the ! sign is used instead of the @ sign.

Question 30

Answers a and b are correct. Two new built-in functions have been introduced: **BIG_COUNT** and **ROWCOUNT_ BIG**. These functions operate in a manner similar to the **COUNT** function and the **@@ROWCOUNT** variable except that they return an integer value of type **bigint**. Answers c, d, and e are invalid function names.

Question 31

Answer b is correct. The **table** data type allows you to store a result set. You declare a **table** data type by using the following syntax:

```
DECLARE @local_variable TABLE <table_definition>
```

Therefore, answers a, c, and d are incorrect.

Question 32

Answers a, b, and d are correct. The **table** data type can be used as an alternative to using the **tempdb** database. **Table** data types are also managed in memory, making them more efficient. Answer c is incorrect because stored procedures that use **table** data types are compiled less frequently than stored procedures using temporary tables. Answer e is incorrect because **table** data types are managed in memory.

Question 33

Answer d is correct. Answer a is incorrect because no return type is specified. Answer b is incorrect because of the invalid syntax (using **RETURNS** as a keyword twice). Answer c is incorrect because of the incorrect syntax in the **SELECT** statement.

Question 34

Answers a and b are correct. User-defined functions can have zero or more input parameters. These functions can return **int**, **sql_variant**, and **bigint** data types; therefore, answers c and d are incorrect.

Question 35

Answers c and d are correct. Both update and delete operations can be cascaded from the referencing table to the referred table. Therefore, answers a and b are incorrect.

Question 36

Answer d is correct. Faster transaction processing is achieved by normalizing data because there are generally fewer columns per record. Answer a is incorrect because performance will degrade if you alter the default optimization settings. Answer b is incorrect because dropping all indexes will not help performance in this case. Answer c is incorrect because updating statistics too infrequently causes slow query performance over time.

Question 37

Answer c is correct. The **NO ACTION** constraint is valid. Answer a is incorrect because it does not specify a valid action. Answer b is incorrect because it specifies **ON UPDATE NO CASCADE** and **ON DELETE ACTION**. Answer d is incorrect because it also does not specify the appropriate action.

Question 38

Answer c is correct. The **@@IDENTITY** global variable returns the last value inserted into an **IDENTITY** column within the same scope. Answer a is incorrect because it uses incorrect syntax. Answer b is incorrect because it specifies a local variable. Answer d is incorrect because it specifies **@@ID** instead of **@@IDENTITY**.

Question 39

Answer a is correct. The **sp_settriggerorder** stored procedure specifies which **AFTER** triggers associated with a table will be executed first or last. Answers b, c, and d are all incorrect because none of those stored procedures exist.

Question 40

Answer b is correct. DTS allows you to move, modify, and join data from different sources into single or multiple destinations. Answer a is incorrect because XML is a subset of the Standard Generalized Markup Language (SGML) used to display and define the data in a document. Answer c is incorrect because T-SQL (Transact-SQL) is a language used to query, update, delete, and administer databases in SQL Server. Answer d is also incorrect. Meta Data Services allows you to manage meta data (or abstract information).

Appendix A
Pubs Database

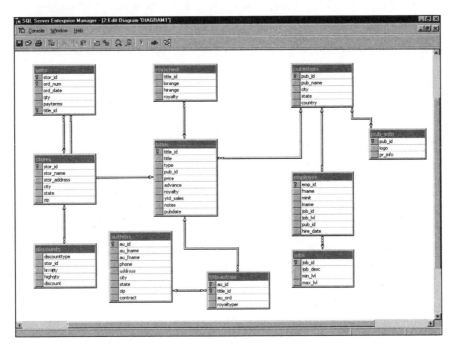

Figure A.1   **Pubs** database diagram.

Pubs SQL

```
EXEC sp_addtype N'empid', N'char (9)', N'NOT NULL'
GO


EXEC sp_addtype N'id', N'varchar (11)', N'not null'
GO


EXEC sp_addtype N'tid', N'varchar (6)', N'not null'
GO
CREATE TABLE [dbo].[stores] (
        [stor_id] [char] (4) NOT NULL ,
        [stor_name] [varchar] (40) NULL ,
        [stor_address] [varchar] (40) NULL ,
        [city] [varchar] (20) NULL ,
        [state] [char] (2) NULL ,
        [zip] [char] (5) NULL ,
        CONSTRAINT [UPK_storeid] PRIMARY KEY  CLUSTERED
        ([stor_id])  ON [PRIMARY]
)
GO


CREATE TABLE [dbo].[publishers] (
        [pub_id] [char] (4) NOT NULL ,
        [pub_name] [varchar] (40) NULL ,
        [city] [varchar] (20) NULL ,
        [state] [char] (2) NULL ,
        [country] [varchar] (30) NULL CONSTRAINT
          [DF__publishers__country__0EA330E9] DEFAULT ('USA'),
        CONSTRAINT [UPKCL_pubind] PRIMARY KEY  CLUSTERED
        ([pub_id])  ON [PRIMARY] ,
         CHECK ([pub_id] = '1756' or [pub_id] = '1622'
                or [pub_id] = '0877' or [pub_id] = '0736'
                or [pub_id] = '1389'
                or ([pub_id] like '99[0-9][0-9]'))
)
GO


CREATE TABLE [dbo].[authors] (
        [au_id] [id] NOT NULL ,
        [au_lname] [varchar] (40) NOT NULL ,
        [au_fname] [varchar] (20) NOT NULL ,
        [phone] [char] (12) NOT NULL
                CONSTRAINT [DF__authors__phone__09DE7BCC]
                    DEFAULT ('UNKNOWN'),
        [address] [varchar] (40) NULL ,
        [city] [varchar] (20) NULL ,
```

```
        [state] [char] (2) NULL ,
        [zip] [char] (5) NULL ,
        [contract] [bit] NOT NULL ,
        CONSTRAINT [UPKCL_auidind] PRIMARY KEY  CLUSTERED
        ([au_id])  ON [PRIMARY] ,
         CHECK (([au_id] like
              '[0-9][0-9][0-9]-[0-9][0-9]-[0-9][0-9][0-9][0-
9]')),
         CHECK (([zip] like '[0-9][0-9][0-9][0-9][0-9]'))
)
GO


CREATE  INDEX [aunmind] ON [dbo].[authors]([au_lname], [au_fname])
        ON [PRIMARY]
GO


CREATE TABLE [dbo].[titles] (
        [title_id] [tid] NOT NULL ,
        [title] [varchar] (80) NOT NULL ,
        [type] [char] (12) NOT NULL
              CONSTRAINT [DF__titles__type__117F9D94]
              DEFAULT ('UNDECIDED'),
        [pub_id] [char] (4) NULL ,
        [price] [money] NULL ,
        [advance] [money] NULL ,
        [royalty] [int] NULL ,
        [ytd_sales] [int] NULL ,
        [notes] [varchar] (200) NULL ,
        [pubdate] [datetime] NOT NULL
              CONSTRAINT [DF__titles__pubdate__1367E606]
              DEFAULT (getdate()),
        CONSTRAINT [UPKCL_titleidind] PRIMARY KEY  CLUSTERED
        ([title_id]       ) ON [PRIMARY] ,
         FOREIGN KEY
        ([pub_id]) REFERENCES [dbo].[publishers] ([pub_id])
)
GO


 CREATE  INDEX [titleind] ON [dbo].[titles]([title]) ON [PRIMARY]
GO


CREATE TABLE [dbo].[discounts] (
        [discounttype] [varchar] (40) NOT NULL ,
        [stor_id] [char] (4) NULL ,
        [lowqty] [smallint] NULL ,
        [highqty] [smallint] NULL ,
```

```
            [discount] [decimal](4, 2) NOT NULL ,
             FOREIGN KEY
            ([stor_id]) REFERENCES [dbo].[stores] ([stor_id])
) ON [PRIMARY]
GO
CREATE TABLE [dbo].[jobs] (
        [job_id] [smallint] IDENTITY (1, 1) NOT NULL ,
        [job_desc] [varchar] (50) NOT NULL
                CONSTRAINT [DF__jobs__job_desc__239E4DCF]
                DEFAULT ('New Position - title not formalized yet'),
        [min_lvl] [tinyint] NOT NULL ,
        [max_lvl] [tinyint] NOT NULL ,
         PRIMARY KEY   CLUSTERED
        ([job_id])   ON [PRIMARY] ,
         CHECK ([max_lvl] <= 250),
         CHECK ([min_lvl] >= 10)
)
GO

CREATE TABLE [dbo].[employee] (
        [emp_id] [empid] NOT NULL ,
        [fname] [varchar] (20) NOT NULL ,
        [minit] [char] (1) NULL ,
        [lname] [varchar] (30) NOT NULL ,
        [job_id] [smallint] NOT NULL
                CONSTRAINT [DF__employee__job_id__2C3393D0]
                DEFAULT (1),
        [job_lvl] [tinyint] NOT NULL
                CONSTRAINT [DF__employee__job_lvl__2E1BDC42]
                DEFAULT (10),
        [pub_id] [char] (4) NOT NULL
                CONSTRAINT [DF__employee__pub_id__2F10007B]
                DEFAULT ('9952'),
        [hire_date] [datetime] NOT NULL
                CONSTRAINT [DF__employee__hire_date__30F848ED]
                DEFAULT (getdate()),
        CONSTRAINT [PK_emp_id] PRIMARY KEY   NONCLUSTERED
        ([emp_id])   ON [PRIMARY] ,
        FOREIGN KEY ([job_id]) REFERENCES [dbo].[jobs] ([job_id]),
         FOREIGN KEY ([pub_id]) REFERENCES
                [dbo].[publishers] ([pub_id]),
        CONSTRAINT [CK_emp_id] CHECK ((([emp_id] like
                '[A-Z][A-Z][A-Z][1-9][0-9][0-9][0-9][0-9][FM]') or
                ([emp_id] like
                '[A-Z]-[A-Z][1-9][0-9][0-9][0-9][0-9][FM]'))
)
```

```
GO

 CREATE  CLUSTERED  INDEX [employee_ind] ON
      [dbo].[employee]([lname], [fname], [minit]) ON [PRIMARY]
GO

CREATE TABLE [dbo].[pub_info] (
      [pub_id] [char] (4) NOT NULL ,
      [logo] [image] NULL ,
      [pr_info] [text] NULL ,
      CONSTRAINT [UPKCL_pubinfo] PRIMARY KEY  CLUSTERED
      ([pub_id])  ON [PRIMARY] ,
       FOREIGN KEY ([pub_id]) REFERENCES
            [dbo].[publishers] ([pub_id])
)
GO

CREATE TABLE [dbo].[roysched] (
      [title_id] [tid] NOT NULL ,
      [lorange] [int] NULL ,
      [hirange] [int] NULL ,
      [royalty] [int] NULL ,
       FOREIGN KEY
      ([title_id]) REFERENCES [dbo].[titles] ([title_id])
) ON [PRIMARY]
GO

CREATE  INDEX [titleidind] ON [dbo].[roysched]([title_id])
      ON [PRIMARY]
GO

CREATE TABLE [dbo].[sales] (
      [stor_id] [char] (4) NOT NULL ,
      [ord_num] [varchar] (20) NOT NULL ,
      [ord_date] [datetime] NOT NULL ,
      [qty] [smallint] NOT NULL ,
      [payterms] [varchar] (12) NOT NULL ,
      [title_id] [tid] NOT NULL ,
      CONSTRAINT [UPKCL_sales] PRIMARY KEY  CLUSTERED
      ([stor_id],[ord_num],[title_id])  ON [PRIMARY] ,
       FOREIGN KEY
      ([stor_id]) REFERENCES [dbo].[stores] ([stor_id]),
       FOREIGN KEY
      ([title_id]) REFERENCES [dbo].[titles] ([title_id])
)
```

```
GO

 CREATE  INDEX [titleidind] ON [dbo].[sales]([title_id])
        ON [PRIMARY]
GO

CREATE TABLE [dbo].[titleauthor] (
        [au_id] [id] NOT NULL ,
        [title_id] [tid] NOT NULL ,
        [au_ord] [tinyint] NULL ,
        [royaltyper] [int] NULL ,
        CONSTRAINT [UPKCL_taind] PRIMARY KEY  CLUSTERED
        ([au_id],[title_id])  ON [PRIMARY] ,
         FOREIGN KEY
        ([au_id]) REFERENCES [dbo].[authors] ([au_id]),
         FOREIGN KEY
        ([title_id]) REFERENCES [dbo].[titles] ([title_id])
)
GO

CREATE  INDEX [auidind] ON [dbo].[titleauthor]([au_id])
      ON [PRIMARY]
GO

CREATE  INDEX [titleidind] ON [dbo].[titleauthor]([title_id])
      ON [PRIMARY]
GO

CREATE VIEW titleview
AS
select title, au_ord, au_lname, price, ytd_sales, pub_id
from authors, titles, titleauthor
where authors.au_id = titleauthor.au_id
   AND titles.title_id = titleauthor.title_id


GO
CREATE  PROCEDURE acur
  @auth_cur cursor varying output,
  @state char(2)  = "CA",
  @ctype int = 1
AS
if (@ctype = 1)
        set @auth_cur = cursor SCROLL for
                select au_lname
                from authors where state = @state
```

```
else
        set @auth_cur = cursor SCROLL for
                select au_lname, au_fname from authors

open @auth_cur
return 1

GO


CREATE PROCEDURE byroyalty @percentage int
AS
select au_id from titleauthor
where titleauthor.royaltyper = @percentage

GO


CREATE PROCEDURE reptq1 AS
select pub_id, title_id, price, pubdate
from titles
where price is NOT NULL
order by pub_id
COMPUTE avg(price) BY pub_id
COMPUTE avg(price)

GO


CREATE PROCEDURE reptq2 AS
select type, pub_id, titles.title_id, au_ord,
   Name = substring (au_lname, 1,15), ytd_sales
from titles, authors, titleauthor
where titles.title_id = titleauthor.title_id
   AND authors.au_id = titleauthor.au_id
   AND pub_id is NOT NULL
order by pub_id, type
COMPUTE avg(ytd_sales) BY pub_id, type
COMPUTE avg(ytd_sales) BY pub_id

GO


CREATE PROCEDURE reptq3 @lolimit money, @hilimit money,
@type char(12)
AS
select pub_id, type, title_id, price
from titles
where price >@lolimit AND price <@hilimit
  AND type = @type OR type LIKE '%cook%'
```

```
order by pub_id, type
COMPUTE count(title_id) BY pub_id, type

GO

CREATE TRIGGER employee_insupd
ON employee
FOR insert, UPDATE
AS
--Get the range of level for this job type from the jobs table.
declare @min_lvl tinyint,
   @max_lvl tinyint,
   @emp_lvl tinyint,
   @job_id smallint
select @min_lvl = min_lvl,
   @max_lvl = max_lvl,
   @emp_lvl = i.job_lvl,
   @job_id = i.job_id
from employee e, jobs j, inserted i
where e.emp_id = i.emp_id AND i.job_id = j.job_id
IF (@job_id = 1) and (@emp_lvl <> 10)
begin
   raiserror ('Job id 1 expects the default level of 10.',16,1)
   ROLLBACK TRANSACTION
end
ELSE
IF NOT (@emp_lvl BETWEEN @min_lvl AND @max_lvl)
begin
   raiserror ('The level for job_id:%d should be between %d and
      %d.', 16, 1, @job_id, @min_lvl, @max_lvl)
   ROLLBACK TRANSACTION
end

GO
```

Glossary

ad hoc connector name
A name that can be used as a table reference when the OLE DB data source is not referenced often enough to warrant configuring a linked server.

aggregate function
A function that performs a calculation on a column in a rowset and produces a single value. The aggregate functions are: **AVG, COUNT, COUNT(*), MAX, MIN, STDEV, STDEVP, SUM, VAR,** and **VARP.**

aggregate query
A SQL statement or query that summarizes multiple rows' information by using an aggregate function.

alert
A response to an event or error condition.

alias
A different name for a table, usually using fewer characters than the full name.

American National Standards Institute (ANSI)
The organization of American industry and business groups that develops communication and trade standards for the United States.

anonymous subscription
A pull subscription for which information about the Subscriber and subscription is not stored.

ANSI
See **American National Standards Institute.**

API
See **application programming interface.**

API server cursor
A server cursor designed to support the cursor functions of an application programming interface (API), such as ODBC, OLE DB, ADO, and DB-Library.

application log
A Windows NT file that records events that SQL Server can then be configured to use.

application programming interface (API)
A set of routines that are available in an application and that are meant to be used by software programmers when they are designing application interfaces.

application role
A SQL Server database role that is created to support an application's security needs.

article
The smallest unit of data involved in replication. An article can be a table or a stored procedure.

authentication
The process of validating user login attempts in SQL Server.

authorization
The process of verifying permissions and access rights that are granted to users.

automatic recovery
Recovery that happens each time SQL Server is restarted. Automatic recovery protects the database in case of system failure and guarantees database consistency.

automatic synchronization
An automatic replication process that synchronizes Subscribers to Publishers when subscriptions are created.

back end
The processing that the database server performs.

backup
The process of copying data to an alternate location so that it can be recovered if the original data is lost.

backup device
A tape, disk file, or named pipe that is used in a backup or restore operation.

backup file
A file that contains a partial or full database, transaction log, or file backup.

backup media
The tape, disk, or named pipe that is used for storing backup sets.

backup set
The output from a single backup operation.

base table
A table that is permanently stored in a database.

batch
A process that contains one or more SQL statements that are executed as a single unit.

BCP utility
A command-line utility that copies SQL Server data to or from an operating system file in a format the user specifies.

binary data type
A SQL Server data type that stores hexadecimal numbers.

Binary Large Object (BLOB)
A SQL Server data type for binary data of an exceptionally large size, such as graphics, sound, or compiled code.

bit data type
A SQL Server data type that has a value of either 1 or 0.

BLOB
See **Binary Large Object.**

blocks
One or more SQL statements enclosed by a **BEGIN** statement and an **END** statement.

Boolean expression
Any operation or expression that can be evaluated as a true, false, or null value.

candidate key
Any unique identifier for a row of data. A candidate key is also called a *surrogate key.*

Cartesian product
The result of joining two tables without using join arguments; it returns all the possible combinations of rows from both tables.

cascading delete
An operation that deletes all of the related rows (or columns) in dependent tables.

cascading update
An operation that updates all related dependent rows (or columns).

character set
The set of characters that SQL Server recognizes in **char, varchar,** and **text** data types. Each character set contains 256 letters, digits, and symbols specific to a country or language. The first 128 characters are the same for all character sets.

char(n) data type
A SQL Server data type that holds between 0 and 8,000 characters.

CHECK constraint
A special type of constraint that defines which data values are acceptable in a column.

checkpoint
An event that causes all modified data pages to be written to disk.

clustered index
An index in which the key values' logical order determines the physical order of corresponding rows in a table.

column
In a table, the area in each row that stores the data value for an object's attribute.

column-level constraint
A constraint definition that is specified in the column definition when a table is made or modified.

commit

A process that saves database changes made since the start of a transaction.

composite index

An index that uses more than one column in a table for data indexing.

composite key

A key composed of more than one column.

concatenation

Combining two or more character strings, expressions, or binary strings into a single character string or expression.

concurrency

The capability of multiple users to access and alter shared data at the same time.

connection

Any successful interprocess communication linkage to SQL Server.

connectivity

The capability of multiple processes to intercommunicate.

constant

A symbol used to represent a specific data value.

constraint

A property of one or more table columns that prevents certain invalid types of data values from being placed in the columns.

control-of-flow language

Transact-SQL statements that control execution flow of SQL statements and statement blocks in batches, stored procedures, and triggers.

correlated subquery

A subquery that refers to a column in the outer statement.

cross join

A join that produces a Cartesian product as its result.

cursor

An entity that enables you to process a result set one row at a time. Cursors can be either client-side cursors or server-side cursors.

Data Control Language (DCL)

The SQL statements used to control permissions on database objects.

Data Definition Language (DDL)

A language used to define a database's attributes and properties.

data dictionary

The set of system tables that have definitions of database structures and related information.

data file

A file that contains the data that is stored in the database, as opposed to the files used to store the transaction log.

data integrity

A state that occurs when all the data values that are stored in a database are accurate.

Data Manipulation Language (DML)
The subset of SQL statements that insert, update, delete, or select data.

data migration
The movement of data from one data source to another.

data mining
Very fast OLAP processing for the purpose of discovering related items inside stored business data.

data source
The location of data that can be accessed through SQL Server.

data transformation
The process that changes a database's data structure or values when you're migrating data.

Data Transformation Services (DTS)
A SQL Server component that can import, export, and transform data.

data type
An attribute of a column that specifies what sort of information can be stored in a column, variable, or parameter.

database catalog
The part of a database that contains the information describing the objects in the database.

database diagram
A graphical representation of the objects contained in a database.

database file
One of the physical files that make up a database.

database management system (DBMS)
A program that controls access to data.

database name
A name uniquely identifying a database on a SQL server.

database object
Any one of the following database components: table, index, trigger, view, key, constraint, default, rule, user-defined data type, or stored procedure.

database object owner
The database user who created the database object.

database owner (dbo)
The user who owns the database; that user does not have to own the associated database objects.

datetime data type
A SQL Server data type that stores date and time values from January 1, 1753, through December 31, 9999. A **datetime** data type consists of two 4-byte integers.

DB-Library
A series of high-level language application programming interfaces (APIs) for the client in a client/server system.

DBMS
See **database management system.**

DCL
See **Data Control Language.**

DDL
See **Data Definition Language.**

deadlock
A situation in which two users have a piece of data locked and are each waiting for the other user to release his or her lock.

decision support system
A database used to analyze business trends.

default database
The database that a user connects to when logging into SQL Server.

default language
The language that SQL Server 2000 uses if the user does not indicate a specific language.

denormalize
The process of introducing redundant data into a table to incorporate data from a related table.

deny
To remove a permission from a user account. Denying a permission also prevents that user account from regaining permission indirectly through group memberships or roles.

differential database backup
A database backup that records only the rows that have changed since the last full database backup.

dirty read
A read that contains data that has been changed but has not been committed to the database.

distributed database
A database implemented on multiple database servers.

Distributor
In the Publish and Subscribe model of replication, the server that holds the distribution database and stores history data and transactions.

DML
See **Data Manipulation Language.**

domain
The set of valid values for an attribute in relational databases.

domain integrity
The set of processes used to ensure that all entries for a column are valid.

DTS
See **Data Transformation Services.**

dynamic cursor
A cursor that shows data modifications (such as updates, deletes, and inserts) made to the underlying data while the cursor is open.

dynamic locking
The SQL Server process that evaluates the most cost-effective locking schema to use with every query.

entity integrity

A process that ensures that a table has a unique primary key and that no row in a database has a **NULL** primary key value.

equality join

A join based on a comparison of scalar values using the operators =, > , >= , < , <= , < >, !<, and !>.

error log

An operating-system ASCII file in which SQL Server records system information.

exclusive lock

A lock that prevents any other process from obtaining a lock on a resource until the original lock on the resource is released at the transaction's end.

explicit transaction

A group of SQL statements placed in between transaction delimiters. The first delimiter must be either **BEGIN DISTRIBUTED TRANSACTION** or **BEGIN TRANSACTION**, and the end delimiter must be one of the following: **SAVE TRANSACTION, ROLLBACK WORK, ROLLBACK TRANSACTION, COMMIT WORK**, or **COMMIT TRANSACTION**.

expression

Any column, function, variable, or subquery, or any combination of column names, constants, and functions connected by an operator and resulting in a single value.

extended stored procedure

A function in an external DLL that is coded using the SQL Server Extended Stored Procedure API.

extent

The unit that SQL Server uses to allocate space to a table or index whenever the object needs more space.

fetch

To retrieve a row or a block of rows during cursor processing.

FK

See **foreign key.**

field

An area in a window that stores a single data value.

file

A basic unit of storage for a database in SQL Server databases.

filegroup

One or more data files in a database that are collected to form a single unit of allocation.

fill factor

A setting used to define free space in an index when the index is created. Fill factors reduce page splitting when a table grows.

fixed database role

A predefined role that controls access in each database.

fixed server role

A predefined role that controls server access and exists at the server level.

float data type

A data type used to hold floating-point numbers from −1.79E+308 through 1.79E+308.

foreign key (FK)

One or more columns in a table whose value matches the primary key of another table.

forward-only cursor

A cursor in which rows can be read only in sequential order from the first row to the last row.

front end

Any program that is used to access a database.

full outer join

An outer join that includes all the rows in both tables, even if the join conditions do not produce a matching row.

full-text catalog

The mechanism that stores all full-text indexes for a database's tables.

full-text index

On a catalog, a special index that, when enabled, allows a full-text search to be performed against a table.

full-text query

A **SELECT** statement that searches for phrases, words, or multiple forms of a word or phrase in character-based columns.

full-text service

The SQL Server component that is used in full-text queries.

grant

Gives permissions to a user, who can then perform an activity or work with data.

guest

A special user account that allows any SQL Server login to have access to a database.

heterogeneous data

Data that comes from two or more data sources that are from different providers, stored in multiple formats.

homogeneous data

Data that comes from two or more data sources but managed by the same software.

horizontal partitioning

A physical design process that splits a single table into multiple tables based on selected rows.

identifier

The name of a database object. The identifier can be from 1 to 128 characters in length.

identity column

In a table, a system-generated column that has the **IDENTITY** property. There can be only one identity column per table.

IDENTITY property
A property that generates the values that uniquely identify each row that is in a table.

image data type
A SQL Server data type used to hold variable-length binary data.

implicit transaction
A SQL Server connection option in which a SQL statement executed by the connection is treated as a transaction by itself.

implied permission
The standard permissions that apply to a server-wide role and to a standard database role. The implied permissions can't be granted, denied, or revoked.

index
A database object that allows SQL Server to use key values to rapidly access data in table rows. Indexing is faster than scanning all rows of data in a table for the results.

index page
A database page containing the rows that make up an index.

inner join
A join that combines two or more tables by using join fields to determine the results.

insensitive cursor
A cursor with a result set that does not reflect modifications to data as the underlying data changes.

int (integer) data type
A SQL Server data type that can be any integer from 2,147,483,647 through −2,147,483,648. Storage size is 4 bytes.

intent lock
A lock that is put on one level of a resource hierarchy to protect shared locks (exclusive locks) on lower-level resources.

isolation level
A setting used to control the locking behavior of SQL Server.

join
The process of combining data from two or more tables to produce a result set incorporating each table's rows and columns.

join condition
Any clause that is used to control how tables are related by their join columns.

kernel
A subset of the storage engine referenced in some error messages in SQL Server 2000.

key
One or more columns that either uniquely identify a row or define the relationships between two tables.

keyset-driven cursor
A cursor that does not show the effects of inserts and deletes to the underlying data but does show any other changes (updates) in the underlying data.

left outer join

An outer join in which all the rows for the first table are included, even if there are no related rows in the second table.

linked server

A remote OLE DB data source that is being used in SQL Server 2000 distributed queries.

local server

The SQL server to which the user is currently connected.

local variable

A user-defined variable given an assigned value.

locale

Information that defines the language and country that a login will use when connecting to SQL Server.

lock

A restriction that affects another user's capability to access resources.

lock escalation

A process of reducing overhead by converting many fine-grained locks to fewer course-grained locks.

log file

A file or set of files that contains a record of the transactions that were made in a database.

Log Reader Agent

A process that replicates information from a database's transaction log to another database.

logical name

The name that SQL Server uses to identify a file; this name can have up to 30 characters.

logical operators

The **AND, OR,** and **NOT** operators, used for search conditions in **WHERE** clauses.

login identification

The account name that must be passed to SQL Server when standard SQL Server security is used.

login procedure

The process of connecting to SQL Server.

login security mode

Identifies what type of security is allowed when users connect to SQL Server 2000. You can use either Windows NT authentication mode or mixed mode.

many-to-many relationship

A relationship in which each row in the first entity has multiple related rows in the second entity, and each row in the second entity has multiple related rows in the first entity.

master database

The SQL Server system database that keeps track of server-wide resources and controls the operation of each instance of SQL Server.

merge replication

A replication type that allows data to be changed on multiple databases and merged back into a central database at a later time.

meta data

The data that describes the database properties, such as the type of data in a column or the column's length. Essentially, it's data about data.

mixed mode

A security mode that allows users to connect using both Windows NT Authentication and SQL Server standard security.

model database

A system database that is used as a template for new user databases.

money data type

A SQL Server data type used to store monetary values with an accuracy of four decimal places. A **money** data type can store values from 922,337,203,685,477.5807 through −922,337,203,685,477.5808.

named pipe

An interprocess communication (IPC) mechanism that permits communication between servers and clients.

nchar data type

A fixed-length data type used to store up to 4,000 Unicode characters.

nested query

A **SELECT** statement containing one or more subqueries.

Net-Library

A communications component of SQL Server 2000 that isolates the SQL Server 2000 client software and database engine from the network APIs.

noise words

Words that are not included in a full-text query search, such as "a," "and," and "the."

nonclustered index

An index in which the physical order of the data isn't the same as the logical order of the index.

nonrepeatable read

A transaction isolation level in which a transaction can read the same table twice and produce different values.

normalization rules

The set of rules that describe how to remove redundant data from a database.

ntext data type

A variable-length data type used to store Unicode data; this data type can contain up to 1,073,741,823 characters.

NULL

An entry that doesn't have a specific assigned value.

nullability

Determines whether a column, variable, or parameter must have a value or can allow nulls.

nvarchar data type

A variable-length data type that can store up to 4,000 Unicode characters.

Object Linking and Embedding (OLE)

An application programming interface (API) for sharing objects among applications.

object owner

The user account that created the object.

object permissions

Attributes that control users' ability to perform operations on objects.

ODBC

See **Open Database Connectivity.**

ODBC driver

A DLL that allows an application to access an ODBC (Open Database Connectivity) data source.

OLAP

See **online analytical processing.**

OLE

See **Object Linking and Embedding.**

OLE DB

A COM-based application programming interface (API) for accessing data. OLE DB can access data in any data-storage format—such as databases, spreadsheets, text files, and so on—for which an OLE DB provider is available.

OLE DB provider

The software that provides access to OLE DB interfaces.

OLTP

See **online transaction processing.**

one-to-many relationship

A relationship in which every row in the first table can be related to many rows in the second table, but every row in the second table can be related to only one row in the first table.

one-to-one relationship

A relationship in which every row in the first table can be related to only one row in the second table, and every row in the second table can be related to only one row in the first table.

online analytical processing (OLAP)

A process that uses multidimensional structures to give fast access to data so it can be analyzed.

online transaction processing (OLTP)

A system for processing data; this system records all of an organization's business transactions as they occur.

Open Database Connectivity (ODBC)
An application programming interface for database material; ODBC supports access to data sources that have ODBC drivers.

outer join
A join that includes all rows from joined tables even when the join conditions do not find a matching row in the other table.

package
A Data Transformation Services (DTS) object that defines the steps to perform while importing and exporting data.

page
SQL Server's internal virtual storage mechanism.

page split
A situation in which inserting or updating data forces the rows on a page to be printed on more than one page. When a page split occurs, half of the rows will be moved to a new page.

parameter
In a stored procedure, a placeholder for a value that is going to be filled in when the procedure is executed. A parameter can be set to a constant or a variable.

Performance Monitor
A Windows NT application that provides status information about system performance and that can be used to monitor SQL Server.

permissions
The authorizations that have been granted or denied on an object or statement.

permissions validation
The process that SQL Server uses to verify whether a user has permissions necessary to perform the SQL statement he or she is trying to execute.

PK
See **primary key.**

positioned update
An update, delete, or insert operation that is performed on a row at the present cursor position.

primary key (PK)
One or more columns that uniquely identify all of the rows contained in a table.

projection
The relational algebraic function that allows you to retrieve a subset of the columns in a table.

proximity search
A full-text query searching for specific words that are close to each other.

publication
One or more articles from one database that are collected together.

publication access list
A list of the login accounts that have access to a publication.

publication database

On the Publisher, a database containing data that is being or can be replicated to other Subscribers.

publish

To mark a set of data as being available for another database to subscribe to during the replication process.

Publisher

In the Publish and Subscribe model of replication, the server that contains one or more publication databases and makes them available to other servers.

pubs database

A sample database that comes with SQL Server 2000.

pull subscription

A subscription that the Subscriber creates and administers.

push subscription

A subscription that the Publisher creates and administers.

range query

A query that gives a specific range of values in its search criteria, such as all rows from 1 through 25.

ranking

In a full-text search, a value showing how closely topics or rows match the specific search criteria. A value of 0 represents a low degree of matching; 1,000 represents the highest degree of matching.

read-only replication

A type of replication in which the replicated data cannot be updated or changed by the Subscriber.

RDBMS

See **relational database management system.**

real data type

A SQL Server data type that is used to store numbers and has seven-digit precision.

record

A group of related columns or fields that are treated as one unit.

recovery interval

The estimated maximum amount of time for a database to come back online when SQL Server is restarted after the system has abnormally shut down.

recursive relationship

A relationship in which a table is related to itself.

referential integrity (RI)

The rules that ensure that a database's foreign key values are valid.

relational data model

A data model based on set theory, relational algebra, and relational calculus.

relational database

A collection of information that is organized into tables.

relational database management system (RDBMS)

A program that supports a relational database and organizes data into related columns and rows.

relationship

A link between tables that associates one table's primary key with another table's foreign key.

remote data

Any data that is stored in an OLE DB data source outside the SQL server you are currently connected to.

remote procedure call (RPC)

An execution of a stored procedure that is not on the local server.

remote server

A SQL server, on a network, that can be accessed by going through the local server of the user.

remote stored procedure

A stored procedure that is found on a remote SQL server and that can be executed through the local SQL server.

remote table

A table stored in an OLE DB data source that is separate from the local SQL server.

replication

The process of keeping data and database objects on one SQL server synchronized with the data on another SQL server (through duplication).

result set

The rows returned from a **SELECT** statement.

return parameters

Parameters in a SQL Server stored procedure that can return data to the caller; return parameters are used in DB-Library APIs and in Open Data Services.

revoke

To remove a permission that was previously granted or denied.

RI

See **referential integrity.**

right outer join

An outer join that includes all the rows in the second table, even when the join conditions do not find a matching row in the first table.

role

A SQL Server security account that can be applied to users or logins to link together similar users.

roll back

To remove the updates from a transaction and return the data modified in the transaction to its original state.

roll forward

A database recovery feature that causes committed transactions to be applied to the data, and causes uncommitted transactions to be rolled back when a SQL server starts up.

row

A collection of the elements that make up a horizontal line in a SQL table. A row is equivalent to a record.

row aggregate

The results of a row aggregate function.

row aggregate function

An aggregate function that generates summary values that appear as additional rows of the result set.

row lock

A lock (access restriction) placed on one row in a table.

RPC

See **remote procedure call.**

rule

A database object used to specify the data values that a column is allowed to contain.

savepoint

A user-defined marker that allows a transaction to be partially rolled back if a minor error occurs.

scalar aggregate

A function applied to all the rows in a table, generating an aggregate value as one of the columns returned.

scheduled backup

An automatic backup that SQL Server Agent accomplishes when the backup is defined and scheduled as a job.

schema

A collection of database objects owned by a single user and making up a single namespace.

scroll

To move a cursor around in directions other than forward-only.

search condition

A part of a **WHERE** or **HAVING** clause that limits the rows being included.

security identifier (SID)

A unique value identifying a user who is logged onto the SQL server.

SELECT

A SQL statement that returns data to another application or statement.

select list

The elements that are being returned in a **SELECT** statement, including column names, functions, or constants.

select query

A query that uses the **SELECT** statement and produces a result set from one or more tables.

self-join

A table that is joined to itself because of matching values in joined fields.

sensitive cursor

A cursor that reflects changes made to underlying data by other users while the cursor is open.

server cursor
Any cursor implemented using SQL cursor statements.

server name
The name by which a SQL server knows itself or other data sources. It can also be the name a client uses to identify a particular SQL server.

shared lock
A lock that allows other users to read the data that is being locked.

SID
See **security identifier.**

smalldatetime data type
A SQL Server data type used to store date and time information that is accurate to the minute.

smallint data type
An integer data type used to store whole numbers from 32,767 through −32,768.

smallmoney data type
A SQL Server data type that stores monetary values. These values range from 214,748.3647 through −214,748.3648, to four decimal places.

snapshot replication
A type of replication that takes periodic snapshots of the published data and does not monitor for changes made to the data.

sort order
The order in which SQL Server evaluates character strings in a collation.

SQL
See **Structured Query Language.**

SQL-92
The latest approved version of the standard for SQL, published in 1992. It is sometimes referred to as ANSI SQL in the United States.

SQL Mail
SQL Server's interface to MAPI mail systems. It allows SQL Server to send and receive email.

SQL Server Agent
A component of SQL Server that creates and manages local or multiserver jobs, alerts, and operators.

SQL Server authentication
The process of verifying attempts to connect to SQL Server.

SQL Server user
A database security account that allows SQL Server logins to use a database.

statement permission
The permission to execute Transact-SQL statements.

static cursor
A cursor that shows the data exactly as it looked when the cursor was opened.

stored procedure
A precompiled collection of one or more Transact-SQL statements that are stored in SQL Server and processed as one unit.

Structured Query Language (SQL)
A database query and programming language.

subquery
Any **SELECT** statement that is used to make up another query. A subquery is sometimes nested in another **SELECT, UPDATE, INSERT,** or **DELETE** statement.

subscribe
To agree to receive a publication as part of replication.

Subscriber
In the Publish and Subscribe model of replication, the server that receives copies of published information.

surrogate key
A candidate key.

system administrator
Any user with the **sysadmin** role.

system catalog
The system tables in the **master** database that contain information about SQL Server.

system databases
The four databases that are provided in a fresh SQL Server installation: **master, tempdb, model,** and **msdb**.

system stored procedures
A set of stored procedures provided by SQL Server that can be used to access the system tables.

system tables
The tables, which are built-in, that make up the system catalog and the database catalog.

table
A database object that is made up of columns and rows and that is used to store data in a database.

table lock
A lock (access restriction) that is on a table and includes all indexes and data.

tabular data stream (TDS)
SQL Server's internal data-transfer protocol for clients and server products.

TDS
See **tabular data stream.**

tempdb database
A system database used to store temporary (working) objects.

temporary stored procedure
A stored procedure created in the **tempdb** database by prefixing the procedure's name with a number sign (#); the temporary stored procedure is erased at the conclusion of the session.

temporary table procedure
A table procedure created in the **tempdb** database by prefixing the procedure's name with a number sign (#); the temporary table procedure is erased at the conclusion of the session.

text data type
A data type used to hold non-Unicode character data (up to 2GB long).

timestamp data type
A data type that generates a unique value within a database. Each new value generated will be one higher than the last value generated.

tinyint data type
An integer data type that is used to store whole numbers from 0 through 255.

Transact-SQL (T-SQL)
SQL Server's implementation of the ANSI SQL-2 standard and SQL Server's extensions to the standard.

Transact-SQL cursor
A server cursor that uses the Transact-SQL extensions to the DE-CLARE CURSOR statement.

transaction
A logical unit of work made up of a group of database operations.

transaction log
A database file in which all changes to the database are recorded before the data changes are written.

trigger
A stored procedure that is automatically executed when certain data is modified.

T-SQL
See Transact-SQL.

tuple
A row of data.

UDF
See user defined function.

Unicode
A set of characters that are stored in the **nchar, nvarchar,** and **ntext** data types and that include characters for most languages.

Unicode collation
The sort order for Unicode data.

union query
A query that combines results from two or more queries into one result set.

UNIQUE constraint
A constraint that enforces the rule that the constrained columns are unique in a table.

unique index
An index in which no two rows are allowed to have the same index value.

uniqueidentifier data type
A SQL Server data type containing a globally unique identifier (GUID) number, which is stored as a 16-byte binary string.

update
To modify data by adding new data, removing existing data, or modifying existing data, usually by using the **UPDATE** statement.

user databases
Any SQL Server database (other than the four system databases) created by users to hold application data.

user-defined data type
A data type that was created by a user and that must be based on one of the SQL Server standard data types.

user-defined function (UDF)
A Transact-SQL function created by a user. A UDF provides the programming-like ability to group your own sets of frequently used steps into reusable subroutines that you can recall at will.

username
The name that a person uses when logging into a SQL Server database.

varbinary data type
A SQL Server data type used to store binary data up to 8,000 bytes long.

varchar data type
A SQL Server data type used to store character data up to 8,000 bytes long.

variables
A defined entity used to temporarily store values. A variable name starts with an at symbol (@).

vertical partitioning
A physical design practice that splits a table into multiple tables for different sets of columns.

view
A logical table defined by using a **SELECT** statement that retrieves data from one or more tables.

wildcard characters
The characters used in pattern matching with the **LIKE** keyword in the **WHERE** clause; wildcards include the underscore, brackets, and the percent sign.

Windows NT authentication
A process that validates and enables a user with a Windows NT user account to connect to SQL Server.

Windows NT Event Viewer
A Windows NT application that views events.

Windows NT Performance Monitor
See **Performance Monitor.**

write-ahead log
The transaction logging method used by most RDBMSs. In this method, the data changes are written to the log before they are committed to the database.

Index